Uncle John's

ULTIMATE BATHROOM READER

The Bathroom Readers'
Institute

Bathroom Readers' Press
Ashland, Oregon

UNCLE JOHN'S ULTIMATE BATHROOM READER
Special Expanded Edition

Cover design by Michael Brunsfeld

Uncle John's Ultimate Bathroom Reader
by The Bathroom Readers' Institute

Printed in the United States of America.

"Honey Bucket," by John Foley, originally appeared in *Alaska Magazine*,
Copyright © 1992 John Foley. Reprinted by permission of the author.

"Knifestyles of the Rich and Famous," from *Marie Claire* magazine. Reprinted by
permission of *Marie Claire* Magazine/Hearst.

"Killing Mass Transit," "Good News for Hitler," "Morgan's Swindle," "Into the
Mouths of Babes," "Reefer Madness," and "Who Helped Hitler?" originally ap-
peared in *It's a Conspiracy!* by The National Insecurity Council. Text © 1992 by
Michael Litchfield. Published by EarthWorks Press. Reprinted by permission of
EarthWorks Press.

Selections from *Primetime Proverbs*, © 1989 by Jack Mingo and John Javna.
Reprinted by permission of the authors.

"Millennium Madness," "The Great Criswell," "Is It 2000?," and assorted inserts
on the year 2,000 from *The Bathroom Readers' Guide to the Year 2000*. Copyright ©
1996, by Eric Lefcowitz. Reprinted by permission of EarthWorks Press.

"One-Hit Wonders," "The Singing Chipmunks", and "The Wild Thing Story"
from Behind the Hits, © 1985, by Bob Shannon and John Javna. Reprinted by
permission of the authors.

THANK YOU!

The Bathroom Readers' Institute sincerely thanks the people whose advice and assistance made this book possible.

John Javna
John Dollison
Lenna Lebovich
Gordon Javna
Erik Linden
Melissa Schwarz
Sharilyn Hovind
Larry Kelp
Andy Sohn
Michael Brunsfeld
Sherry Powell
Benjamin Brand
Steve Rosebrough
Jennifer Massey
Chris Rose-Merkle

Gordon Van Gelder
Eric Lefcowitz
Malissa Nelson
Morgan Smith
Max, Lucy & Alice
Julie Roeming
Lonnie Kirk
Paul Stanley
Bennie Slomski
Gordon Javna
Thomas Crapper
Jesse & Sophie, *B.R.I.T.*
...and all the bathroom readers
Hi to Emily and Molly!

Special thanks to Leder Norahs

★　★　★

PREDICTION FOR THE YEAR 2000

"When Jane cleans house she simply turns the hose on everything... Why not? Furniture (upholstery included), rugs, draperies, unscratchable floors—all are made of synthetic fabric or waterproof plastic. After the water has run down a drain in the middle of the floor (later concealed by a rug of synthetic fiber), Jane turns on a blast of hot air and dries everything." —*Popular Mechanics,* 1950

CONTENTS

NOTE:
Because the BRI understands your reading needs, we've
divided the contents by length as well as subject.
Short—A quick read
Medium—1 to 3 pages
Long—For those extended visits, when something
a little more involved is required

Key for expanded edition: # means an entry is from the 5th B.R.;
• means it's from 6th B.R." ; and * means it's from the 7th B.R.

AN ARTFUL HOAX

On display: Vincent Van Gogh's ear (that's how it was labeled).

Where: In New York's Museum of Modern Art in 1935, during the first exhibition of Van Gogh's art in the U.S.

Background: Hugh Troy, a New York artist, suspected that most Americans were more interested in Van Gogh the man than they were in Van Gogh the artist. To prove this, he mounted a shrivelled object in a velvet shadow box and wrote: "This is the ear which Vincent Van Gogh cut off and sent to his mistress, a French prostitute, Dec. 24, 1888." Then he visited the Van Gogh exhibit, and when no one was looking he put it out on display.

What Happened: The "ear" was mobbed, while Van Gogh's paintings were virtually ignored. It wasn't until later that Troy admitted that he had fashioned the ear out of a piece of chipped beef.

INTRODUCTION

This is a special edition of the *Ultimate Bathroom Reader*.

The first printing was a solid 324 pages of all-new material. But we got to thinking—some dedicated bathroom readers crave even *more* bulk. So we've created this expanded edition. We've flushed out 200 pages of classic bathroom reading from our *Fifth, Sixth,* and *Seventh Bathroom Readers* and added them to this volume.

If you've already got a copy of *The Best of Uncle John's Bathroom Reader*, you'll be relieved to know that the book you're holding now is completely different, with a whole new set of articles, quotes, stories and trivia.

But you'll also find that it's just as much of a gas to read—for us as well as you. We at the BRI often feel that we have the best job in the world. We get to spend the year flipping through old magazines, newspapers, and obscure books, looking for off-the-wall subjects to write about...and then we get to "field-test" the materials.

Of course, it's a challenge to figure out how to condense whole books into a few pithy pages. But after all, someone's got to do it.

Maybe you think that after nine years—and over 2,000 pages—of *Bathroom Readers*, it'd be getting hard to find things to write about. Nope; the material, so to speak, keeps on coming. In fact, by the time we finished this volume, we'd gathered so much information that we had enough to get started on the next one, too—our 10th Anniversary special. (Keep on the look out for that.)

Keep those cards and letters coming—let us know what you like, and send us your own favorite bathroom reading material. Share and share alike, you know.

Happy reading—go with the flow.

BRAND NAMES

You already know these names.
Here's where they came from.

CLOROX. In 1913, the Electro-Alkaline Company of Oakland, California, started selling bleach in jugs carried by horse-drawn carts. A supplier pointed out that their name sounded industrial—even dangerous. He suggested combining "chlorine" and "sodium hydroxide" (two of the product's ingredients), to create *Clorox*.

BRILLO. From the Latin word *beryllus*, which means "shine."

LEE JEANS. At the turn of the century, Henry D. Lee was one of the Midwest's biggest wholesalers of groceries, work clothes, and other items. In 1911, because he wasn't getting shipments of work clothes on time, he decided to build his own factory. In 1924, he started making jeans for cowboys. In 1926, Lee's made the first jeans with zippers.

FORMULA 409. The two scientists who invented the "all-purpose cleaner" in the late 1950s didn't get the formula right until their 409th attempt.

CONVERSE ALL-STARS. Named for Marquis M. Converse, who founded the Converse Rubber Company in 1908. He introduced the canvas-topped All-Star—one of the world's first basketball shoes—in 1917.

BAUSCH & LOMB. In the 1850s, Henry Lomb invested his life savings ($60) in an eyeglass business run by John Bausch. By 1908, they were selling over 20 million lenses a year.

TURTLE WAX. In the early 1940s, Ben Hirsch mixed up a batch of car wax in a bathtub. He called it Plastone Liquid Car Wax, and started selling it around the country. Several years later, he was walking along Turtle Creek in Beloit, Wisconsin, when "he made a mental connection between the hard shell of a turtle and his product." *Plastone* became *Turtle Wax*.

SPECIAL AFFECTS

*Here are a few unexpected ways that movies have
made their mark on the American public.*

COMA (1978)

"In 1978," writes historian Scot Morris, "there was a reported 60% drop in human organs donated to U.S. hospitals, as compared to the previous year. Why?...The decline in donors occurred just after the release of *Coma*, a film in which hospital patients are murdered so their organs can be harvested and sold."

FORREST GUMP (1994)

The title character carries his favorite book, *Curious George*, around in a suitcase. Later, he gives a copy to his son. In the first three weeks after the film's release, sales of *Curious George* books jumped 25%—and have stayed high since.

IT HAPPENED ONE NIGHT (1934)

Clark Gable took off his shirt in the Oscar-winning comedy, and America saw he was bare-chested underneath. Overnight, undershirt sales plummeted.

E.T. (1982)

"In one of the film's more dramatic moments," writes Carolyn Wyman in *I'm a Spam Fan*, "the alien opens up his clenched fist and out drops—not the expected weapon—but brown, yellow, and orange pieces of both boy and extraterrestrial's favorite candy"—Reese's Pieces. "Those few minutes of screen time sent sales of Reese's Pieces into outer space. Sales increased 65%, causing the company to keep two factories open round the clock."

LOVE HAPPY (1949)

The Marx Brothers' final film was so badly underfinanced that the producer had to invent what is now known as "product placement." He devised a rooftop chase scene where the characters jumped from one neon sign to another. It was one long commercial and corporations paid to be a part of it.

"Republican" and "Democrat" are both towns in North Carolina.

PLITZ-PLATZ I WAS TAKING A BATH

As kids, we were all told that trains go "choo-choo" and cars go "beep beep." Check out the sounds they make in other languages.

AAH-CHOO!
Portuguese: Ah-chim!
German: Hat-chee!
Greek: Ap tsou!
Japanese: Hakshon!
Italian: Ekchee!

SPLASH!
Hindi: Dham!
Russian: Plyukh!
Danish: Plump!
Spanish: Chof!
Greek: Plitz-platz!

EENY-MEENY-MINY-MO
Arabic: Hadi-badi
Italian: Ambaraba chichicoco
Japanese: Hee-foo-mee-yo
Swedish: Ol-uh dol-uh doff
Polish: Ele mele dudki

CHOO-CHOO!
Chinese: Hong-lung, hong-lung
Danish: Fut fut!
Japanese: Shuppo-shuppo!
Swahili: Chuku-chuku!
Greek: Tsaf-tsouf!

ZZZZZZ...
Arabic: Kh-kh-kh...
Chinese: Hulu...
Italian: Ronf-ronf...
Japanese: Gah-gah...

UPSY-DAISY!
Arabic: Hop-pa!
Italian: Opp-la!
Japanese: Yoisho!
Russian: Nu davai!
Danish: Opse-dasse!

KITCHY-KITCHY-KOO!
Chinese: Gujee!
French: Gheely-gheely!
Greek: Ticki-ticki-ticki!
Swedish: Kille kille kille!

UH-OH!
Chinese: Zao le!
Italian: Ay-may!
Japanese: Ah-ah!
Swahili: Wee!
Swedish: Oy-oy!

BEEP BEEP!
Chinese: Dooo dooo!
Hindi: Pon-pon!
Spanish: Mock mock!
French: Puet puet!
Japanese: Boo boo!

CHUGALUG!
Arabic: Gur-gur-gur!
Hindi: Gat-gat!
Hebrew: Gloog gloog!
Russian: Bool-bool!
Chinese: Goo-doo, goo-doo!

Native Americans spoke more than 133 different languages.

FAMILIAR PHRASES

Here are some origins of everyday phrases.

KNUCKLE UNDER

Meaning: Give in to someone of superior strength.

Origin: Today only the joints in your fingers are known as knuckles, but before the 14th century *all* joints in the body were called knuckles. In those days, "knuckling under" meant getting down on your knees before your master or conqueror.

BRAND-NEW

Meaning: Obtained very recently.

Origin: The German word for "fire" is *Brand*. Horseshoes, as well as other items that were fresh from the fire of a blacksmith's forge, were said to be *brandneu*, or "brand-new" in English.

DOUBLE-CROSS

Meaning: Betray.

Origin: Comes from boxing and describes a fixed fight. If a fighter deliberately loses, he "crosses up" the people who have bet on him to win; if he wins, he "crosses up" the people paying him to lose. Someone is betrayed no matter how the fight turns out; hence the name *double*-cross.

FINISH IN A DEAD HEAT

Meaning: Tie for first place.

Origin: Racing term from the days when horses ran several races, or "heats," to determine a winner. (A horse had to win two out of three, three out of five, etc.) When two horses tied in a heat, it was considered "dead," because it didn't count.

HAVING KITTENS

Meaning: Acting hysterically.

Origin: In the Middle Ages, when a pregnant woman experienced severe pains that didn't appear to be labor pains, people thought she was bewitched and "had kittens clawing at her inside her womb." A common excuse given in court for obtaining an abortion was "to remove cats in the belly."

Q: When did cars first come with seatbelts?   A: 1950.

HERE'S THE STORY…

Inside facts on The Brady Bunch, *the syrupy TV sitcom that aired from September 26, 1969 to August 30, 1974. Like* Star Trek, *it was never very popular in prime time, but has become a monster cult show.*

HOW IT STARTED

In 1964, while TV producer Sherwood Schwartz was working on his hit show *Gilligan's Island*, he began fleshing out ideas for a new family sitcom.

In the mid-'60s, the standard *Leave It to Beaver* sitcom family was already out of date; you had to have a gimmick to have a hit. So Schwartz came up with the idea of making the wife a widow, and the husband a widower. It was a TV first—a blended family, with three kids from the dad and three from the mom. He called it *Yours and Mine*.

Schwartz wrote the script for a 1/2-hour pilot episode in which Carol and Mike Brady get so lonely on their honeymoon that they return home to get Alice and the kids. He showed it to the networks and got a mixed response. NBC liked the idea, but thought the pilot was unrealistic (who'd leave their honeymoon to be with kids?); ABC wanted Schwartz to expand it to a 1-1/2 hour TV movie (he refused because it would be too boring); CBS rejected it outright—they had their own widow-marries-widower show in the works (it never aired). So *Yours and Mine* was dead in the water.

Then four years later in 1968, Lucille Ball and Henry Fonda starred in a fairly successful movie with a plot similar to Schwartz's show, called *Yours, Mine, and Ours*. It reminded someone at ABC of the pilot they'd seen in 1964; they called Schwartz and bought the program. Once ABC was committed, Schwartz had no trouble getting Paramount TV to finance it. The show was on its way.

INSIDE FACTS

Name That Show

Paramount immediately ran into a problem with the name. A lawyer for the owners of *Yours, Mine, and Ours* threatened to sue them if they kept the title *Yours and Mine*. Schwartz wanted to fight— he'd registered *his* title first. But no one else thought it was worth the effort. The choice came down to *The Brady Bunch*, or *The Brady Brood*. "Bunch" sounded like juvenile delinquents; "brood" sounded like a horror flick. Finally, they just picked one and started production.

The Bradys vs. the Censors

• It was officially established in the early episodes that Mike Brady was a widower—but the fate of Carol's first husband was never discussed. Why? Schwartz wanted to leave open the possibility that Carol was a divorcée, even though the network wouldn't allow it explicitly.

• 1969 was the peak of the "sexual revolution," and Carol and Mike joined in. They became the first TV sitcom couple to actually sleep together. Until then, censors had always required twin beds— even for married couples. But the Bradys had...a double bed!

• One thing the Bradys weren't allowed to have: a toilet. ABC removed the toilet from the Brady bathroom, leaving only a sink and tub. The running joke on the set was that the Bradys used the restroom at the corner gas station.

The Blended Family

• Schwartz interviewed 464 boys and girls to find the Brady kids.

• He wanted the sons and daughters to have the same hair color as their parents. The reason: he didn't want viewers confused about which kids belonged to whom. But when the Brady kid auditions started, Schwartz didn't know who was going to play the parents. So he hired two sets of Brady kids—blonde and brunette. When Robert Reed and Florence Henderson were hired as the parents, he fired the blonde boys and brunette girls.

In the Cast

• Barry Williams was the most popular Brady kid. He was an instant pop star, getting 6,500 letters a week in 1971.

• Robert Reed didn't want to play Mike Brady. A classically trained actor, he had the lead role in the Broadway play *Barefoot in the Park*. He wanted to star in the TV version planned for the 1970 season, and only took the *Brady Bunch* part after ABC decided that all the actors in their *Barefoot* sitcom would be African Americans.

More than 50% of Americans fall asleep on their sides.

WHEN YOUR HUSBAND GETS HOME...

Here's a bit of advice taken directly from a 1950s Home Economics text book. It was sent in by a reader, along with the comment: "Times have changed!" No kidding. Believe it or not, this was part of a course intended to prepare high school girls for married life.

Have dinner ready: "Plan ahead, even the night before, to have a delicious meal—on time. This is a way of letting him know that you have been thinking about him and are concerned about his needs. Most men are hungry when they come home and the prospects of a good meal are part of the warm welcome needed."

Prepare yourself: "Take 15 minutes to rest so you will be refreshed when he arrives. Touch up your makeup, put a ribbon in your hair and be fresh-looking. He has just been with a lot of work-weary people. Be a little gay and a little more interesting. His boring day may need a lift."

Clear away the clutter: "Make one last trip through the main part of the house just before your husband arrives, gathering up school books, toys, paper, etc. Then run a dust cloth over the tables. Your husband will feel he has reached a haven of rest and order, and it will give you a lift, too."

Prepare the children: "Take a few minutes to wash the children's hands and faces (if they are small) comb their hair, and if necessary, change their clothes. They are little treasures and he would like to see them playing the part."

Minimize all noise: "At the time of his arrival, eliminate all noise of washer, dryer, dishwasher or vacuum. Try to encourage the children to be quiet. Be happy to see him: Greet him with a warm smile and be glad to see him."

Some don'ts: "Don't greet him with problems or complaints. Don't

A record: 60.2% of the U.S. TV audience watched the last episode of M*A*S*H in 1983.

complain if he's late for dinner. Count this as minor compared with what he might have gone through that day."

Make him comfortable: "Have him lean back in a comfortable chair or suggest he lie down in the bedroom. Have a cool or warm drink ready for him. Arrange his pillow and offer to take off his shoes. Speak in a low, soft, soothing and pleasant voice. Allow him to relax—unwind."

Listen to him: "You may have a dozen things to tell him, but the moment of his arrival is not the time. Let him talk first."

Make the evening his: "Never complain if he does not take you out to dinner or to other places of entertainment. Instead, try to understand his world of strain and pressure, his need to be home and relax."

THE BEST & WORST TIPPERS

According to a poll in Bartender *magazine:*

• Lawyers and doctors are the worst tippers. Normally, doctors are the #1 tightwads. In rougher times, it's lawyers. The reason: "There are more lawyers and less work."

• The biggest tippers are bartenders and "service personnel."

• As smoking gets more restricted, cigar and cigarette smokers —who are now forced to smoke at the bar instead of at restaurant tables—are becoming notably good tippers.

• Other leading tightwads: teachers, computer people, musicians, professional athletes, and pipe smokers.

• Other top tippers: hairstylists, mobsters, tavern owners, regular customers.

• Vodka drinkers are good tippers. People who order drinks topped with umbrellas are bad tippers.

• Democrats tip better than Republicans.

One in 500 humans have one blue eye and one brown eye.

FAMOUS TIGHTWADS

For some bizarre reason, really rich people are often the most uptight about spending money. Here are a few examples of people who've gone over the deep end about loose change.

MARGE SCHOTT, owner of the Cincinnati Reds. Told her staff in 1995 she couldn't afford Christmas bonuses and gave candies instead. They turned out to be free samples from a baseball-card company …and they came with coupons inviting consumers to "win a trip to the 1991 Grammys."

CARY GRANT. Nicknamed "El Squeako" by Hollywood friends, he counted the number of firewood logs in his mansion's garage and used a red pen to mark the level of milk in the milk bottles in his refrigerator, both to keep his servants from taking them.

FRANKLIN D. ROOSE-VELT, U.S. president. Mooched dollar bills off of his valet to drop in the collection plate at church.

GOUCHO MARX. Wore a beret, which became one of his trademarks, "so he wouldn't have to check his hat."

CORNELIUS VANDER-BILT, American financier. When his doctor told him on his deathbed that a glass of champagne a day would moderate his suffering, Vanderbilt —then the wealthiest man in America—replied, "Dammit, I tell you Doc, I can't afford it. Won't sodywater do?"

J. PAUL GETTY, oil baron. Installed a pay phone in his mansion to keep visitors from running up his long-distance bill; put locks on all the other phones. "When you get some fellow talking for ten or fifteen minutes," the billionaire explained, "well, it all adds up."

LEE IACOCCA, former head of Chrysler Corp. Threw himself lavish holiday parties and charged the gifts to underlings. Popular saying at Chrysler: "If you have lunch with someone who looks like Iacocca and sounds like Iacocca, rest assured—if he offers to pick up the check, it's not Iacocca."

ALLENISMS

Truths from one of America's leading wits, Woody Allen.

"Sex without love is an empty experience, but as empty experiences go it's one of the best."

"I am at two with nature."

"There's no garbage in California. That's because they turn it into television shows."

"To *you* I'm an atheist; to God, I'm the Loyal Opposition."

"The difference between sex and death is that with death you can do it alone and no one is going to make fun of you."

"The lion and the calf shall lie down together...but the calf won't get much sleep."

"More than any other time in history, mankind faces a crossroads. One path leads to despair and utter hopelessness. The other, to total extinction. Let us pray we have the wisdom to choose correctly.

"Death is one of the few things that can be done just as easily as lying down."

"I took a speed reading course and read *War and Peace* in twenty minutes. It involves Russia."

"When I was a little child, I was breast fed from falsies."

"I will not eat oysters. I want my food dead. Not sick—not wounded—dead."

"I'm not the heroic type. I was beaten up by Quakers."

"What if everything is an illusion and nothing exists? In that case, I definitely overpaid for my carpet."

"I never want to marry. I just want to get divorced."

"Why are our days numbered and not, say, lettered?"

"The worst thing you can say about Him is that basically, He's an underachiever."

"I should have stayed in college...I was in the black studies program. By now I could have been black."

CELEBRITY SWEEPSTAKES

There's an old saying in advertising: "If you haven't got anything to say about your product, have a celebrity say it for you." Sometimes celebrity endorsements work, sometimes they don't. Here are a few examples.

ROSEANNE AND TOM ARNOLD
In 1993, CelebSales, a clothing manufacturer, hired the outspoken couple to endorse a line of large-sized clothing.

What they wanted: A positive image. Roseanne had TV's #1 show and she was unapologetic about her size. "I think the sexiest thing a woman can do," she said, "is be as fat as me—or fatter." Roseanne also attracted publicity. *People* magazine, for example, shot an entire fashion layout for the line, with Roseanne modeling the clothes herself.

What they got: A lawsuit. A week before the clothes were to premiere in a fashion show, Roseanne pulled out of the deal, obtained a court order canceling the show, and sued CelebSales, claiming they owed her $750,000 in licensing fees. CelebSales countersued for $24 million, arguing that the Arnolds "not only reneged on agreements to market the clothes on television, but generated publicity so vile that nobody would want to buy their product."

What happened: The clothing line was canceled. In 1996, a court awarded the Arnolds the $750,000 they said they were owed. By that time, they weren't even a couple anymore.

CYBILL SHEPHERD & JAMES GARNER
In 1986, the Beef Industry Council announced that it had hired Shepherd, an ex-model and star of TV's "Moonlighting," and Garner to represent them in a $30 million "Beef: Real Food for Real People" campaign.

What they wanted: To change beef's image as an unhealthy food. "We're thrilled that two stars of such magnitude have agreed to join the beef team," one council spokesperson told reporters. "I don't think we could have two celebrities and an industry more suited for one another."

What they got: Egg on their face. A few months later, Shepherd was interviewed in *Family Circle* magazine. "Asked to name her latest beauty tip," said a news report, "the star was quoted as saying, 'I've cut down on fatty foods and am trying to stay away from red meat.'" Shepherd claimed her publicist had made the quote up. "The comments attributed to me were released by my publicity office, but they were not entirely correct," she explained. "I do avoid 'fatty foods,' but I have retained red meat in my diet."

Then, in April 1988, Garner underwent a quintuple bypass surgery to correct clogged arteries. Was beef the cause? "It could very well be due to something else," a beef board spokesman protested. Newspapers reported that Garner was recovering. "According to his spokesman," said one, "he is 'beginning to eat a normal diet.' No word on whether beef is included."

What happened: The Beef Industry Council pledged that it would stand by Shepherd and Garner…then quietly dumped each of them when their contracts expired.

JACK KLUGMAN

The star of TV's "Odd Couple" and "Quincy" was hired as spokesperson for Canon USA copiers in 1982.

What they wanted: A recognizable TV pitchman

What they got: Unexpected competition. In 1984, Minolta hired Klugman's "Odd Couple" co-star, Tony Randall, to endorse its *own* line of copiers. Randall played a compulsive cleaner on the show; Klugman played a slob—which was why Minolta wanted Randall, as *Fortune* magazine reported in 1985:

> The Minolta ads, which according to his agent riled Klugman, played up the Odd Couple stereotypes and even made a thinly veiled reference to Klugman when Randall ad-libbed, "Of course, I'm not a slob like, uh…" and gave his you-know-who-I-mean look. Minolta's marketing coup was to associate Canon machines in consumers' minds with Klugman's mess: jammed paper, perhaps, or ink-blackened hands.

What happened: The Randall ads boosted sales of Minolta copiers, but they didn't hurt Canon's sales, so the company retained Klugman as their spokesman.

Survey result: 33% percent of respondents refuse to participate in surveys when asked to do so.

TOASTER FOODS

We wrote about how the toaster was invented back in BR #2—now here's the origin of America's two biggest-selling toaster foods.

EGGO WAFFLES

The *Eggo* name has probably been around longer than you think. It was coined in 1935, when three brothers—Frank, Tony, and Sam Dorsa—borrowed $35 to buy a waffle iron and started experimenting with waffle batter. When they got a batter they liked, they sold it to restaurants in Northern California. A fourth brother, George, suggested they call their product "Eggo" because "the batter has lots of eggs." In 1937, the company went public, and the brothers built a big waffle-batter factory in San Jose.

After World War II, when Americans began buying home freezers in record numbers, the Dorsas guessed there was a bigger market for frozen waffles than for waffle batter. So in 1950, they gambled and switched their entire production to ready-made waffles. Within a year, they were cranking out 10,000 an hour…and still couldn't keep up with demand. Kellogg's bought the company in 1968. Today, the brand controls an estimated 60% share of the $500 million frozen waffle industry.

POP-TARTS

The Pop-Tart story starts with dogfood, not cereal…and not with Kellogg's but with its rival, Post. According to Steve Hymon, in the *Chicago Tribune*:

> In 1957, Post's pet-food division came out with Gaines Burgers [which] were a novel concept because the dog food was semi-moist but didn't have to be refrigerated—a convenience many humans coincidentally sought in their breakfast food.
>
> In 1963, the Post research and development department, using some of the same technology that made Gaines Burgers possible, figured out a way to keep fruit filling moist while inhibiting the growth of spoilage-causing bacteria. The obvious application: a fruit-filled pastry that could be shipped and stored without having to be refrigerated.

On Feb. 16, 1964, Post unveiled its new product, Country Squares. The food industry oohed and aahed; the business press buzzed; grocers waited expectantly.

And waited.

Post blundered. It took so long to get its product to grocery stores that Kellogg's had had a chance to catch up. In just six months, Kellogg's created *and* test-marketed Pop-Tarts. People at Post knew they were sunk. Hymon goes on:

> The names given to the two products were one more indication of Kellogg's superior marketing savvy. Kellogg appreciated that kids were the primary target audience for Pop-Tarts because they had yet to establish breakfast habits of their own. Post seems to have been more confused. As awful a name as Country Squares seems in 1994, it was arguably worse in 1964, when the word "square" was widely used to mean "nerdy." When paired with "country," it seemed to describe a food for middle-age rubes from the sticks.

POPPING OFF

The original Pop-Tarts came in four flavors: Strawberry, Blueberry, Brown Sugar, and Apple-Currant (which Kellogg's quickly changed to Apple-Berry when it realized most consumers didn't know what currants were). Kellogg's put its marketing muscle behind the new product, blitzing kid's TV shows with commercials featuring Milton the Toaster. By 1967, they had both created and locked up the $45 million toaster pastry market. The brand maintained a 75% market share into the 1990s, with $285 million in sales in 1990...and nearly $500 million by 1993.

What happened to Country Squares? Post changed the name to Post Toast-Em Pop-Ups, but it was too late. Post finally gave up in the early 1970s and sold the marketing rights to someone else.

TOASTER FLOPS. *Not every toaster food works. Here are some other ideas that bit the big one...and the reasons why.*
- **Downyflake Toaster Eggs.** Too weird.
- **ReddiWip's Reddi Bacon.** Bacon fat dripped to the bottom of the toaster, creating a fire hazard.
- **Toaster Chicken Patties.** Same problem, with chicken fat.
- **Electric French Fries.** Stamped out in slab form, they "looked like a picket fence, tasted like a picket fence."

PRIMETIME PROVERBS

TV tidbits from the book Primetime
Proverbs, *by Jack Mingo and John Javna.*

ON DIVORCE

"Actress Robin Givens has filed a libel suit against her estranged husband Mike Tyson, claiming he told a reporter she was after his money…She's asking $125 million."
—**NBC News**

"Did you ever notice that alimony is like keeping up payments on a car with four flats?"
—*Laugh-In*

ON CHILDBIRTH

"Home delivery is for newspapers, not babies."
—**Oscar Madison,**
The Odd Couple

ON POLITICIANS

Rush: "Lincoln wasn't a crook."
Wainwright: "We don't know that. He never finished his term."
—*Too Close for Comfort*

ON RACISM

"Bigotry started a long time ago—nobody knows where. Personally, I think the French started it."
—**Johnny Fever,**
WKRP in Cincinnati

SUSPICIOUS ADVICE

"Never trust a woman. Even the four-legged variety."
—***The Prisoner***

"My dad once gave me a few words of wisdom which I have always tried to live by. He said, 'Son, never throw a punch at a redwood.'"
—**Thomas Magnum,**
Magnum P.I.

ON TV

"No wonder they call it a medium; it's so seldom rare or well-done."
—**Mighty Mouse,**
***The New Adventures
of Mighty Mouse***

ON MONEY

"There's only one thing more important than money, and that's more money."
—**Pappy Maverick**
Maverick

"Money seems to have a rubberlike quality, because you can bounce a check or stretch a dollar."
—**Mork,**
Mork and Mindy

FAMOUS
FOR 15 MINUTES

Here it is again—our feature based on Andy Warhol's prophetic comment that "in the future, everyone will be famous for 15 minutes." Here's how a few people are using up their allotted quarter-hour.

THE STAR: Cory McDonald

THE HEADLINE: *Clown's Coins Create Controversy*

WHAT HAPPENED: McDonald made his living as the balloon-sculpting Mr. Twister the Clown, performing at fairs and birthday parties. For six years, he also enjoyed wandering the streets of Santa Cruz, California, in his clown costume, putting quarters in expired parking meters. One day in 1995, a frustrated meter maid handed him a citation; she'd found a local law that prohibited "good samaritans" from feeding other people's meters. McDonald was outraged. A lawyer agreed to take his case "pro-Bozo"; together they waged a campaign to embarrass the city and change the law.

THE AFTERMATH: It worked. Newspapers all over the U.S. picked up the story, and Mr. Twister became the symbolic victim of all bad laws and frivolous prosecutions in America. Anti-government editorials referred scathingly to the Santa Cruz city government. Finally, Santa Cruz city council members—eager to put the matter to rest—donned big red clown noses at a council meeting and repealed the ordinance. Mr. Twister expressed his appreciation by twisting balloon animals for them.

THE STAR: Lya Graf, a 20-year-old circus midget

THE HEADLINE: *Millionaire Mogul Meets Midget & Mellows*

WHAT HAPPENED: J. P. Morgan—one of the world's most feared robber barons—was in the Senate Caucus Room on June 1, 1933, waiting to testify before the Senate Banking and Currency Committee. Suddenly a publicity man for the Ringling Brothers Barnum & Bailey Circus popped a midget onto his lap. At that instant, a newspaper photographer who was in on the stunt snapped a picture. The whole room froze; Morgan was not known for his sense of humor...and didn't like physical contact. But to everyone's

---

Why a 7th-inning stretch instead of some other inning? 7 is considered a lucky number.

surprise, he smiled and chatted with her. The next day, the photo *and* Lya Graf were famous all over the world.

THE AFTERMATH: The photograph changed public perception of the robber barons. As John Brooks writes in *American Heritage* magazine:

> Morgan, and even Wall Street as a whole, profited adventitiously from the encounter. From that day forward until his death a decade later, he was in the public mind no longer a grasping devil whose greed and ruthlessness had helped bring the nation to near ruin, but rather a benign old dodderer. The change in attitude was instantaneous and Morgan took advantage of it.

Lya Graf wasn't so lucky. "She was shy and sensitive," writes Brooks, and though she could tolerate employment as an "ordinary circus freak," she couldn't stand being a "celebrity freak."

> Two years later, hounded by fame, she left the United States and returned to her native Germany. She was half Jewish. In 1937 she was arrested as a "useless person" and in 1941 was shipped to Auschwitz, never to be heard from again.

THE STAR: Alvin Straight, a 73-year-old farmer

THE HEADLINE: *A Lawn Day's Journey: Laurens Man Mows Path to Fame*

WHAT HAPPENED: In the spring of 1994, Alvin Straight found out that his 80-year-old brother, Henry, had had a stroke. He hadn't seen Henry in seven years, and decided he'd better go see him "while I had the chance." The only problem: Alvin lived in Laurens, Iowa...and Henry lived 240 miles away in Mt. Zion, Wisconsin. Alvin didn't have a driver's license, didn't want anyone else to drive him, and wouldn't take public transportation. So he hitched a 10-foot trailer to his lawn tractor and started driving the back roads at 5 mph. It took him six weeks, and by the time he got to Mt. Zion, he was so sore "I could barely make it with two canes." CNN broadcast the story, and Alvin was an instant celebrity.

THE AFTERMATH: He was bombarded with offers to appear on talk shows—with Letterman, Leno, etc.—but he wouldn't go, because he refused to fly or take the train to either coast. He did sign a contract to make a TV movie of his life, but nothing ever came of it.

The term "rookie" comes from the Civil War slang "reckie," which was short for "recruit."

THE STAR: George Holliday, general manager of an L.A. plumbing company.

THE HEADLINE: *Camcorder Creates King Controversy*

WHAT HAPPENED: George Holliday gave his first wife a camcorder for Valentine's Day. He was playing with it on the evening of March 2, trying to figure out how it worked...so when sirens awoke him early the next morning, he instinctively grabbed for it. He pulled on some pants and stood shivering on his balcony, filming while some L.A. cops beat the hell out of a man named Rodney King. The next day, he took the tape to a local TV station and for $500, let them broadcast it. The broadcast was fed to CNN and in hours, the whole world knew about it. In a few days, Holliday was famous. Camera crews were at his door, and major news publications were interviewing him.

THE AFTERMATH: Holliday had lots of offers to cash in on his celebrity: a film company wanted to make *The George Holliday Life Story*, a producer talked about *The George Holliday TV Show*, a company wanted him to endorse a George Holliday "crimebuster" toy. All but a $39.95 video called *Shoot News and Make Money with Your Camcorder* fell through. He filed a $100 million lawsuit against the TV stations that had aired his film clip without his permission, but lost. By the time he met his second wife a few years later, says one report, "his notoriety had waned to the point where he had to tell her who he was."

THE STAR: Fred and Selena Payton, owners of a carpet and upholstery cleaning service in Rockville, Maryland

THE HEADLINE: *Selena and Fred are Giving It Up for Arsenio*

WHAT HAPPENED: In July 1993, Arsenio Hall—looking for a ratings boost for his TV show—announced that he would host one show at a viewer's house. He picked the Paytons. For some reason, this was national news—and the Paytons, now famous for 15 minutes...for being famous for 15 minutes...were interviewed by all the major news organizations.

THE AFTERMATH: The night went off without a hitch, as 1,200 people from the neighborhood hung out with the Paytons and watched Patti LaBelle and Bobcat Goldthwait entertain. Then the Paytons' 15 minutes were up. Hall's show went off the air soon afterward.

In 1789, the total U.S. federal government debt was $190,000.

A MUSICAL IS BORN

Some musicals are so famous that they are familiar even to people who never go to plays. Here are the origins of some favorites.

SHOWBOAT (1927)

Oscar Hammerstein, Jerome Kern, and producer Florenz Ziegfield were sick of the light, upbeat musicals that had made them famous. The wanted to do something with adult themes like alcoholism, interracial relationships, and marital troubles—even if no one came to see it. But they needn't have worried. Their adaptation of Edna Ferber's novel about life on a riverboat opened in 1927 to rave reviews and sold out so often that Ziegfield considered staging a second production in a nearby theater to handle the overflow. So far the show has had five Broadway revivals, more than any other play in history.

OKLAHOMA! (1943)

Based on a play called *Green Grow the Lilacs*, which had a limited run in the 1930-1931 Broadway season. A woman who'd helped produce it thought it would make a good musical and approached composer Richard Rodgers with the idea. He was interested, but his partner Lorenzo Hart—who'd become an unreliable alcoholic—wasn't. Rodgers's solution: he teamed up with lyricist Oscar Hammerstein...who hadn't had a hit in years and was considered a has-been. Together they wrote a musical called *Away We Go!* When it got to Broadway, it was renamed *Oklahoma!* and played to sellout crowds. It established Rodgers and Hammerstein as a team.

MAN OF LA MANCHA (1965)

In the late 1950s, a TV/film writer named Dale Wasserman went to Madrid to do research for a movie. The local press mistakenly reported that he was there to write a play about Don Quixote—which sparked his curiosity. Wasserman became so interested in Quixote and author Miguel Cervantes that he traveled all over Spain, retracing their steps. This, in turn, inspired him to write a TV drama called *I, Don Quixote*, which aired on CBS in 1959. He expanded it into *Man of La Mancha* in the early 1960s.

Julie Andrews didn't get to play Eliza in the film version of *My Fair Lady* because she wasn't

GREASE (1972)
Originally a five-hour rock 'n' roll musical written by two amateur actor-writers for a Chicago community theater. A producer bought the rights and had it trimmed by more than half before taking it to New York. Interesting sidelight: George Lucas's film, *American Graffiti*, is usually credited with starting the 1950s nostalgia boom, but this play opened off-Broadway on Feb. 14, 1972—a year before *American Graffiti* premiered. It ran for 3,388 performances, and the 1978 film version was the #1 box-office film of the year.

ANNIE (1977)
Lyricist Martin Charnin was browsing in a bookstore, doing some last-minute Christmas shopping, when he saw a book called *Arf: The Life and Hard Times of Little Orphan Annie*. He bought it for a friend and intended to wrap it and give it away. Instead, he stayed up that night reading it...and decided to turn it into a musical. Ironically, although the musical was a smash, the movie it inspired in 1982 was such a huge disaster that it even caused the *play's* ticket sales to plummet...and ultimately forced it to close in 1983.

CATS (1982)
When T. S. Eliot first wrote *Old Possum's Book of Practical Cats*, a children's book of verses, he only circulated it to his friends; it wasn't published until years later. The same thing happened when Andrew Lloyd Webber, a fan of the book, put some of the poems to music. At first, he only entertained friends with them. Eventually he decided to turn them into a short, one-act musical...then changed his mind and began working on a full-length performance. *Cats* is now the longest-running musical in Broadway history, earning more than $100 million since it opened.

LES MISERABLES (1987)
French playwright Alain Boubil got the idea after seeing *Jesus Christ Superstar* on Broadway: he figured that if pop-rock music could be used to tell the story of Jesus, why not tell the story of the French Revolution? Boubil wasn't sure how to do it...until he saw *Oliver!*, adapted from the Charles Dickens novel *Oliver Twist*. He decided to adapt a classic novel from the period...and settled on Victor Hugo's novel *Les Miserables*.

a "big enough star." So she signed as Mary Poppins...and won the Oscar for Best Actress.

INTO THE
MOUTHS OF BABES

*In the late 1970s, Beech-Nut Baby Foods marketed "100% pure" apple
juice that contained no apples at all. Were they trying to profit
at the expense of our children...or were they the victims of
unscrupulous business practices themselves?*

B eech-Nut Foods, one of the oldest and most respected food
labels in America, had fallen on hard times by the late 1970s.
One by one, its most profitable divisions had been sold off,
leaving only its baby food products—which had never turned a
large profit.

• In 1979, after the Nestlé Company bought Beech-Nut, there was
even greater pressure to make the baby food line profitable.

• Company executives had already been cutting costs wherever
they could. To squeeze profits out of their apple products, for example, Beech-Nut bought its apple concentrate from Universal Juice,
a wholesaler whose price was 20% below the market average.

WHAT HAPPENED

• Beech-Nut employees became suspicious of Universal almost immediately. In 1978, when Beech-Nut employees inspected Universal's plant in Queens, New York, they were "denied access" to the
apple-concentrate processing facility. (In fact, there wasn't any.)
Nonetheless, Beech-Nut continued buying from Universal Juice.

• By 1981, Beech-Nut's director of research, Jerome LiCari, had
become concerned that the bargain concentrate might be tainted,
so he suggested the company replace its wholesaler. When his boss-
es ignored him, he quit. Shortly after, however, the FDA began
paying attention.

THE FDA

• In 1982, an FDA investigator found that despite Beech-Nut's
claims of the product being "100% apple juice," it actually contained "beet sugar, malic acid, apple flavor, caramel color, corn syrup and cane sugar—but *no* apple juice" (*FDA Consumer*).

Cleopatra wasn't Egyptian; she was Greek. And she was the seventh queen by that name.

- Beech-Nut executives first claimed that they had no proof their product was not juice, then said that even if it were true, "Who were we hurting?"
- In 1986, the FDA indicted Beech-Nut, its suppliers, and its top executives for "conspiring to defraud the public by willingly distributing phony apple juice." There were more than 800 charges in all.
- According to *Financial World*: "In the end, the company pleaded guilty to 215 counts of introducing adulterated food" from 1981 to 1983, paid $2.5 million in fines, and lost 20% of their market because of bad publicity.

WAS THERE A CONSPIRACY?
Did Beech-Nut knowingly sell adulterated apple juice, then stonewall the FDA while the company dumped its inventory? Some facts to consider:

- When the FDA told Beech-Nut execs that their product was adulterated, instead of recalling it, they moved it out of their New York warehouse to avoid a New York state embargo, shipped much of it to the Caribbean to make it difficult to track, and dumped it on the market at "tremendous discounts."
- According to *Financial World*, Beech-Nut's president, Neils Hoyvald, explained in a letter to Nestlé: "If the recall had [occurred when the FDA first ordered it], over 700,000 cases in inventory would have been affected...due to our many delays, we were faced with having to destroy only 20,000 cases."
- An anonymous letter sent to the FDA in 1983 said Beech-Nut executives were laughing at federal authorities and stalling the FDA's investigation. It was signed "Johnny Appleseed."

FOOTNOTE
- Hoyvald's lawyer was Brendan Sullivan, who also defended Oliver North. Sullivan recommended that instead of sending Hoyvald to jail, he "be placed on probation and required to teach [ethics] to business students." Hearing of this, one professor quipped, "We may see CEOs deliberately polluting streams [or] using banned food additives, just so they can be convicted and sentenced to a job at Harvard." He added: "You can't overlook the fact that this Beech-Nut character and Ollie North have the same lawyer...I wouldn't be surprised if somebody started selling a Jollie Ollie Apple Juice that tastes like shad" (*Barron's*).

Women in Switzerland did not win the right to vote until 1971.

THE "ODD ELVIS" QUIZ

Elvis is one of the greatest rock singers of all time...as well as one of the most unusual people ever to walk the earth. Here's a little quiz based on some of the stranger recollections of his friends and associates.See if you are on the same wavelength as the King. (Answers start on p. 507.)

1. Elvis' friends learned not to show pain around him. Why not?

a) He hated weaklings.

b) He'd burst out crying if a friend was hurt, and wouldn't stop blubbering for hours.

c) He thought he had the power to "cure the sick." They'd have to sit there while he "laid hands" on them...then pretend he'd cured them.

2. The King was a big eater. Take breakfast, for example: Elvis usually ate a pound of bacon, six scrambled eggs, "a platter of butter-soaked biscuits with sausage," and pots of black coffee to wash it all down. Occasionally, though, Elvis experimented with new diets—like the time he developed an interest in vegetarianism. "Because the spiritual teachings say that you have to eat right," Elvis told friends over dinner one evening in 1973, "I'll be eating a lot of vegetables now, a lot of salads, and raw fruits. I'm telling the maids, and that's what they're going to make for me." How long did Elvis's vegetarian phase last?

a) Two hours.

b) Two days.

c) Two months.

3. Elvis liked TV, but he hated the show *The Streets of San Francisco.* "We made damn sure that *The Streets of San Francisco* was never on when Elvis was around," his bodyguard once said. "I promise you, Elvis was very likely to blow a television set out with his gun if it had come on the screen." It wasn't because the plots were dull, or because the acting was bad. What was the reason?

a) He didn't like the size of Karl Malden's nose.

b) He didn't like the sponsor.

c) He didn't like the character's name.

First president to wear long pants instead of breeches: James Madison (1809-1817).

4. Elvis hated dieting and exercise and often asked his doctor, George Nickopoulos, about other methods of losing weight. One night, "Dr. Nick" mentioned the possibility of an intestinal bypass or "shunt" that would cause food to pass through the King's body before it was completely digested. What was Elvis' reaction?
a) He said he wanted the operation that night.
b) He was so grossed out that he threw up.
c) He said he didn't want the operation himself, but wanted to watch Dr. Nick perform it on someone else "for scientific reasons."

5. In 1961, a friend of Elvis' on the Memphis police force died. What odd request did Elvis have?
a) He wanted to sing "Hound Dog" as they lowered the coffin into the grave.
b) He wanted to watch the mortician embalm his friend.
c) He wanted to prop his friend's body up in a police car and drive around Memphis with the sirens and lights on.

6. Elvis once met country singer Jimmy Dean. How did he greet him?
a) He pulled out a gun and stuck it up against his head.
b) He complained that he didn't look "anything like your cousin, *James* Dean."
c) He started running around, snorting and mooing.

7. Being asked to perform for the president in the White House is one of the biggest honors a musician can receive. Elvis was once asked to play at a party thrown by President Richard Nixon. It didn't work out because...
a) They insisted Elvis wear a business suit while he performed.
b) His manager snorted, "Elvis doesn't play for free."
c) Conservatives threatened to boycott the event if Elvis showed up.

8. Elvis is the only person we've ever heard of who actually died while reading in the bathroom. What was he reading?
a) A book about Nostradamus.
b) A book about the Shroud of Turin.
c) *Uncle John's Bathroom Reader.*

If you're an average American, you spend 4-6 hours/day watching TV.

FAMOUS LAST WORDS

It's never too early to get yours ready.

"Don't let it end like this. Tell them I said something."
—**Pancho Villa**

"I'd rather be fishing."
—**Jimmy Gass,** *murderer*

"O.K. I won't."
—**Elvis Presley,** *responding to his girlfriend's request that he not fall asleep in the bathroom*

"It's very beautiful over there."
—**Thomas A. Edison**

"Why not? Why not?"
—**Timothy Leary**

"Make my skin into drum-heads for the Bohemian cause."
—**John Ziska,** *Czech rebel*

"I've never forgiven that smart-alecky reporter who named me 'Butterfingers'."
—**Thomas Moran,** *pickpocket*

"I'm tired of fighting. I guess this is going to get me."
—**Harry Houdini**

"Remember me to my friends, tell them I'm a hell of a mess."
—**H. L. Mencken,** *essayist*

"Monsieur, I beg your pardon."
—**Marie Antoinette,** *to her executioner, after stepping on his foot accidentally*

"Dying is a very dull affair. My advice to you is to have nothing whatever to do with it."
—*Author* **Somerset Maugham**

"But, but, Mister Colonel—"
—**Benito Mussolini,** *executed 1945*

"This isn't the worst. The worst is that they stole twenty-five years of my life."
—*Director* **Erich von Stroheim's** *last words to Hollywood*

"I'm not afraid to die, Honey …I know the Lord has his arms wrapped around this big fat sparrow."
—*Blues singer* **Ethel Waters**

"I am about to, or, I am going to die. Either expression is used."
—**Dominique Bouhours,** *grammarian*

"Never felt better."
—**Douglas Fairbanks, Sr.**

GROUCHO GETS ELECTED, ACT I

Here's a script from a recently rediscovered radio show featuring Groucho and Chico Marx. Close your ears and listen with your eyes as you enjoy an episode of Five Star Theater, performed on March 13, 1933.

SCENE: *The office of Beagle, Shyster & Beagle, Attorneys at Law. Miss Dimple, the receptionist, is typing. Judge Maxwell, a local politician, is waiting for Waldo T. Flywheel, attorney, to arrive. Ravelli(Chico Marx), Flywheel's assistant, is sleeping in the corner.*

The door opens.

MISS DIMPLE: Good morning, Mr. Flywheel.

GROUCHO: Can't you think of anything else to say? You say that to me every morning.

JUDGE: (Stepping forward) Oh, Mr. Flywheel, you remember me, Judge Maxwell. I've been planning for a long time to drop in and talk to you about the coming election.

GROUCHO (impatiently): I know. I know.

JUDGE: (Surprised): Really? How did you know?

GROUCHO: Why, you just told me.

JUDGE: Mr. Flywheel, my re-election is being bitterly fought by a group of crooked politicians.

Their leader is Big Boss Plunkett, who is going to be tried for bribery shortly after the election. He doesn't want me on the bench because he knows I can't be tampered with.

GROUCHO (indignantly): See here, Judge Maxwell. Did you come here to buy my vote?

JUDGE: Why, no, of course not.

GROUCHO: Then you're wasting my time...and my time is valuable. Do you realize that while you're here talking nonsense, I could be at my desk, sleeping?

JUDGE: You don't understand, Mr. Flywheel. I am here to enlist your support in my campaign.

RAVELLI (waking up): Attsa fine. I take two bottles.

JUDGE: Two bottles of what?

RAVELLI: Two bottles of campaign. (Laugh.) Attsa some joke!

JUDGE (Indignant): Gentlemen! From your attitude I can only conclude that you are in sympathy with Boss Plunkett and his crooked politics. I'm going. Good day.

First president to greet people with a handshake: Thomas Jefferson. Earlier presidents bowed.

Door slams.

GROUCHO: Ravelli, I'm ashamed of you. I saw you taking your hand out of Judge Maxwell's pocket.

RAVELLI: Well, I had to take it out sometime.

Knock, door opens.

MISS DIMPLE: Why, it's Boss Plunkett, the politician!

GROUCHO: Ravelli, take Plunkett's hat.

CHICO: You take it, boss. It won't fit me.

PLUNKETT: Flywheel, my pal. Joe Crookley tells me that if it hadn't been for the way you defended him in court, he would have gone to prison for 20 years. He says you're a pretty smart lawyer.

GROUCHO (Coyly): Oh! I don't take his flattery seriously. That Joe Crookley is just a silly old cutthroat.

PLUNKETT: Listen, Flywheel, I want to talk turkey to you.

GROUCHO (Whispering): I think you'd better talk English. I don't want Ravelli to understand.

PLUNKETT: Look here, I'm against Judge Maxwell. If you join our party, I'll see to it that you get the nomination for judge.

GROUCHO: Plunkett, I'm willing to accept the nomination, but I can't join your party.

PLUNKETT: Why not?

GROUCHO: Frankly, I haven't a thing to wear.

Does Groucho get the nomination? Find out in Act II, page 262.

BIG NUMBERS: A TRILLION

Trillions are the numbers we use to express the national debt. But few of us have a sense of how big they are. Tim Gutmann, a New Hampshire mathematician, came up with a way of getting proper perspective. He asks: "Where were you one trillion seconds ago?"

His answer: "One trillion seconds is over thirty one thousand six hundred and eighty-eight years. That's 31,688 years. Lots and lots longer than recorded history; indeed, writing was developed in Sumeria only 252 billion (not trillion) seconds ago. Humans were around, but they hadn't been for long. Lucy (*Australopithecus afarensis*—one of the oldest known human descendents) walked the earth around 110 trillion seconds ago."

Napoleon Bonaparte, a Frenchman, designed the flag of Italy.

OOPS!

*Everyone's amused by tales of outrageous blunders—probably because
it's comforting to know that someone's screwing up even worse
than we are. So here's an ego-building page from the BRI.
Go ahead and feel superior for a few minutes.*

LEFT OUT

In 1994, Susan Leury was commissioned to create a 9-foot, 800-lb. bronze statue of native son Babe Ruth for the new baseball stadium in Baltimore. "During the many months of modeling and molding...Leury met countless experts and aficionados. Details were researched and debated. Did the Babe wear his belt buckle on the left or right? Was his hat cocked to the side or worn straight? No fact was too small to escape scrutiny. Except one.

"The bronze Babe, unveiled at the northern Eutaw Street entrance of Oriole Park, is leaning on a bat and clutching on his hip a right-handed fielder's glove. The real Babe was a lefty."

—from *Parade* magazine, 1/1/96

BOMBS AWAY!

"In 1994, the *Northwest Herald* of Crystal Lake, Illinois, ran a story about the controversy surrounding the Smithsonian Insitution's exhibit of the Enola Gay, the B-29 Superfortress that dropped the atomic bomb on Hiroshima in 1945.

"Apparently, the crack journalist who wrote the headline either failed to read the story, or had forgotten how World War II ended.

"The headline read: 'Atomic Bombers Criticize Enola Homosexual Exhibit.' 'It was a stupid thing on deadline,' the editor said. 'I'm not discussing it anymore.' "

—from the San Francisco *Chronicle*, 10/23/94

ASHES TO ASHES

"In 1990 the Wilkinsons, a family in Sussex, England received what they thought was a gift package of herbs from Australian relatives. They stirred the contents into a traditional Christmas pudding, ate half of it and put the remainder in the refrigerator.

"Soon thereafter, a member of the family relates, 'We heard from

Auntie Sheila that Uncle Eric had died, and had we received his ashes for burial in Britain.'

"Shocked, the Wilkinsons quickly summoned a vicar to bless, and bury, Uncle Eric's leftovers."

—from the *Wall Street Journal*, 12/18/90

A STIFF DRINK

"Coca-Cola is fixing an embarrassing typo in the word 'disk' in copyright information on about 2 million 12-packs of the drink.

"In the misprint, the 's' is replaced by a 'c.' The error appeared on boxes of Olympic promotional packages of Coca-Cola Classic distributed in the Atlanta area.

"Normally, the small type under the copyright information states that the 'red disk icon and contour bottle are trademarks of the Coca-Cola Co.' 'Everybody recognizes that it was an innocent mistake,' said a company spokesman, who wouldn't say how the error occurred. 'It's obviously a misprint.' "

—from wire service stories, 7/96

OOPS—WRONG AIRPORT

"Edward Valiz and Jose Gonzales were headed for the tiny Turlock, California airport, but when they emerged from their rented plane, they discovered instead that they'd landed at Castle Air Force Base…in the middle of a training exercise.

"Base officials said they had tried to warn off the plane, but never got any radio response.

"The pair were arrested when drug-sniffing police dogs found two pounds of methamphetamine, along with $1,300 in cash."

—from the *San Francisco Examiner*, 1994

WHICH PARTS?

"People calling an 800-number for Sears, Roebuck and Co. listed in the local phone directory were offered, instead, the chance to listen to 'the kinkiest group orgy line in America.'

"Apparently, a phone company clerk mistyped the number. 'I was amazed and shocked at first,' said one caller. 'After a few seconds, it seemed pretty funny. I mean, what a message to get when you're trying to reach a parts department.' "

—from wire service stories, 8/96

Medical studies show that intelligent people have more copper and zinc in their hair.

FABULOUS FLOPS

*Some consumer products are popular the moment they hit
the market, while others never get off the ground.
Their only legacy is a few bathroom laughs.*

Cheese-Filtered Cigarettes. In 1963, a Wisconsin businessman looking for new ways to use local cheese had a brainstorm: If smoke can be used to flavor cheese, why can't
cheese be used to flavor smokes? According to the *Wall Street Journal*, Univ. of Wisconsin chemists found that Parmesan and Romano were the best filter cheeses, using "a combination of one-third
charcoal and two-thirds cheese." The cigarette industry didn't bite.

Grubbies Sneakers. You've heard of pre-washed jeans. In 1966,
B.F. Goodrich came up with a similar idea: "pre-tattered" sneakers.
You didn't have to wait months for your sneakers to look beat-up.
With Grubbies, all you added was the foot odor.

Indoor Archery. In the early '60s, bowling was one of America's
hottest sports. Hoping to "do for archery what automatic pin-
setters have done for bowling," a number of entrepreneurs opened
"archery lanes," with automatic arrow-returns. They expected to
have thousands around the United States by 1970.

Look of Buttermilk/Touch of Buttermilk Shampoo. A 1970s
"health product." Were you supposed to eat it or wash with it? Did
you *want* to wash with it? Rubbing dairy products into their hair
didn't exactly conjure up images of cleanliness in the minds of most
consumers. "Touch of Yogurt Shampoo" also flopped.

Plastic Snow. Before snowmaking machines, how did ski resorts
keep people skiing during dry spells? In the mid-'60s, plastics
seemed like the answer. One resort spread tons of styrofoam pellets
on their ski runs; they quickly blew away. Another company offered mats with nylon bristles, like Astroturf, and New Jersey's
Great Gorge ski area laid them out on its slopes. They worked
well...unless you fell down. "The bristles were needle-sharp and
everybody tore his pants," founder Jack Kurlander told reporters,
"There was blood, blood, blood. Boy were we embarrassed!"

FLUBBED HEADLINES

These are 100% honest-to-goodness headlines.
Can you figure out what they were trying to say?

Man Robs, Then Kills Himself

KHRUSHCHEV IS BUR-IED IN ENCYCLOPEDIA

Carter Plans Swell Deficit

LIVING TOGETHER LINKED TO DIVORCE

MAYOR SAYS D.C. IS SAFE EXCEPT FOR MURDERS

Town Okays Animal Rule

Deer Kill 130,000

BOYS CAUSE AS MANY PREGNANCIES AS GIRLS

Prostitutes Appeal to Pope

DEADLINE PASSES FOR STRIKING POLICE

Stiff Opposition Expected to Casketless Funeral Plan

DRUNK GETS NINE MONTHS IN VIOLIN CASE

Bar Trying to Help Alcoholic Lawyers

Criminal Groups Infiltrating Pot Farms

Teenage Prostitution Problem Is Mounting

Delegate sex switch advocated

DEAD EXPECTED TO RISE

LEGALIZED OUTHOUSES AIRED BY LEGISLLATURE

Lot of Women Distressing

"Dead" Woman Doesn't Recall What Happened

Blind workers eye better wages

SUN SUED IN PUERTO RICO BY CONSERVATION TRUST

Milk Drinkers Turn to Powder

U.S., China Near Pact on Wider Ties

TWO CONVICTS EVADE NOOSE; JURY HUNG

MRS. COLLINS BURNED AT DUMP

Hospitals Are Sued by 7 Foot Doctors

Farmer Bill Dies In House

JUMPING BEAN PRICES AFFECT POOR

LAWMEN FROM MEXICO BARBEQUE GUESTS

Columnist gets urologist in trouble with his peers

Antique Stripper to Demonstrate Wares at Store

Strange stat: More boys than girls are born during the day; more girls are born at night.

THE BIRTH OF RAMBO

Who created Rambo? If you said Sylvester Stallone, you're wrong—it was a mild-mannered Canadian college professor teaching at the University of Iowa.

Young David Morrell could not tolerate conflict of any kind. Whenever violence appeared on TV, he had to leave the room. Until his early teens, even news reports panicked him; he was convinced someone would suddenly announce that a new war had begun. As he got older, Morrell found that writing was a way to get over some of his fears.

AN IDEA IS BORN

In 1969, while studying American literature at Penn State University, Morrell saw a TV news program that sparked his imagination and changed his life. The first report of the evening showed soldiers sweating out a battle in Vietnam. The second was about National Guardsmen dodging rocks, bottles, and bullets trying to put down urban riots.

If a viewer turned the sound off, he mused, it would seem that both film clips were a part of the same story. That gave him an idea for a tale in which the Vietnam war literally came home to America. He imagined a disaffected Vietnam veteran returning, disturbed and embittered by his Vietnam experiences, wandering aimlesssly around the backroads of the country.

THE PLOT THICKENS

Another news story provided further inspiration. "In a Southwestern American town," Morrell recalled, "a group of hitchhiking hippies had been picked up by the local police, stripped, hosed, and shaved. I wondered what my character's reaction would be if he were subjected to the insults those hippies had received."

Morrell decided his character would probably go nuts. He began writing a novel about a longhaired Vietnam vet who's driven over the edge when he's arrested and abused by a small-town Kentucky sheriff.

The naked truth: People in nudist colonies play volleyball more often than any other sport.

The character still didn't have a name. But that changed one afternoon when—an hour after Morrell had read a poem by Arthur Rimbaud (pronounced "Rambo") for his French class—his wife returned from the supermarket with a type of apple she'd never heard of before...the Rambo.

Morrell rushed to his typewriter and typed: "His name was Rambo, and he was just some nothing kid, for all anybody knew, standing by the pump of a gas station on the outskirts of Madison, Kentucky."

FIRST BLOOD

It took years to complete *First Blood*. Morrell finally finished it in 1971, while he was a professor at the University of Iowa. Although the book was intended to be an antiwar novel, it was extremely violent. By the end of the book, the Kentucky town is destroyed, the sherriff is killed along with 200 National Guardsmen, and Rambo is executed by his former instructor, who blows the top of his head off with a shotgun.

That summer Morrell sent the manuscript to a literary agent. He was so unsure of how people would react to it—Was it too bloody? Too violent?—that he included his Ph.D. dissertation in the package, too. That way, he figured, the agent would still have something respectable to sell if publishers hated the novel.

He needn't have worried. *First Blood* was sold in three weeks... and it was a huge success. *Time* magazine put it at the top of its book review page, observing that it was the first in a new genre of fiction—"carnography," the violence equivalent of pornography.

Columbia Pictures snapped up the movie rights for $90,000 and then sat on it for a year. They then sold it to another studio...which passed it on to someone else, and so on. Over the next ten years, 18 different screenplays based on *First Blood* were developed. Nearly every Hollywood tough guy—Clint Eastwood, Paul Newman, Robert De Niro, Nick Nolte, and even George C. Scott—was considered for the lead role and rejected.

"The novel became a Hollywood legend," Morrell says. "How could so much money and so much talent be expended on an enterprise that somehow could not get off the page?"

For Part II of the Rambo story, turn to page 250.

Vultures fly without flapping their wings.

NOT WHAT THEY SEEM TO BE

We take a lot of things for granted, based on image. But things (and people) often aren't what we think they are. Here are some examples.

AMERICAN GOTHIC

Image: Grant Wood's famous painting of an old Indiana couple posing in front of their farmhouse is considered the definitive portrait of the straitlaced Midwestern farmer.

Actually: They aren't farmers...or a couple. Wood's sister, Nan, was the model for the woman; a dentist friend named Byron McKeeby posed as the man. And the "farmhouse" in the picture was once used as a bordello.

WILLIAM ENO

Image: Considered the "Father of Traffic Safety." According to David Wallechinsky in *Significa*, he "originated stop signs, one-way streets, taxi stands, pedestrian safety islands, and traffic rotaries."

Actually: He never learned to drive. He thought cars were a passing fad. And he preferred horses anyway.

THE CHRISTMAS SONG

Image: A classic of the Christmas season. With lyrics like "Chesnuts roasting on an open fire...Jack Frost nipping at your nose," it evokes the feeling of a cold December perfectly.

Actually: It was written during a summer heat wave in Los Angeles. According to one account: "Mel Torme and his lyricist... wrote it in less than an hour, while consuming cold drinks at the piano and putting ice to their foreheads."

THE BEACH BOYS

Image: The Kings of California Surfing. Led by Brian Wilson, who wrote and sang hits like "Surfin' Safari" and "Surfin' USA," they started a national surfing craze in the early 1960s.

Actually: Brian Wilson (and three other Beach Boys) never surfed. "I didn't really know anything about surfing at all," he admitted in

---

Shoot 'em up: Actor John Wayne made more than 200 movies.

1995. In fact, says Stephen Gaines in his Beach Boy biography:

> Although the Beach Boys had sold an estimated 80 million records—20 million of them with surfing as a major theme—and Brian had splashed around in the water with his brothers for publicity photos, he had never mounted a surfboard....Indeed, photographing Brian in the surf was almost a cruel joke, because Brian had a deep, abiding fear of the water, and in his childlike manner he would warble in a thin voice, "The ocean *scares* me!"

Actually, the only Beach Boy who ever surfed was Brian's brother Dennis, the group's drummer, who drowned in 1983.

AIR JORDANS
Image: The first "air-cushioned" sneakers.
Actually: Nike tried air, and it didn't work—it leaked through the "airbag" material. They had to replace it with a gas that has larger molecules than air.

THE WEEKLY READER
Image: A benign weekly newspaper for elementary school kids.
Actually: Not so benign. In October 1994, the magazine ran an article "that discussed smokers' rights and the harm done to the tobacco industry by smoking restrictions. The article said nothing about smoking as a cause of lung cancer and heart disease." It turned out that the *Weekly Reader*'s owners were also the largest shareholders in RJR Nabisco, makers of Camel cigarettes.

THE "BLACK BOX"
Image: Whenever an airplane goes down, the first thing investigators say they're looking for is the "black box" that contains a recording of all conversations in the cockpit.
Actually: It's a yellow box.

KARL MARX
Image: Enemy of American capitalism.
Actually: Years *after* he had become famous as the author of the *Communist Manifesto*, he gratefully accepted a job as the London correspondent of the New York *Tribune*. His reason: His anti-capitalist political writing hadn't earned him enough to live on.

THE GREENING OF AMERICA

Here's a fad you've probably never heard of—chlorophyll. Does it sound silly? Well, think of all the things popular today that are going to be just as laughable in 40 years.

THE GREEN STUFF

In the 1930s, Dr. Benjamin Gruskin found a way to make chlorophyll—the green stuff in plants that turns sunlight into chemical energy—soluble in water. This discovery interested scientists but didn't appear to have much practical use.

That didn't bother O'Neill Ryan, Jr. and Henry T. Stanton, two ad executives. They decided to get into the chlorophyll business and patented Gruskin's process. Then, they tried to get manufacturers to use chlorophyll in products as a breath freshener and odor-killer—even though they had no proof (or reason to believe) it worked as either.

A GREENER AMERICA?

Somehow, in 1950, Ryan and Stanton managed to talk Pepsodent into coming out with a chlorophyll-based toothpaste called Chlorodent. Backed by Pepsodent's advertising muscle, it sold so well that other toothpaste companies rushed their own versions to market. By mid-1951, 30% of all toothpastes sold in the United States contained chlorophyll.

Other companies began adding chlorophyll to *their* products. By the end of 1952, stores were filled with chlorophyll soaps, cigarettes, dog foods, mothballs, toilet paper, diapers, shoe insoles, even popcorn. Chlorophyll beer, men's shorts, and Hebrew National chlorophyll-treated salami were in the works.

The End: In 1953, the American Dental Association and the FDA announced that chlorophyll did not cure bad breath—or any other odor. As the New York State Medical Society put it, "chlorophyll has certainly…swept the nation clean, not of odors, but of money." The public got the message. In less than a year, sales of chlorophyll-based products plunged from $120 million to $10 million—and most of them were pulled from the market.

STRANGE LAWSUITS

These days, it seems that people sue each other over practically anything. Here are a few real-life examples of unusual legal battles.

THE PLAINTIFF: Robert Lee Brock, an inmate at the Indian Creek Correctional Center in Chesapeake, Virginia

THE DEFENDANT: Robert Lee Brock, an inmate at the Indian Creek Correctional Center in Chesapeake, Virginia

THE LAWSUIT: Brock (serving 23 years for grand larceny) sued himself "for getting drunk and violating his civil rights." In a handwritten brief, he said: "I partook of alcoholic beverages in 1993. As a result I caused myself to violate my religious beliefs. This was done by my going out and getting arrested." Since Brock is imprisoned and can't work, he asked the state of Virginia to pay him and his family $5 million.

THE VERDICT: The judge acknowledged Brock's "innovative approach to civil rights litigation," then dismissed it as "ludicrous."

THE PLAINTIFF: Gloria Quinan, owner of Banner Travel in Santa Rosa, California

THE DEFENDANT: Pacific Bell

THE LAWSUIT: Pac Bell made a slight error when they listed Quinan's travel agency in their 1988 "Smart" Yellow Pages. Her ad was supposed to say she specialized in "exotic" travel; they changed it to "erotic" travel. Quinan's business dropped off by more than 50 percent, and most of the calls she *did* get were "from people genuinely interested in erotic services." Pac Bell said they wouldn't charge Quinan for the ad. She preferred to sue for $10 million.

THE VERDICT: Settled quietly out of court.

THE PLAINTIFF: Thomas Zarcone, food truck operator

THE DEFENDANT: William M. Perry, a Suffolk County, New York, judge

THE LAWSUIT: On April 30, 1975, Judge Perry was presiding over night court in Hauppage, New York. He sent a deputy sheriff out to buy coffee from Zarcone, who ran a food truck outside the courthouse. Fifteen minutes later, the deputy sheriff returned with three police officers. "He told me that Judge Perry wanted to see me about the coffee, because it was terrible," Zarcone recounted. "I said, 'You must be joking.'" They weren't. At the judge's orders, they handcuffed him and hauled him into the courthouse while bystanders gawked. "People were saying, 'Look, they're locking up the frankfurter man,'" Zarcone told a reporter. He was taken to Perry's chambers, where the judge screamed that his coffee was "garbage" and insisted it had been watered down. Zarcone sued the state.

THE VERDICT: Zarcone was awarded an unspecified amount for damages. Perry was removed from the bench for lying to the appellate court about the incident.

THE PLAINTIFF: Bob Glaser, a San Diego attorney

THE DEFENDANT: City of San Diego

THE LAWSUIT: In 1995, Glaser attended a Billy Joel / Elton John concert. He had to pee, and while he was in the men's room, women started using it because the lines for the women's room were so long. Glaser, "angered when a woman used a urinal in front of him," sued for $5.4 million for "embarrassment and emotional trauma."

THE VERDICT: Still pending.

THE PLAINTIFF: Rhonda Cook

THE DEFENDANTS: Des Moines Chrysler-Plymouth and Fred Owens, an ex-employee

THE LAWSUIT: In 1995, Cook stopped at the Iowa car dealership to look at a new Chrysler Concorde. Salesman Fred Owens convinced her to climb into the trunk "to check out its spaciousness." Then he slammed the trunk shut and bounced the car a few times. Cook claimed emotional distress and false imprisonment, and sued for unspecified damages. She pointed out that the sales manager had previously offered $100 to anyone who could get a customer to climb in the trunk.

THE VERDICT: Still pending.

Mel Brooks fought in the Battle of the Bulge in World War II.

MISS AMERICA,
PART I: The Origin

There she is...on TV, in the newspapers, on cereal boxes. It's Miss America. You may think of it as an institution, but for all its pomp and pretension today, the Miss America Pageant started off as just a crass little money-making gimmick. See for yourself. This story may surprise you.

SUMMER'S TALE

S H. Conrad Eckholm was the owner of Atlantic City's Monti-cello Hotel in the 1920s. The hotel made a lot of money during the summer, but business always dropped off drastically after the Labor Day weekend.

Eckholm figured that a festival of some sort, held at the end of September, might keep families at the beach a week or two longer. He pitched the idea to the Atlantic City Business Men's League, and they agreed to sponsor the "Fall Frolic" of 1920, which featured a masquerade ball and a "Rolling Chair Parade."

PUBLICITY STUNT

The Frolic was a success; the Business Men's League decided to sponsor a second one in 1921. This time, however, an Atlantic City newspaperman named Harry Finley suggested adding a new event to the schedule: a "popularity contest" for young women.

His idea was to have several Northeastern newspapers select young women to represent their cities. They'd be picked from photographs sent in by readers, and would compete against each other in Atlantic City to see who was the most popular of all.

Everyone would benefit from the contest: the newspapers would sell more papers, and Atlantic City hoteliers would get free publicity...which would draw paying customers to the boardwalk. So the Atlantic City Chamber of Commerce and the Hotelmen's Association got behind it. They agreed to add the event to the 1921 Fall Frolic.

CHOOSING A NAME

What would the popularity contest be called? At the first organizing committee meeting in 1921, someone suggested "Miss America." But the rest of the committee thought that sounded weak. They insisted on "The Most Beautiful Bathing Beauty in America" instead. (Winning contestants did assume the title "Miss America" as early as 1925, but the pageant itself didn't officially take the name until 1941.)

JUST IN CASE
Perhaps to guarantee that at least some genuine beauties would show up, organizers divided the Beauty category into two groups. The "professional" division was open to "actresses, motion picture players, or professional swimmers"; the "amateur" division was composed of the newspaper nominees and any other nonprofessionals who wanted to enter.

The winners from each category would face off against one another for the grand prize, a mermaid statue "valued at $5,000"...but actually only worth about $50.

THE FIRST PAGEANT
No one remembers how many "professionals" competed that first year, but Miss America Pageant records show that newspapers from only eight cities—Atlantic City, Camden (NJ), Newark, Ocean City (NJ), Harrisburg (PA), Pittsburgh, Philadelphia, and Washington, D.C.—nominated contestants.

Of these, only seven actually competed for the title: Miss Atlantic City, citing a potentially unfair hometown advantage, dropped out of the competition and assumed the role of hostess. For the next 40 years—until the "Miss Atlantic City" contest was abolished in 1960—Miss Atlantic City hosted the Miss America Pageant, but did not actually compete.

LITTLE MISS WASHINGTON
One of the unintended consequences of letting *anyone* nominate a candidate for the newspaper competition was that some of the young ladies chosen didn't even know about the contest.

Margaret Gorman, a 15-year-old schoolgirl from Washington D.C., was playing marbles in the dirt with some friends when some reporters from the Washington *Herald* tracked her down and told her she'd just won the Miss Washington D.C. pageant.

Her parents had never heard of it and were a little apprehensive—but they weren't about to pass up a free trip to Atlantic City. They agreed to play along. The decision was a good one: Gorman won the amateur division and went on to beat Virginia Lee, winner of the professional division, for the bathing-beauty crown. She became the very first Miss America.

A GOLDMINE

With its eight contestants and $27,000 budget, the 1921 pageant was extremely modest by today's standards. Even so, an estimated 90,000 to 100,000 people turned out to see it, making it a huge success. It was just a swimsuit contest, not a polished TV ceremony draped in patriotism like today's pageants, but that didn't matter. What counted most was that it made money for Atlantic City merchants. As A. R. Riverol writes in *Live from Atlantic City: The History of the Miss America Pageant Before, After and in Spite of Television,*

> The pageant's original aim was not to promote pageantry, beauty, scholarship, or any other such lofty ideal. Its creation was to make money, a point that many aficionados still feel uncomfortable admitting. That the pageant provided a variety of events, diversions, and entertainment was a peripheral amenity to the organizer's aims—business and self-promotion.

"We brought people here by the thousands," Mayor Edward Bader observed dryly, "and if they wished to purchase anything, the merchants profited."

Not what you expected? That's just the beginning.
For part II of the Miss America story, turn to page 112.

✳   ✳   ✳   ✳

RANDOM THOUGHT

"When I go to the beauty parlor, I always use the emergency entrance. Sometimes I just go for an estimate."

—*Phyllis Diller*

Phone survey: 61% of Americans like to hear music when put on hold; 22% prefer silence.

IS IT REALLY 2000?

*On Dec. 31, 1999, we'll be getting ready to celebrate a new millennium
...or maybe expecting the end of the world. But according to this piece from*
The Bathroom Reader's Guide to the Year 2000, *it's all a mistake.*

A NEW BEGINNING

Prior to the 6th century, the European calendar was based on the years counted from the founding of Rome or A.U.C. (Anno Urbis Conditae—"the year of the founding of the city.")
• In 1288 A.U.C. (534 A.D.), a Ukrainian monk named Dionysius Exiguus decided that the Christian calendar ought to be based on Jesus' birth. Under the patronage of Pope John I, he set out to try to figure exactly when Jesus had been born.
• It was a near-impossible task: the date of Jesus' birth isn't mentioned anywhere in the Bible. Still, working from vague gospel accounts, official Roman records, and astrological charts, Dionysius eventually settled on 754 A.U.C. as Christ's birthday. He called it 1 A.D. (for Anno Domini, or the Year of the Lord).

IT ISN'T 2000

"Unfortunately, Dionysius Exiguus was wrong in his calculations," writes Isaac Asimov in *The March of the Millennia.*
• The proof is found in the New Testament, where it clearly states that King Herod was ruler of Judea at the time Jesus was born. Since Herod's death is firmly dated at 4 B.C., Jesus must have been born about then. (Some argue it may have been as early as 12 B.C.)
• "If we were really counting from the birth of Jesus, the year we call 2000 is really somewhere between 2004 and 2020, and the actual year of A.D. 2000 may already have passed," writes Asimov.

IT ISN'T THE MILLENNIUM

• Dionysius' decision to began his new calendar with year 1, instead of the year 0, meant that by the beginning of year 2 A.D., only one year had elapsed; by 10 A.D., only nine years had passed; and by 100 A.D., only 99 years had been completed.
• Extend this logic to the present day and you realize by the year 2000, only 1999 years will have elapsed. So it's the first day of the year 2001, not of 2000, that starts the next millennium.

SEEDLESS FRUIT

In most cases, if there are no seeds, there is no fruit. Over time, however, several types of fruit that are good for eating have been found or created without pesky seeds inside. This piece is by Prof. David Sugar (no kidding!).

SEEDLESS WATERMELONS

The Seedless watermelon is not truly seedless—the seeds are so underdeveloped that they can be eaten while barely being noticed. It was developed by selecting watermelon strains in which the seeds matured much later than the flesh. So when the flesh is ripe for eating, the seeds still have a long way to go.

Where do seeds for planting seedless watermelon come from? When grown in parts of the world with very long, hot growing seasons, the seeds will finally mature. By that time, the flesh has deteriorated and is no longer good to eat.

SEEDLESS GRAPES

This is probably the best-known seedless fruit, especially the Thompson Seedless. In seedless grape varieties, the seed begins to form (which stimulates the grape berry's growth), but it stops developing while still very small, and becomes insignificant to the eater.

When grape seeds do develop, they produce hormones that stimulate the fruit and make it larger. So some seedless grape growers spray on a synthetic version of that hormone when the grapes are growing...to get those really big seedless grapes.

Making new seedless grape plants doesn't require seeds—pieces of grapevine cut in the winter will make new vines after rooting in moist soil.

SEEDLESS PEARS AND APPLES

Normally, apples and pears must have seeds. Each apple or pear has the capacity to develop 10 seeds, and needs at least one for the fruit to grow. However, a good load of seeds helps the fruit to become large and have a normal shape. An apple or pear with only one or two seeds may be misshapen—since the fruit grows more in the area near the seed than in other parts of the fruit.

But warm temperatures during flowering can sometimes over-come the need for seeds. For example, the Bartlett pear grown in Oregon and Washington generally needs seeds for fruit to form. In the warmer spring weather of California, on the other hand, Bartlett pears often grow without seeds. This is called "parthenocarpy" or "virgin fruit" (the Parthenon in Greece is the temple of virgins).

SEEDLESS "STONE" FRUITS

The "stone" fruits—peaches, nectarines, plums, apricots, cherries, and almonds—all have a single seed. While an occasional fruit may be found in which the seed did not fully develop, this type of fruit will usually fall off the tree if it doesn't have a seed inside.

By the way: you may be surprised to see almonds on this list of fruits. Actually, an almond tree is very much like a peach tree... except that in the almond, the *seed* grows large; the fleshy "fruit" part dries up and usually splits open before harvest.

☞   ☞   ☞   ☞

NAME THAT YEAR

How do you pronounce "2001"? Thanks to Stanley Kubrick's film *2001: A Space Odyssey*, most people think of it as "Two Thousand and One."

That's no accident. Fred Ordway, who advised Kubrick on the film, recalls: "Stanley asked me if we should say 'two thousand and one' or 'twenty-oh-one.' And we decided that 'two thousand and one' sounded better." He adds: "We often wondered...whether [the film's title] would have an influence on the English language when we got into the 21st century."

It did. But William Safire, who writes a weekly column called "On Language" for the *New York Times*, opts for "twenty-oh-one." Safire explains: " 'Two thousand and one' may sound mysterious and futuristic today but by the time we get there, it will be a laborious mouth filler."

Apparently, Safire is in the minority. A poll conducted by the *Futurist* in 1993 showed that 62% of people surveyed favored "two thousand one," 18% preferred "two thousand and one," and only 10% approved of Safire's choice of "twenty-oh-one."

Chopsticks are known as "quick little fellows" in China.

OLYMPIC CHEATERS

*Some people become famous at the Olympic games because they win a
medal. Others become infamous because they don't play by the rules.
Here's a look at the BRI's Olympic Hall of Shame.*

ROMAN EMPEROR NERO
Year: 67 A.D.
Place: Olympia

What happened: Nero decided to compete in the chariot race. In
the middle of the event, however, he fell off his chariot and was
left behind in the dirt. He never completed the course.

Reaction: The Olympic judges, "under extreme pressure," declared
him the winner anyway.

SPRIDON BELOKAS, Greek marathon runner
Year: 1896
Place: Athens, Greece (the first modern-day Olympics)

What happened: These Olympics were a matter of national pride
for Greeks. So Belokas became a national hero when he won the
bronze medal. But shortly after the games ended, he admitted
"hitching a ride in a horse-drawn carriage" during the race.

Reaction: He was stripped of his medal and running shirt, and
became a national disgrace overnight.

MEMBERS OF THE EAST GERMAN LUGE TEAM
Year: 1968
Place: Grenoble, France (Winter Games)

What happened: The East Germans placed first, second, and
fourth in the luge competition. Then Olympic officials discovered
that they'd "used a chemical to heat the runners of their toboggans
to increase speed."

Reaction: They were disqualified and forfeited their medals. But
the East German team never admitted guilt, blaming the incident
on a "capitalist plot."

Most, if not all, polar bears are left-handed.

JOHN CARPENTER, American runner, 400-meter finals

Year: 1908

Place: London

What happened: Scottish champ Wyndham Halswelle, the fastest qualifier and the person favored to win, was rounding the final bend neck-and-neck with three U.S. runners when one of them—Carpenter—shoved him sideways. John Taylor, another of the Americans, "won" the race, but not before a British official broke the tape and declared "no race."

Reaction: Carpenter was disqualified; Halswelle and the other two American finalists were invited to re-run the race two days later, "this time in lanes separated by strings." The Americans refused. Halswelle re-ran the race alone and won the gold medal automatically, the only person ever to win the gold in a "walkover."

FRENCH OLYMPIC AUTHORITIES AND THE FINNISH OLYMPIC COMMITTEE

Year: 1924

Place: Paris

What happened: Finland's Paavo Nurmi was the world champion long-distance runner. But for some reason, French officials didn't want Nurmi to sweep the gold medals in the 1500-, 5000-, and 10,000-meter events. So they scheduled the 5000-meter final just 55 minutes after the 1500-meter final, hoping Nurmi would be too tired to win the second race. Then Finnish officials arbitrarily dropped Nurmi from the 10,000-meter race so Ville Ritola, Finland's second-best runner, would have a shot at a gold medal.

Reaction: Nurmi was furious, but there was nothing he could do about it. He ran the 1500-meter event...and won in record time. Then, less than an hour later, he ran the 5000 meter...and won *that* in record time. Finally, according to legend, "as Ritola won the 10,000 meters by half a lap in world record time, Nurmi ran a lone 10,000 meters *outside* the stadium and beat Ritola's time."

RANDOM THOUGHT: "It's strange that men should take up crime when there are so many legal ways to be dishonest."

On some Caribbean islands, the oysters can climb trees.

IN ONLY 66 YEARS...

This comparison of the Wright brothers' first flight and that of Apollo 11, only 66 years apart, was supplied to Uncle John by NASA back in 1980. Uncle John recently found it among some old research papers, and immediately took it to the bathroom. It's a fascinating reminder of how fast things have changed.

WRIGHT BROTHERS		APOLLO 11
December 17, 1903	**Date**	July 16-24, 1969
Kitty Hawk, NC	**Place**	Cape Kennedy, FL; moon; Pacific Ocean
Less than $1,000 (including spare parts and round-trip rail tickets)	**Cost**	$355 million (Office of Manned Space Flight), or $375 million (Manned Spacecraft Center)
12 seconds	**Duration**	195 hours, 19 minutes, 35 seconds
15 feet	**Altitude**	242,000 statute miles (210,000 nautical miles)
120 feet	**Distance**	952,700 miles, 363 feet
3 pounds, 3 ounces	**Fuel Weight**	6.6 million pounds
Gasoline	**Fuel**	Liquid oxygen, liquid hydrogen, and kerosene
12 horsepower	**Power**	192,000,000 horsepower (7,600,000 pounds of thrust)
605 pounds	**Craft Weight**	6.4 million pounds
10 feet/second (31 mph)	**Speed**	35,000 feet/second
5	**Witnesses**	500,000,000 (est.)

The Wright brothers made four flights on December 17, 1903; the first was the shortest.

WRIGHT ON

Existential wisdom from comedian Steven Wright.

"Right now, I'm having amnesia and déjà vu at the same time. I think I've forgotten this before."

"I put tape on the mirrors in my house so I don't accidentally walk through into another dimension."

"A friend of mine once sent me a postcard with a picture of the entire planet Earth taken from outer space. On the back it said, 'Wish you were here.' "

"If you were going to shoot a mime, would you use a silencer?"

"I have the world's largest collection of seashells. I keep it on the beaches of the world. Perhaps you've seen it."

"I was cesarean-born. You really can't tell, although whenever I leave a house, I go out through a window."

"I locked my keys in the car the other day. But it was all right. I was still inside."

"I had amnesia once or twice."

"I have an existential map. It has 'you are here' written all over it."

"I'm writing a book. I've got the page numbers done, so now I just have to fill up the rest."

"If toast always lands butter side down, and cats always land on their feet, what happens if you strap toast on the back of a cat and drop it?"

"I walked into a restaurant. The sign said 'Breakfast Served—Any Time.' I ordered French toast...during the Renaissance."

"I like to reminisce with people I don't know. Granted, it takes longer."

"Cross-country skiing is great if you live in a small country."

"I used to work in a fire hydrant factory. You couldn't park anywhere near the place."

"I eat Swiss cheese, but I only nibble on it. I make the holes bigger."

WEDDING SUPERSTITIONS

If this book was Modern Bride, *we'd probably call these wedding "traditions" rather than superstitions. But think about it—most of them were started by people who believed in evil spirits and witches and talismans.*

THE BRIDAL VEIL: The veil has served a number of purposes throughout history, including: (1) protecting the bride from the "evil eye," (2) protecting her from jealous spinsters (who might also be witches) and (3) protecting the groom, his family, and other wedding guests from the bride's psychic powers—just in case she has any.

THE WEDDING KISS: A toned-down but direct throwback to the days when the couple was required to consummate their marriage in the presence of several witnesses, to insure that the consummation actually took place.

THE BRIDE'S GARTER AND GARLAND OF FLOWERS: Originally the groomsmen fought with each other to see who would get the bride's garter, which was supposed to bring good luck to the person who possessed it. But the Catholic Church frowned on the rowdy practice, and it was eventually replaced by a milder custom: the bride throwing a garland of flowers to her bridesmaids. Today the customs exist side by side.

WEDDING RINGS: One of the most ancient wedding practices The Egyptians, Romans, and Greeks all exchanged rings during their wedding ceremonies. Because a circle is a round, unending shape, it came to symbolize the ideal love that was supposed to come from marriage: it flowed from one person to the other and back again, forever. The ring has always been worn on the left hand—and was originally worn on the thumb. It was later moved to the index finger and then to the middle finger, and eventually ended up on the third, or "medical," finger. Reason: the third finger was believed to lead straight to the heart, via a single nerve.

Celebrated dropout: Mark Twain didn't even make it through elementary school.

HONEYMOON: This European tradition dates back hundreds of years and gets its name from the fact that newlyweds were expected to drink honey (believed to be an aphrodisiac) during the period of one full cycle of the moon (about a month).

THROWING RICE OR CONFETTI: Originally a fertility ritual. Wedding guests threw wheat at the bride only, in the hope that she would bear children the same way that wheat produced bread.

WEDDING CAKE: Guests originally gave "bride-cakes" to a just-married woman to encourage fertility.

JUNE WEDDING: It was customary for Romans to marry in June to honor the queen of the gods, Juno—who was also the goddess of women. They hoped to win her favor to make the marriage last, and make childbirth easier.

CARRYING THE BRIDE OVER THE THRESHOLD: Romans thought good and evil spirits hung around at the entrance of a home. They also believed that if you walked into your house left foot first, the evil spirits won. So to be sure the bride—whom Romans figured was "in a highly enotional state and very apt to be careless"—didn't accidentally step into her new home with the wrong foot, the groom just picked her up and carried her.

THE RECEPTION SPEECH: In pre-Christian Rome, newlyweds hired an "official joker" to tell dirty stories to guests during the reception. The Romans believed that "unclean" thoughts in the minds of guests turned the attention of vengeful gods away from the newlyweds, which helped protect them from evil.

DECORATING THE WEDDING CAR. In medieval France, when a couple was unpopular, people derided them publicly by banging on pots, kettles, etc. This was a *charivari*, or "rough serenade." In America it became a *shivaree*, and people got the treatment from friends. This gave way to a new custom—trying to keep a couple from consummating their marriage by making noise at their window. When newlyweds began leaving weddings by car, the only way to harass them was to deface the vehicle.

Tsunamis travel as fast as jet planes.

GOOD NEWS FOR HITLER

After William Randolph Hearst, America's most powerful newspaper publisher, visited a German spa, he had new respect for Hitler. Was there gold in the waters? Here's a piece from It's a Conspiracy!, by the National Insecurity Council.

In September 1934, William Randolph Hearst went to the world-famous spa at Bad Nauheim to "take the waters." The Nazi government welcomed him. After a month of socializing with prominent Germans, Hearst was invited to meet the new chancellor, Adolph Hitler. According to German newspapers, "Hearst was charmed and converted by the Nazi leader."

The German newspaper may have been right. When he returned to the United States, Hearst completely changed the editorial policy of his 19 daily newspapers and began praising the Nazi regime. For example, a September 1934 editorial signed by Hearst began:

> Hitler is enormously unpopular outside of Germany and enormously popular in Germany. This is not difficult to understand. Hitler restored character and courage. Hitler gave hope and confidence. He established order and utility of purpose....And the Germans love him for that. They regard him as a savior.

Was Hearst offering his praise for free, or was he paid?

SUSPICIOUS FACTS

As George Seldes reported in *Even the Gods Can't Change History:*

• Hearst's change in editorial policy came less than a month after the Nazi Ministry of Propaganda first subscribed to his International News Service (INS), a wire service that Hearst had created to compete against AP and UPI. INS was considered by journalists to be, by far, the worst of the three services.

• Even so, the Nazis paid Hearst more than $400,000 a year for their subscription to INS, at a time when other customers were only paying $50,000 to $70,000 for the same service. (The Nazis paid only $40,000 for their subscription to AP.)

• Hitler appears to have gotten what he paid for. According to legal

---

Time yourself: If you're an average adult, you spend 11-13 minutes in the shower.

papers filed in a lawsuit involving Hearst in the 1930s, "Promptly after the visit with Adolph Hitler and the making of... arrangements for furnishing INS material to Germany...William Randolph Hearst instructed all Hearst press correspondents in Germany, including those of INS, to report happenings in Germany only in a 'friendly' manner. All of such correspondents reporting happenings in Germany accurately and without friendliness, sympathy and bias for the actions of the then German government, were transferred elsewhere, discharged, or forced to resign."

• Week after week, Hearst papers ran pieces sympathetic to the Nazis. One article, which justified German rearmament to the American people, was written by Hitler's Minister of Aviation, Hermann Goering.

WAS IT A CONSPIRACY?

Was Hitler's payment a bribe to get Hearst to print pro-Nazi propaganda? The U.S. ambassador to Germany, William E. Dodd, thought so:

• According to Dodd, who was ambassador to Germany from 1933 to 1937, Hitler sent two of his chief propagandists to meet with Hearst at Bad Nauheim, to see how his image could be polished. When they found Hearst receptive, they set up a meeting and cut the deal.

• When Dodd found out about the arrangement, he "did not hesitate to tell the president that this was not a legitimate business deal; it was buying political support."

• Dodd noted that Hearst newspapers also began praising Italian dictator Mussolini after "Giannini, president of the Bank of America, had loaned Hearst some millions of dollars." Giannini was an avid Mussolini supporter.

• George Seldes wrote that in the 1940s, Hearst's deals with the two dictators were widely rumored in the industry, but he was so powerful that "of the 1,730 daily newspapers" Hearst *didn't* own, "not 1 percent ever said a word about the situation."

• Hearst, untouched by the scandal, continued to smear the patriotism of "socialists, liberals and other un-Americans" until the day he died. Ironically, no one seemed to question his motives.

George Washington and Abraham Lincoln were both descended from England's King Edward I.

BEHIND THE TITLE

What does it take to come up with just the right book title? Here are a few stories about famous titles that might give you an idea. For more of the same, read Now All We Need Is a Title, *by André Bernard.*

JAWS, by Peter Benchley

Benchley, a first-time author, struggled for months to come up with a title for his book about a man-eating shark. He tried hundreds—from *The Shark* and *Great White* to *A Silence in the Water*. His father, writer Nathaniel Benchley, suggested *What's That Noshin' on My Laig?* Finally, Benchley's editor said the only *word* he liked in any of the titles was "jaws." By then, Benchley didn't even care anymore: "Nobody reads first novels anyway," he said.

CATCH-22, by Joseph Heller

In 1961, Simon & Schuster was all set to publish Heller's first novel as *Catch-18*. Then another publisher protested that it was too similar to Leon Uris's new book, *Mila-18*—which they were about to release. Uris (who wrote *Exodus*) was a big name, Joseph Heller was an unknown. Simon & Schuster gave in and changed the title. Ironically, the phrase *Catch-22* has become part of the English language, and is arguably America's most famous modern book title.

BONFIRE OF THE VANITIES, by Tom Wolfe

During the 15th century, a monk named Savonarola inspired residents of Florence, Italy, to build a bonfire and burn all their worldly possessions—their vanities. After two such fires were built, the citizens built a third—this one for Savonarola. Tom Wolfe came upon the story during a trip to Italy. The idea of a bonfire for destroying one's "vanities" intrigued him.

SEX AND THE SINGLE GIRL, by Helen Gurley Brown

Cosmopolitan editor Helen Gurley Brown wanted to "write a book about sex being okay for single women." Her original title, *Sex for the Single Girl*, was considered immoral; she didn't want readers to think she was *promoting* sex after all. By changing one three-letter word, the title became morally acceptable. The book was a huge bestseller and helped create the "sexual revolution of the 1960s."

Gas guzzlers: 76% of U.S. commuters drive to work alone.

THE POSTMAN ALWAYS RINGS TWICE, by James M. Cain

Cain has given two different versions. He's said that while he was working on the manuscript, the mailman would ring the bell twice when delivering bills, once for personal letters. He's also said that the mailman would ring twice when delivering rejection letters from publishers. (On the day Alfred Knopf decided to publish the novel, the postman only rang once.) Cain named the novel as a memorial to his early failures.

A MOVEABLE FEAST, by Ernest Hemingway

Hemingway spent over 30 years writing this memoir about his life as a struggling writer in Paris. He died before it was published, and still hadn't come up with a satisfactory title (rejects: *The Paris Nobody Knows*; *To Write It Truly*). Finally, Hemingway's widow thought of a letter he'd written a decade earlier: "If you are lucky enough to have lived in Paris as a young man," he wrote, "then wherever you go for the rest of your life, it stays with you, for Paris is a moveable feast."

THE MALTESE FALCON, by Dashiell Hammett

Hammett had this title before he had written the book. But his publisher, Alfred Knopf, tried to talk him out of it. "Whenever people can't pronounce a title or an author's name," he said, "they are…too shy to go into a bookstore and try." The word Knopf objected to? *Falcon.* Hammett stuck to his guns, and the title is a part of American pop culture.

CAT ON A HOT TIN ROOF, by Tennessee Williams

Williams created the character of Brick in a short story called "Three Players of a Summer Game." Later, he turned the story into a play, adding Brick's wife—Maggie the Cat. That reminded him of something his father always used to say: 'Edwina, you're making me as nervous as a cat on a hot tin roof!' "

WHO'S AFRAID OF VIRGINIA WOOLF?, by Edward Albee

Albee found the phrase scrawled on a mirror in a Greenwich Village bar.

When he didn't wear a pocketwatch, George Washington used a small sundial to tell the time.

MARILYN'S SECRETS

*Marilyn Monroe's life has been examined and re-examined so often,
you may feel there's nothing you don't know about her...but thanks
to the diligence of BRI member Jack Mingo, we're able to
bring some interesting little-known facts to light.*

Her mother was a film-negative cutter in Hollywood. Her father could have been any of several men her mother was sleeping with at the time, but later in life Marilyn Monroe convinced herself that Clark Gable was her biological father.

• Two weeks after her birth, she was placed with a religious foster family that taught her that going to movies was a sin.

• Her closest playmate was a stray dog she adopted. Just after her seventh birthday, a neighbor killed him with a shotgun. That same day, her mother suddenly appeared and took her back.

• Still working as a film cutter, her mom used movie houses as a form of day care, knowing her daughter would stay cool and safe while she worked. The devout seven-year-old spent hours praying that her shockingly amoral mother wouldn't be condemned to hell.

• When Monroe was 10, her mother was committed to a mental institution. She went to live with an aunt, who dyed young Marilyn's hair platinum blonde and bought her only white clothes.

• As a child, she vowed she would never get married. She was going to become a schoolteacher and have lots of dogs, instead.

• She quit high school at 16 to marry a 21-year-old. She took a job spraying varnish on fabric for airplanes, but soon became a model. Her agent said she was "too plump" and "smiled too high on her face," but two years later she had appeared on 33 magazine covers.

• As a young adult, she spent her small income on acting classes and rent. She filled the gaps by providing quick in-car sex in exchange for restaurant meals, and began getting movie parts by sleeping with movie executives.

• Monroe's beauty wasn't all natural. Her hairline was heightened by electrolysis, her teeth were bleached, and an overbite was corrected. A plastic surgeon removed a lump of cartilage from the tip of her nose and inserted a crescent-shaped silicone implant into her jaw to give it a softer line.

PRIMETIME PROVERBS

Television wisdom from the book Primetime Proverbs, *compiled by Jack Mingo and John Javna.*

ON AMERICA

"You know what makes this country great? You don't have to be witty or clever, as long as you can hire someone who is."
—**Ted Baxter,**
The Mary Tyler Moore Show

"There's about three great moments in a man's life: when he buys a house, and a car, and a new color TV. That's what America is all about."
—**Archie Bunker,**
All in the Family

ON ARTISTS

"Artists are always ready to sacrifice for art—if the price is right."

—**Gomez Addams,**
The Addams Family

ON TELEVISION

"This show is ridiculous. I can't recommend this to children. I couldn't even recommend it to a Marine. Parents, you should be ashamed to let your children watch this show. Let 'em read a book, go out and play, watch the fruit ripen. Anything but this."

—**Dick Loudon,**
Newhart

ON EMPLOYEES

"Nobody has ever stood up to me the way you did. I find you bold, forceful, a man of conviction—three qualities I *despise* in an employee."
—**Mr. Wainwright III,**
Too Close for Comfort

ON WINNING

"As my Great Aunt Maude always said, 'If you can't win the game, the next best thing is to upset the chessboard.'"
—**Artemus Gordon,**
The Wild, Wild West

Jane Hathaway: "Chief, haven't you ever heard of the saying, 'It's not whether you win or lose, it's how you play the game'?"
Mr. Drysdale: "Yes, I've heard it. And I consider it one of the most ridiculous statements ever made."
—*The Beverly Hillbillies*

"There's nothing to winning, really. That is, if you happen to be blessed with a keen eye, an agile mind, and no scruples whatsoever."

—**Alfred Hitchcock,**
Alfred Hitchcock Presents

Armadillos can get leprosy.

FAMILIAR PHRASES

Here are the origins of some everyday phrases.

HIGHTAIL IT

Meaning: Leave quickly.

Origin: Dates back to the Old West. Cowboys on the Great Plains noticed that wild horses jerked their tails very high just before galloping off. Soon anyone who left quickly was said to have "hightailed it."

RED HERRING

Meaning: Distraction; diversionary tactic.

Origin: Comes from hunting. When herring is smoked, it changes from silvery gray to brownish red and gives off a strong smell. Hunters use red herrings to train dogs to follow a scent...and, by dragging a red herring across the trail, they can also throw a dog *off* a scent.

STUFFED SHIRT

Meaning: Braggart or pompous person.

Origin: In the days before mannequins, clothing shops displayed shirts in their windows by stuffing them with tissue paper or rags. The shirt looked broad-chested, like a strong man, but was really light and flimsy.

RIGHT-HAND MAN

Meaning: Important assistant.

Origin: In 17th-century cavalries, the soldier at the far right of a line of troops had a position of special responsibility or command.

AT THE DROP OF A HAT

Meaning: Quickly; without delay.

Origin: The term dates back to the days when races, prizefights, and other sporting events were literally started with the wave or the drop of a hat.

WIENERS ON WHEELS

*Here's a BRI inside look at the Oscar Mayer Wienermobile,
perhaps the most popular pop-culture icon on four wheels.*

THE EVOLUTION OF THE WIENERMOBILE
In the beginning, there was the "Weiner Wagon," a horse-drawn cart that the Oscar Mayer Company sent to Chicago-area butcher shops to promote its products. A German band rode on the back, oom-pahing for crowds wherever the wagon stopped.

Modern thinking. In the mid-1920s, Oscar's nephew, Charlie, joined the company right out of college. He came up with the idea of hiring a midget to dress up in a chef's uniform and make appearances with the band. Dubbed "Little Oscar, the world's smallest chef," the midget sang, plugged Oscar Mayer products, and gave away prizes at each stop.

Rolling along. In the 1930s, there was a nationwide craze for vehicles in the shape of products. There were milk bottle-mobiles, vacuum cleaner-mobiles, cheese-mobiles, and so on. Mayer's nephew decided to create a special vehicle for Little Oscar. He paid the General Body Company of Chicago $5,000 to convert an old car into a 13-foot, open-cockpit hot dog—the first "Wienermobile." It rolled off the assembly line in 1936.

Wieners everywhere. Putting the world's smallest chef behind the wheel of the World's Largest Wiener, as Oscar Mayer called it, generated plenty of publicity. In fact, it was such a good promotional gimmick that by the 1940s the company had an entire fleet of Wienermobiles. Every time they opened a new meat-packing plant, they commissioned a new Wienermobile to go with it. The vehicles were on the road continuously from 1936 to 1977, stopping only during World War II gasoline rationing.

Dead dog. By the mid-1970s, it looked like the Wienermobile's days were running out. Oscar Mayer wanted to move away from its regional meat plant promotions toward nationwide TV advertising campaigns...and who knows, maybe it thought the dogs-on-wheels were getting too dorky. So, in 1977, the entire wienie fleet was put up on blocks.

On a roll. The giant wieners might have stayed there forever. But in 1986, the company decided to commemorate the 50th anniversary of the original Wienermobile. As Wienermobile manager Russ Whitacre explains, "We brought the last working one out of storage and put it on the road, driven by two college students for the summer. We got a great deal of response...a lot of nostalgia. Boomers said it was a piece of their lives." When thousands of fans wrote to Oscar Mayer about the vehicles, company officials decided they had something worth preserving, and ordered a brand-new fleet of six to be built. They hit the road in 1988.

LAMBORWIENIE

The pre-1980s Wienermobiles had been pretty spartan as sausages go, but the 1988 models were genuine Wienerbagos, complete with microwave ovens, refrigerators, CB radios, cellular phones, and stereo systems capable of belting out 21 different renditions of the Oscar Mayer Wiener song, including country, rap, and rock 'n' roll versions. Even the car's exhaust system was improved—in addition to ordinary automobile fumes, the Wienermobiles give off a "fondly familiar hot dog scent" during appearances.

The car's V6 engine has a top speed of 110 mph. But the only person known to have driven the car that fast was Al Unser Jr., who took one of the wienies for a spin at the Indianapolis Motor Speedway. Oscar Mayer hotdoggers (the company's name for Wienerdog drivers) are pretty much stuck driving at the legal speed limit. As Whitacre explains, "Because of the vehicle's visibility, we hear about it if someone drives a Wienermobile in an unsafe manner."

WIENERMOBILE 2000

By 1994, the new Wienermobiles had logged an average of 200,000 miles apiece on American highways and byways, so Oscar Mayer hired California auto designer Harry Bradley—creator of the original Mattel Hot Wheels—to design a Wienermobile for the 21st century. Among his improvements: He extended the wienie theme to the *inside* of the vehicle, giving it a hot dog dashboard and glove box, a condiment control panel, and relish-colored captain's chairs for the driver and passengers. Estimated total cost of each vehicle: $150,000.

WIENERMOBILE FACTS

• Nine different men played Little Oscar; the last one retired in 1971. Why wasn't he replaced? Oscar Mayer is mum on the subject. Our theory: As times changed, dressing midgets up as chefs could be considered "bad taste."

• What happens to old Wienermobiles? Most are sent to Canada, Mexico, and other countries where Oscar Mayer has affiliates, but at least one is always kept on hand as a "loaner wiener" in case any of the new ones break down.

• Which is harder to get into: Harvard Law School, or the driver's seat of the Wienermobile? Hint: Every year, more than 1,000 recent college graduates apply for the coveted position of "hotdogger"; only 12 get the nod. Oscar Mayer says "outgoing personalities and impressive academic credentials" are key qualities for the job.

• Once you're hired on as a hot dogger, you have to put in a week of on-the-dog training at Hot Dog High, the company's Wienerdog training facility. "The curriculum takes about seven days," hotdogger Brian Spillane explains, "including one day to learn how to drive the 'Dog,' just so no one gets in a pickle when they miss a turn."

• Mastery of hot dog puns is another must. "Go ahead and grill us," Dan Duff, another hotdogger, challenges. "In this job, we're trained to cut the mustard. It's a job to relish...and that's no bologna."

• Wienermobiles log an average of 1,000 miles per week visiting baseball games, children's hospitals, grocery stores, etc. Even so, there have been very few traffic accidents involving the Wienermobile—although there was at least one accident involving a Wienermobile fan. As one hotdogger admits: "One guy saw the Weinermobile, and laughed so hard, his false teeth fell out—right into the big air vents on the buns. We never did find them. He really sank his teeth into our buns."

Clothes horses: 9% of Americans buy their pets clothing on birthdays and holidays.

THE FIRST PHONE BOOKS

Today, the phone directory is the most widely used book in America. Practically every household has at least one. Here's how they got started.

THE FIRST WHITE PAGES

The first personal phone directory was issued in 1878—just two years after Alexander Graham Bell invented the telephone—by Boston's Telephone Dispatch Company. It was different from today's White Pages in two major respects:

1. It was only one page long, because only 97 Bostonians owned telephones in 1878.

2. It didn't list any phone numbers. Why not? There weren't any. Direct dial hadn't been invented; you just picked up the receiver and turned a hand crank that rang a bell alerting the operator. When she came on the line, you told her who you wanted to talk to. That was it.

THE FIRST YELLOW PAGES

The first business directories were actually printed on white paper. The R.R. Donnelley Company, a Chicago printing firm, was already publishing listings of local companies with their addresses. When phones came along in 1877, Donnelley just noted which businesses had them.

The first *Bell* Telephone business directory followed almost immediately in 1878; like the first personal directories, it was only one page long. Businesses were divided into seven listings: Physicians; Dentists; Stores; Factories, etc.; Meat and Fish Markets; Miscellaneous; and Hack [horses for hire] and Boarding Stables.

The number of phone customers grew exponentially over the next decade, and as directories got larger, printing costs soared. In the late 1880s, telephone companies around the country began selling advertising space in their directories to defray expenses. Today

Approximately 56,000 courier pigeons "fought" in World War II.

the ads actually *make* money—a lot of it—for phone companies: U.S. businesses bought more than $10 billion worth of yellow-page ads in 1995.

THE COSMIC QUESTION

Of course, we still haven't answered the *real* question: why are yellow pages yellow? Well, research conducted by Bell Laboratories has shown that black ink on dark yellow paper is the second-most visible paper-and-ink combination—after black ink on white paper. But nobody knew that in 1881, when the first yellow pages were printed.

Here's what happened: The Wyoming Telephone and Telegraph Co. hired a printer in Cheyenne to print its first business directory. But he didn't have enough white paper to complete the job. So, rather than lose the phone company's business altogether, he used the stock he had on hand—yellow paper.

Like the first personal directories, the first "yellow pages" were actually a yellow *page*—a single sheet that contained only 100 business listings, under such headings as Boots, American Indian Jewelry, and Soda Water Companies. Most of the telephone numbers on it were just one, two, or three digits long.

✤　　✤　　✤

PHONE PRANKS

In April 1996, some hackers tapped into the main number that directs callers to New York City's 76 police precincts and replaced the standard recording with the following message:

> You have reached the New York City Police Department. For any real emergencies, dial 911. Anyone else—we're a little busy right now eating some donuts and having coffee. (In the background, the *New York Post* reported, a second voice could be heard saying "A *big* cup of coffee. And masturbating.")

The recording ended, "You can just hold the line. We'll get back to you. We're a little slow, if you know what I mean. Thank you."

THE BIRTH OF "THE SIMPSONS"

It may be the most popular prime-time cartoon in history. But how did such an outrageous show make it onto the air in the first place? Read on.

OFF THE WALL

In the mid-1980s, producer James L. Brooks was hired to develop a comedy series called "The Tracey Ullman Show" for the fledgling Fox TV network. Ullman was immensely popular in England...but Brooks wasn't sure her humor would play well in the United States. He figured that inserting short cartoon segments between her comedy sketches might help keep the show interesting to American audiences.

Brooks was a fan of counterculture cartoonist Matt Groening (pronounced *Graining*), whose weekly cartoon strip *Life in Hell* runs in *The Village Voice* and more than 200 other "alternative" newspapers. He had a *Life in Hell* poster in his office, and one day he remarked to an assistant, "We should get this guy and have him animate for us."

LOST IN SPACE

So Fox officials approached Groening about animating *Life in Hell* and making its characters—two humans named Akbar and Jeff and three rabbits named Binky, Sheba, and Bongo—part of the show. At first, Groening agreed. Then he ran into a problem: "Fox told me outright, 'We must own the characters and the marketing rights.' The studio was still getting over the fact that a few years ago it gave George Lucas all the licensing rights to *Star Wars*."

Groening was making a pretty good living licensing the *Life in Hell* characters for calendars, mugs, T-shirts, etc., and didn't want to give it up. But rather than walk away from Fox's offer, he came up with another idea. He dashed off a short story based on his real-life family—Homer and Marge Groening (his parents); Lisa and Maggie (his sisters); and an autobiographical character named Bart (an anagram of the word "brat"). He proposed using them instead of the *Life in Hell* characters. Fox agreed to give it a try.

A NEW FAMILY

As Groening developed these characters for TV, they began to lose their resemblance to his real family. (His father, for example, isn't bald, and his mother no longer wears "big hair.") He changed their last name to the all-American sounding "Simpson," and fashioned their lives after old sitcom characters. "I used to spend hours transfixed in front of a TV set watching family situation comedies," he told the *San Francisco Chronicle* in 1990. "It's no accident that the Simpsons live in Springfield—that's the town in 'Father Knows Best.' " Later, he added: "What is 'The Simpsons' but a hallucination of the sitcom? And that has to be the ultimate American nightmare."

The original sketches were only 15 to 20 seconds long, so Bart was the only well-developed character. "He was like what would have happened if 'Leave It to Beaver's' Eddie Haskell got his own show," Groening says. "He was a deviant." Homer—his voice, at least—was a Walter Matthau impersonation, Lisa was supposed to be a "female Bart," and Marge and Maggie weren't much more than backdrops for the other characters.

BUST AND BOOM

The "Tracey Ullman Show" debuted in 1987. It was a critical success, but ratings were terrible. Despite this, "The Simpsons" attracted a huge cult following, and Fox responded by increasing the length of the sketches from 20 to 90 seconds. Then they introduced a line of Simpsons T-shirts, posters, and other items to cash in on the fad.

But the biggest boost to the Simpsons' popularity came from a candy bar company. The makers of Butterfinger and Baby Ruth licensed the Simpson characters for their candy bar ads—which aired on network TV. So kids who'd never heard of "The Tracey Ullman Show" (or Fox, for that matter) finally got a glimpse of Bart and his family. Their popularity grew.

ON THEIR OWN

In 1988, Fox decided to spin "The Simpsons" off into their own show. It was scheduled to premiere in September 1989. But when the initial 13 episodes came back from Korea, where they were being animated, Groening discovered that the director had added a

Three Mile Island is only 2 1/2 miles long.

few unauthorized "jokes" of his own. In one episode, for example, when the Simpsons are watching a TV show called "The Happy Little Elves Meet the Curious Bear Cubs," the animators inserted a scene in which a bear cub rips off the head of an elf and drinks its blood.

"Not exactly a minor addition," Groening told *The New York Times* in 1990. "When we watched it, we sat in the dark for about two minutes in silence. Then we ran for the door. I thought my career in animation had sunk to the bottom of the sea. Had that gotten on the air, there would be no show today." The director and animators were fired, and the show was postponed until January 1990 while new animators fixed the episodes.

SHOWTIME

"The Simpsons" as we know it today finally made it onto TV on January 13, 1990. It earned the second-highest ratings in its time slot—pretty impressive when you consider that Fox didn't have as many affiliates around the country as ABC, CBS, or NBC. ("The Tracey Ullman Show" went off the air five months later.) "The Simpsons" went on to become Fox's highest-rated show. In March 1990, it placed 20th in the weekly Nielsen ratings, and in June went all the way to #3. It has, without question, played a key role in establishing Fox as a viable fourth network.

SOUR GRAPES

In 1992, Tracey Ullman filed suit against Fox for $2.25 million, arguing that since "The Simpsons" got their start on her show ("I breast-fed those little devils," she told a reporter), she was entitled to a share of the merchandising profits. In court, however, she admitted that she did not create "The Simpsons," write any of the shows, or take part in any of the merchandising. She lost the case.

cᴆ   cᴆ   cᴆ

"The creativity of the way people respond to the show is fantastic. You should see the fan mail. Kids send in their pictures of Bart beating up other cartoon characters."

— *Matt Groening*

Henry Ford was Charles Lindbergh's first passenger in the Spirit of St. Louis.

FAMOUS INDIAN IMPOSTORS

It's common for North Americans to romanticize the traditions
of Native Americans, so it shouldn't be surprising that the "Indian way"
is fertile ground for hoaxes and impostors. Here are two notable examples.

GREY OWL

In the 1930s, Grey Owl was one of the most famous naturalists in the world. "He is no stuffed Indian," *The New York Times* reported at the time. "He is real and honest."

Who He Said He Was: Grey Owl claimed to be the son of a Scottish man and his Apache wife. At the age of 15, his story went, he went to live with the Ojibway tribe near Ontario, Canada. They named him Wa-Sha-Quon-Asin, which translates as "He-Who-Flies-by-Night" (an appropriate name), or "Grey Owl." They also taught him how to trap beavers…but when his traps killed a mother beaver and left its young as orphans, he decided to stop killing animals and start protecting them.

The Canadian government was impressed. They made a film about his work and gave him a job as a conservationist in their national parks. His fame grew; he wrote two bestselling books (in 1931 and 1935) and toured England twice, speaking in packed lecture halls to more than 250,000 people. He was even invited to meet with King George…whom he greeted as an equal, extending his hand and saying, "I come in peace, brother."

Who He Really Was: A few days after He-Who-Flies-by-Night died in 1938, an Ontario newspaper discovered that he was actually Archibald Stansfeld Belamey, an Englishman who'd moved to Canada at the age of 18. Once there, he quickly acquired four wives, several children, a police record, and a reputation for public drunkenness. He abandoned them all for the fantasy world of a half-Indian beaver lover.

What Happened: Belamey is still held in high esteem. As *History Today* reported in 1994, "Grey Owl has never been forgotten. His

Terminator 2 cost $647,000 per minute of film to make.

books remain in print. His cabins in the National Parks where he worked have been restored, and some of his canoe routes have been mapped for park visitors."

LITTLE TREE

In 1976, Delacorte Press published *The Education of Little Tree*, by Forrest Carter. The book became a #1 bestseller on the *New York Times* nonfiction list. More than a million copies were in print by the late 1980s, and in 1991 the American Bookseller's Association voted it the book "they most enjoyed selling."

Who He Said He Was: Carter said *The Education of Little Tree* was an autobiographical account of the way his Cherokee grandmother and her Scottish husband taught him how to weave baskets, make moccasins, hunt wild game, and live off the land.

Who He Really Was: In 1991, an historian was researching a biography of segregationist Alabama governor George Wallace when he discovered Forrest Carter's true identity. Incredibly, he was really Asa Carter, a violent white supremacist and former speechwriter for Wallace. As the historian wrote in *The New York Times*:

> Between 1946 and 1973, [Asa] Carter carved out a violent career in Southern politics as a Ku Klux Klan terrorist, right-wing radio announcer, home-grown American fascist and anti-Semite....He even organized a paramilitary unit of about 100 men that he called the Original Ku Klux Klan of the Confederacy.

In time, Carter became too bigoted even for the Wallace campaign. So he ran against Wallace for governor in 1970 (he got 15,000 votes out of more than 1 million cast). Then he dropped out of sight, moved to Texas, and began writing novels as Forrest Carter (after Nathan Bedford *Forrest,* the Confederate general who founded the Ku Klux Klan). His two most successful novels were *Gone to Texas,* which Clint Eastwood made into the film *The Outlaw Josey Wales,* and *The Education of Little Tree.* Carter died in 1979...and his true identity remained a secret until 1991.

What Happened: *The New York Times Book Review* moved *The Education of Little Tree* from its nonfiction list to its fiction list. Carter's books are still in print, and sales remain strong.

SPEAK OF THE DEVIL

Here are some random bits of information about the Devil.

THE DEVIL YOU SAY

• The Devil as we think of him—with the horns, pitchfork, etc.—dates back to the 10th and 11th centuries; his popular image was not taken from the Bible. According to the New Testament, the devil takes the form of a lion, a wolf, a dragon, and a serpent. Early Christians sometimes thought of him as a three-headed dog.

So where does the Devil we know come from?

• His beard (goatee), horns, hooves, hairy legs, pointy ears, etc. were borrowed from the goat. Scholars cite two reasons:

1. "The domestic goat was renowned for the size of its phallus," writes historian J. C. J. Metford, and, according to legend, "tempted saints by whispering in their ears lewd details of the sexual pleasures they had relinquished."

2. One of the ways the Church discouraged interest in other religions was by literally "demonizing" gods that competed with theirs. So a lot of the imagery is derived from pagan sources: the goatlike features also come from Pan, the Greek god of shepherds, fertility, and nature.

• His red skin is the color of blood and fire.

• His three-pronged fork, or *triton*, was borrowed from Poseidon, the nasty-tempered Greek god of the sea and of earthquakes, whose main symbol was a three-pronged spear.

DEVOLUTION

• Modern mythology paints the Devil as the kind of all-powerful, evil being who possesses little girls in *The Exorcist* or tries to destroy the world in *The Omen* But that hasn't always been the case.

• During the Middle Ages in parts of Europe, he was seen as more of a mean-spirited, clumsy, dimwitted lout with a fondness for pranks—like Bluto in the *Popeye* cartoons—that the wise and the holy could easily outsmart. "There was nothing grand about their Satan," historian Charles Mackay writes in his book *Extraordinary Popular Delusions and the Madness of Crowds.*

Mary Stuart became Queen of Scotland when she was six days old.

On the contrary, he was a low, mean devil, whom it was easy to circumvent, and fine fun to play tricks with....It was believed that he endeavored to trip people up by laying his long invisible tail in their way, and giving it a sudden whisk when their legs were over it; that he used to get drunk, and swear like a trooper, and be mischievous. ...Some of the saints spat in his face, to his very great annoyance; others chopped off pieces of his tail, which, however, always grew on again.

• Of course, some countries were extremely serious about Satan. Historians estimate that from 1450 to 1750, more than 200,000 alleged witches were executed in Europe and America for "dealing with the Devil."

DEVIL'S FOOD

• How did devil's food cake get its name? One theory: The stuff was so tasty that people assumed that the inventors had to sell their soul to the Devil to get the recipe.

• You've probably eaten pumpernickel bread before...but did you know the word *Pumpernickel* means "Devil's fart" in German? Apparently, when German bakers invented the bread centuries ago, it was awful. The 1756 book *A Grand Tour of Germany* described it as bread "of the very coarsest kind, ill-baked and as black as coal, for they never sift their flour." Locals joked that it was so difficult to digest that even the Devil himself got gas when he ate it.

• In some countries, the Devil is nicknamed "the good man," "the old gentleman," and even "the great fellow." Why? Tradition had it that if you "spoke of the Devil," he would appear. So people didn't.

SATAN ON TRIAL

In 1971, a man named Gerald Mayo filed suit against Satan in the U.S. District Court in Pennsylvania, alleging that "Satan has on numerous occasions caused plaintiff misery and unwarranted threats, against the will of plaintiff, that Satan has placed deliberate obstacles in his path and has caused plaintiff's downfall. Plaintiff alleges that by reason of these acts Satan has deprived him of his constitutional rights."

The case, "Gerald Mayo v. Satan and His Staff," was thrown out of court after Mayo failed to provide the U.S. marshall with instructions on how to serve Satan's subpoena, and could not prove that Satan lived within the jurisdiction of the District Court.

What's the most-shoplifted book in the United States? The Bible.

THE CREATION OF FRANKENSTEIN

You might assume that the flat-headed, bolts-in-the-neck monster we all know was taken directly from Mary Shelley's original novel. Nope. It was created specifically for the movies. Here's the story of how the world's most famous monster was born.

FIRST FRIGHT

History books credit Thomas Alva Edison with inventing the lightbulb, the phonograph, the movie camera, and many other things. But one invention they usually leave off his resume is the horror movie. His Edison Film Company invented it in 1910, when they put Mary Shelley's 1818 novel *Frankenstein* on film for the first time.

Edison's *Frankenstein* was barely 16 minutes long and was only loosely based on the original. The filmmakers thought the book was too graphic, so they eliminated "all the...repulsive situations and concentrated on the mystic and psychological problems found in this weird tale."

CREATIONISM

But one scene in Shelley's book wasn't graphic *enough* for Edison executives: the "creation scene" in which Dr. Frankenstein brings the monster to life. Shelley devoted only two sentences to it:

> I collected the instruments of life around me, that I might infuse a spark of being into the lifeless thing that lay at my feet. It was already one in the morning; the rain pattered dismally against the panes, and my candle was nearly burnt out, when, by the glimmer of the half-extinguished light, I saw the dull yellow eye of the creature open; it breathed hard, and a convulsive motion agitated its limbs.

That was all Shelley wrote. So the folks at Edison used their imagination and decided to make a "cauldron of blazing chemicals" the source of the monster's life. Edison's monster looked nothing like the Frankenstein we know now. It was a white-faced hunchback with matted hair and a hairy chest.

ON THE ROAD

Following the success of Edison's *Frankenstein*, other studios filmed their own versions of the story. The first full-length Frankenstein film, called *Life Without a Soul*, hit the silver screen in 1916, and an Italian film called *Il Mostro di Frankenstein* followed in 1920.

But the Frankenstein monster might never have become a Hollywood icon if it hadn't been for Hamilton Deane, an English actor who ran (and starred in) a traveling *Dracula* show during the 1920s. Tired of performing *Dracula* night after night, Deane began looking for material he could use as an alternate. He settled on *Frankenstein*.

In 1927 he asked a member of the *Dracula* troupe, Peggy Webling, to adapt *Frankenstein* into a play. Like the folks at Edison, she got creative with the story. For example:

- Webling saw the monster—whom Mary Shelley called *Adam*—as an alter ego of Dr. Victor Frankenstein. She became the first person ever to refer to both the man *and* the monster as Frankenstein. To make the connection obvious, she dressed the characters in identical clothing throughout the play.
- She changed the ending. In the novel, Dr. Frankenstein pursues the monster to the Arctic circle, where the monster strangles him, jumps onto an ice floe, and drifts off to a sure death. The scene made good reading, but it was boring on stage. So Webling had the monster jump off a cliff instead.

Unfortunately, Hamilton Deane, who played the monster, wasn't much of an athlete. As troupe member Ivan Butler recalled years later, the new ending was "very tame indeed, because of Deane's tentative jump." So Webling wrote a more exciting ending. "The final version was quite a bloodthirsty affair," Butler recalled, "with the monster apparently tearing his maker's throat out before being destroyed by lightning. Old Deanie revelled in it."

CLASSIC FRANKENSTEIN

Universal Pictures bought the screen rights to Deane's *Dracula* and cast Bela Lugosi in the starring role. Even before the film was released in 1931, studio executives knew it would be a hit. So they commissioned a *Frankenstein* film, too. They bought the rights to Webling's play, then hired fresh screen writers to craft a brand-new script.

A WHALE OF A TALE

First, Universal hired director James Whale to work on the film. Whale had just finished work on *Hell's Angels* and *Journey's End*, two films about World War I, and Universal officials were so impressed with them that they offered Whale his pick of any of the dozens of film projects they had in the works. He chose *Frankenstein*. Why? As he later recalled:

> Of thirty available stories, *Frankenstein* was the strongest meat and gave me a chance to dabble in the macabre. I thought it would be amusing to try and make what everybody knows is a physical impossibility seem believable....Also, it offered fine pictorial chances, had two grand characterizations, and had a subject matter that might go anywhere, and that is part of the fun of making pictures.

And besides, Whale was sick of working on war movies.

BEG, BORROW, AND STEAL

Once again, writers changed Shelley's story. Universal's screenwriters followed the novel only loosely, adding and deleting details as they saw fit. They also appropriated ideas from other films:

• An early draft of the script said the lab should be filled with electrical gadgets that were "something suggestive of the laboratory in *Metropolis*," a 1926 German film about a mad scientist.

• Dr. Frankenstein's lab was moved from the top floor of his house to an old watchtower. This idea was taken from *The Magician*, a 1926 film in which a student of the occult finds "the secret of the creation of human life...in an ancient sorcerer's tower."

• *The Magician* was also an inspiration for the creation scene. As in *Frankenstein*, lightning bolts that strike the tower create life.

• Both *Metropolis* and *The Magician* provided ideas for the character of Igor, Dr. Frankenstein's assistant. In both films, the mad scientist has a dwarf for an assistant. Whale's scriptwriters changed him from a dwarf to a hunchback.

• Universal scriptwriters moved the final scene to an abandoned windmill, where angry peasants trap Dr. Frankenstein and the monster inside and burn it to the ground. Why was a windmill chosen? Scriptwriter Robert Florey remembers, "I was living in a [Hollywood] apartment above a Van de Kamp bakery," which had a windmill as its company symbol. The sight of the company's "windmill rotating inspired me to place the final scene in an old mill."

• In Mary Shelley's *Frankenstein*, the monster is extremely articulate and drones on for entire chapters without stopping. But movie audiences were still getting used to the idea of *people* talking (and screaming) in movies, let alone monsters—so the scriptwriters decided to make the Frankenstein monster a mute. Throughout the film, all he does is grunt.

CREATING THE MONSTER

Whale cast an actor named Colin Clive to play Dr. Frankenstein and selected a woman named Mae Clarke to play Dr. Frankenstein's fiance. (Bette Davis was also considered for the part.)

Casting the monster turned out to be more difficult. Bela Lugosi, probably Universal's first choice for the part, filmed a full-dress screen test. But because the *Frankenstein* makeup hadn't yet been finalized, the makeup department gave Lugosi a big, fat head "about four times normal size," and "polished, clay-like skin."

Nobody knows if Lugosi's performance was any good; the screen test was lost shortly after it was filmed. But it didn't really matter—Lugosi figured the nonspeaking role was beneath him and worried that his fans wouldn't recognize him under all that makeup. The role went to someone else, someone who was almost completely unknown in Hollywood.

For Part II of the Frankenstein story, turn to page 277.

☆   ☆   ☆

BLACKENSTEIN

In 1972, a "blaxploitation" version of Frankenstein was released—*Blackenstein*. The plot: Dr. Stein experiments on a black Vietnam vet. Something goes awry...and a "crazed monster with a square Afro" is created. A planned sequel, *Blackenstein Meets the White Werewolf*, was never made.

WARHOLISMS

Don't let the blank look fool you. Andy Warhol had insight.

"If a person isn't generally considered beautiful, they can still be a success if they have a few jokes in their pockets. And a lot of pockets."

"The most beautiful thing in Tokyo is McDonald's. The most beautiful thing in Stockholm is McDonald's. Peking and Moscow don't have anything beautiful yet."

"Good B.O. means good box office. You can smell it from a mile away."

"If the lines on your hands are wrinkles, it means your hands worry a lot."

"When I look around today, the biggest anachronism I see is pregnancy. I just can't believe that people are still pregnant."

"After you pay somebody back, you never run into them anymore. But before that, they're everywhere."

"In the '60s, everybody got interested in everybody. In the '70s, everybody started dropping everybody."

"They say that time changes things, but actually you have to change them yourself."

"People look the most kissable when they're not wearing makeup. Marilyn's lips weren't kissable, but they were very photographable."

"Changing your tastes to what other people don't want is your only hope of getting anything."

"Even beauties can be unattractive. If you catch a beauty in the wrong light at the right time, forget it."

"If people want to spend their whole lives creaming and tweezing and brushing and gluing, that's really okay too, because it gives them something to do."

"I really do live for the future, because when I'm eating a box of candy, I can't wait to taste the last piece."

"The best time for me is when I don't have any problems that I can't buy my way out of."

Medical Alert for Vince Lombardi: "Telesphobia" is the name given to "the fear of being last."

LUCKY FINDS

*Ever found something valuable? It's a great feeling. Here's
a look at a few people who found really valuable stuff...
and got to keep it. You should be so lucky.*

FLEA MARKET TREASURE

The Find: A copy of the Declaration of Independence, printed on the evening of July 4, 1776

Where It Was Found: Inside a picture frame

The Story: In 1989, an unidentified "middle-aged financial analyst from Philadelphia" paid $4 for a painting at a flea market. He didn't even like the painting, but liked the frame, so he took the picture apart...and when he did, a copy of the Declaration of Independence fell out. "It was folded up, about the size of a business envelope," says David Redden of Sotheby's Auction House. "He thought it might be an early 19th-century printing and worth keeping as a curiosity."

A few years later, the man showed the print to a friend, who suspected it might be valuable and encouraged him to look into it. He did, and learned that only hours after finishing work on the Declaration in 1776, the Continental Congress had delivered the handwritten draft to a printer with orders to send

copies of the Declaration...to the several Assemblies, Conventions & Committees...and the Commanding Officers of the Continental troops, that it be proclaimed in each of the United States & at the head of the Army.

This was one of those original copies. No one is sure how many were printed that night; today only 24 survive, and most are in poor condition. But the one in the picture frame was in mint condition, having spent the better part of two centuries undisturbed. In 1991, it sold at auction for $2.4 million.

UNCLAIMED MERCHANDISE

The Find: More than 20,000 previously unreleased recordings by Bob Dylan, Elvis Presley, Johnny Cash, Roy Orbison, Frank Sinatra, Louis Armstrong, and other music stars.

Mussolini dodged the Italian draft.

Where It Was Found: At a Nashville warehouse sale

The Story: In 1990, Douglas and Brenda Cole went to an auction in Nashville. On a whim, they paid $50 for the contents of a storage locker that a recording engineer had abandoned. Among the contents: boxes of used recording tapes that Nashville's Columbia Studios had apparently sold the engineer between 1953 and 1971 as scrap. "They were considered waste material, waste tape," an attorney explains. After listening to a few of them, the Coles realized they had something special, but they couldn't get Columbia Records interested. So, in 1992, they sold the tapes for $6,000 to Clark Enslin, owner of a small New Jersey–based record label.

Enslin contacted Sony Records (Columbia's parent company) about the tapes—and they filed suit against him, claiming he'd acquired the tapes illegally. The case was in court for three years and ended in a mixed verdict. Sony won commercial control over the 30% of the tapes recorded by artists who were signed with Columbia at the time the recordings were made; Enslin kept control of the remaining 70%—including songs by Presley, Sinatra, Williams, Armstrong, Orbison, and Jerry Lee Lewis. Actual estimated value of the tapes: $100 million. "It's very exciting," Enslin says. "It's hard to describe what it's like, knowing I have the best collection of recorded music in the world."

TREASURE IN THE TRASH

The Find: The $200,000 grand prize–winning cup in a Wendy's Restaurant fast food contest

Where It Was Found: In the garbage

The Story: In 1995, Craig Randall, a 23-year-old trash collector in Peabody, Massachusetts, noticed a Wendy's contest cup sitting in some garbage he was collecting. "I won a chicken sandwich the week before," he told reporters, "and I figured, hey, I'd get some fries to go with it." Instead, when he peeled off the sticker he saw: "Congratulations. You have won $200,000 towards a new home." The fact that he *found* the cup didn't matter; Wendy's gave him the money anyway. "I have no idea where it came from," he said. "It was just sitting there."

Q: Who invented the talking doll?   A: Thomas Edison, in 1888.

I'M GAME

You've played them. You've loved them.
Now here's a look at where they came from.

THE GAME OF LIFE
In 1860, young Milton Bradley's lithography company was in trouble; sales of his bestselling product, pictures of a clean-shaven Abraham Lincoln, had fallen off drastically when Lincoln grew a beard. Desperate, he printed up a board game called "The Checkered Game of Life." Players who landed on "Idleness" were told to "Go to disgrace"; the "Bravery" square led to "Honor"; and so on. It was perfect for the puritanical Victorian era, and sold so well that Bradley became America's first game mogul.

In 1960, the Milton Bradley Company came out with the 100th-anniversary "Game of Life." It became the second bestselling game of all time (after Monopoly).

PARCHEESI

In the late 1800s, a manufacturer approached Sam Loyd, one of America's premier game designers, with a problem: His company had a surplus of cardboard squares. Could Loyd devise some sort of game that would use the squares, so his company could get rid of them?

Borrowing from a centuries-old Indian game called *pachisi*, Loyd created a "new" game he called Parcheesi. It didn't take him very long. In fact, it was so easy that he only charged the manufacturer $10 for his services. Within a few years, the game became one of the most popular in the United States—but that $10 was the only money Loyd ever got for it.

TWISTER

In the early 1960s, Reynolds Guyer worked at his family's sales-promotion company designing packages and displays. He also created premiums—the gifts people get for sending in boxtops and proofs-of-purchase.

One day in 1965, the 29-year-old Guyer and his crew started work on a premium for a shoe polish company. "One idea," he says, "was to have kids standing on this mat with squares that told them where to put their feet....but I thought, this is bigger than just a premium."

He expanded the mat to 4' x 6' and turned it into a game. "I got the secretaries and the designers and everyone together to play. You know, in 1965 no one ever touched. It really broke all the rules of propriety having people stand so close together."

At first it was a flop. No one knew what to make of a game where people were the main playing pieces. But when Johnny Carson and Eva Gabor played it on the "Tonight Show" in 1966, America got the point. Overnight, it became a runaway hit.

TRIVIAL PURSUIT

In December 1979, Scott Abbott, a sports editor with the *Canadian Press*, and Chris Haney, a photographer with the *Montreal Gazette*, sat down to play Scrabble. Then they realized their game was missing four pieces. Haney went out to buy a new game...and was astonished that he had to cough up $16 for it. Abbott suggested that they invent their own game. They tossed around some ideas until they came up with the magic word "trivia."

"I was the sports buff," Abbott remembers, "and Chris was the movie and entertainment buff. We sat down...and started doodling a game board. The whole thing was done in about 45 minutes."

They offered $1,000 shares in the game to friends and co-workers, but hardly anyone was interested. "I heard people call them small-time shysters," one colleague remembers. As Haney puts it, "Of course, it was no, no, no, and they all came to us later, and of course we said no, no, no." Abbott and Haney eventually raised the money to produce 20,000 games...and managed to sell them all, mostly in Canada. Still, according to Matthew Costello in *The World's Greatest Games*:

> Trivial Pursuit might have stayed just a moderate success if the daughter of the Canadian distributor for Selchow & Righter (ironically, the maker of Scrabble) hadn't discovered "this terrific new game." She told her father, and Selchow & Righter bought the rights to it. With their marketing push, North America was besieged by Trivial Pursuit.

Since then, more than 60 million sets—over *$1 billion* worth of the games—have been sold in 33 countries and in 19 languages around the world.

Approximately 90% of Americans mail at least one holiday greeting card a year.

WOULD YOU BELIEVE?

According to Webster's Dictionary, *a cynic is "one who believes that human conduct is wholly motivated by self-interest." Does that describe you? Find out by taking this handy-dandy, 100% all-true quiz.*
(*Answers begin on page 507.*)

POLITICS

1. Presidential security advisor Oliver North testified in 1987 that information leaked by Congress had "seriously compromised intelligence activities" during an incident involving Egyptian terrorists. Actually...
a) North made the incident up.
b) North was the one who'd leaked the information.
c) Since Oliver North never lies, everyone believed him.

GOOD CAUSES

2. As a spokesperson for AIDS awareness, pop singer Madonna advised Americans that using condoms is "the best way to say I love you." However in her own life, she explained...
a) She never uses condoms.
b) She doesn't trust most condoms, so she has them custom-made.
c) When she *really* loves someone, she says, "The hell with the condom."

3. Candy Lightner founded Mothers Against Drunk Driving (MADD) in 1980 when her daughter was killed by a drunk driver. In 1994, she took a job as...
a) A paid lobbiest for a liquor industry trade group.
b) A nightclub comedian doing a "drunk" act.
c) An advisor to Seagram's.

EDUCATION

4. In May 1996, an 18-year-old crusader for sexual abstinence named Danyale Andersen was in the news. After spending more than 100 hours preaching abstinence to younger students in her high school and appearing before the school board in her hometown to support an "abstinence-only health curriculum," she...
a) Posed for Playboy.
b) Became a nun
c) Had a baby out of wedlock.

Ancient Egyptian tombs are decorated with pictures of watermelons.

SPORTS

5. Japan's Yasuhiro Yamashita overcame a torn leg muscle to win a gold medal in judo at the 1984 Olympics. His opponent, Mohamed Ali Rashwan of Egypt, told reporters he hadn't attacked Yamashita's leg because "I would not want to win this way." For his sportsmanship, he received the 1985 Fair Play Trophy. Actually...
a) The first thing Rashwan did was attack Yamashita's leg.
b) Japanese businessmen had bribed Rashwan to lose.
c) He only found out the leg was injured *after* the match was over.

6. The National Football League presents itself as an advocate of "family values." So when David Williams, a lineman for the Houston Oilers, missed a game to be with his wife during the birth of their son, the Oilers' front office...
a) Gave him a special award.
b) Gave him two weeks of paternity leave.
c) Docked him a week's pay.

FINANCES

7. Benjamin Franklin, America's "apostle of thrift," coined phrases like "A penny saved is a penny earned." Historians now say that Franklin's own bank account...
a) Was with a Mafia bank.
b) Was perpetually overdrawn.
c) Had the lowest interest rate in the Colonies.

8. The IRS says it's every American's duty to keep good, accurate financial records. But a 1994 audit showed that...
a) No one understands what they're talking about.
b) Even the IRS's records are a mess.
c) Only about 47% of Americans keep any records at all.

THE NEWS MEDIA

9. *The New York Times*' well-known slogan is "All the News That's Fit to Print." But when the *Times* summarized the Supreme Court's decisions in 1973, it omitted one. Why?
a) It was a paternity suit brought against their publisher, Arthur Ochs Sulzberger.
b) It involved obscene grafitti, and they refused to print the four-letter words involved.
c) It was a libel suit against a major news organization, and they didn't want to publicize it.

THE GREAT CRISWELL

This is excerpted from a book called The
Bathroom Reader's Guide to the Year 2000.

BACKGROUND

Although he's best known for his cameo appearance in the worst movie of all time—*Plan Nine from Outer Space*—Jeron Criswell was also a famous (or infamous) psychic. In 1968 he wrote *Criswell Predicts—From Now to the Year 2000*, which has become a classic of millennial weirdness.

Criswell claims his predictions have an 86% accuracy rate. "Over the next thirty years," he tells readers, "you may keep your own score as to their accuracy. After that, it will not matter."

But in case you have the urge to take him seriously, you should know that Criswell also predicted the following events on these specific days:

- Fidel Castro is assassinated on August 9, 1970
- Earthquake destroys San Francisco on April 7, 1975
- Women in Missouri will lose their hair on February 11, 1983
- Meteor destroys London on October 18, 1988
- Denver is destroyed on June 9, 1989
- The First Interplanetary Convention is held on March 10, 1990

MORE PREDICTIONS

Here are a few more of Criswell's bizarre predictions:

Aphrodisiac Spray

"I predict that our own United States will, in the future, be swept by the popular clouds of an Aphrodisian fragrance. It will be invented by a scientist who is searching for an improved antiseptic spray. Instead he will invent a spray that is almost odorless but when breathed stimulates the most basic sexual erotic areas.

"This aroma will fill every man and woman who inhales it with uncontrollable passion...I predict that the sex urge will advance rapidly, and many men will flagrantly expose themselves in public...I predict a wealthy San Francisco attorney will announce his

---

Heavy thought: The average adult male has 40 lbs. of bone and 65 lbs. of muscle in his body.

marriage to his mother and a Hollywood producer will openly declare his daughter is going to bear his child, and a young man in Arkansas will ask to be legally wed to his pet cat."

Birth Control

"I predict that birth control will no longer be a major problem in the United States. Placed in the water system of the country, in every city, regardless of size, will be chemicals which will act as contraceptives on the entire populace. In addition to this, the electricity that comes into each home will have certain ionic particles that cause contraception."

The Destruction of Denver

"I predict that a large city in Colorado will be the victim of a strange and terrible pressure from outer space, which will cause all solids to turn into a jelly-like mass."

Men Become Cannibals

"I predict an outburst of cannibalism that will terrorize the population of one of the industrial cities in the state of Pennsylvania—Pittsburgh!...I predict that over one thousand flesh-mad and blood-crazed men will wander through the streets suddenly attacking unsuspecting victims."

The End

"The world as we know it will cease to exist...on August 18, 1999.

"A study of all the prophets—Nostradamus, St. Odile, Mother Shipton, the Bible—indicates that we will cease to exist before the year 2000! Not one of these prophets even took the trouble to predict beyond the year 2000! And if you and I meet each other on the street that fateful day, August 18, 1999, and we chat about what we will do on the morrow, we will open our mouths to speak and no words will come out, for we have no future...you and I will suddenly run out of time! Who knows but what future generation from some other planet will dig down through seven layers of rubble and find us some 2,000 years hence, and crowd around a museum glass containing a fragment of a Coke bottle, a bent hairpin and a parched copy of our Bible which managed to escape destruction! They will wonder what on earth was meant by the words 'Ford' or 'Hollywood'... and what in heaven's name was a *Criswell*."

CAB CALLOWAY'S JIVE DICTIONARY

In the '30s and '40s, Cab Calloway and his band were famous for tunes like "Minnie the Moocher" and "St. James Infirmary." But he was also known as a "hep-cat," identified with outrageous zoot suits and jive talk. His guide on how to talk like a hipster was published in the 1940s. It was unearthed by BRI member Gordon Javna.

APPLE: The big town, the main stem

BARBEQUE: The girlfriend, a beauty

BARRELHOUSE: Free and easy

BATTLE: Crone, hag

BEAT IT OUT: Play it hot

BEAT UP THE CHOPS: To talk

BEEF: To say, to state

BLIP: Something very good

BLOW THE TOP: To be overcome with emotion or delight

BUDDY GHEE: Fellow

BUST YOUR CONK: Apply yourself diligently, break your neck

CLAMBAKE: Every man for himself

COOLING: Laying off, not working

CORNY: Old-fashioned, stale

CUBBY: Room, flat, home

CUPS: Sleep

CUT RATE: Low, cheap person

DICTY: High-class, nifty, smart

DIME NOTE: $10 bill

DRAPE: Suit of clothes, dress

DRY GOODS: Dress, costume

DUKE: Hand, mitt

FALL OUT: To be overcome with emotion

FAUST: An ugly girl

FEWS AND TWO: Money or cash in small quantity

FRAME: The body

FROMPY: A frompy queen is a battle or faust

FRUITING: Fickle, fooling around with no particular object

GATE: A male person

GLIMS: The eyes

GOT YOUR BOOTS ON: You know what it is all about, you are wise

GOT YOUR GLASSES ON: You are ritzy or snooty, you fail to recognize your friends

GUTBUCKET: Low-down music

HARD: Fine, good

HEP CAT: A guy who knows all the answers, understands jive

HOME-COOKING: Something very nice

ICKY: A stupid person, not hip

IN THE GROOVE: Perfect

JACK: Name for all male friends

JEFF: A pest, a bore

JELLY: Anything free, on the house

JITTER BUG: A swing fan

KILL ME: Show me a good time, send me

KILLER-DILLER: A great thrill

LAY YOUR RACKET: To jive, to sell an idea

LEAD SHEET: A coat

LILLY WHITES: Bed sheets

MAIN IN GRAY: The postman

MAIN ON THE HITCH: Husband

MAIN QUEEN: Favorite girl friend, sweetheart

MESS: Something good

METER: Quarter, twenty-five cents

MEZZ: Anything supreme, genuine

MITT POUNDING: Applause

MOUSE: Pocket

MURDER: Something excellent or terrific

NEIGHO POPS: Nothing doing, pal

OFF THE COB: Corny, out of date

OFF TIME JIVE: A sorry excuse, saying the wrong thing

PIGEON: A young girl

PINK: A white person

POPS: Salutation for all males

POUNDERS: Policemen

QUEEN: A beautiful girl

RUG CUTTER: A very good dancer

SALTY: Angry or ill-tempered

SEND: To arouse the emotions (joyful)

SET OF SEVEN BRIGHTS: One week

SHARP: Neat, smart, tricky

SLIDE YOUR JIB: Talk freely

SOLID: Great, swell, okay

SQUARE: An un-hip person

STAND ONE UP: To assume one is cut-rate

TAKE IT SLOW: Be careful

TOGGED TO THE BRICKS: Dressed to kill

TRILLY: To leave, to depart

TRUCK: To go somewhere

WHIPPED UP: Worn out, exhausted

WRONG RIFF: Saying or doing the wrong thing

THANKSGIVING MYTHS

Historian Samuel Eliot Morison says that "more bunk has been written about Pilgrims than any other subjects except Columbus and John Paul Jones." After reading this, maybe you'll agree.

It's one of American history's most familiar scenes: A small group of Pilgrims prepare a huge November feast to give thanks for a bountiful harvest and show their appreciation to the Indians who helped them survive their first winter. Together, the Pilgrims and Indians solemnly sit down to a meal of turkey, pumpkin pie, and cranberries.

Just how accurate is this image of America's first Thanksgiving? Not very, it turns out. Here are some common misconceptions about the origin of one of our favorite holidays.

MYTH: The settlers at the first Thanksgiving were called Pilgrims.

THE TRUTH: They didn't even refer to *themselves* as Pilgrims—they called themselves "Saints." Early Americans applied the term "pilgrim" to *all* of the early colonists; it wasn't until the 20th century that it was used exclusively to describe the folks who landed on Plymouth Rock.

MYTH: It was a solemn, religious occasion.

THE TRUTH: Hardly. It was a three-day harvest festival that included drinking, gambling, athletic games, and even target shooting with English muskets (which, by the way, was intended as a friendly warning to the Indians that the Pilgrims were prepared to defend themselves).

MYTH: It took place in November.

THE TRUTH: It was some time between late September and the middle of October—after the harvest had been brought in. By November, says historian Richard Ehrlich, "the villagers were working to prepare for winter, salting and drying meat and making their houses as wind resistant as possible."

MYTH: The Pilgrims wore large hats with buckles on them.

THE TRUTH: None of the participants were dressed anything like the way they've been portrayed in art: the Pilgrims didn't dress in black, didn't wear buckles on their hats or shoes, and didn't wear tall hats. The 19th-century artists who painted them that way did so because they associated black clothing and buckles with being old-fashioned.

MYTH: They ate turkey.

THE TRUTH: The Pilgrims ate *deer*, not turkey. As Pilgrim Edward Winslow later wrote, "For three days we entertained and feasted, and [the Indians] went out and killd five deer, which they brought to the plantation." Winslow does mention that four Pilgrims went "fowling" or bird hunting, but neither he nor anyone else recorded which *kinds* of birds they actually hunted—so even if they did eat turkey, it was just a side dish. "The flashy part of the meal for the colonists was the venison, because it was new to them," says Carolyn Travers, director of research at Plymoth Plantation, a Pilgrim museum in Massachusetts. "Back in England, deer were on estates and people would be arrested for poaching if they killed these deer....The colonists mentioned venison over and over again in their letters back home." Other foods that may have been on the menu: cod, bass, clams, oysters, Indian corn, native berries and plums, all washed down with water, beer made from corn, and another drink the Pilgrims affectionately called "strong water."

A few things definitely *weren't* on the menu, including pumpkin pie—in those days, the Pilgrims boiled their pumpkin and ate it plain. And since the Pilgrims didn't yet have flour mills or cattle, there was no bread other than corn bread, and no beef, milk, or cheese. And the Pilgrims didn't eat any New England lobsters, either. Reason: They mistook them for large insects.

MYTH: The Pilgrims held a similar feast every year.

THE TRUTH: There's no evidence the Pilgrims celebrated again in 1622. They probably weren't in the mood—the harvest had been disappointing, and they were burdened with a new boatload of Pilgrims who had to be fed and housed through the winter.

An adult giraffe's tongue is 17 inches long.

TRUE CONFESSIONS

A little bathroom pastime: Match the intimate revelation with the celebrity who said it. Inspired by Jon Winokur's book of quotes, True Confessions.

1. "Brain the size of a pea, I've got."

2. "I never wanted to be famous; I only wanted to be great."

3. "I learned the way a monkey learns—by watching its parents."

4. "If only I had a little humility, I would be perfect."

5. "The only reason they come to see me is that I know life is great—and they know I know it."

6. "It costs a lot of money to look this cheap."

7. "I guess I look like a rock quarry that someone has dynamited."

8. "Sometimes, at the end of the day when I'm smiling and shaking hands, I want to kick them."

9. "I left high school a virgin."

10. "I never had a date in high school or in college."

11. "I'm not smart enough to lie."

12. "I'm at the age where food has taken the place of sex in my life. In fact, I've just had a mirror put over my kitchen table."

13. "I pretended to be somebody I wanted to be until I finally became that person. Or he became me."

14. "Sitting on the toilet peeing—that's where I have my most contemplative moments."

A. Tom Selleck

B. Cary Grant

C. Sally Jesse Raphael

D. Charles Bronson

E. Richard Nixon

F. Ronald Reagan

G. Madonna

H. Ray Charles

I. Princess Diana

J. Clark Gable

K. Dolly Parton

L. Prince Charles

M. Ted Turner

N. Rodney Dangerfield

ANSWERS 1-I, 2-H, 3-L, 4-M, 5-J, 6-K, 7-D, 8-E, 9-A, 10-C, 11-F, 12-N, 13-B, 14-G

Maine is the only U.S. state with a one-syllable name.

THE REMOTE CONTROL

Over 400 million TV remote controls are currently in use in the United States. Here's the story of their creation.

THE FIRST TV REMOTE

• Commander Eugene MacDonald, Jr., president of the Zenith Radio Co., hated TV commercials. He figured other Americans did too, so he told his researchers to create a system that would mute all ads by remote control.

• Zenith wasn't the only one working on this idea. In 1953, another company introduced a TV remote control that operated with radio waves. Unfortunately, the waves traveled through walls and down the street, and tended to operate *neighbors'* TV sets as well.

TRY, TRY AGAIN

• In 1953 and 1954, Zenith developed two remote-control systems, both of which flopped:

1. The "Lazy Bones" connected to the TV with a long cable. It worked, but among other problems, it kept tripping people.
2. The more advanced "Flashamatic" used four photo cells, one in each corner of the TV cabinet. Each cell controlled one function—volume, channels, etc. All a viewer had to do was aim a flashlight at the right cell. Unfortunately, first-generation couch potatoes couldn't remember which cell did what...and direct sunlight operated all of them at once.

• In 1955, Robert Adler, a Zenith acoustics expert, developed a remote system using high-frequency sound. The device contained an aluminum rod that rang when hit by a hammer. Called the Space Command 200, it debuted in 1956. Retail price: $399.95. Unfortunately, any noise produced by small pieces of metal, such as jingling keys or dog chains, produced tones similar to the remote's, so channels changed and sets turned on and off unpredictably.

• By 1962, the kinks in the Space Command were worked out. Bulky vacuum tubes were replaced with transistors, making the remote smaller and cheaper. But Adler's development of ultrasound remained *the* technique for all remote controls until the early 1980s, when new semiconductors make infrared remote controls capable of transmitting digital codes.

Q: How did Levi's 501 jeans get their name?   A: The original version had 501 copper rivets.

FAMILIAR PHRASES

More origins of everyday phrases.

START WITH A CLEAN SLATE
Meaning: Make a fresh start.
Origin: From the days when tavern keepers used slate blackboards to keep track of money owed by customers. When a person paid off a debt, their name was erased, and they literally got to "start with a clean slate."

HARP ON SOMETHING
Meaning: Dwell obsessively on the same topic.
Origin: The modern expression is a shortened version of the old phrase, "harping on one string," which meant playing the same note of a harp over and over.

BAIL OUT
Meanings: (1) Remove water from a ship; (2) pay to get someone out of jail; and (3) jump out of a plane in an emergency.
Origin: The expression and all of its meanings come from a time when English sailors used buckets known as *beyles* to remove unwanted water from their ships.

BIGWIG
Meaning: Important person.
Origin: Judges and lawyers have worn wigs in British courts since the 18th century. Lawyers wear short wigs, but the judge wears a long wig, sometimes down to his shoulders. That makes the judge —the most important person in the room—literally a "bigwig," because he wears the biggest wig.

CANARY / CANARY ISLANDS / CANARY YELLOW
Meanings: Species of bird; islands near Africa; a shade of yellow.
Origin: When ancient Romans first set foot on an archipelago off the coast of West Africa, they quickly discovered that the islands were crawling with wild dogs. They named the islands *Canariae Insulae*, "Dog Islands." In time, they became known as the "Canary

Islands" and the small gray and green finches that lived there became known as "canaries." When selective breeding resulted in a
bright yellow variety of the bird, the color itself became known as
"canary yellow."

THROW INTO STITCHES

Meaning: Make someone laugh hard.
Origin: This stitch has nothing to do with sewing: it comes from
stice, an Old English word that means "to sting." When you throw
someone into stitches, you make them laugh so hard that it hurts.

TURN A BLIND EYE

Meaning: Deliberately overlook something.
Origin: Goes back to the British admiral Lord Nelson, who was
blind in one eye. In 1801, Nelson was second-in-command during
a naval attack on Copenhagen. The commanding admiral signaled
an order to cease fire. Rather than obey it, Nelson held his tele-
scope up to his blind eye, turned toward the admiral's ship, and
told a subordinate, "I don't see anything." The attack continued,
and the Danish eventually surrendered.

EAT HUMBLE PIE

Meaning: Admit you're wrong; humiliate yourself.
Origin: In the Middle Ages, when the lord of a manor returned
from deer hunting, he and his noble guests dined on *venison* (deer
meat), considered the finest part of the deer. His servants and other
commoners ate a pie made from the *umbles*—the heart, liver, en-
trails, and other undesirable parts. Originally, "umbles" and "humble" were unrelated words. But eating the pie was such a humble
act that when the word *umble* disappeared, *humble* took its place in
this expression.

FORK IT OVER

Meaning: Surrender something.
Origin: Centuries ago, most of the farmland in England was owned
by great lords. Farmers were supposed to pay the lords their rent
with silver coins. When the farmers had no coins, landlords took
wagons into the fields and demanded that the farmers use pitch-
forks to "fork over some" of the crop instead.

Survey result: 70% of employers don't like hiring married couples to work in the same office.

CELEBRITY MUMMIES

Here are a few contemporary mummies of note.

JOHN WILKES BOOTH (aka John St. Helen)

After he shot Lincoln, Booth was a fugitive for 12 days. The government said that federal troops tracked him down and shot him in a Virginia tobacco barn. Then, to prevent his gravesite from becoming a Confederate shrine, they quickly buried him in an unmarked grave at the Washington Arsenal. But this made people suspicious. Why so fast—were they hiding something? Was the man they buried really Booth...or had the assassin escaped?

Over the years, more than 40 people made deathbed "confessions" claiming they were Booth. One of these was John St. Helen. In 1877, thinking he was about to die, St. Helen confessed to a man named Finis L. Bates that he was Lincoln's assassin.

St. Helen actually survived and lived until 1903. When he finally died, Bates had St. Helen's body mummified and moved to his basement, where it was stored for the next 20 years. Then, when Bates died in 1923, his wife sold the mummy. It ended up in the hands of carnival operators who exhibited it as Booth until the mid-1970s. It then disappeared, and hasn't been seen since.

ELMER J. MCCURDY

In 1976, an episode of TV's "The Six Million Dollar Man" was filmed at the Nu-Pike amusement park in Long Beach, California. There was a dummy hanging from a fake gallows in the fun house; when a technician tried to move it out of the way, its arm came off at the elbow...exposing human bones. It was a mummy, not a dummy!

The film crew was horrified. The mummy's face had been painted and shellacked so many times that the amusement park owners thought it was made of *wax*. But who was the mummy? And how did it wind up in the park?

The L.A. County coroner had one clue: the mummy's mouth was stuffed with carnival ticket stubs. They were traced to Oklahoma, and, working with Oklahoma historians, the coroner finally identified the body as Elmer J. McCurdy, a long-forgotten bandit.

The Pacific Ocean is twice as large as the Atlantic...and larger than all the continents combined.

According to a 1993 *Wall Street Journal* article:

> Eighty years ago, [McCurdy] robbed the wrong train and rode off with $45 and a load of whiskey. When the posse caught him two days later, the whiskey was gone and he was having a nice nap. According to local legend, he decided to shoot it out anyway. That was another mistake. An…undertaker in Pawhuska, OK, mummified his body and put it on display for 5¢ a view until 1916, when two men posing as Mr. McCurdy's brothers claimed the corpse. They were actually carnival promoters. For decades, the unfortunate Mr. McCurdy crisscrossed the country as a sideshow attraction.

The town of Guthrie, Oklahoma, paid for McCurdy's trip back to the state and gave him a Christian burial. His grave (which has been sealed in concrete to ensure that it is his *final* resting place) is now the town's biggest tourist attraction.

EVA "EVITA" PERON

Juan Peron was the president of Argentina from 1948 to 1954. His wife, Eva, a former actress and a crusader for the poor, was extremely popular. When she died of cancer in 1952 at age 33, Peron had her mummified and put on public display. The procedure took about a year and cost $100,000.

Peron fell from power while his wife was still lying in state, and went into exile in Spain before he could arrange her burial. Evita was put in storage in Buenos Aires. Then her body disappeared.

It turned out that anti-Peronists—making sure the body was never again used as a pro-Peron political symbol—had stolen the coffin, sealed it in a packing crate, and eventually buried it in a Milan cemetary. In 1971—19 years later—a sympathetic Spanish intelligence officer told Peron where his wife was buried. Peron had her exhumed and brought to Spain. When the ex-dictator pried open the coffin, his wife was so well preserved that he cried out, "She is not dead, she is only sleeping!"

Rather than bury his Evita again, Peron kept her around the house; he and his third wife, Isabel, propped her up in the dining-room and ate in her presence every evening, even when they entertained guests. The arrangement lasted until 1973, when Peron returned to power in Argentina and left his beloved mummy in Spain. Later, Evita was brought across the Atlantic and was buried in Argentina.

If you want to hardboil an ostrich egg, bring along something to do. It takes up to four hours.

GROUCHO SEZ...

A few choice words from the master, Groucho Marx.

"I've had a perfectly wonderful evening. But this wasn't it."

"I was married by a judge. I should have asked for the jury."

"Remember men, we're fighting for this woman's honor—which is probably more than she ever did."

"If I held you any closer, I'd be on the other side of you."

"Those are my principles. If you don't like them I have others."

"From the moment I picked up your book until I laid it down, I was convulsing with laughter. Someday I intend to read it."

"The husband who wants a perfect marriage should learn how to keep his mouth shut and his checkbook open."

"Oh, are you from Wales? Do you know a fellow named Jonah? He used to live in Wales for a while."

"Blood's not thicker than money."

"He may look like an idiot and talk like an idiot, but don't let that fool you. He really is an idiot."

"The secret of success is honesty and fair dealing. If you can fake those, you've got it made."

"Well, Art is Art, isn't it? Still, on the other hand, water is water! And East is East and West is West and if you take cranberries and stew them with applesauce they taste more like prunes than rhubarb does.... Now you tell me what *you* know."

"I've been around so long I can remember Doris Day before she was a virgin."

"Outside of a dog, a book is a man's best friend. Inside of a dog it's too hard to read."

"Who are you going to believe, me or your own eyes?"

"Well, I hardly know where to begin. I hardly know when to stop, either; just give me a few drinks and see for yourself."

SILENT PARTNERS

Everyone knows that Hollywood is a world of fiction and fantasy; even so, it's hard to believe that people who appear to like one another on TV and in film sometimes loathe each other in real life. Some examples:

FRED AND ETHEL MERTZ ("I LOVE LUCY")

How we remember them: Fred and Ethel (William Frawley and Vivian Vance) were like everybody's next-door neighbors. Both were frumpy and grumpy, but underneath, they had an abiding love for one another…at least in front of the cameras.

How they really were: Frawley and Vance could barely stand each other from the moment they began working on the show… and things got worse from there: Vance, who was 25 years Frawley's junior (39 to his 64), hated the idea that viewers believed she could be married to someone so old. "He should be playing my *father*, not my husband," she routinely complained. Another thorn in her side: there was a clause in her contract that allowed the show to dump her if Frawley died or became too ill to work.

Frawley wasn't any happier: his nicknames for Vance were "Old Fat Ass" and "that old sack of doorknobs," and he was famous for frequently asking Desi, "Where did you dig up that bitch?"

Silent treatment: Things came to a head near the end of the "I Love Lucy" run, when Desi Arnaz approached Vance about spinning off the Fred and Ethel characters into their own show. As Vance later recounted,

> I loathed Bill Frawley, and the feeling was mutual….There was no way I could do a series with him on our own, so when Desi asked me, I refused. I still wouldn't budge when he offered me a bonus of $50,000 just to do a pilot. When Bill found out, he was furious, not because he wanted to work with me any more than I did with him, but because he stood to earn a lot more money than he did on "Lucy." He never spoke to me again except when work required it.

A few years after "I Love Lucy" ended, someone asked Frawley if he'd kept in touch with Vance. "I don't know where she is now and she doesn't know where I am," he replied, "and that's exactly the way I like it."

Why are all the continents wider in the north than in the south? Nobody knows.

ABBOTT AND COSTELLO

How we remember them: The quintessential buddy comedy team of the 1930s, 1940s, and 1950s. Sure, they fought onstage, but that was part of their act...and it never seemed to get in the way of their warm friendship.

How they really were: According to Penny Stallings in *Forbidden Channels*, Abbott and Costello's relationship deteriorated toward the end of their careers. Abbott was one of showbiz's greatest straight men, but Costello came to believe that he'd "carried" Abbott for years. Mel Blanc, who worked on Abbott and Costello's TV show in the 1950s, recalled, "They hated each other. Especially Costello. Even at the end he was still trying to get other straight men, but he could just never find one as good."

Silent treatment: The pair frequently hosted "The Colgate Comedy Hour," but Costello stormed off the set after an argument one day and never returned. Instead, he became a frequent guest on a competing show hosted by Steve Allen. Abbott was so upset by the split that he fell ill and had to check into a hospital. The relationship remained troubled from then on: Costello later sued Abbott for $222,000 in unpaid royalties, but he dropped dead of a heart attack in 1959 before the suit was resolved.

SONNY AND CHER

How we remember them: The ultimate hippie power couple of the 1960s and early 1970s, Sonny and Cher were a beacon of stability at a time when people were questioning the merits of traditional relationships. In their songs, on their show, and in their marriage—or so we thought—Sonny and Cher proved that two people didn't have to be square to be devoted to one another.

How they really were: Not long after they hit superstardom with their variety TV show, Sonny and Cher's private life began to crumble. In November 1972, Sonny says, Cher announced she was having an affair with their guitarist. Sonny was devastated, but within a few months, he realized their marriage was over for good...at least behind the scenes. Public perception was another story, as Bono recounts in his autobiography *And the Beat Goes On*.

Despite their differences, he and Cher decided to stay together for the sake of their bank accounts:

> I told Cher that she had to realize that we were involved in a business, a highly profitable business, and though the marriage was gone and the love lost, it was silly to give up the tremendous sums of money we were making. I'd come to terms with the reality of our situation. I accepted it…and I was OK with her pursuing whatever personal life she wanted. I'd do the same. But Sonny and Cher were names too valuable to simply walk away from. She agreed.

Silent treatment: For the last year of their marriage and their variety show, Sonny and Cher lived a lie: pretending to be happily married, they set up separate households in different parts of their 54-room mansion, Sonny with his lover in one corner and Cher with hers in another. The charade lasted until February 1974, when Cher moved out and filed for divorce on grounds of "involuntary servitude." They've been taking potshots at each other in the media ever since.

"Cher wants to run like a racehorse, but she can't find a track," Bono laments in his autobiography. "I used to be the jockey, but Cher quite nicely shoved the saddle up my ass."

SISKEL AND EBERT

How we think of them: The best film critics on TV. "The fat one" (Ebert) and "the other guy" (Siskel) seem to get along pretty well despite their different opinions about movies.

How they really are: As *Time* magazine reported in 1987, "The two have little in common outside the TV studio.…They rarely socialize…Nor are their fights confined to the TV cameras. In the middle of an interview, for example, Ebert will complain that Siskel won't let him plug his books on TV. And Siskel will deride his partner for his "megalomania." "He thinks the world revolves around him," Siskel sneers to the reporter. Are they just kidding? No one knows.

Silent treatment: Siskel and Ebert don't even sit together during their film screenings. Siskel sits at the rear of the screening room, and Ebert sits closer to the front, *Time* reports, "usually munching from a box of Good & Plenty."

I SCREAM, YOU SCREAM

We've uncovered a lot of food origins in the Bathroom Readers, but
until now, we never got around to one of the best foods of all.

ICE AGES

Which is oldest—ice cream, sherbet, or snow cones?

As far as anyone can tell, snow cones are the oldest: they date back at least as far as Roman emperor Nero (37 A.D. to 68 A.D.), who had snow brought down from mountaintops to cool his wine cellars. On hot days he'd mix some of the extra snow with honey, juices, and fruit pulps, and eat it as a snack.

Sherbet—which has more fruit and less milk or cream than ice cream—came next. In the late 13th century, Marco Polo brought a recipe for sherbet from China to Italy. Only a few people knew about it. "Recipes [for sherbet] were secrets, closely guarded by chefs to the wealthy," explains Charles Panati in *Extraordinary Origins of Everyday Things*.

Historians estimate that sometime in the 16th century one of these chefs—no one knows who—increased the milk content in the recipe and reduced or eliminated the fruit entirely...inventing ice cream in the process.

RICH DESSERT

Iced dessert remained an exclusive, upper-class treat for over a century. "With refrigeration a costly ordeal of storing winter ice in underground vaults for summer use," Panati says, "only the wealthy tasted iced desserts." Then, in 1670, a Sicilian named Francesco Procopio dei Coltelli opened Paris's first coffeehouse, Cafe Procope. It was the first business ever to make ice cream available to the general public.

This inspired other coffeehouses around Europe to do the same. By the mid-17th century, ice cream could be found in most of the continent's major cities...and by the end of the century, people were addicted to it. Beethoven wrote from Vienna in 1794: "It is very warm here....As winter is mild, ice is rare. The Viennese are afraid that it will soon be impossible to have any ice cream."

ICE CREAM IN AMERICA

Meanwhile, ice cream had gotten a foothold in the New World. It was first brought over in 1690, and by 1777 it was being advertised in New York newspapers. Ice cream was popular with many of the Founding Fathers, including Alexander Hamilton, George Washington (who ran up a $200 ice cream tab with one New York merchant in the summer of 1790), and Thomas Jefferson (who had his own 18-step recipe for ice cream and is believed to be the first president to serve it at a state dinner). First Lady Dolly Madison's ice cream parties helped make ice cream fashionable among the new republic's upper crust.

CRANKING IT OUT

By the 1790s, ice cream was becoming more readily available in the United States, but it was still a rare treat due to the scarcity and high price of ice—and the difficulty in making it. Most ice cream was made using the "pot freezer" method: the ingredients sat in a pot that, in turn, sat in a larger pan of salt and ice. The whole thing had to be shaken up and down by one person, while another vigorously stirred the mixture.

Over the next 50 years, two developments made ice cream an American staple:

1. In the early 1800s, "ice harvesting" of frozen northern rivers in winter months, combined with insulated icehouses that sprang up all over the country, made ice—and therefore ice cream—cheap for the first time. By 1810, ice cream was being sold by street vendors in nearly every major city in the United States.

2. In 1846, Nancy Johnson created the world's first hand-cranked ice cream freezer. With this invention, ice cream was both affordable *and* easy to make for the first time. By 1850, it was so common that *Godey's Lady's Book* could comment: "A party without it would be like a breakfast without bread."

WE ALL SCREAM

By 1900, electricity and mechanical refrigeration had given rise to a huge domestic ice cream industry. And it had become so closely identified with American culture that the people in charge of Ellis Island, determined to serve a "truly American dish" to arriving immigrants, served them ice cream at every meal.

End to end, the number of Crayola crayons made in a year would circle the globe 4-1/2 times.

WEIRD BAR SPORTS

Here's a look at some of the more unusual ways that bar owners have tried to keep customers busy and entertained while they drink.

D WARF TOSSING
How It's Played: A dwarf dresses up in body padding, a crash helmet, and a harness. Then contestants hurl him across the room into a pile of mattresses. The "winner" is the person who throws the dwarf the farthest. In some contests, dwarfs have been thrown as much as 30 feet. Why do the dwarfs do it? They can make as much as $2,000 a night.

History: Invented at a Queensland, Australia, bar in 1985. It later produced an offshoot—dwarf bowling: "A helmeted dwarf is strapped to a skateboard or mechanic's creeper and rolled headfirst into bowling pins, which are made of plastic."

In 1987, a few American bars tried out this "sport," and it was a commercial success. But the bad publicity—combined with lobbying by groups like Little People of America—killed it.

THE HUMAN (BAR)FLY

How It's Played: Wearing a velcro suit, bar patrons sprint down a runway, leap on a small trampoline, and hurl themselves onto a wall covered with velcro hooks. First prize goes to the person whose feet stick highest on the wall. Getting off the wall can be fun, too. "One of our rules is that the men peel off the women, and the women peel off the men," says a bar owner. "Sometimes it takes three women to peel off one guy."

History: Inspired by David Letterman, who performed the stunt on his show in 1984. The Cri Bar and Grill in New Zealand began holding "human fly" contests in 1991, and other New Zealand bars followed suit. *Sports Illustrated* covered it in 1991; it quickly spread to the United States, where it flourished for a few years.

SUMO SUIT WRESTLING

How It's Played: Participants don 43-pound rubberized vinyl and nylon suits that make them look like 400-pound sumo wrestlers—

complete with the traditional Japanese sumo "diaper" and a crash helmet with a sumo wig glued on the outside. Then they slam into each other on a big padded mat. (Not to be confused with human cockfighting, in which—no kidding—people dress up in padded chicken costumes and peck, bump, and scratch each other.)

History: Englishman Peter Herzig invented the suits after seeing sumo wrestlers in a Miller Beer commercial. Miller then bought hundreds of the suits and began promoting the "sport" in nightclubs in the early 1990s.

HUMAN BOWLING

How It's Played: Like real bowling, you have to knock down as many pins as you can...but in this sport, the pins are five feet tall and made of canvas and styrofoam; the bowler is strapped *inside* a huge metal-frame bowling ball. A partner rolls them down the 30-foot lane toward the pins. "Just because you're in the ball doesn't mean you have no obligations to the team," says Lori Fosdick, a regular bowler. "I've seen some pretty maneuvers—but I've also seen people who seemed to be going straight and rolled right around the pin."

History: Creator Thomas Bell got the idea in the early 1990s after watching some gerbils running on an exercise wheel. He figured humans might enjoy doing the same thing. "Bowling has always been a competitive sport," he says straight-faced. "We're just taking it to a more competitive level."

GERBIL RACING

How It's Played: Eight gerbils race in a portable race track that's set up on the wall behind the bar. Betting is not allowed, but customers who pick the winning gerbil win free drinks.

History: Invented in 1992 by a bar in Alberta, Canada, with the blessings of the Canadian SPCA. "My gerbils live to the age of two, unlike wild gerbils, which have a lifespan of only eight months," says Morley Amon, owner of the Alberta track. "They aren't running against their will. They run just to see what's on the other side."

BRAND NAMES

*Here's another look at brand names you
know and where they come from.*

Q-TIPS. In the early 1920s, the owner of the Gerstenzang Infant Novelty Company noticed that his wife cleaned their daughter's ears by wrapping cotton around a toothpick. Inspired, he built a machine that made "ready-to-use cotton swabs." At first he called the product Baby Gays. In 1926, they became Q-Tips ("Q for Quality") Baby Gays...and finally just Q-Tips.

ZIPPO LIGHTERS. Introduced as a revolutionary windproof lighter in 1932 and named after another revolutionary invention of the time—the zipper.

MAYBELLINE. In 1915, Mabel Williams created an eye makeup for herself out of black pigment and petroleum jelly. Her brother decided to sell it in his mail-order catalog as Lash-Brow-Ine. It sold extremely well, and in 1920 he changed the name to Maybelline, as a gesture to her.

SARAN WRAP. In 1933, Dow researchers discovered a plastic called *monomeric vinylidene chloride*. They called it VC Plastic. In 1940, a salesman suggested they rename it Saran (the name of a tree in India). Dow liked the new name because it had only five letters and had no negative connotations. During World War II, Saran was used in everything from belts to subway seats. In 1948, it was marketed to housewives as a plastic film called Saran Wrap.

MAX FACTOR. In the early days of the movie industry, Max Factor devised a new makeup that made actors look natural on film. It established his reputation as Hollywood's premier cosmetics authority, which gave him cachet with the general public.

RAY-BANS. Originally called "Anti-Glare goggles" in 1936. Bausch & Lomb, the manufacturer, decided "anti-glare" would be too hard to protect as a trademark, so the glasses—designed to "inhibit ultraviolet and infrared rays"—were re-christened Ray-Bans.

MISS AMERICA, PART II:
The Early Years

Here's more of the history of the Miss America Pageant. (Part I is on page 49.) One aspect we find fascinating: The same "traditionalists" who call Miss America their own and fight to preserve it whenever it's threatened today were its biggest enemies in the 1920s and 1930s. It goes to show how transient some notions of "decency" and "morality" can be.

RAKING IN THE DOUGH

The 1921 Fall Frolic was such a moneymaker that the Atlantic City government increased its contribution from $1,000 to $12,500 the following year. The number of participating newspapers also increased in 1922, from 8 to 57 (this time the entire country was represented). As the pageant grew, so did the crowds that thronged to see it. In 1922, 250,000 people visited Atlantic City during the pageant; 300,000 came the following year.

To maximize the time (and money) that tourists spent in Atlantic City, organizers spread the events out over three days in 1922, and then to five days in 1924 and afterward. As A. R. Riverol writes in *Live from Atlantic City*:

> The ingenuity in the pageant was that it was structured to keep the people at the resort happily spending their money. Most events were scheduled either on separate days or on the same day but hours apart....To enjoy all of the offerings of the Miss America pageant, the day tripper would either have to wait for hours or travel to Atlantic City the next day. The answer? Stay overnight.

A MAJOR SETBACK

But as the Atlantic City festivities grew in popularity, they also attracted increasing opposition. Even in the "Roaring '20s," bathing suit contests were as controversial as wet T-shirt contests are today. Women's groups and civic and religious organizations condemned the pageant for being indecent, for exploiting women for money, and for corrupting the youthful contestants.

On top of the general criticism, there were also a number of "scandals" that muddied the pageant's reputation. In 1923, for

For every gallon of sea water, you get more than a quarter of a pound of salt.

example, Miss Brooklyn and Miss Boston turned out to be married; Miss Alaska was not only married, but also a resident of New York City—not Alaska.

As the '20s wore on, hotel owners began to lose faith in the pageant as a moneymaker. Frank Deford writes in *There She Is:*

> They became convinced that the pageant, for all its notice, was starting to give Atlantic City a bad name, and cost the hotels respectable cash-and-carry patrons.

HARD TIMES

Finally in 1928, after years of negative publicity and vehement opposition from conservative groups, the Atlantic City hotel operators decided to shut Miss America down, stating that it had degenerated into a "worn out and useless...cheap exploitation of physical beauty."

From the very beginning critics had charged that the pageant lured "bad" women to the boardwalk and turned innocent young girls into hussies; now the organizers believed it themselves. The Hotelmen's Association declared:

> There has been an epidemic recently of women who seek personal aggrandizement and publicity by participating in various stunts throughout the world, and the hotelmen feel that in recent years that type of woman has been attracted to the Pageant in ever-increasing numbers....Many of the girls who come here turn out bad later and though it may happen in other cities, it reflects on Atlantic City.

SECOND TRY—THE 1933 PAGEANT

"Miss America" seemed to be dead and buried. But memories of the big bucks the pageant had brought in lingered on...and in 1933, in the middle of the Great Depression, a handful of organizers decided to bring it back to life.

The Hotelmen's Association and the Chamber of Commerce refused to support it, and the newspapers—who'd sponsored earlier beauty contests—declined to participate. So the pageant had to turn to carnivals, amusement parks, theaters, and other seedy businesses to find beauty queens to compete in the 1933 event.

How were presidents Franklin D. Roosevelt and Theodore Roosevelt related? Fifth cousins.

There were so many problems during Pageant Week that the 1933 contest became, arguably, the biggest disaster in Miss America history. For example:

- Miss West Virginia had to drop out because of stomach pains after she ate lobster with her ice cream.
- Miss New York State collapsed onstage from an abscessed tooth.
- Miss Oklahoma was rushed to the hospital for an emergency appendectomy.
- Miss Arkansas was revealed to be married.
- Misses Iowa, Illinois, and Idaho were disqualified because they actually resided in neither Iowa, Illinois, nor Idaho.

The 1933 crown ultimately went to Miss Connecticut, 15-year-old Marian Bergeron, but her shining moment was tarnished. "The crown was so big it came right down over my eyes, and it made me look retarded," she recalled years later. The crown was stolen the day after and was never recovered.

IF AT FIRST YOU DON'T SUCCEED...

The 1933 pageant was such a loser that until the mid-'50s, organizers of the Miss America pageants never recognized it as an "official" pageant...or acknowledged Bergeron as a genuine Miss America.

Nonetheless, in 1935, "respectable" members of Atlantic City society decided to hold another one. Why? They were probably motivated by competition. In 1934 an "American Queen of Beauty" was crowned in Madison Square Garden. And a year later, a "Miss America" was named at the San Diego County Fair. These contests were even sleazier than their Atlantic City predecessor. According to *There She Is*, the San Diego crown was conferred upon the winner by "the two gentlemen who ran the midget and nudist concessions at the fairs." And the San Diego Miss America didn't get a cash prize, a college scholarship, or anything like that. Instead, she won "the 'right' to pose in the buff for two years."

Rather than let a good thing get away—and perhaps also to keep the Miss America name from sinking deeper into the muck, if such a thing were possible—Atlantic City decided to give the pageant one more chance in 1935.

Stay tuned—there's more on page 151.

Ben and Jerry's Ice Cream gives its ice cream waste to Vermont farmers, who use

SIBLING RIVALRY

Brothers who go into business together don't always stay close. In fact, going into business with a relative might be the best way to lose a family. Here are 4 classic cases.

ADIDAS / Adolf & Rudolf Dassler

Background: According to *Everybody's Business*, "Adolf and Rudolf Dassler were the sons of a poor laundress who grew up in the tiny Bavarian milltown of Herzogenerauch, near Nuremburg. Before World War II, they started a factory there to make house slippers, then branched to track shoes and soccer boots."

Rivalry: "They had a violent falling out and after the war went their separate ways. Rudolf left Adidas and started a rival athletic shoe company, Puma. Before long Adidas and Puma—both head-quartered in Herzogenerauch—were battling head-to-head all over the world. When Adolf died in 1978, the two brothers hadn't spoken to each other in 29 years."

GALLO WINE / Ernest, Julio & Joseph Gallo

Background: Ernest, Julio, and Joseph Gallo inherited the family vineyard in 1933 when their father murdered their mother and then committed suicide. 24-year-old Ernest and 23-year-old Julio used their inheritance to start the Gallo Winery. At the same time, they raised their teenage brother, Joseph—who went to work for them as a vineyard manager when he was old enough. After toiling for his brothers for 18 years, Joseph bought a nearby ranch. He grew grapes (which he sold to the Gallo Winery) and raised cattle.

Rivalry: In 1983, Joseph expanded his dairy operation to include Gallo cheese…but his brothers said he was infringing on their trademark. In 1986 they sued him. Joseph retaliated with a counter-suit, claiming that his 1/3 share of his father's inheritance entitled him to 1/3 of the winery. As the family fell apart, the fight got nastier. During the trial, the winemakers accused Joseph of "running a rat-infested cheese plant;" Joseph shot back that his brothers specialized in making cheap wine for drunks. Ernest and Julio won both suits.

it as pig feed. The pigs love it all…except for Mint Oreo, which they refuse to eat.

REVLON / Charles, Joseph & Martin Revson

Background: According to *Everybody's Business*: "The cosmetics giant was founded in 1932 by Charles Revson, his older brother Joseph, and Charles Lachman. A younger brother, Martin, joined the firm later. But it was Charles who led the company's drive to the top."

Rivalry: "Joseph left the company in 1955 because he didn't agree with Charles that Revlon should go public. He sold all his stock to the company for $2.5 million. (If he'd waited four years, the stock would have been worth $35 million.) Martin left in 1959 after bitter fights with his older brother. He sued the company, charging that his brother Charles 'engaged in a practice of mistreating executives and abusing them personally.' The brothers didn't speak to each other for 13 years. 'What brother?' Charles once said. 'I don't have a brother.' "

KELLOGG'S / John & William Kellogg

Background: In 1876, 25-year-old Dr. John Harvey Kellogg became head of the Battle Creek Sanitarium. His first official act was to hire his younger brother, William, as "chief clerk." To make the institution's vegetarian food more palatable, the brothers invented a number of foods—including corn flakes. Then they set up a company on the side, manufacturing and distributing their cereal around the country.

Rivalry: John, a world-famous doctor by 1900, insisted that Kellogg's cereals be "health foods." So he forbade the use of white sugar. William just wanted something that would sell...and when he added sugar to the flakes while John was out of the country, the partnership fell apart. "Will set out on his own...in 1906," writes William Poundstone in *Bigger Secrets*. "By 1909 the brothers weren't on speaking terms. Both spent much of the following decade suing each other. These complex legal actions resulted in the ruling that only Will's company could market cereal under the Kellogg's name, and in lifelong mutual enmity for the two brothers." When John Harvey died in 1942, the two hadn't spoken in 33 years.

Quickie: Robert, James & Edward Mead Johnson started *Johnson & Johnson* in an old wallpaper factory. Edward left and started Mead Johnson, which now competes with Johnson & Johnson.

MONTHS OF THE YEAR

Here's where the names of the months come from.

JANUARY. Named for the Roman god *Janus*, a two-faced god who "opened the gates of heaven to let out the morning, and closed them at dusk." Janus was worshiped as the god of all doors, gates, and other entrances. Consequently, the opening month of the year was named after him.

FEBRUARY. The Roman "Month of Purification" got its name from *februarius*, the Latin word for purification. February 15 was set aside for the Festival of Februa, in which people repented and made sacrifices to the gods to atone for their wrongdoings.

MARCH. Named for Mars, the Roman god of war. The Roman empire placed great emphasis on wars and conquest, so until 46 B.C. this was the first month of the year.

APRIL. No one knows the origin of the name. One theory: it comes from *Aprilis* or *aphrilis*, which are corruptions of *Aphrodite*, the Greek name for Venus, the goddess of love.

However, many experts think the month is named after the Latin verb *aperire*, which means "to open." (Most plants open their leaves and buds in April.)

MAY. Some people think the month is named after *Maia*, the mother of the god Mercury; other people think it was named in honor of the *Majores*, the older branch of the Roman Senate.

JUNE. It may have been named in honor of *Juno*, the wife of Jupiter; or it may have been named after the *Juniores*, the lower branch of the Roman Senate.

JULY. Named after Julius Caesar.

AUGUST. Named after Gaius Julius Caesar Octavianus, heir and nephew of Julius Caesar. The Roman Senate gave this Caesar the title of "Augustus," which means "revered," and honored him further by naming a month after him.

SEPTEMBER. Comes from the Latin word *septem*, which means "seven." September was the seventh month until about the year 700 B.C., when Numa Pompilius, the second Roman king, switched from a 304-day calendar to a 355-day lunar calendar.

OCTOBER. From *octo*, the Latin word for "eighth." When Romans changed the calendar, they knew October was no longer the 8th month, and tried to rename it. Some candidates: *Germanicus* (after a general), *Antonius* (an emperor), *Faustina* (the emperor's wife), and *Herculeus* (after Emperor Commodus, who had nicknamed himself the "Roman Hercules.") None of the new names stuck.

NOVEMBER. From *novem*, the Latin word for "nine." November was also referred to as "blood-month." Reason: It was the peak season for pagan animal sacrifices.

DECEMBER. From *decem*, the Latin word for "tenth." Attempts to rename it *Amazonius* in honor of the mistress of Emperor Commodius failed.

DAYS OF THE WEEK

When Anglo-Saxons invaded the British isles, they brought their language and pagan gods with them. The names of the days of the week are a legacy.

SUNDAY. Originally called *Sunnan daeg*, which, like today, meant "sun day."

MONDAY. Originally called *Monan daeg*, "moon day."

TUESDAY. *Tiwes daeg* was named in honor of Tiw, the Anglo-Saxon (and Norse) god of war.

WEDNESDAY. Named *Wodnes daeg* and dedicated to Woden, the king of the gods in Valhalla.

THURSDAY. *Thu(n)res daeg* commemorated Thor, the god of thunder, and the strongest and bravest god of all.

FRIDAY. Originally named *Frige daeg* after Thor's mother Frigga, the most important goddess in Valhala. (That's one theory; the day may be also named after Freyja, the Norse goddess of love.)

SATURDAY. Named *Saeter daeg* in honor of Saturn, the Roman god of agriculture. It's the one day of the week whose name *isn't* derived from Anglo-Saxon/Norse myths.

Q: Why do helium-filled balloons float?   A: Helium is seven times lighter than air.

DUMB CRIMINALS

Many Americans are worried about the growing threat of crime. Well, the good news is that there are plenty of crooks who are their own worst enemies. Here are a few true-life examples.

T AKE ALL YOU WANT
"SEATTLE — Police got an early morning call from the owners of a motor home parked on a Seattle street. When officers arrived, they found sewage and what looked like vomit on the ground. Nearby, they found a man curled up ill next to the car.

"The man admitted he had been trying to siphon gas and had plugged his hose into the motor home's sewage tank by mistake. The motor home's owner declined to press charges, calling it the 'best laugh he's ever had.' "

—The Eugene *Register-Guard*, Aug. 6, 1991
(*Submitted by BRI member Karen Roth, Eugene, Oregon*)

DOG YUMMIES
"SPRING VALLEY, Calif. — Thieves broke into a commercial meat freezer in Spring Valley and are not being pursued as a high priority. The freezer is located equidistant between two buildings. The thieves undoubtedly thought the freezer belonged to a restaurant and that they were stealing frozen steaks for resale; in reality, it belongs to the restaurant's next-door neighbor, the Paradise Valley Road Pet Hospital, which reported nine euthanized dogs missing."

—*News of the Weird*, March, 1996

MAKING TRACKS
"SPOKANE, Wash. — Police had little difficulty catching up with a woman who robbed the Five Mile branch of the Washington Trust Bank last Saturday. The woman, who walked into the bank and showed the teller what appeared to be the handle of a gun, was given an undetermined amount of cash. She then walked out of the bank, got into a waiting cab and left. Police traced the taxi and got the woman's address. She was arrested without incident.

—Wire service story, March 8, 1996

A watermelon is 92% water; a raw apple is 84% water.

EYE DID IT

"EL CERRITO, Calif. — Robbery suspect Aaron Lavell Harris has given new meaning to the word *eyewitness*. Police searching the scene of an aborted armed robbery last week found one clue—a glass eye with Harris's name stenciled on it. Apparently, it popped out when Harris jumped from a second-story window to escape."

—San Francisco *Chronicle*, March 24, 1993

BALED OUT

"LANCASTER, Calif. — An inmate who fled prison by hiding in a garbage truck found himself trapped in a compacted bale of trash on Thursday. The prisoner thought he could escape the minimum-security prison by hiding in a trash bin. But the bin was collected by a truck that crushes garbage into a bale about one-fifth the size of the original load. The bale and prisoner were dumped at a landfill. He was discovered by the operator of a tractor breaking up garbage. He is listed in fair condition with broken bones."

—The *Oregonian*, Jan 14, 1996

THANKS FOR THE RIDE

"OSLO, Norway — Thomas Braendvik was walking to the local police station to report the theft of his bicycle, when a kind bicyclist headed his way offered him a lift. Braendvik accepted, and took a seat on the luggage rack.

" 'I thought the bike looked suspiciously like mine, so I asked if he minded me trying my key in the lock,' Braendvik told a reporter. The key fit, proving that the bike belonged to Braendvik. A policeman happened to have been watching the whole episode. He arrested the thief on the spot."

—Associated Press, July 7, 1996

WRONG BAR

"CHICAGO — Two would-be robbers could not have picked a worse place than Z's Sports Tap for their holdup attempt. Much to their chagrin, there was a retirement party going on…for a police officer. There were more than 100 cops in the bar. They quickly subdued the robbers and called on-duty police. 'That's what makes this job interesting,' said a police spokesman. 'Dumb people.' "

—Wire service reports, December 21, 1995

According to our resident astronomer, 41% of the moon is not visible from earth at any time.

WILL ROGERS SAID...

A tiny piece of the rich legacy left by America's national humorist in the 1920s and early 1930s. (He died in 1935.)

"Even if you are on the right track, you'll get run over if you just sit there."

"If stupidity got us into this mess, why can't it get us out?"

"We can't all be heroes... because someone has to sit on the curb and clap as they go by."

"Alexander Hamilton started the U.S. Treasury with nothing—and that was the closest our country has ever been to being even."

"There's no trick to being a humorist when you have the whole government working for you."

"I belong to no organized party. I am a Democrat."

"You can't say civilizations don't advance...In every war they kill you a new way."

"The man with the best job in the country is the Vice-President. All he has to do is get up every morning and say, 'How is the president?'"

"Diplomacy is the art of saying 'Nice doggie' until you can find a rock."

"Nothing you can't spell will ever work."

"If you make any money, the government shoves you in the creek once a year with it in your pockets. All that don't get wet you can keep."

"Liberty don't work as good in practice as it does in speeches."

"I see we are starting to pay attention to our neighbors in the south. We could never understand why Mexico wasn't just crazy about us; for we have always had their good will, and oil and minerals, at heart."

"Half our life is spent trying to find something to do with the time we have rushed through life trying to save."

"I never expected to see the day when girls would get sunburned in the places they do today."

A female mackerel lays 500,000 eggs at a time.

CELEBRITY SUPERSTITIONS

They're only human, after all.

Luciano Pavarotti: "I won't sing a note or act a word until I find a bent nail onstage. It's like a good-luck charm for me. If I can't spot my nail onstage, I search the wings."

Larry Bird (basketball player): Always makes sure to rub his hands on his sneakers before a game, to give him "a better feel" for the ball.

Lena Horne (singer): Thinks peanut shells in her dressing room bring bad luck.

Winston Churchill: Thought it was unlucky to travel on Fridays. Tried to arrange his schedule so he could "stay put" on that day.

Tony Curtis (actor): Wears only slip-on shoes. Thinks laces are unlucky.

Cornelius Vanderbilt (America's richest man in the 1860s): Had the legs of his bed placed in dishes of salt, to ward off attacks from evil spirits.

Drew Barrymore (actor): Says "peas indicate good luck."

Jim Kelly (Buffalo Bills quarterback): Vomits for good luck before each game. He's been doing it since high school.

Queen Elizabeth II: Insists on making a token payment for scissors used to cut ribbons at official openings. (It's bad luck to accept scissors as a gift and return nothing.)

Babe Ruth: Always stepped on first base when he came in from his right field position.

Zsa Zsa Gabor: Thinks it's bad luck to have goldfish in the house.

Wayne Gretzky (the NHL's all-time leading scorer): Puts baby powder on his stick before every game, and tucks only one side of his jersey into his pants.

Joan Rivers: "I knock on wood so often I have splinters in all ten knuckles."

Princess Diana: Had a lock of hair sewn into her wedding dress. (For luck?)

Great name: In some parts of England, garbage collectors are known as "swill solicitors."

FAMILY REUNIONS

You know how strange it seems when you find out you have an unexpected connection to someone. But what if the person were closely related to you? These stories are almost too weird for words, but they're all true. Inspired by an article sent by BRI member Joann McCracken in Boston.

WHO: James Austin and Yvette Richardson / Brother and sister

SEPARATION: When Yvette was three years old and James was seven months old, their father and mother separated. The father took James; the mother took Yvette. That was the last time the siblings saw or heard of each other.

TOGETHER AGAIN: James went to school in Philadelphia and got a job at the main post office. He worked the 4 p.m. shift, along with 4,100 other people. One day, he was talking to his shop steward, Barrie Bowens, about his life. As the *Boston Globe* reported:

> Austin told her that his father died young and that he never knew his mother. Bowens asked his mother's name and realized it was the name of Richardson's mother, too.
>
> For two years, James and Yvette had worked side by side, shooting the breeze but never prying into each other's personal life....Now they discovered they were brother and sister.

They were stunned. "Working in the same department side by side," the 34-year-old Richardson said, shaking her head. "The same place, the same time, every day. What are the odds of that?"

WHO: John Garcia and Nueng Garcia / Father and son
SEPARATION: During the late 1960s, John Garcia was stationed in Thailand with the Air Force. He lived with a woman named Pratom Semon, and in 1969, they had a son. Three months later, Garcia was shipped back to the States; he wanted to take Semon, but she refused to go. For two years, Garcia regularly wrote and sent checks to support his son. Then Semon started seeing another man and told Garcia to end his correspondence. Garcia lost touch with his son. Although he tried to find him, even sending

letters to the Thai government requesting an address, he was unsuccessful. He reluctantly gave up.

TOGETHER AGAIN: In 1996, John (who lived in Pueblo, Colorado) was driving through Colorado Springs when he decided to stop at a gas station. He filled up and bought two lottery tickets, then handed the clerk a check for $18. According to news reports, when the clerk saw the name on the check, the conversation went like this: "Are you John Garcia?" "Yes." "Were you ever in the Air Force?" "Yes." "Were you ever in Thailand?" "Yes." "Did you ever have a son?"

"With that question," writes the *San Francisco Chronicle*, "the two stared at each other and realized at the same moment that they were the father and son who had been separated 27 years ago and half a world away." Nueng's mother, it turned out, had married an American and moved to Colorado in 1971.

Incredibly, the elder Garcia had never been to that gas station before and wasn't even particularly low on fuel. "I don't even know why I stopped for gas," he admitted on "Good Morning America." "I started thinking—this couldn't be. I was totally shocked."

WHO: Tim Henderson and Mark Knight / Half-brothers

SEPARATION: When Mark Knight was a year old, his parents divorced. His father remarried and had a son named Tim. His mother remarried, too, and Mark took his stepfather's last name. The brothers met once, when Mark was five and Tim three, but the families fought and never saw each other again.

TOGETHER AGAIN: In February 1996, Henderson had to travel from Newcastle, England, to London. He couldn't afford the train fare, so he called the Freewheelers Lift Share Agency, which matches hitchhikers and drivers. They have 16,000 names on file. The name they gave him was Mark Knight.

According to a report in the *Guardian*: "As they drove, they started talking about friends and relatives. 'There was a moment of complete silence as we both stared at each other in disbelief,' said Mr. Henderson. 'Then one of us said, "You must be my brother." It was pretty mind-blowing. I always knew I had a half-brother but never thought we would meet.' "

A FOOD IS BORN

*These foods are such a big part of our lives that sometimes it's
hard to believe they weren't always around. Here's
a brief history of how they got to your house.*

HEINEKEN BEER. In the 1860s, a young Dutch man
named Gerard Adriaan Heineken wanted to start his own
business. He didn't have any money...but his mother did.
Heineken knew she hated the way drunks wandered the streets of
Amsterdam on Sunday mornings after all-night Saturday binges.
So he suggested that if she helped him start a brewery, local men
might drink *beer* all night instead of hard liquor, and public drunkenness might decrease. It was a pretty strange sales pitch...but it
worked. Today, Heineken N.V. is the largest beer producer in Europe, and the second largest in the world.

MIRACLE WHIP. Early in the Great Depression, prepared mayonnaise went from a household staple to an expensive luxury item
that few could afford. Kraft began researching ways to make an in-
expensive substitute and eventually came up with something made
of oil, egg yolks, cooked starch paste, and seasonings. It had less oil
than regular mayonnaise, so it was cheaper to produce...but was
also harder to make. Kraft invented a new mixer they called the
"miracle whip" to give the product its creamy consistency. Then
they named the product after the machine.

INSTANT COFFEE. In the early 1930s, Brazilian coffee harvests
were so huge that the worldwide price of coffee nearly collapsed. In
desperation, the Brazilian Coffee Institute started looking for new
ways to use the coffee beans. They approached the Nestle Company with the idea for "coffee cubes," which would convert quickly
into coffee when immersed in water.

Nestle took on the project...then gave up. But Max Morgenthal-
er, a company researcher, continued on his own time, using coffee
he bought himself. In 1937, he finally found a way to turn coffee
into powder without destroying its flavor. Nestle awarded him a
gold medal and a percentage of the profits. They marketed the "in-

stant" coffee under the brand name Nescafe, leaving it in powdered form (rather than cubes) so consumers could make their brew as strong as they wanted. It was issued to American GIs as part of their daily rations during World War II, and soldiers brought their taste for it home when the war was over.

BEN & JERRY'S ICE CREAM. In the late 1970s, Bennett Cohen and Jerry Greenfield, friends since high school, moved to Vermont to start a business. They weren't sure what kind of business, except that it would involve food. "We were both big into eating," Jerry says. Their first idea was bagels, but they gave that up when they learned that bagel-making equipment costs at least $40,000. So they paid $5 for a five-day ice cream–making correspondence course, rented an old gas station in Burlington, and began turning out ice cream by hand. Today, Ben & Jerry's ice cream is sold all over the world, and their factory in Waterbury is Vermont's leading tourist attraction.

CRISCO. You've probably seen "hydrogenated vegetable oil" on ingredients lists of cookies or crackers. It means that hydrogen was added to the oil to harden it. Crisco was the first food product to use this process: In the early 1900s, Proctor & Gamble experimented with hydrogenation to "harden" liquid cottonseed oil so it could be used as a substitute for lard. After they came up with a "creamy shortening" they could sell, they held an employee contest to name the new product. "Cryst" was rejected for religious reasons; "Krispo" was nixed because it was already trademarked. In the end, the company combined the two to get "Crisco," an acronym for "crystallized cottonseed oil."

ICED TEA. "While tea drinking is a nearly 5,000-year-old pleasure that began in China," Maureen Sajbel writes in the *Los Angeles Times*, "Sipping iced tea is a fairly recent American invention. The story goes that on a hot, humid day at the St. Louis World's Fair, a discouraged vendor wasn't having much success in selling Indian hot tea. With a scratch of the head and a burst of American inventiveness, he added ice. Within hours, fair-goers were drinking glass after glass of the thirst-quenching iced drink."

Mosquitoes aren't fond of citronella. Why? It irritates their feet.

MYTH AMERICA

*Here are a few more stories about America
that we've been taught are true...*

THE MYTH: Jackie Robinson broke baseball's color barrier in 1947 when he joined the Brooklyn Dodgers.

THE TRUTH: Robinson was *not* the first black man to play major league baseball; in fact, he came along more than 60 *years* after Moses "Fleet" Walker, a catcher who played 42 games for the Toledo Mudhens of the American Association in 1884. Walker's brother joined him later in the season, but only played five games. When the season ended, both Walkers were gone. Apparently, a country with dozens of Jim Crow laws still on the books wasn't ready to integrate their national pastime just yet.

THE MYTH: Machine Gun Kelly coined the expression "G-men" (for government men). In 1933, the story goes, FBI agents surrounded him on a Tennessee farm. Rather than shoot his way out, Kelly threw up his hands and shouted to the government agents, "Don't shoot, G-men, don't shoot!"

BACKGROUND. FBI director J. Edgar Hoover recounted the tale in a 1946 issue of the *Tennessee Law Review*.

THE TRUTH: Hoover made it up to generate publicity for the Bureau and to give his agents a nickname. The FBI wasn't even responsible for capturing Kelly; he was actually caught by a posse of lawmen led by W. J. Raney, a Memphis police officer. And, according to contemporary accounts, what Kelly really said was, "Okay, boys, I've been waiting for you all night."

THE MYTH: The *Spirit of '76*, the famous painting showing a flag-carrier, a drummer, and a man playing a fife (flute), was inspired by an actual scene in the Revolutionary War.

THE TRUTH: It started off as a *Civil War* painting. Archibald Willard, a Civil War veteran himself, first painted a cartoonish version, depicting three imaginary war recruits parading around "in lighthearted fashion." It wasn't until a friend talked him into painting a more somber version that he added the revolutionary themes and gave the painting its now-famous name.

THE MYTH: George Washington was a great military tactician.

THE TRUTH. "So notorious was his reputation for losing battles ineptly," writes Michael Korda in *Success*, "that John Adams called him 'an old muttonhead' and Jefferson commented, with great delicacy, that Washington was 'not a great tactician.'"

> As a young officer, he once constructed a fort at Great Meadows, Pennsylvania, on a swampy creek bottom, hemmed in on all three sides by wooded hills. This position for a fortress was so ludicrous that the French, in this case Washington's enemies, captured him immediately, and generously released him with the advice to take up some other line of work.
>
> Giving up fortifications, Washington then…became the personal aide to Lt. General Edward Braddock, whom Washington persuaded to divide the forces in the siege of Fort Duquesne. The result? Braddock lost the battle, his army, and his life.

After taking over the command of the Continental army,

> Washington proceeded through 1775 and 1776 to retreat from Long island to Brooklyn Heights, from Brooklyn Heights to Kips Bay, from Kips Bay to Washington Heights, from Washington Heights to White Plains, and from there across the Hudson into New Jersey. …It can be truly said that…Washington beat the British by retreating faster than they could advance.

THE MYTH: Geronimo was the name of a famous Apache chief.

THE TRUTH: His name was actually Govathlay, which doesn't sound anything like Geronimo. Mexican settlers, who couldn't pronounce Govathlay, referred to the chief as "Jerome," or "Geronimo" in Spanish. And there's nothing in the historical record to suggest that Govathlay ever shouted "Geronimo!" as he jumped from a cliff into a river to escape the U.S. Cavalry. That scene was invented for a 1940 movie, which probably led directly to the legend. (World War II paratroopers *did*, however, frequently shout "Geronimo!" when they jumped out of planes.)

DR. STRANGELOVE

Dr. Strangelove is considered one of the best satires of the Cold War era…if not one of the funniest movies ever made. Here are some little-known, behind-the-scenes details.

BUT SERIOUSLY, FOLKS

In the late 1950s, a 28-year-old film maker named Stanley Kubrick began reading up on the U.S.-Soviet arms race. He subscribed to *Aviation Week* and the *Bulletin of the Atomic Scientists*, and over the next six years read more than 70 books on the subject. As he read, he became fascinated by what he called "people's virtually listless acquiescence in the possibility—in fact, the increasing probability—of nuclear war."

One of the books Kubrick read was *Red Alert*, a novel about a paranoid U.S. military general who goes insane and launches an unprovoked nuclear attack on the Soviet Union. The book, by former Royal Air Force officer Peter George, was so intriguing that Kubrick bought the film rights and hired George to help him write a screenplay from the book.

BLACK HUMOR

The screenplay was supposed to be serious…but Kubrick's dark sense of humor kept intruding. Finally, he stopped fighting it and placed a phone call to satirist Terry Southern. Kubrick hadn't actually met Southern, but he'd read one of his books—*The Magic Christian*. A few years earlier, Peter Sellers had bought 100 copies of it and sent it to his friends…including Kubrick. Southern recalls Kubrick telling him on the phone that

> he had thought of the story as a "straightforward melodrama" until …he "woke up and realized that nuclear war was too outrageous, too fantastic to be treated in any conventional manner." He said that he could only see it now as "some kind of hideous joke." He told me he had read a book of mine which contained, as he put it, "certain indications" that I might be able to help him with the script.

So Southern became a co-writer on the world's first black comedy about nuclear war.

A SELLERS' MARKET

That wasn't Sellers's only behind-the-scenes contribution. For some reason, the corporate geniuses at Columbia Pictures decided that the movie *Lolita*, which Kubrick had directed in 1962, had succeeded because of "the gimmick of Peter Sellers playing several roles." So before *Strangelove* even had a title, they agreed to give Kubrick the green light for it...as long as it "would star Peter Sellers in at least four major roles."

Kubrick made that promise...but it turned out to be impossible to fulfill. Sellers did play *three* parts in the film brilliantly: Dr. Strangelove, President Merkin Muffley, and Group Captain Lionel Mandrake. Unfortunately, at the last minute, he was injured and had to give up the role of Major T. J. "King" Kong. Southern remembers:

> Kubrick's response was an extraordinary tribute to Sellers as an actor: "We can't replace him with another actor, we've got to get an authentic character from life, someone whose acting career is secondary—a real-life cowboy."...He asked for my opinion and I immediately suggested big Dan ("Hoss Cartwright") Blocker...of the TV show *Bonanza*....
>
> [Kubrick] made arrangements for a script to be delivered to Blocker that afternoon, but a cabled response from Blocker's agent arrived in quick order: "Thanks a lot, but the material is too pinko for Dan. Or anyone else we know for that matter."
>
> As I recall, this was the first hint that this sort of political interpretation of our work-in-progress might exist.

It was only then that Slim Pickens, a former rodeo clown, was hired for the part. (Ironically, Pickens was more conservative than Blocker, even supporting presidential candidate George Wallace.)

MIXED REVIEWS

As the film progressed, Kubrick had a growing uneasiness about the reception that awaited it. At one point, Mo Rothman, the executive producer assigned by Columbia Pictures, called with the message that "New York does *not* see anything funny about the end of the world!" Ultimately, many critics agreed. When it premiered in January 1964, Bosley Crowther wrote in *The New York Times*:

When your face blushes, the lining of your stomach turns red, too.

Dr. Strangelove...is beyond any question the most shattering sick joke I've ever come across....I am troubled by the feeling, which runs all through the film, of discredit and even contempt for our whole defense establishment, up to and even including the hypothetical Commander in Chief....Somehow, to me it isn't funny. It is malefic and sick.

Columbia was spooked and distanced itself from the film. "Even when *Strangelove* received the infrequent good review," Southern wrote, "the studio dismissed the critic as a pinko nutcase." At one point, Columbia's publicity department called the film "a zany novelty flick which does not reflect the views of the corporation in any way." But of course, when the Library of Congress listed *Strangelove* as one of the "50 greatest American films of all time," former Columbia execs were "in prominent attendance."

THE LOST SCENE

Something to look for: In many of the scenes filmed in the Pentagon war room, a long table filled with cakes, pies, and other desserts can be seen off to one side. The table isn't there by accident—Kubrick originally intended to end the movie with a pie fight. He even filmed the scene, as set director Ken Adams remembers:

It was a very brilliant sequence with a *Hellzapoppin* kind of craziness. Undoubtedly one of the most extraordinary custard pie battles ever filmed. The characters were hanging from chandeliers and throwing pies which ended up by covering the maps of the General Staff.... The sequence ended with the President of the United States and the Soviet ambassador sitting on what was left of the pies and building 'pie castles' like children on a beach.

But Kubrick removed the scene. Why? He forgot to tell the actors to play it straight. As the scene progressed, it was obvious that they were having a great time—which didn't fit with the rest of the film. Unfortunately, there was no time or money left to reshoot it.

FINAL THOUGHT

"Confront a man in his office with a nuclear alarm, and you have a documentary. If the news reaches him in his living room, you have a drama. If it catches him in the lavatory, the result is comedy."

— *Stanley Kubrick*

Only two words in the English language end in "gry"—angry and hungry.

LANGUAGE OF LOVE

*They say that it's international, but a good vocabulary can help. Here
are some forgotten Victorian words that might come in handy.*

THE GOOD:

Ravary: A fit of passion

Babies-in-the-eyes: The reflection of oneself in a loved one's pupils

Lavolt: A lively dance

Frike: Lusty, bawdy

Enterbathe: To bathe together, literally, to mix tears

Fairhead: A beauty

Amoret: A loving look, glance

Smick: To kiss

Fardry: To paint the face with white make-up for cosmetic benefit

Greade: A woman's bosom

Loveship: Act of love-making

Bridelope: Wedding

Frim: Fleshy, vigorous

Halch: To embrace tightly

Fucus: A kind of rouge made from lichen

Half-marrow: A husband or wife

Modesty-piece: A lace cloth that covers a woman's chest

Muskin: A term of endearment for a woman; sweetheart

THE BAD:

Curtain-sermon: A lecture given by a wife at bedtime

Grandgore: Infectious disease

Acharne: To thirst for blood

Chichevache: A thin, ugly face

Gandermooner: A man who chases other women during the first month after his wife has given birth

Clarty-paps: A slovenly, dirty wife

Delumbate: To sexually maim

Mormals: Inflamed sores

Winchester goose: A sexually transmitted disease

Fulyear: A man who dishonors women

Rush ring: To "wed" without a ring; to convince a woman that a false marriage was legal

Bespawled: Covered with spittle and saliva

Flesh-shambles: A dirty, ill-reputed brothel

Lib: To castrate

Stewed prune: Madam in a brothel

Longest word in Shakespeare's plays: "honorificabilitudinitatibus" (*Love's Labour's Lost*)

HONESTLY, ABE

A few random thoughts from our 16th president, Abraham Lincoln.

"It's better to be silent and thought a fool than speak and remove all doubt."

"People are just about as happy as they make up their minds to be."

"Whatever you are, be a good one."

"If I were two-faced, would I be wearing this one?"

"How many legs does a dog have if you call the tail a leg? Four. Calling a tail a leg doesn't make it a leg."

"If both factions, or neither, shall abuse you, you will probably be right. Beware of being assailed by one, and praised by the other."

"If you intend to go to work, there is no better place than right where you are."

"A woman is the only thing that I am afraid of that I know will not hurt me."

"The severest justice may not always be the best policy."

"Things may come to those who wait, but only the things left by those who hustle."

"The loss of enemies does not compensate for the loss of friends."

"If this country cannot be saved without giving up that principle [equality]....I would rather be assassinated on this spot than surrender it."

"A fellow once came to me to ask for an appointment as a minister abroad. Finding he could not get that, he came down to some more modest position.... When he saw he could not get that, he asked me for an old pair of trousers. It is sometimes well to be humble."

"It is said an Eastern monarch once charged his wise men to invent him a sentence...which should be true and appropriate in all times and situations. They presented him the words: 'And this, too, shall pass away.'"

"A universal feeling, whether well- or ill-founded, cannot be safely disregarded."

Poll results: What kind of flowers do most U.S. women want on Valentine's Day? Roses.

TAKE ME OUT TO THE BORU GAME

This is a page for baseball fans.

The Japanese have adopted baseball as their national game. They've also taken a number of American baseball terms and made them Japanese. Here are some of the words, written phonetically. Some are easy, some confusing. See if you can tell what they mean. Answers are at the bottom of the page.

1. Batta
2. Boru
3. Kochi
4. Besuboru
5. Besu-ryne
6. Chenji appu
7. De Gemu
8. Era
9. Herumetto
10. Mitto
11. Maneja
12. Suisaido sukuiizu

13. Homuran
14. Auto
15. Fain Puray
16. Kyatcha
17. Pasu boh-ru
18. Sukoa bodo
19. Batta bokkusu
20. Kuriin hitto
21. Foku boru
22. Wairudo pitchi
23. Banto
24. Pitchingu sutaffu

25. Furu kaunto
26. Puray boru!
27. Senta
28. Gurobu
29. Fauru
30. Pinchi ranna
31. Hitto endu ran
32. Battingu sutansu
33. Foa boru
34. Daburu Hedda
35. "Gettsu"
36. Katto ofu puray

ANSWERS: 1. Batter; 2. Ball; 3. Coach; 4. Baseball; 5. Baseline; 6. Change-up; 7. Day game; 8. Error; 9. Helmet; 10. Mitt; 11. Manager; 12. Suicide squeeze; 13. Home run; 14. Out; 15. Fine play; 16. Catcher; 17. Passed ball; 18. Score board; 19. Batting box; 20. Clean hit; 21. Fork ball; 22. Wild pitch; 23. Bunt; 24. Pitching staff; 25. Full count; 26. Play ball!; 27. Center field or center fielder; 28. Glove; 29. Foul ball; 30. Pinch runner; 31. Hit-and-run; 32. Batting stance; 33. Four balls (a walk); 34. Double-header; 35. "Get two" (double-play); 36. Cutoff play

In 1995, world population was almost 6 billion; about 1/3 of the people are under age 15.

KILLING MASS TRANSIT

"Some people say that the people of Los Angeles chose the automobile over the trains, chose paved highways over palm trees, chose smog over clean air—all for the freedom and mobility associated with automobile travel. In fact, the people of L.A. had no say in the matter." —Russell Mokhiber

Before the Second World War, nearly every major city in the U.S. had a network of low-polluting public transportation—streetcars, electric trains, or trolleys. Los Angeles, for example, had the largest electric train system in the world. It linked the 56 towns of greater L.A. and carried 80 million passengers a year.

Many public transit systems around the country were owned by electric companies. They had been built in the years before most homes were wired for electricity, to increase sales of electric power.

But in the mid-1930s, Congress began breaking up the utility monopolies. In 1935, it passed antitrust laws that forced them to sell their mass-transit holdings.

MOTOR POOLS

• These mass-transit companies were put up for sale at a time when the nation's automakers, mired in the Great Depression, were looking for ways to increase sales.

• "The [auto] industry was in a vulnerable position," writes Russell Mokhiber in his book *Corporate Crime and Violence*. "It was not clear that the four-wheeled buggy would become the transportation method of choice for a nation in the midst of its worst economic depression...[but] the industry knew that without efficient rail systems, city-dwellers around the country would be forced to find alternative means of transportation. So General Motors, determined to sell more cars and buses, decided to destroy the rail systems."

GM GOES TO WORK

• In 1932, GM formed a holding company called United Cities Motor Transit. Through UCMT, the automaker bought three mass- transit companies in Ohio and Michigan, converted them to buses, then sold them back to local companies with the stipulation that they buy only GM buses in the future. GM had hoped to use

---

A world record: Mrs. Myra Franklin saw the film *The Sound of Music* more than 900 times.

these "showcase" bus lines to persuade other companies to make the switch, but there was little interest.

• When GM tried to use the same technique in Portland, Oregon, it ran into trouble. The American Transit Assn. publicly exposed GM's plan and censured it. GM was forced to dismantle UCMT.

• That didn't stop GM however. In fact, it then decided to skip the small companies and wipe out New York's trolley system—America's largest. To protect itself from criticism, GM worked with an existing bus company, the Omnibus Corporation, rather than setting up its own. It took only 18 months to dismantle New York's massive public transportation system.

THE SECOND STAGE

• GM was now ready to take on the rest of the country. Using a small Illinois bus company as a front, it began buying up dozens of mass-transit companies. "Tracks were literally torn out of the ground, sometimes overnight," writes journalist Jonathan Kwitny. "Overhead power lines were dismantled, and valuable off-street rights of way were sold." In East St. Louis, for example, the transition from streetcars to buses took less than 24 hours. (*Harper's*)

• Soon the front company became too big for GM to finance. So GM transformed it into a holding company called National City Lines, Inc., and approached other companies that would also benefit from the destruction of electric transit. By 1937, Greyhound Bus Lines, the Firestone Tire and Rubber Company, Mack Manufacturing, Standard Oil of California, and Phillips Petroleum had also joined up, investing $10 million altogether.

• NCL finished dismantling transit systems after the end of World War II; by the time it was done, it had eliminated lines carrying hundreds of millions of passengers in more than 45 cities, including New York, Philadelphia, Baltimore, St. Louis, Oakland, Salt Lake City, and Los Angeles. By 1955, only 5,000 streetcars remained nationwide out of a fleet that had numbered 40,000 in 1936.

WAS IT A CONSPIRACY?

In 1949, GM and the other conspirators were indicted for violating antitrust laws. They defended themselves by claiming that their investments in the enterprise were small, that they had exerted no managerial control over National City Lines, and that a nationwide switch to buses had already begun.

SUSPICIOUS FACTS

• The conspirators claimed that they had put money into National City Lines because transit lines were a good investment. But internal documents showed they knew they were going to lose money. The real profits would come later, by selling products to the new *bus* lines. According to Kwitny, internal Mack memos admitted to "probable losses" on the bus stocks, but predicted that the losses would be made up by future sales to the newly created bus lines.

• The companies investing were very secretive about their involvement with National City Lines: Standard Oil of California invested its money through two other companies, because, a company official later admitted, "We didn't want to be criticized." Firestone channeled its investments through two of its employees who posed as independent investors.

• Though National City Lines was supposed to be independent, the agreements under which the conspirators provided money specified that all buses, tires, and petroleum products had to be purchased from the companies that owned stock in National City Lines. Moreover, NCL and its branches were run by employees of the stockholding companies.

• Kwitny also notes that the contracts forbade transit companies from buying streetcars or any other piece of equipment that ran on anything but gasoline. (The contracts were later changed to permit the purchase of *diesel* buses, which became popular in the 1940s).

END OF THE LINE

• Once the light rail systems were gone, big business got out of the transit business: GM, Standard Oil, Firestone, Phillips, Mack, and Greyhound all dumped their stocks. Even the holding company itself, National City Lines, got entirely out of mass transit.

• Meanwhile, a federal court decided that the companies had engaged in an illegal conspiracy. GM, National City Lines, Firestone Tire and Rubber, Phillips Petroleum, Mack Manufacturing, and Standard Oil of California were all convicted of violating the Sherman Antitrust Act.

• Their penalty? A slap on the wrist. Each company was fined $5,000. Company officials found guilty were each fined a dollar.

FAMILIAR PHRASES

More origins of everyday phrases.

RIDE PIGGYBACK

Meaning: Ride on the back of something.

Origin: "Piggyback" has nothing to do with pigs—it is a corruption of "pick-a-back"...which, in turn, came from "pick back" and "pick pack." All of these referred to packs that people threw on their back to carry things.

COAT OF ARMS

Meaning: Design showing a family crest.

Origin: In the Middle Ages, knights wore a special coat over their armor to keep it clean and protect it from the weather. The coat was usually decorated with the knight's family crest, showing that the knight was of noble birth and thus entitled to bear arms. As gunpowder made suits of armor obsolete, coats of arms became purely decorative.

HAVING A FIELD DAY

Meaning: Having a great time; easily overwhelming an opponent.

Origin: "Field days" began as special days set aside by the military for troop maneuvers and exercises. By the 19th century, the expression expanded to include civilian festivities as well. Eventually, it was used to mean any pleasurable experience.

GET COLD FEET

Meaning: Become wary; back out of a commitment.

Origin: In the early 17th century, having cold feet meant having no money (and thus no shoes). In the 18th century, the meaning changed, probably in reference to soldiers with cold or frozen feet, who are more likely to retreat than those with warm ones.

BEAT A HASTY RETREAT

Meaning: Leave quickly; back down.

Origin: In the 14th century, European armies used trumpets and other instruments to call troops back to camp. Centuries later, drums were used. Drummers literally "beat the signal to retreat."

Something to ponder: Elvis Presley got a "C" in his eighth grade music class.

BUTTONHOLE A PERSON
Meaning: Stop a passer-by; detain someone.
Origin: The expression was originally "buttonhold" a person. It referred to the practice of grabbing a person by their buttons and holding on while you tried to sell them something.

HEARD THROUGH THE GRAPEVINE
Meaning: Heard some gossip.
Origin: During the Civil War, soldiers said that rumors came in "on the grapevine telegraph"—a reference to the fact that there were no real telegraph lines in camp to supply accurate information...just grapevines.

INDIAN SUMMER
Meaning: The period of warm weather after summer has gone and before fall is over.
Origin: Dates back to the days of mistrust between settlers and Native Americans. The term "Indian" acquired a derogatory connotation and was used in expressions like "Indian giver" and "Indian summer"—weather that appeared to be summer but wasn't.

DRINK A TOAST
Meaning: Drink in honor of another person.
Origin: Literally comes from drinking toast. In the Middle Ages people added a piece of spiced toast to their tankards of ale to improve the taste. The practice was abandoned as brewing methods improved, but the term continued to apply to the practice of drinking to someone's health.

FLY IN THE OINTMENT
Meaning: One thing wrong with an otherwise-perfect situation.
Origin: Ointment used to mean a sweet-smelling cosmetic. The phrase comes from a verse in the Bible, Ecclesiastes 10:1: "Dead flies make the perfumer's ointment give off an evil odor."

DRESSED TO THE NINES
Meaning: Well-dressed.
Origin: Probably comes from the Old English expression *dressed to then eyne*, which means "dressed to the eyes."

CELEBRITY SWEEPSTAKES

Celebrity endorsements are a multi-billion-dollar business. If you get the right celebrity to pitch your product, it can be worth millions. But if you pick wrong...well, take a look at these examples.

GERALDINE FERRARO
Pepsi hired the 1984 Democratic vice-presidential candidate—the first woman ever nominated by a major political party—to do a Diet Pepsi commercial in 1985.

What they wanted: People "who represent America's new generation of leaders" to go with their "Choice of a New Generation" campaign. Roger Enrico, Pepsi's CEO, explained that "Ferraro is [no longer] a despised Democrat; she's a living symbol of women's possibilities." He added, "As the first woman vice-presidential candidate, she'll get us on every news show in America."

What they got: Angry customers. Liberals attacked Ferraro for selling out, conservatives attacked Pepsi for promoting a liberal agenda. But the worst criticism came from anti-abortion protesters, as Enrico recalled in his book, *The Other Guy Blinked:*

> As the commercial started to air, a whole other kind of protest began. It was about "The Choice of a New Generation." No, it was about the word *choice*....Did it ever enter our minds that, in politics, that word has a very different meaning? Nope. So we were very, very surprised when we start getting letters. Angry letters. Letters that said, "Your commercials are 'pro-choice.' You favor the right of women to have abortions on demand.'

What happened: Pepsi pulled the ads. "I felt sorry for Ferraro," Enrico writes, "but I learned to keep Pepsi's nose out of politics."

RUSH LIMBAUGH

In 1994, the Florida Citrus Department bought $1 million worth of ads on Limbaugh's show to get him to promote orange juice.

What they wanted: A big audience for their "health-oriented" ads. The 300-pound Limbaugh might not be a good spokesperson for health food, but he did have upwards of 15 million listeners. "True,

Mr. Limbaugh is no plain-vanilla guy," wrote *Advertising Age* in February. "He's popular because of his conservative opinions. And he dotes on baiting liberals. But that's a plus in today's market...where ad messages delivered by popular hosts carry extra weight with loyal listeners."

What they got: An instant public-relations disaster. Groups like the National Organization for Women (NOW) and the NAACP started a "Flush Rush–Drink Prune Juice" campaign. "Limbaugh's hate-mongering is being underwritten by state and federal tax dollars," NOW's president complained. And Democrats—particularly Florida's governor—were outraged. "We're looking for people who will present the best possible image for Florida citrus—not people who will engender hate, disregard for minorities or represent any political philosophy," said a Democratic state representative. Even the citrus commissioners' jobs wound up in jeopardy. The following month, Democrats held up the otherwise-routine appointment of three members of the Citrus Board in the Florida legislature as a protest.

What happened: Sales of orange juice dropped after the campaign went on the air, and the board dumped Limbaugh after his six-month contract expired. Limbaugh predictably blamed his firing on "liberals, both in government, in special interest groups like the militant National Organization for Women, and in the press."

⊗　　⊗　　⊗

SELLING OUT?

Terri Garr on why she made a Yoplait commercial:

"They give you a lot of money, and I come from a...relatively poor background. So I go, '*That* much money for a day's work? Yessss!' But my management people said it's not enough. And I say, 'What do you mean it's not enough?' So they came back with even more money. It's crazy. But what am I going to do, be in the Motion Picture Country Home, 86 years old, saying to my pal, Farrah Fawcett: 'In 1986, I could have done a commercial for a million dollars but nooooo, I was too fine.' I don't want to be telling that story. I want to be on my own estate, in the south of France, telling my servants, 'I got this commercial....' "

THE TRUTH ABOUT "KILLER BEES"

Since 1964 we've read news reports of "killer bees" working their way up from South America to the United States. They finally arrived in 1990 ...and nothing much happened. Is the killer bee crisis for real, or is it an example of media exaggeration fueling public hysteria?

IN THE BEEGINNING

In 1956, the Brazilian government wanted to improve Brazil's honey industry. Although Brazil is the fifth-largest country in the world, it ranked only 47th in world honey production. So it hired Dr. Warwick E. Kerr, an American entomologist. Kerr's solution was to import African honeybees, which produce far more honey than the European bees that had been brought to Brazil by Western colonists in the 16th and 17th centuries.

Because African bees are more aggressive than Brazilian bees, Kerr decided not to release the bees directly into the environment. Instead, he planned to interbreed them with the gentler Brazilian bees, then release their hybrid offspring.

Kerr's plan didn't work as he had hoped. About a year after he began the project, 26 swarms of the purebred African bees escaped from his laboratory in São Paulo and quickly began overrunning the Brazilian honeybee population. His efforts to create a kinder, gentler honeybee had failed—and the aggressive bees were taking over.

NO BEEG DEAL

No one was too excited by this development. True, Africanized bees *are* more aggressive than European honeybees—for instance, they attack by the hundreds instead of by the dozens when their hives are disturbed. But they can still only sting once before they die. Brazil actually had a larger problem with its native wasps, which can sting someone many times without dying. About the only people who noticed the difference were Brazilian beekeepers, who found the new bees harder to manage.

POLITICAL ANIMAL

For the next eight years, the Africanized bees attracted little or no attention at all. Then, on April 1, 1964, the Brazilian army overthrew President Joao Goulart and set up a military dictatorship. When Kerr spoke out against human rights abuses, the new regime used the government-controlled press to portray him as a modern-day mad scientist. Professor Robert Morse describes what happened next in his book *Bees and Beekeeping*:

> In an effort to discredit Kerr as a scientist, the military played upon the fear that many people have of stinging insects. Since most people do not know the difference between bees and wasps, any stinging incident, many of which were caused by wasps, was blamed on Professor Kerr's [accidental release of Africanized bees].
>
> The Brazilian military called the bees, in Portuguese, the language of Brazil, *abelhas assassinas* (killer bees). So far as I can determine, the first mention of the words "killer bees" in the United States was in *Time* magazine in the September 24, 1965, issue that picked up one of these military press releases.

Some Brazilian newspapers even claimed that Dr. Kerr had *taught* the bees to be mean.

Other magazines and newspapers followed *Time*'s lead and printed the Brazilian junta's propaganda as if it were the truth. In the process, they created a wave of hysteria that swept across South America, then Central and North America as the Africanized bees moved inexorably northward.

HARD TO BEELIEVE

When will the killer bees arrive in the United States? Actually, they've been here since 1959, thanks to a U.S. Department of Agriculture program that distributed—no kidding—*Africanized bee semen* to domestic beekeepers. "It's common knowledge among larger commercial beekeepers," says Dee Lusby, an Arizona beekeeper. "The USDA bee lab in Baton Rouge, Louisiana, received Africanized bee semen from Brazil 30 years ago and made the offspring available to beekeepers in this country and around the world. It was part of an ongoing program to breed superior honey-producing bees, just like Dr. Kerr's experiments in South America."

Coincidence? William Shakespeare and Miguel De Cervantes died on the same day in 1616.

And that probably wasn't their first trip to the United States. According to *Bee World* magazine, other bee breeders may have brought them over from Africa as early as the mid-1800s. So the killer bees aren't coming, they're already here, and they've probably been here for over a century.

For that matter, most beekeepers say that the *German* bee, which has been in the United States for over two centuries, is even meaner than the Africanized bees. But even these extra-mean bees aren't much of a public nuisance, beekeepers note, and say many predict that the Africanized bees aren't either. "You're more likely to be killed by lightning than attacked by Africanized honeybees," says Dr. Anita Collins, a research geneticist with the Department of Agriculture.

SO WHAT'S THE DIFFERENCE?

• Anatomically speaking, Africanized bees are virtually indistinguishable from European bees, except that they're slightly smaller. Even the experts have a hard time telling them apart without studying them in a lab.

• Africanized bee venom is no stronger than that of European bees. In fact, Africanized bees carry slightly less venom than European bees do.

• The only real difference is behavior: Africanized honey bees are much more active, both as honey producers and defenders of the hive. They're more easily angered, and, once agitated, take longer to calm down—sometimes as long as 24 hours. They also defend the hive in greater numbers than European bees do. "They get eight to ten times as many bees out to defend the colony and sting," Dr. Collins says. "It's not any different sting for sting," adds Stormy Sparks, a Texas A&M entomologist, "but there's just a much bigger potential for multiple stings."

• A positive note: Africanized bees evolved in a hot climate, so they have very little tolerance for cold compared to European bees, and will probably never go above the southern third of the United States.

The average 10-gallon hat holds only 3 quarts of water.

HOORAY FOR HOLLYWOOD

*Hollywood is so closely identified with the glamorous film industry,
it's hard to imagine that it started out as a prim Victorian town...but it did.*

HISTORY. In 1886 Kansas prohibitionists Harvey and Daeida Wilcox "bought a 120-acre citrus farm in sleepy Cahuenga Valley, a suburb of Los Angeles, for $150/acre." They built an elaborate Victorian house in the middle of a fig orchard, then began subdividing the property. Liquor wasn't allowed, and only "well-educated, worldly, decent" people were offered the property.

In 1903, the subdivision was big enough to become the city of Hollywood. But it didn't last long. In 1910, the citizens voted to make Hollywood an official district of L.A. The reason: They wanted access to L.A.'s water system. Since then, one historian laments, "Hollywood has been reduced to a mere 'northwest sector of the city of Los Angeles.'"

NAME. While her California house was being built in 1886, Daeida Wilcox went East to visit her family. On the train, she met a woman who described a lovely Illinois summer estate, called Hollywood, that was sprinkled with holly trees.

Mrs. Wilcox was taken with the idea. She repeatedly tried to grow holly on her citrus farm before deciding that the climate wasn't suitable. Perhaps to console herself, she named their ranch Hollywood anyway. In 1887 she registered the name with the Los Angeles recorder.

MAIN INDUSTRY. In the early 1900s the film industry was centered in both New York City and Fort Lee, New Jersey. But soon movie companies were headed west:

• **The First West Coast Studio.** In 1907 Colonel William Selig was producing crude silent movies in Chicago, "whenever the sun was shining—which was not frequently enough to make [his business] a profound success." He happened to read a promotional

---

The French writer Voltaire drank 70 cups of coffee a day.

pamphlet sent east by the Los Angeles Chamber of Commerce that mentioned the city was "bathed in sunshine some 350 days of the year." This impressed Selig, and he sent two men—Francis Boggs and Thomas Parsons—to see if it was true.

To give the area a true test, Boggs and Parsons set up a temporary studio in L.A. and began making pictures, recruiting actors off the streets of the city. When they'd completed several pictures, they left to test another location—Colorado—where they compared the climate and photographic possibilities to those on the coast. The West Coast won. Not only was there almost unlimited sunshine, but the varied scenery—mountains, rivers, deserts, and ocean—was unbeatable. Boggs and Parsons shared their discovery with other filmmakers in the east, and in early 1909, Selig went to Los Angeles to build the first L.A. studio.

The First Hollywood Studio. Ironically, it was the Wilcoxes' puritanism that brought moviemakers to Hollywood. When the couple subdivided their estate, one plot of land wound up in the hands of a tavern owner…who opened a bar there. The outraged Victorians passed a law prohibiting booze, bankrupting the bar. So when the Nestor Moving Picture Company arrived from New Jersey in 1911, they were able to buy the abandoned tavern cheap and convert it into the first Hollywood studio. Within a week, Nestor's had produced Hollywood's first film, *Her Indian Hero*, a western featuring real indians. Within three months, they were sharing Hollywood with fourteen other film companies—despite the "Actors Not Welcome" signs posted all over town.

HOLLYWOOD FACTS

• Early filmmakers who moved West weren't just looking for a place in the sun; they were looking for a place to hide. So many were violating Thomas Edison's motion picture patents that a legal battle known as the Patents War erupted. Southern California was the perfect refuge—as far from the federal government as possible and close enough to the Mexican border for a quick getaway.

• The famous "HOLLYWOOD" sign in the hills above the film capital originally said "HOLLYWOODLAND." It was built in 1923 to promote a real estate development. The last four letters fell down during WW II.

No wonder they grunt: Most of a hog's sweat glands are in its snout.

TEST YOUR GRAMMY IQ

Every year, the news media make a big deal about who won the Grammy Awards. Have you been paying attention? Here's a little quiz to see how much you really know about the "coveted" music awards.
(Answer pages start on page 507.)

1. Which of these groups has never won a Grammy?
a) Alvin and the Chipmunks   **b)** The Beach Boys   **c)** Aerosmith

2. An assassination ended the meteoric career of the 1962 winner of Album of the Year. Who was it?
   a) Vaughn Meader   **b)** Sam Cooke   **c)** Clark Taylor

3. In 1965, the bestselling record of the year was "Satisfaction"; the Beatles recorded *Help!*; Motown was tearing up the charts. The Grammy winner that year for Best Vocal Group was:
   a) The Beatles   **b)** The Supremes   **c)** The Anita Kerr Quartet
   d) Steve Brummet & His Polka Pals   **e)** The Mamas & the Papas

4. When did Elvis win his first Grammy?
a) 1960, for "Are You Lonesome Tonight?" (Best Male Singer)
b) 1965, for *Blue Hawaii* (Best Movie Sountrack)
c) 1967, for *How Great Thou Art* (Best Inspirational Performance)
d) 1974, for "In the Ghetto" (Song of the Year)

5. The first artist ever to refuse a Grammy was
   a) Nina Simone   **b)** Bob Dylan   **c)** Sinead O'Connor

6. In the decade following the Beatles break-up in 1970, each member of the group won a Grammy for a non-Beatle effort... except one. Which one?
   a) John   **b)** George   **c)** Ringo   **d)** Paul

7. Although this rock group—considered one of the world's best by most critics—had never won a Grammy, they received a Lifetime

Achievement Award in 1985. "Thank you," said the group's leader, "the joke's on you." What band was it?

    a) The Doors   **b)** The Rolling Stones   **c)** The Who

8. What performer won a Best Vocalist Grammy for a song she'd written about *not* receiving the award a few years earlier?

    a) Roseanne Cash   **b)** Dolly Parton   **c)** Carole King

9. Which Grammy winner told a reporter: "My nomination must have been an accident. Either that, or a lot of people have a perverse sense of humor."

    a) Bobby McFerrin   **b)** Bob Newhart   **c)** Frank Zappa

10. What was notable about the Grammys won by Jimi Hendrix and Janis Joplin?

a) What Grammys?

b) They were withheld because of the artists' overt drug use.

c) They were given for a little-known duet they did of the Beatles' old hit, "She Loves You."

11. Who was the first African-American ever to win the *Best New Artist* award?

    a) Chubby Checker, 1960   **b)** Little Stevie Wonder, 1962

       c) O. C. Smith, 1968   **d)** Natalie Cole, 1975

12. What was surprising about 1966's Best Folk Artist winner, Cortelia Clark?

a) It turned out he'd undergone a sex-change operation.

b) He couldn't afford to rent a tux to go to the awards ceremony.

c) There *was* no Cortelia Clark—it was really B. B. King, recording under a different name.

13. In 1996 John Popper, harmonica player for Blues Traveler, pulled off a Grammy first when he jumped out of his seat to get an award, and…

    a) Tore a ligament in his leg   **b)** His pants fell down

       c) He tripped and fell

Desire. The other one was named Cemetery.

O'ROURKE-ISMS

P. J. O'Rourke, the "Republican party animal," on a few random topics.

"Never wear anything that panics the cat."

"Wearing a hat implies that you are bald if you are a man and that your hair is dirty if you are a woman."

"There is no way to make vomiting courteous. You have to do the next best thing, which is to vomit in such a way that the story you tell about it later will be amusing."

"People who don't smoke have a terrible time finding something polite to do with their lips."

"Drugs have taught an entire generation of American kids the metric system."

"How much fame, money, and power does a woman have to achieve on her own before you can punch her in the face?"

"Don't send funny greeting cards on birthdays or at Christmas. Save them for funerals, when their cheery effect is needed."

"Feminism seems to be a case of women having won a leg-wrestling match with their own other leg. There is only one thing for men to do in response to this confusing situation, which is the same thing men have always done, which is anything women want."

"Dates used to be made days or even weeks in advance. Now dates tend to be made the day after. That is, you get a phone call from someone who says, 'If anyone asks, I was out to dinner with you last night, okay?'"

"There is one thing women can never take away from men. We die sooner."

"After equality, wage parity, [and] liberation...Women still can't do the following: Start barbeque fires; hook up a stereo; shine shoes; anything on a roof; decide where to hang a picture; investigate mysterious house noises at night; kill and dispose of large insects; walk past a mirror without stopping to look."

If your stomach didn't produce a new layer of mucous every two weeks, it would digest itself.

THE CHEW-CHEW MAN

Where did the low-calorie diet come from? It started with a guy known as the "Chew-Chew Man" to critics and the "Great Masticator" to fans.

THE BIRTH OF "FLETCHERISM"

In 1895, 44-year-old Horace Fletcher was turned down for life insurance because he weighed 217 pounds (at 5'6" tall), and he drank excessively. "I was an old man at forty, and on the way to a rapid decline," he recalled years later.

In 1898, Fletcher performed an experiment on himself. He began chewing each bite of food 30 to 70 times—even milk and soup, which he swished in his mouth—and never ate when he was upset or wasn't hungry. After five months of "Fletcherizing" each morsel of food, he lost 60 pounds and regained his health. He also found that he could live happily on 1,600 calories a day, far less than the 3,500 to 4,500 calories recommended at the turn of the century.

THE GREAT MASTICATOR

The experience helped Fletcher find a new calling—pitching his chewing habits to the masses. His slogan: "Nature will castigate those who don't masticate." Fletcher's lecture tours and bestselling books attracted tens of thousands of followers, including John D. Rockefeller and Thomas Edison. Adherents formed "Fletcher clubs," where they met to eat slowly and chant ditties like:

> I choose to chew, Because I wish to do, The sort of thing that
> Nature had in view, Before bad cooks invented sav'ry stew;
> When the only way to eat was to chew! chew! chew!

Fletcher died from bronchitis in 1919 at the age of 69, and his chewing theories soon followed him to the grave. But one thing that did survive him was his low-calorie diet: In 1903, a Yale University professor named Russell Chittenden examined Fletcher, found him to be in excellent health, and decided to try the diet himself. Soon after, his rheumatic knee stopped bothering him and his chronic headaches went away, prompting Chittenden to launch a series of studies into diet and health. These and other pivotal studies led to a ratcheting down of the recommended calorie intake from 3,500 a day to the 2,000 recommended today.

The Sanskrit word for "war" also translates as "desire for more cows."

MISS AMERICA, PART III:
Creating An Institution

Here's where Miss America starts to look like the pageant we know today. It's interesting that one person is so responsible for its success—which makes her either an unsung hero, if you like the pageant...or the culprit, if you don't. It's also interesting to see that the key to turning a "moneymaking scheme" into an "institution" is finding a way to make it seem patriotic.

WONDER WOMAN
The 1935 pageant would probably have been another dud. But Eddie Corcoran, the person in charge of organizing the event, had a stroke of luck: he read an article praising Lenora Slaughter, assistant to Florida Baseball Commissioner Al Lang. The article lauded Slaughter's work on the "Festival of the States" parade and pageant in Saint Petersburg, Florida. Corcoran had never organized a pageant, and knew he needed help. He wrote a letter to Lang asking to "borrow" Slaughter for the six weeks leading up to the contest. He offered to pay her $1,000 for the work.

Slaughter hesitated...but Lang urged her to "go up there and show those damn Yankees how to do a *real* job with a pageant." Finally, she consented to go to Atlantic City. But only for the agreed-upon six weeks.

She ended up staying for more than 30 years.

CULTURAL REVOLUTION

Slaughter had spent her career working with civic-minded, upper-crust society women, and she put this background to work on the Miss America Pageant's #1 problem: its reputation for sleaze. For the rest of the 1930s and into the 1940s, she tore the pageant down to its barest essentials and rebuilt it into the kind of event that even high-class society matrons could love. Or as Bess Myerson, Miss America 1945, put it, "She picked the pageant up by its bathing suit straps and put it in an evening gown."

One of the ways Slaughter cleaned up the contest's image was by drawing attention away from the swimsuit competition. She did this by adding a talent category to the competition, and by bringing back family-oriented events. She also excluded children from the competition for the first time, requiring that all entrants be 18 years old by the first day of competition.

MRS. ATLANTIC CITY

Despite all these changes, the pageant's surivival remained in doubt. Conservatives and women's organizations kept up their criticism, and groups like the Federated Women's Clubs of New Jersey denounced the contest as "the work of the devil."

Her back to the wall, Slaughter made a brilliant move to stave off an attack by the Atlantic City government—then run by conservative Quakers. She asked the wife of Mayor C. D. White to head the pageant's hostess committee, which organized the chaperones and escorts for contestants during Pageant Week. Mrs. White, whom Slaughter described as "the Quakerest of Quakers," was perfect for the job. She recruited people from the "best" families in town to volunteer in the pageant. The 1935 and 1936 pageants were considered successes.

CLOSE CALL

Putting Mrs. White in charge of the hostess committee helped the pageant survive its next big scandal. In 1937, a 17-year-old girl named Bette Cooper won the Miss America crown before anyone realized she was too young to compete. Then, the morning she was supposed to be crowned, she ran off with her pageant-appointed escort—an Atlantic City man named Lou Off. Cooper never returned, and the title remained vacant for the rest of the year.

It turned out later that Cooper ran away simply because she didn't want to drop out of Junior College to fulfill her "queenly duties," and didn't know how else to get out of them. Even so, newspapers all over the East Coast covered the drama in lurid— and inaccurate—detail. Ordinarily, the pageant would have been doomed, but not this time. "The pageant escaped a lot of heat," Deford writes, "because nobody wanted to take on Mrs. White."

FOR WOMEN ONLY

After the scandal blew over, Slaughter and White took steps to make sure it would never happen again. They instituted a ban,

forbidding contestants from having *any* contact with any men—
even their fathers—during Pageant Week. The young women were
also barred from nightclubs, bars, and taverns, and had to avoid any
public events where alcohol was served. They had to observe an
ironclad 1:00 a.m. curfew, and even taxicabs were declared off-
limits except in emergencies, to avoid even the hint of scandal.
Nearly all of the rules set down in the 1930s are still in effect today.

GOING FURTHER

Once Slaughter got the Miss America Pageant and its contestants
firmly under control, she set her sights on the pageant's other major problem: the cheesy state and local "franchise" pageants that
fed their winners into the Miss America contest.

Over the next several years, Slaughter phased out contests run
by newspapers and amusement parks and began regulating operators of the state and local pageants that were left. For-profit
pageants were out. One by one, Slaughter took control of them
and turned them over to local chapters of the nonprofit Jaycees
(Junior Chamber of Commerce) to run as a public service.

Today more than 300,000 volunteers around the country run the
2,000 local contests that feed into the Miss America Pageant.

ALL THIS AND WORLD WAR II

Slaughter was still implementing her reforms when the Japanese
bombed Pearl Harbor and the United States entered World War II.
Once again, the future of the pageant seemed in doubt (although
this time, at least, it wasn't the pageant's fault). Who could justify
all of the effort and expense that went into the pageant when
America's sons were shipping off to war?

The federal government, that's who.

The War Finance Department, which had the power to cancel
frivolous and wasteful public events during wartime, decided that
the pageant could—and should—continue during the war. Why?
"They knew we could do a good job selling war bonds," Slaughter
explained, "and agreed to pay $2,500 if I would chaperone Miss
America on a trip around America selling war bonds in 1943."

For the next three months, Slaughter and that year's Miss

Long odds: Only one person in 2 billion will live to the age of 116.

America, a 19-year-old UCLA coed named Jean Bartel, toured the United States selling bonds. They made 469 appearances in 24 different states and autographed 50,000 pictures.

When it was done, they'd sold $2.5 million worth of bonds—more than any other individual Americans during the war.

WRAPPED IN THE FLAG

This was an amazing accomplishment. But it was even more amazing to see who *bought* the bonds. More than 80% of Bartel and Slaughter's customers were women—a total surprise, since traditionally, women did not like swimsuit contests or beauty pageants.

This illustrated how effective the bond sales had been as an image-building tool. Before the drive, the pageant was generally seen as an overhyped swimsuit contest. Afterward, it was regarded as a wholesome search for the ideal American woman—a beauty pageant the entire family could enjoy.

More than all of Lenora Slaughter's reforms combined, wrapping the pageant in the flag had transformed Miss America into an "all-American" institution.

MISS AMERICA FACT

During a bond-selling visit to the University of Minnesota, the student council there approached Bartel and Slaughter with a suggestion. "I don't know any of the names," recalled Slaughter, "but I remember that an ugly little girl with spectacles—never a potential beauty—was at the head of it."

The ugly duckling noted that while plenty of scholarships were available for male students, there were almost none for females, and the pageant could help change that. Slaughter—always on the lookout for ways to improve the contest's image—was immediately enthusiastic.

Today, the Miss America Pageant is the largest source of scholarship money for U.S. women, handling over $25 million a year.

For Part IV of the story, turn to page 202

OOPS!

More examples of Murphy's law—anyting that can goe wroong, will.

BORDER CROSSING
"If you closely examine a map of South Dakota, you'll see that the man-made western border of the state has a slight bump in it as it runs north-south. When the territory was being surveyed, the boundary was set to fall on the 27th meridian west from Washington, D.C. As the surveyors working down from the north met those coming up from the south, they missed each other by a few miles. This error remains on every map to this day."

—from *Oops*, by Paul Smith

HAPPY BIRTHDAY!

"A Dutch couple tried to have a baby for more than five years. Finally, they turned to the University Hospital at Utrecht, one of the Netherlands' most prestigious fertility clinics. An in-vitro fertilization took place in March, 1993; in December, the woman had twins—Teun and Koen.

"Apparently, however, the clinic made a mistake. 'Little Teun,' said news reports, 'is as white and blonde as his father and mother. Little Koen is black.' After first denying responsibility, the clinic had to admit they'd 'accidentally inseminated the mother's eggs with sperm from another man along with that of her husband.' "

—from the *San Francisco Chronicle*, 6/29/95

HEAR, HEAR

"In the 1950s Harold Senby of Leeds, England began experiencing difficulty hearing. He was fitted for a hearing aid, but his hearing did not improve.

In fact, he seemed to be hearing worse than before. During the next 20 years, he was refitted several times, but each time his hearing stayed the same. Finally, during a visit to his doctor in March 1978, the hearing aid was removed entirely.

Miraculously, Senby's hearing began to improve. After a closer medical examination, the doctor discovered that "in the 1950s, the hearing aid had been made for his left ear, not the right ear, which was the one giving him trouble."

—from *The Blunder Book,* by M. Hirsch Goldberg

FUNNY MONEY
In 1960, the Brazilian government discovered that the cost of printing a 1-cruziero note was 1.2 cruzieros. They immediately stopped issuing it.

—from *Oops,* by Paul Smith

GOOD BET
In 1995, Pizza Hut scheduled a commercial featuring Pete Rose. According to news reports, "a young boy asks Pete Rose about his accomplishments in baseball. At the end, Rose asks if the boy likes Pizza Hut pizza, and the boy replies, 'You bet!' " After reviewing the script, the company canceled its plans. "That's not the best choice of words," explained Rose.

—from the *San Francisco Chronicle,* 6/21/95

WHAT A GAS!
"When a cow has an attack of bloat (actually methane gas generated in the stomach), it must obtain relief promptly or die.

"A Dutch veterinarian was summoned recently to treat a cow suffering from this affliction, an agricultural news service reported. He tried a standard remedy, which is to insert a tube carefully up the beast's rear end.

"A satisfying rush of gas followed. With misplaced scientific zeal, the vet, perhaps seeking a source of cheap heat and light, then applied a match. The resulting torchlike jet set the barn ablaze. It burned to the ground. The flames spread to the nearby fields, which were consumed.

"The vet was convicted of negligence and fined. The cow remained serene."

—from *Remarkabilia,* by John Train

WHAT A DOLL!

*Here are five of the more unusal
dolls sold in America in recent years.*

THUGGIES

Introduced in the summer of 1993, Thuggies came with something that no dolls had ever had before—criminal records. There were 17 different characters, with names like "Motorcycle Meany," "Dickie the Dealer," "Bonnie Ann Bribe," and "Mikey Milk 'em." They were outlaw bikers, dope pushers, white-collar criminals, even "check-kiting congressmen."

But despite their "personal histories," the dolls were designed to *discourage* crime, not encourage it. Each one came packaged in a prison cell and had its own rehabilitation program. Children were supposed to set them on the straight-and-narrow. (Bonnie Ann Bribe, for example, doing time for trying to bribe her way through school, had to read to senior citizens one hour a day.) The dolls even came with a gold star to wear when they successfully completed rehab.

"It works, believe me," Carolyn Clark, co-founder of Thuggies, Inc., told reporters. "It's not going to turn the kid into a criminal. ...It lets them know that they can correct this kind of behavior."

TONY THE TATTOOED MAN

Comes with tattoos and a "tattoo gun," that kids can use to apply the tattoos to the doll or to themselves. Additional tattoos—including "brains, boogers, bugged-out eyes and other anatomical atrocities"—are sold separately.

BABY THINK IT OVER

Like Thuggies, Baby Think It Over was designed to teach kids a lesson—in this case, "Don't get pregnant." The dolls are issued to junior-high and high school students so they can experience what it's really like to have a baby. Each doll weighs 10 pounds, and contains electronics that make it cry "at random, but realistic, intervals, simulating a baby's sleeping and waking patterns to its demand for food," says Rick Jurmain, who invented the doll with his wife, Mary.

Like a real baby, there's no way to stop the doll from crying once it starts except by "feeding" it, which is done by inserting a special key into the baby's back, turning it, and holding the baby in place with pressure for as long as 15 minutes. The key is attached to the "parent's" arm with a tamper-proof hospital bracelet, which prevents them from handing off the responsibility to someone else. And the teenagers have to respond quickly—once the baby starts crying, a timer inside the baby records how long it cries. It also records any shaking, drops, or harsh handling that takes place. If the crying baby is left unattended for longer than two minutes, the timer registers that as neglect.

There's also a "drug-addicted" version that's more irritable, has a "higher pitch, a warbling cry," and a body tremor. Priced at $200 apiece, Baby Think It Overs are sold as instructional aids, not toys.

RHOGIT-RHOGIT

Sexual abstinence is simply not an option for Rhogit-Rhogit. "Elegant, intellectual, and extremely sexy, Rhogit-Rhogit will seduce you with his male prowess, his animal sexuality, his vision, and his depth," says the sales catalog from BillyBoy Toys, the Paris company that manufactures it. "He feels equally comfortable in butch, tough-boy clothes as he does in the most avant-garde French and Italian designer clothes and the most utterly formal attire."

Rhogit-Rhogit also has a male sidekick, Zhdrick, who, according to the catalog "is, perhaps, the most sophisticated, sensual, and provocatively sexual doll ever made." The dolls retail for $1,000 apiece, which includes one designer outfit and one condom. If you want wigs, jeans, lassos, boots, underwear, top hats, or other accessories from the company's "Boy Stuff" collection, you have to pay extra. (A lot extra—outfits run $600 to $900 apiece.)

TALKING STIMPY DOLL

From the cartoon series, *Ren & Stimpy*. "Yank the hairball in Stimpy's throat and he talks. Squeeze his leg and he makes 'rude underleg noises.'" Recommended for "ages 4 and up."

UNUSUAL AWARDS

*You've heard of the Oscars and the Emmys,
but how about these awards?*

THE BOZOS

Awarded during the 1980s by Bozo the Clown (Larry Harmon) to the "biggest bozos in the news." Winners included Jim and Tammy Bakker, Oliver North, Vanna White, Geraldo Rivera (twice), and Cher. The prize: a Bozo telephone.

SITTING DUCK AWARD

Presented annually by the National Society of Newspaper Columnists to "the target most useful to a columnist on a slow news day." Winners include: Roseanne Arnold, O. J. Simpson's houseguest Kato Kaelin, and Millie, the dog belonging to former first lady Barbara Bush.

HARLON PAGE HUBBARD LEMON AWARD

Awarded annually by consumer, public health, and environmental groups to "the year's most unfair, misleading, and irresponsible advertising." Hubbard pioneered America's first nationwide advertising campaign for "Lydia Pinkham's Vegetable Compound," a cure-all health tonic with a 20% alcohol content. Winners include: Walt Disney's "movie news" ads, which look like real news reports, and GMC truck, for bragging about the safety of its Safari minivan when it actually ranked "near the bottom" in crash tests.

GOLDEN FLEECE AWARDS

Awarded from 1975 to 1988, by Senator William Proxmire, to government agencies that wasted the most money. Winners included the Department of Agriculture, which spent $46,000 to find out how long it takes to cook two eggs for breakfast, and the National Science Foundation, which awarded a $9,992 grant to an anthropologist to study the "political significance of bullfighting in Spain."

Count 'em yourself: Ears of corn *always* have an even number of rows of kernels.

GOLDEN RASPBERRIES (RAZZIES)

Awarded by "460 film professionals, journalists, and fans for the worst films and performances of the year." Winners get a golfball-sized raspberry glued to a film reel and spray-painted gold. "It costs us about $2 to make and is every bit as tacky as the movies and performances they are given to," says John Wilson, the ceremony's organizer. Winners include *Showgirls*, *Mommie Dearest*, *Howard the Duck*, and Sylvester Stallone (who's won eight times, including a special award for worst actor of the decade).

MILLARD FILLMORE MEDAL OF MEDIOCRITY

Presented by "The Society for the Preservation and Enhancement of the Recognition of Millard Fillmore, the Last of the Whigs" to "recognize mediocrity in high places." The award is named after America's 13th president, who was denied his own party's nomination for re-election in 1852. "We felt that underachievers needed somebody to look up to, or down on, and that's Fillmore," says the group's president. "He was the Gerald Ford of the 19th century."

Winners include ex-President Bush (for winning a 90% approval rating at the end of the Gulf War...and then losing the 1992 election to the governor of Arkansas); Roseanne Arnold (for botching the national anthem at a baseball game in 1990); the canceled baseball season of 1995; former Vice President Dan Quayle (do we need to explain?); Billy Carter; Ed McMahon; Prince Charles and Princess Diana; and James Watt, Reagan's Secretary of the Interior.

✣ ✣ ✣

BRI's nominee for the "Did-We-Really-Need-This Award?" Award: The Liberace Legend Award. Presented since 1994 by the Liberace Foundation, in "a gala benefit at the famed Liberace Mansion." Winners are selected "for major contributions to the community and the world of entertainment." They include Debbie Reynolds, Siegfried and Roy, and Liza Minelli. According to a press release: "The presentation is the highlight of a series of festivities surrounding the May 16 birthday celebration of Liberace."

THE MYSTERIOUS OUIJA BOARD

Why did Uncle John write this chapter? Maybe his porcelain Ouija board told him to.

GHOSTWRITER

In the 1890s, spiritualism was a big fad. In the midst of it, someone came up with a new tool for communicating with the dead: a small piece of wood called a "planchette." People would gather around a table or other flat surface, place their hands on the planchette, and watch how it moved. Some had pencils attached that wrote out messages; others pointed at letters, numbers, and words painted on the table and spelled out messages that way. No one could explain why the planchette moved. Skeptics charged that the people who held the planchette were moving it—perhaps unconsciously. But true believers insisted that spirits guided the little thing across the table.

SPELLING IT OUT

William and Isaac Fuld thought the whole thing was a bunch of nonsense, but wanted to cash in on it. They owned a toy company in Maryland, and figured the planchette would make a good game. So they took a board about the size of a cafeteria tray, painted the letters of the alphabet across the middle, and put the numbers 0 through 9 underneath. They also put the words "Yes" and "No" in the left and right corners, and the word "Goodbye" across the bottom. Then they painted the name of the game, "Ouija"—a combination of *oui* and *ja,* the French and German words for "yes" — across the top. Their "Ouija Talking Board" was patented in 1892.

DEAD SERIOUS

It wasn't until World War I that Ouija boards became a big commercial success.

Company legend has it that not long before the war broke out, William Fuld's favorite Ouija board told him to "prepare for big business." So he expanded production...and sure enough, during the war people began using the Ouija to "keep in touch" with loved ones who'd been sent into battle. Sales skyrocketed, and the money poured in.

Since then, Ouija sales have always boomed in times of national crisis, tailed off when conditions improved, then increased again when the next crisis hit. The Ouija board sold well during World War II, the Korean War, and the Vietnam War, and dipped in between. The Fuld Family manufactured Ouija Boards until 1967, when they sold the rights to Parker Brothers.

OUIJA FACTS

• At the time World War I started, the IRS collected a 10% tax on every game sold in the United States and the Fulds didn't want to pay. So they declared the Ouija board to be a "scientific instrument" that didn't qualify for the tax. They fought the case all the way to the Supreme Court...and lost.

• No one can explain how the Ouija planchette moves across the board. "There's nothing special about Ouijas to give it any supernatural powers," one Parker Brothers spokesperson insists. "It's simply a game."

• One reasonable theory: the game works through an "idiomotor action" in much the same way that a dowsing rod finds water. "Unconsciously picturing what you want to have happen can cause your muscles to make it happen," psychology professor Ray Hyman explains. "People think they're not doing anything and that some outside force is making it happen."

*   *   *   *

TRUE STORY

At age 47, the Rolling Stones' bassist, Bill Wyman, began a relationship with 13-year-old Mandy Smith, with her mother's blessing. Six years later, they were married, but the marriage only lasted a year. Not long after, Bill's 30-year-old son Stephen married Mandy's mother, age 46. That made Stephen a stepfather to his former stepmother. If Bill and Mandy had remained married, Stephen would have been his father's father-in-law and his own grandpa.

WEIRD TALES OF THE OUIJA BOARD

Here are some of the strangest stories
from the annals of the Ouija board.

GHOST WRITING?

The most famous Ouija board user in history was Pearl Curran, a St. Louis, Missouri, housewife. She was playing the game with some friends in 1913 when, legend has it, the planchette began moving around the board with surprising strength. It spelled out this message: "Many moons ago I lived. Again I come, Patience Worth my name." The "spirit" identified itself as a woman who'd been born in 1625 in Dorsetshire, England, and had migrated to New England...where she was murdered by an Indian.

For the next six years (according to Curran), the spirit fed her poems, aphorisms, and other works through the Ouija board. Paul Sann writes in *Fads, Follies and Delusions of the American People,*

> Between 1913 and 1919 the pent-up Patience transmitted to Curran no less than 1,500,000 pearls of wisdom heavy with moral and religious dissertations, garnished with 2,000 items of blank verse and six novels. Mrs. Curran said that in one busy ten-day stretch alone her whirling planchette recorded 30,000 words. She said she could take 2,000 words an hour off the board when both she and the virginal puritan were on the right wavelength.

One thing that made Curran's story believable was the fact that while she'd had no formal training as a writer, the prose she produced was surprisingly good, often using very antiquated language. All of it was "far beyond the ken of Mrs. Curran, who," one critic wrote, "has never exhibited a shred of literary talent or enthusiasm." Curran's story was still intact when she died in 1937 at the age of 46—although many psychology experts explained away her writings as either a fraud or the product of an "alternating personality," the same phenomenon that causes people to speak in tongues.

COMMAND PERFORMANCES

A handful of people have actually committed murder when their Ouija boards "told" them to.

• In the early 1930s, for example, a 15-year-old girl named Mattie Turley murdered her father with a shotgun, apparently with the help of her mother, Dorothea Turley, who wanted to leave Mattie's father for another man. "The Ouija board told me to do it so that Mama can be free to marry a handsome cowboy, that's all that happened," the 15-year-old testified at her trial, "Mother told me the Ouija board couldn't be denied and that I would not even be arrested for doing it." Both mother and daughter were convicted of murder: Mrs. Turley's 10- to 25-year sentence was overturned three years later, and she was freed, but Mattie Turley didn't get out until she was 21.

• In 1932, a 77-year-old railroad worker named Herbert Hurd murdered his wife after their Ouija board falsely accused him of having an affair. As he later testified:

> The spirits told her through her Ouija board that I was too fond of another woman and had given her $15,000 of a hidden fortune. The Ouija board lied. I never was friendly with another woman and I never had $15,000, but Nellie beat me and burned me and tortured me into confessing all those lies, so I finally had to kill her.

• In 1956, a wealthy Connecticut woman named Helen Dow Peck left nearly her entire $178,000 estate to John Gale Forbes, a name her Ouija board had spelled out in 1919. The only problem: There was no John Gale Forbes—a court-ordered search failed to turn up a single person by that name in the entire United States.

OUIJA BOARDS IN THE NEWS

"Britain's Appeal Court was asked today to review a murder trial because three jurors allegedly used a Ouija board to contact one of the victims before finding a man guilty. Lawyers for Stephen Young told the court they had received information from another juror about a seance in the hotel where the jury stayed the night before they found Young guilty of shooting newlyweds Harry and Nicola Fuller. The three jurors 'contacted' Harry Fuller, who named Young, 35, as the killer, they said. The 12-person jury went on to convict Young unanimously." —*San Jose Mercury News, 1994*

Whale oil was used in automobile transmission fluids as late as 1973.

PRIMETIME PROVERBS

Pearls of television wisdom from Primetime Proverbs, *compiled by John Javna and Jack Mingo.*

ON BEAUTY
"You could throw her in the river and skim ugly for two days."

—Granny,
The Beverly Hillbillies

ON WISDOM
"A truly wise man never plays leapfrog with a unicorn."

—Banacek,
Banacek

"What insight could you possibly hope to gain from a man whose I.Q. wouldn't make a respectable earthquake?"

—Diane Chambers,
Cheers

ON HISTORY
L.P.: "She's from one of California's first families."
Chico Rodriguez: "Oh, is she Mexican, too?"

—*Chico and the Man*

ON MATH
"If you've enjoyed this program just half as much as we've enjoyed doing it, then we've enjoyed it twice as much as you."

—Michael Palin,
Monty Python's Flying Circus

ON RELATIONSHIPS
"You're nothing but a tiny dot, a speck, a minute insignificant nothing. But I'm proud to call you my friend."

—Warren Ferguson,
The Andy Griffith Show

"I've never felt closer to a group of people. Not even in the portable johns of Woodstock."

—Jim Ignatowski,
Taxi

ON THINGS TO LOOK FORWARD TO
"If you make it to one hundred, that fat weather guy will say your name on TV."

—George Utley,
Newhart

ON THE LEGAL PROFESSION
"It's not enough that all the lawyers are crooks. Now the crooks are becomin' lawyers."

—Donegan,
Kaz

ON HOPE
"One good, solid hope is worth a carload of certainties."

—The Doctor,
Dr. Who

When a cat died in ancient Egypt, its owners shaved off their eyebrows as a sign of mourning.

FAMOUS TIGHTWADS

Who are the cheapest guys around? Often, the richest ones.
Here are more examples of extreme tightfistedness.

JOHN D. ROCKEFELLER, founder of Standard Oil. Gave a groundskeeper a $5 Christmas bonus...then docked it from the man's pay when he took Christmas Day off to spend with his family.

WALT DISNEY. Timed employees' trips to candy and soda machines.

CLARK GABLE, movie star. Often argued with his grocer about the price of jelly beans.

PAUL VOLCKER, chairman of the Federal Reserve Board. Rather than pay for a laundromat, he packed dirty laundry into a suitcase every week and drove it to his daughter's house.

TY COBB, baseball legend. As an early investor in Coca Cola stock, he was extremely wealthy—but still collected bars of soap from locker room showers and hotel rooms and sent them back to his Georgia farm.

J. PAUL GETTY, oil baron.
• When his son was kidnapped and held hostage, he refused to pay ransom money until the kidnappers sent the boy's ear to him in the mail.

• He calculated the wages of his gatekeeper by counting the number of times the main gate of his estate was opened and closed on a given day, then multiplied the number "by some minute sum" to arrive at a salary.

CALVIN COOLIDGE, U.S. president. Personally oversaw and approved all White House expenditures; reportedly bought food for state dinners at the local Piggly Wiggly.

ARTHUR FIEDLER, conductor of the Boston Pops. Rather than repair the holes in the walls of his home, he stuffed them with "moldering bits of carpet." He was also famous for skipping out on the tab when dining with his musicians.

The average caterpillar has 2,000 muscles in its body; the average human, 700.

THE PINBALL STORY

If you like pinball (and who doesn't?), here's the next best thing to actually having a machine in the bathroom. Hmm…interesting idea. Imagine what it would sound like to people waiting to use the toilet. "What are you doing in there? What's that noise? Hey, are you playing pinball?!!?"

ROLLING STONE

Have you ever heard of a game called Bagatelle? No one plays it anymore, but for centuries it was one of the most popular pastimes of the European upper classes. Originally, it was played outside. People threw stones up a hill and hoped that, as the stones rolled down, they'd fall into holes that had been dug in the hillside.

By the middle of the 17th century, the game was played indoors. Players pushed small balls up an inclined felt board with a stick, then let the balls go. Again, the object was to get the balls to drop into holes. But now each hole was surrounded by small pins (actually brass nails) to make it harder. The more points a hole was worth, the more pins were nailed around it. That, of course, is how *pinball* got its name.

THE NEXT STEP

Bagatelle remained popular in various forms for centuries. But modern pinball didn't evolve until 1931, when game manufacturer David Gottlieb created a version called Baffle Ball. He made two important changes to Bagatelle:

1. He incorporated a spring-loaded mechanism (virtually indistinguishable from modern-day pinball shooters), so balls were *launched* rather than pushed or dropped.

2. He made it a coin-operated machine, designed to sit on retailers' countertops.

There weren't any lights, bells, mechanical bumpers, or even flippers. Players shook and jostled the machine (technically, they weren't even supposed to do *that*) to get the ball into one of the high-scoring holes.

But it was an appealing diversion during the Great Depression, and was very popular.

Female canaries cannot sing.

As Russell Roberts wrote in the *Chicago Tribune*:

> To an American public haunted by economic disaster, facing day upon dreary day of hanging around street corners with nothing to do and no hope in sight, the new games were a welcome respite. For either a penny or a nickel (for which you got 7 or 10 balls, respectively), you could forget, for a few minutes anyway, the world and all its troubles. Soon every drugstore, bar and candy store had at least one.

Baffle Ball was also a source of employment. The games sold for only $16. Anyone who had the money could buy one, put it in a store, and split the profits with the store owner. "Pinball routemen," explains Candice Ford Tolbert in *Tilt: The Pinball Book*, "were anyone and everyone who could come up with a little cash and who had the time to service and collect from machines out on locations."

THE BIG THREE

Demand for Baffle Ball was so great that Gottlieb couldn't fill all his orders. So some of his distributors started to build their own games. In 1932, Gottlieb's biggest distributor, Ray Moloney, invented a game called Ballyhoo. It was so successful that he formed the Bally company and began designing games full-time.

Another distributor—an aspiring Disney cartoonist named Barry Williams—came up with so many innovations that Gottlieb offered him a royalty for his designs. (Later, Williams formed his own company.) Their first joint venture was a game called Advance. Roger Sharpe writes in *Popular Mechanics*:

> One of the breakthrough attractions of Advance was its delicately counterbalanced gates, which were vulnerable to jabs and nudges from players. One day, in 1932, Williams went to a drugstore and saw a player hit the bottom of Advance to score points without having to aim. This so enraged Williams that he took the game off location and hammered five nails through the bottom of the machine. In Williams' words, "Anybody who tried to affect the play of the game by slapping the flat of his hand against the game's undersurface, would now think twice before trying it again."

However, Williams knew this was a cruel and temporary solution. So, he developed a simple, effective device that stopped play if the machine was handled roughly. The device consisted of a small ball balanced on a pedestal. If the game was shaken or pounded, the ball fell from the pedestal and struck a metal ring that immediately stopped play.

Williams called the device a stool pigeon...but not for long. "I never quite liked the name 'stool pigeon,' " he recalled years later, "but I just couldn't come up with anything else." So he set one of the games up in a nearby drugstore and waited to watch the response. Sure enough, a player came along and handled the game too roughly, setting off the stool pigeon. "Damn, I tilted it!" he exclaimed. From then on, the mechanism was known as the *tilt*.

OTHER MILESTONES

There were four other important steps in creating the pinball machine as we know it:

1. Themes. In 1933, David Rockola (later a jukebox tycoon) came up with *Jigsaw*. Players could put a puzzle together by hitting certain targets and holes. Its popularity showed that the public wanted variety and novelty in their pinball games.

2. Electricity. Williams introduced *Contact*, the first pinball game to use electricity, also in 1933. It had an electrified "kick-out hole" that returned a ball to play after awarding points, and a bell that rang every time a player scored. Features like automatic scoring and "lighted back glass" quickly appeared on new machines.

3. Bumpers. Bally introduced *Bumper* in 1937. It used the first "electrically operated wire and spring bumpers."

4. Flippers. The first flippers appeared in a Bally game called *Humpty Dumpty*, in 1947. Before this breakthrough—created by accident when a technician touched two loose wires together—pinball machines were almost entirely games of chance. In *Humpty Dumpty*, the balls jumped around at the player's command. This feature quickly became indispensable on the machines...and turned pinball into a worldwide phenomenon. "In most of Europe, in fact, they're called flipper games and flipper machines," Roger Sharpe writes in *Pinball!* "Today, we have ramps, drop holes, underground networks, multiball games, drop targets and spinners, but they all don't necessarily have to be on every game. A flipper does."

At birth, a Panda is smaller than a mouse.

PINBALL AND THE LAW

In 1933, pinball manufacturers made a mistake that would haunt them for decades. They decided to compete directly against slot machines, electronic bingo, and other gambling machines by building "payout" pinball machines, which rewarded successful players either with cash or tokens that could be redeemed for cash.

To many people, the move made pinball machines synonymous with gambling. And when communities outlawed other types of gambling machines—before and after World War II—they often got rid of all types of pinball machines as well.

Fighting Back. Pinball manufacturers countered by introducing "free play," machines that rewarded players with extended games instead of cash. But even these were controversial. Free games are objects of value, and therefore a kind of gambling payoff. Tamer "add-a-ball" features were condemned, too. In fact, it wasn't until America was exposed to the excesses of the 1960s that pinball finally regained acceptance as the lesser of many evils.

Believe it or not, however, many cities and states still have anti-pinball laws on the books, although they're seldom enforced anymore. Ironically, Chicago—home of Gottlieb, Bally, and Williams, the big three manufacturers of pinball machines—is one of the cities that had a long-term ban on the game. It wasn't until 1976 that pinball was finally legalized in its own hometown.

PINBALL FACTS

• David Gottlieb may have invented pinball, but he didn't have much faith in it. His second game was called *Five Star Final*, supposedly named after his favorite newspaper, the *Chicago Tribune*'s end-of-the-day edition. Actually, though, Gottleib figured the pinball "fad" was over and this was his "final" game. A few decades later, in the "golden age" of pinball, new machines were being designed and shipped every *three weeks*.

• It takes a team of six designers about nine months to invent and perfect a pinball game.

• Pinball designers work toward these ideals: the game should be easy enough to keep novices from getting discouraged, yet challenging enough to keep "wizards" interested; the average game should last from 2 1/2 to 3 minutes, or roughly 47 seconds a ball; and the player should get one free game for every four played.

MAKING HIS MARK

Mark Twain is one of America's greatest humorists...and maybe one of our great philosophers, too. Here are examples of what we mean.

"A banker is a fellow who lends you his umbrella when the sun is shining and wants it back the minute it begins to rain."

"Clothes make the man. Naked people have little or no influence on society."

"Every time you stop a school, you have to build a jail. What you gain at one end you lose at the other. It's like feeding a dog on his own tail. It won't fatten the dog."

"If you pick up a starving dog and make him prosperous, he will not bite you. This is the principal difference between a dog and a man."

"The human race has one really effective weapon, and that is laughter."

"The man who sets out to carry a cat by its tail learns something that will always be useful and which never will grow dim or doubtful."

"The surest protection against temptation is cowardice."

"There is no distinctly native American criminal class ...except Congress."

"Keep away from people who try to belittle your ambitions. Small people always do that, but the really great make you feel that you, too, can become great."

"The rule is perfect: in all matters of opinion our adversaries are insane."

"It usually takes more than three weeks to prepare a good impromptu speech."

"The best way to cheer yourself up is to try to cheer somebody else up."

"Nothing so needs reforming as other people's habits."

"Put all your eggs in the one basket and *WATCH THAT BASKET!*"

CRANK CALLS

*Ever make a "phony phone call"? What if you tried it and reached the
president or vice president...and they took you seriously?
Here are a few times when it really happened.*

THE PRESIDENT IS DEAD!

Call for: Vice President Thomas Marshall

What happened: Marshall was in the middle of a speech at
Atlanta's Civic Auditorium on November 23, 1919, when he was
interrupted by a member of his staff. They'd just received a call
from the White House telling them that President Woodrow Wilson, who'd recently had a stroke, had died. "I cannot continue my
speech," the stunned vice president told his shocked audience,
"I must leave at once to take up my duties as chief executive of this
great nation."

Aftermath: Marshall was stunned again when he found out the call
was a fake. He denounced it as a "cruel hoax."

WE WANT TO NEGOTIATE

Call for: President George Bush

What happened: In March 1990, an Iranian official called the
White House to say he'd been instructed to set up a phone conference between Bush and Iranian president Ali Akbar Hashemi Rafsanjani concerning U.S. hostages held in Lebanon. Bush took the
call "on the off chance that it might be real." Two days later, when
the White House tried to return the call, they realized it had been
a put-on.

Aftermath: Even the Iranians thought the Bush administration's
response to the crank call was a little weird. "Can it be that such a
global power, with all its intelligence capabilities, talks to a person
it cannot identify?" the real President Rafsanjani asked in Teheran.
"This is a strange occurrence."

THE PRESIDENT IS DEAD!

Call for: CNN (Cable News Network)

What happened: In 1992, three hours after President Bush had collapsed during a banquet in Tokyo and vomited in the Japanese

---

The most popular Campbell's soup in Hong Kong is watercress and duck gizzard.

prime minister's lap, the CNN newsroom got a call from the president's personal physician, who was with Bush in Japan. He had terrible news: the president had just died. CNN staffers thought the story was real and typed it into their news computer. Fortunately for them, the caller had left his phone number...and they traced it to Idaho, not Tokyo.

The story was quickly wiped off the computer and never made it onto CNN's main news channel. But downstairs at Headline News, staffers saw it moments before it was erased. They rushed the tragic information to anchor Don Harrison. "This just in to CNN Headline News!" he told viewers urgently. Then, as he opened his mouth to read the bulletin, he heard someone off-camera yell, "No! Stop!" "We are now getting a correction...," he ad-libbed.

Aftermath: The call was traced to the Garden City, Idaho, home of James Edward Smith, 71, who was arrested and placed in a mental hospital.

WHAT DO YOU THINK OF QUEBEC?

Call for: Queen Elizabeth

What happened: In October 1995, Pierre Brassard, a disc jockey at Montreal's Radio CKOI, called Buckingham Palace and said he was Canadian Prime Minister Jean Chretien; he asked to speak to the queen. Palace officials checked with Chretien's office to verify that the call was genuine, but Chretien wasn't in. Still, an official said that Chretien "probably wanted to speak with her."

So Queen Elizabeth got on the line...and chatted for 17 minutes. She didn't realize it was a prank, even when Brassard "started talking about Halloween and suggesting she put on a nice hat."

Aftermath: The English public was not amused. "We think it's annoying," a Palace spokesperson said. In retaliation, one British newspaper published Radio CKOI's phone number and urged readers to call when Brassard was on the air. Another paper had a reporter call Brassard, posing as a Scotland Yard detective, and threaten legal action. But the London tabloid *News of the World* got the best revenge: it offered Brassard an $80,000 trip to London for an exclusive story...then reneged on the deal when he accepted, telling him it was a prank.

Spinach consumption in the U.S. rose 33% after the Popeye comic strip became a hit in 1931.

ALL ABOUT CHESS

For chess lovers, books about how to play the game are essential bathroom reading. For the rest of us, three pages about chess—one of the oldest and most popular board games in history—are plenty.

FIRST MOVES

• Chess began in northern India sometime before 500 A.D. and was probably based on an Indian military game called *chaturanga* —*chatur* meaning "four," and *anga* meaning "parts of an army." Like real Indian armies of the day, the game had four types of pieces: elephants, chariots, cavalry, and infantry. It was largely a game of chance; how well you did depended on how well you rolled the dice.

• Chaturanga was later combined with *petteia*, a Greek game of reason. The result was a game close to modern chess. The dice were eliminated, and the emphasis of the game shifted from chance to strategy. There were 16 pieces per player, just like in modern chess: one king, one vizier, or adviser, two elephants, two horses, two chariots, and eight foot soldiers.

• The new game became a worldwide phenomenon. By 800 A.D., it had spread east to China, Korea, and Japan…and west to the Arab world. In Persia, the game was known as *shāh māt*—"the king is dead." This is the direct linguistic predecessor to the English word "checkmate."

• When the Moors conquered Spain in the ninth century, they brought chess with them. From there it spread all over Europe, and continued to evolve into the game we know today.

THE PIECES

How did the game go from the original pieces to what we have now?

• **The elephant.** According to *The Greatest Games of All Time,* Arabs didn't approve of the elephant piece because "physical representations are forbidden in the Islamic religion." They replaced it with "a minaret-shaped piece with a nick cut into it." Later, when Europeans saw it, the pointed top with a nick reminded them of a bishop's hat…so they called it a bishop.

- **The chariot.** Hadn't been used for centuries in European warfare. It was changed to something more familiar: a castle (or rook).

- **The vizier.** Never a part of European culture, it was replaced by the queen—a king's most important *un*official advisor.

- **The cavalry pieces and foot soldiers.** Stayed the same—the names were simply changed to knights and pawns.

SLOW MOTION

About the only thing that separated medieval chess from today's version was the way the pieces moved. Most were considerably weaker. The queen, for example—the most powerful piece today—could only move one space at a time. But in the 15th century, the rules abruptly changed.

- The queen was suddenly able to go any distance in any direction, as long as she wasn't blocked by other pieces.

- The bishop became able to move any distance diagonally, as long as no one was in the way.

- Even the pawns were strengthened a little: they became able to move two spaces on the first move.

Chess historians believe these changes were connected to the introduction of artillery into modern warfare. Artillery enabled armies to shoot weapons over previously unthinkable distances, so the short distances traveled in chess no longer made military sense. When the game was brought up to date, pieces naturally became more powerful.

THE RIGHT MOVES

Today, the way some pieces move seems pretty arbitrary. For example, the pawns can only move straight ahead, except when they are attacking; then they can only move diagonally. And the knight (horse) can jump over other pieces. But these moves actually made a lot of sense when they were introduced:

- The pawn is based on a soldier known as a *pikeman.* As pikemen marched forward into battle, they held their shields directly in front of them and stuck their pikes (spears) out on either side. The shield was so bulky that it was literally impossible for the pikeman to attack anything directly in front of him. That's why a pawn can only attack pieces that are diagonally to the left or right.

• Knights were the only people in the battlefield on horseback—and thus are the only ones who can leap over their opponents.

CHESS AND REVOLUTION

Because many court officials—kings, queens, etc.—are represented in chess, the pieces have traditionally been seen as symbols of the establishment. This has made them unpopular with revolutionaries. Often, when a king was overthrown, the people who toppled him would try to replace the country's chess pieces as well.

• After the Revolutionary War, for example, many American chessmakers replaced kings with acorn-shaped pieces. One editor who hoped to make chess "better adapted to our feelings as citizens of a free republic," suggested calling the kings, queens, and pawns *governors*, *generals*, and *pioneers*. The idea never caught on.

• At the beginning of the French Revolution, the Convention decreed that kings, queens, knights, rooks, bishops, and pawns would henceforth be known as *flags*, *adjutants*, *dragoons*, *cannons*, *volunteers*, and *troops of the line*. These changes were rejected by chess players…although many French sets still contain crownless queens.

CHANGING SIDES

The most bizarre example of "revolutionary chess" came in the late 1920s, when the Marx and Engels Institute in Moscow invented a communist chess board for the USSR. The board was divided into red and white teams, with Joseph Stalin serving as the red king and other prominent Communists filling out the ranks of the red queen, bishops, knights, and rooks. Prominent opponents of the Communists filled out the white ranks.

But as Stalin began wiping out his political enemies in the purges of the 1930s, many Communists represented by the red pieces fell out of favor—which meant they could no longer be represented on the red side. These "enemy of the people" pieces had to be bleached white and moved to the other side of the board; owners who didn't comply risked being sent to Siberia. As the purges progressed, it became so difficult to keep track of who belonged on which side of the board that the chess sets had to be abandoned.

IS *THIS* BATHROOM READING?

Here's a surprise entry—the Bill of Rights. Actually, Uncle John's been thinking about including this for some time. After all, what better chance to read the document than in the bathroom? You know, you can read one of the Amendments, then flip to the history of bubblegum or something. If they'd taught it that way in school, we'd all know it by heart now. We at the BRI like to think that the Founding Fathers would be proud of us.

BILL OF RIGHTS

Here's the complete text of the first 10 Amendments to the U.S. Constitution.

1. Congress shall make no law respecting an establishment of religion, or prohibiting the free exercise thereof; or abridging the freedom of speech, or of the press; or the right of the people peaceably to assemble, and to petition the Government for a redress of grievances.

2. A well regulated militia, being necessary to the security of a free State, the right of the people to keep and bear Arms, shall not be infringed.

3. No Soldier shall, in time of peace be quartered in any house, without the consent of the Owner, nor in time of war, but in a manner to be prescribed by law.

4. The right of the people to be secure in their persons, houses, papers, and effects, against unreasonable searches and seizures, shall not be violated, and no Warrants shall issue, but upon probable cause, supported by Oath or affirmation, and particularly describing the place to be searched, and the persons or things to be seized.

5. No person shall be held to answer for a capital, or otherwise infamous crime, unless on a presentment or indictment of a Grand Jury, except in cases arising in the land or naval forces, or in the

Militia, when in actual service in time of War or public danger; nor shall any person be subject for the same offence to be twice put in jeopardy of life or limb; nor shall be compelled in any criminal case to be a witness against himself, nor be deprived of life, liberty, or property, without due process of law; nor shall private property be taken for public use, without just compensation.

6. In all criminal prosecutions, the accused shall enjoy the right to a speedy and public trial, by an impartial jury of the State and district wherein the crime shall have been committed, which district shall have been previously ascertained by law, and to be informed of the nature and cause of the accusation; to be confronted with the witnesses against him; to have compulsory process for obtaining witnesses in his favor, and to have the Assistance of Counsel for his defence.

7. In Suits at common law, where the value in controversy shall exceed twenty dollars, the right of trial by jury shall be preserved, and no fact tried by a jury, shall be otherwise re-examined in any Court of the United States, than according to the rules of the common law.

8. Excessive bail shall not be required, nor excessive fines imposed, nor cruel and unusual punishments inflicted.

9. The enumeration in the Constitution, of certain rights, shall not be construed to deny or disparage others retained by the people.

10. The powers not delegated to the United States by the Constitution, nor prohibited by it to the States, are reserved to the States respectively, or to the people.

*   *   *   *

FOOD FOR THOUGHT

In a recent survey, a randomly selected group of American citizens were shown a list of freedoms. Then they were asked by pollsters if they would vote for those rights. Not only did many respondents fail to recognize that the freedoms on the list were already guaranteed by the Bill of Rights—they said they'd vote *against* the rights if they were on the ballot.

The average 1995 luxury car had more than one mile of wiring.

BRAND NAMES

You already know these names. Now you know where they come from.

KOOL-AID. Originally named Kool-Ade, until bureaucrats in the Food and Drug Administration banned the use of "ade" because it means "a drink made from..." So inventor E. E. Perkins simply changed the spelling to "aid," meaning "help."

SONY. Originally called Tokyo Tsushin Kogyo. Founder Akio Morita wanted a name he could market internationally. He looked through a Latin dictionary, picked out the word *sonus* (sound), and combined it with "sunny."

CHEERIOS. Originally Cheery Oats. In 1946, Quaker Oats threatened to sue, claiming it had exclusive rights to the name "Oats." Rather than fight, General Mills switched to Cheerios.

BISSELL CARPET SWEEPER. Melville Bissell owned a crockery shop in Grand Rapids, Michigan. He was so allergic to the straw his crockery was packed in that he started sneezing whenever he had to sweep it up. So he invented—and ultimately manufactured—the first carpet sweeper.

HAMILTON-BEACH. L. H. Hamilton and Chester A. Beach perfected a "high-speed, lightweight universal electric motor" and used it in the first commercial drink mixer in 1912. They went on to build small appliances for home use.

GREY POUPON DIJON MUSTARD. Sound classy? Actually, it's named for the Briton who invented it—a Mr. Grey—and his French business partner—Monsieur Poupon—who put up money to open a mustard factory in (where else?) Dijon, France.

CARNATION. In 1901, while walking down a street in Seattle, the head of the Pacific Coast Condensed Milk Company noticed a box of Carnation Brand cigars in a store window. He decided it was a good name for his milk, too. With a picture of a flower on the label, it would be recognizable even to children.

Sound like someone you know? An ostrich's eyes are bigger than its brains.

PHRASE ORIGINS

More origins of everyday phrases.

TURN OVER A NEW LEAF

Meaning: Start over.

Origin: Trees have nothing to do with it—the leaf in the expression is actually the page of a book. Just as the plot of a novel changes from page to page, so too can people change their lives.

IN THE DOLDRUMS

Meaning: Unhappy or depressed; sluggish.

Origin: *Doldrum* is believed to be a corruption of the word *dullard* —meaning "dull or sluggish person." Early cartographers applied it to the dullest areas of the ocean, near the equator, where the waters are calm and winds are very light. With little or no wind in their sails, ships might literally spend weeks "in the doldrums."

WORKING FREELANCE

Meaning: Working independently, for more than one employer.

Origin: The novelist Sir Walter Scott first used this term to describe soldiers-for-hire in the Middle Ages. Because they owed loyalty to no one, he reasoned, they were *free* to hire out their skill with *lances* to anyone who could afford them.

PUT SOMEONE ON THE SPOT

Meaning: Put someone in a difficult position.

Origin: Gangster slang from the 1920s. A person *on the spot* was marked for execution. Probably originated in reference to witnesses, who were "on the spot" where a crime was committed.

ON THE NOSE

Meaning: Perfect; right on time.

Origin: In the early days of radio broadcasting, directors used hand signals to communicate with announcers in soundproof studios. A finger across the throat meant "cut," and a finger *on the nose* meant that the show was right on schedule.

The man who created the Thighmaster was once a Bhuddist monk.

PLEASE LEAVE A MESSAGE...

Telephone answering machines are a bathroom reader's friend. We owe the inventor a debt of gratitude, because they let us read in peace. After all, who wants to jump off the toilet and race madly for the phone every time it rings?

T**HE FIRST EFFORT**
You may not know this, but when Thomas Edison played "Mary Had a Little Lamb" on his first crude recording device in 1877, he was really trying to create a telephone answering machine. The problem with the telephone, he reasoned, was that—unlike the telegraph—it didn't take messages. Unfortunately, the Wizard of Menlo Park couldn't come up with a viable answering device; he had to "settle" for the phonograph instead.

THE FIRST MACHINE
A Danish technician named Valdemar Poulsen invented the answering machine in the summer of 1898. Poulsen's device, called the "telegraphone," was meant to be used exclusively as an answering machine, but was actually the world's first magnetic recorder—the direct precursor to the tape recorder. In 1903, his company, the American Telegraphone Company, tried to crack the U.S. market. It failed miserably, for three reasons:

1. Poor sound quality.
2. It was too expensive for most homes or businesses.
3. The Bell companies refused to allow "outside" machines to be hooked up to their phone lines—which virtually eliminated the entire U.S. market.

American Telegraphone then tried to market their machine as a dictaphone instead, but that failed, too. They went bankrupt in 1919.

THE PHONEMATE
Then, in the late 1960s, Neal Buglewicz, a California inventor, decided to buck the phone company. He developed an answering

---

Male hospital patients fall out of bed twice as often as female patients.

machine that used two tape recorders and called it the Phonemate 700. His second version, the "streamlined" Phonemate 400, became the first answering machine made widely available to consumers. By today's standards, it was laughably primitive: It weighed 10 pounds, used reel-to-reel tapes, could only record voice messages 30 seconds long, and required earphones to retrieve messages. But it opened the door for other designs. Soon other companies were offering similar machines.

AT&T did what it could to prevent the answering machine from succeeding. In 1972, they announced that phone customers had to buy special equipment to connect answering machines to the telephone company network. But Phonemate and its competitors went to court to have the regulations thrown out, and in 1976 they won.

☞　　☞　　☞　　☞

FARTS IN THE NEWS

• Frank Lathrop is the proud inventor of the TooT TrappeR, a special seat cushion that instantly absorbs the odor of unwanted gas. Lathrop got the idea after too many complaints from his wife. "You just sit on it, and it goes to work," Lathrop explains. "We call this the perfect thing for the person who has everything, including gas." The TrappeR's air filter "uses the same technique that was used in gas masks during the Desert Storm War."

• Biologist Dr. Colin Leakey has devoted his entire career to figuring out what makes people pass wind. "We believe that by looking at chemicals in the flatus, we can look at what is being broken down and where these particular chemicals come from," he says. To accomplish this, Leakey (*Leakey?!!?*) has invented the *flatometer*, a device that measures flatulence.

• Johnson & Johnson, which produces drugs for gas and indigestion, once conducted a survey and found that almost one-third of Americans believe they have a flatulence problem. However, according to Terry Bolin and Rosemary Stanton, authors of *Wind Breaks: Coming to Terms with Flatulence*, most flatulence is healthy. What is unhealthy, the authors argue, is that we spend too much time dwelling on it.

Coffee beans aren't beans—they're fruit pits.

THE ODD TITLE AWARD

*Q: What do the Pulitzer Prize and the Odd Title Award have in common?
A: None of Uncle John's Bathroom Readers have won either of
them. Here are some real-life books that have won Bookseller
magazine's annual award for the most unusual book title.*

THE NAME GAME

Every year, tens of thousands of new books are published.
Some are pretty strange...and in 1978, the staff at *Bookseller*
magazine decided to honor a few with the Odd Title of the Year
Award. Every year, they give a bottle of champagne to the person
who finds the most unusual book title of the year. The only rules:
the book itself has to be serious, and "gratuitously eye-catching academic works" are automatically disqualified. The title has to be
weird without trying to be. (That's why *New Guinea Tapeworms &
Jewish Grandmothers; Tales of Parasites and People,* lost out in 1994.)
Here are all the winners. Remember: These are *real* book titles!

1978: *Proceedings of the Second In-
ternational Workshop on Nude Mice*
(Also won the Oddest of the Odd
Book Title Award, given in 1994
to the oddest title in the contest's
15-year history)
Runners-up:
• *Cooking with God*
• *Iceberg Utilization*
• *Fight Acne and Win*

1979: *The Madam as Entrepreneur:
Career Management in House
Prostitution*
Runners-up:
• *Macrame Gnomes*
• *100 Years of British Rail Catering*

1980: *The Joy of Chickens*
Runner-up:
• *Children Are Like Wet Cement*

1981: *Last Chances at Love:
Terminal Romances*
Runner-up:
• *Waterproofing Your Child*

1982: Two winners: *Braces Own-
ers' Manual: A Guide to the Care
and Wearing of Braces,* and *Popula-
tion and Other Problems*
Runners-up:
• *Tourist Guide to Lebanon*
• *Scurvy Past and Present*
• *Keeping Warm with an Axe*

1983: *The Theory of Lengthwise Rolling*

Runners-up:

- *Practical Infectious Diseases*
- *Nasal Maintenance: Nursing Your Nose Through Troubled Times*
- *Atlas of Tongue Coating*

1984: *The Book of Marmalade: Its Antecedents, Its History and Its Role in the World Today*

Runners-up:

- *Big and Very Big Hole Drilling*
- *Picture Your Dog in Needlework*
- *Napoleon's Glands and Other Ventures in Biohistory*

1985: *Natural Bust Enlargement with Total Power: How to Increase the Other 90% of Your Mind to Increase the Size of Your Breasts*

Runner-up:

- *Anorexia Nervosa in Bulgarian Bees*

1986: *Oral Sadism and the Vegetarian Personality*

1987: No prize awarded

1988: *Versailles: The View from Sweden*

Runner-up:

- *Detecting Fake Nazi Regalia*

1989: *How to Shit in the Woods: An Environmentally Sound Approach to a Lost Art*

1990: *Lesbian Sado-masochism Safety Manual*

1991: No prize awarded

1992: *How to Avoid Huge Ships*

Runner-up:

- *Watermark Diseases of the Cricket Bat*

1993: *American Bottom Archaeology*

Runners-up:

- *Liturgy of the Opening of the Mouth for Breathing*
- *The Complete Suicide Manual*

1994: *Highlights in the History of Concrete*

Runners-up:

- *Septic Tanks and Cesspools: A Do-It-Yourself Guide*
- *Butchering Livestock at Home*
- *Best Bike Rides in the Mid-Atlantic*
- *Gymnastics for Horses*
- *Psychiatric Disorders in Dental Practice*

1995: *Reusing Old Graves* ("a study of cemetery etiquette")

Runners-up:

- *Amputee Management: A Handbook*
- *Mucus and Related Topics*
- *Simply Bursting: A Guide to Bladder Control*
- *Fun Games and Big Bangs: The Recreational Use of High Explosives*
- *Rats for Those Who Care*
- *Teach Your Cat to Read*
- *Virtual Reality: Exploring the Bra*

The U.S. Post Office sold a record 123 million Elvis Presley commemorative stamps in 1993.

INCOME TAX TRIVIA

You may not like to pay them, but reading about them isn't so bad. And when you're done with the page, you can always tear it out and...

A UDIT INFO
Do you worry about being audited? Actually, the odds you'll be audited are pretty low: In 1994 the IRS audited about 93,000 individual income tax returns out of 114 million submitted, or about .08% of all returns filed. That's way down from 1914, when every single one of the 357,598 tax returns submitted was audited. The IRS didn't take any chances with the signatures that year, either: each taxpayer had to sign their return under oath in the presence of IRS officials.

KISS & TELL
Believe it or not, the IRS actually pays people to tattle on tax cheats. In fiscal year 1993, for example, it payed out $5.3 million to tipsters. The money was rewarded to more than 14,000 different informants, whose tips led to the collection of $172 million in previously unpaid taxes. The most "useful" tattlers earned an average of $1,772 apiece. But they had to file Form 211, the official IRS informer form, to claim their "reward."

TAX RANKINGS
Sweden has the highest taxes of any modern economy on earth—its taxes make up 56.9% of the country's total income. The United States comes in ninth behind Sweden, France, Italy, Germany, Canada, Britain, Switzerland, and Japan. Taxes make up about 29.9% of its total income.

LEGAL DEADBEATS
According to a 1990 IRS study, 1,219 taxpayers with incomes over $200,000 legally paid *no* federal income tax at all that year—and 1,114 of these people paid no income taxes anywhere else in the world, either.

DEDUCTIONS

According to the 1995 tax code, Nobel Prize money is exempt from taxation, and the cost of a police officer's uniform can be deducted. But the meals a firefighter eats in the firehouse are taxable, because the IRS considers the fire station to be a "home."

THE FIRST "LOOPHOLE"

In 1915 a U.S. Congressman, complaining about the increasing complexity of the tax code, lamented, "I write a law. You drill a hole in it. I plug the hole. You drill a hole in my plug." His words were reported in newspapers all over the country, and a new word—*loophole*—was born.

IT'S OUR TIME, TOO

How much time do you spend each working day to pay your federal income taxes? Over the years the National Tax Foundation, an income tax lobbying group, has kept track of how much of the average American's working day is used to earn enough to make payments to Uncle Sam. Their findings:

1929: 19 minutes per day	1969: 1 hour, 48 minutes
1939: 40 minutes	1979: 1 hour, 48 minutes
1949: 1 hour, 16 minutes	1989: 1 hour, 47 minutes
1959: 1 hour, 36 minutes	

CHANGING VIEWS

In a 1972 poll by the Advisory Commission on Intergovernmental Relations, Americans ranked the federal income tax as "the fairest of all taxes." In a similar study in 1989, American taxpayers ranked the tax as "the *least* fair of all taxes."

THE DREADED DATE

In 1954, the IRS moved the deadline for filing tax returns back a month, from March 15 to April 15. Reason: The tax code had become so complicated that Americans needed more time to fill out the forms.

AS SMART AS BAIT

A lot of stuff on the internet makes great bathroom reading. For example: Here's a list of "35 Politically Correct Ways to Say Someone's Stupid," taken off the Internet and sent to us by BRI member John Dollison.

1. A few clowns short of a circus.
2. A few fries short of a Happy Meal.
3. An experiment in Artificial Stupidity.
4. A few beers short of a 6-pack.
5. Dumber than a box of hair.
6. A few peas short of a casserole.
7. Doesn't have all his corn flakes in one box.
8. The wheel's spinning, but the hamster's dead.
9. One Fruit Loop shy of a full bowl.
10. One taco short of a combination plate.
11. A few feathers short of a whole duck.
12. All foam, no beer.
13. The cheese slid off his cracker.
14. Body by Fisher, brains by Mattel.
15. Has an IQ of 2, but it takes 3 to grunt.
16. Warning: Objects in mirror are dumber than they appear.
17. Couldn't pour water out of a boot with instructions on the heel.
18. Too much yardage between the goal posts.
19. An intellect rivaled only by garden tools.
20. As smart as bait.
21. Chimney's clogged.
22. Doesn't have all his dogs on one leash.
23. Doesn't know much but leads the league in nostril hair.
24. Elevator doesn't go all the way to the top floor.
25. Forgot to pay his brain bill.
26. Her sewing machine's out of thread.
27. Her antenna doesn't pick up all the channels.
28. His belt doesn't go through all the loops.
29. If he had another brain, it would be lonely.
30. Missing a few buttons on her remote control.
31. No grain in the silo.
32. Proof that evolution *can* go in reverse.
33. Receiver is off the hook.
34. Several nuts short of a full pouch.
35. He fell out of the Stupid tree and hit every branch on the way down.

"The Alphabet Song," "Twinkle, Twinkle Little Star," and "Baa, Baa Black Sheep" are

THE ROOSEVELTS

*The Roosevelt family has been a big part of the
American 20th century. They're quotable, too.*

"The best executive is one who has sense enough to pick good people to do what he wants done, and self-restraint enough to keep from meddling."
—*Theodore Roosevelt*

"A conservative is a man with two perfectly good legs who has never learned to walk forward."
—*Franklin D. Roosevelt*

"No man is justified in doing evil on the ground of expediency."
—*Theodore Roosevelt*

"No one can make you feel inferior without your consent."
—*Eleanor Roosevelt*

"To destroy our natural resources, to skin and exhaust the land instead of using it so as to increase its usefulness, will result in undermining, in the days of our children, the very prosperity which we ought by right to hand down."
—*Theodore Roosevelt*

"Every time an artist dies, part of the vision of mankind passes with him."
—*Franklin D. Roosevelt*

"I think we consider too much the good luck of the early bird, and not enough the bad luck of the early worm."
—*Franklin D. Roosevelt*

"If you can't say something good about someone, come and sit by me."
—*Alice Roosevelt Longworth*
(Theodore's daughter)

"My father gave me these hints on speechmaking: Be sincere… be brief…be seated."
—*James Roosevelt* **(FDR's son)**

"Never underestimate a man who overestimates himself."
—*Franklin D. Roosevelt*

"Calvin Coolidge looks like he was weaned on a pickle."
—*Alice Roosevelt Longworth*

"When they call the roll in the Senate, the Senators do not know whether to answer 'Present' or 'Not guilty.' "
—*Theodore Roosevelt*

"The gains of education are never really lost. Books may be burned and cities sacked, but truth…lives in the hearts of humble men."
—*Franklin D. Roosevelt*

---

all sung to the same music: a 1765 French song titled *"Ah! Vous Diraije Maman."*

THE ICEMAN COMETH

*Not all mummies are wrapped in bandages. Here's one
who was buried in ice, fully clothed, for 5,000 years.*

SURPRISE ENCOUNTER

On September 19, 1991, some people hiking in the Alps along the Austrian/Italian border spotted a body sticking out of a glacier. The corpse was brown and dried out and looked like it had been there for a long time. But neither the hikers nor the Austrian officials who recovered it four days later had any idea *how* long.

When scientists carbon-dated the remains, the "Iceman" (as he was dubbed in the press) turned out to be more than 5,300 years old. It was the world's oldest fully preserved human body, and the first prehistoric human ever found with "everyday clothing and equipment"—including an axe, dagger, and bow and arrows. Other bodies that have been found were either buried following funerals or sacrificed in religious ceremonies…which means they had ceremonial objects and clothing that didn't shed much light on what everyday life was like.

CLOSE CALL

Because no one realized how old or valuable the Iceman was until five days after he was discovered, no one took any precautions to ensure he wasn't damaged during removal and shipment to the morgue. In fact, it seems they did just about everything they could to *damage* him. An Austrian police officer tried to free the Iceman from the ice by using a jackhammer—shredding his garments and gashing his left hip to the bone. He probably would have done more damage, except that he ran out of compressed air for the jackhammer and had to quit.

Next, as word of the unusual discovery spread, locals and gawkers traveled to the site to view the remains. Many pocketed the Iceman's tools and shreds of garment as souvenirs. And when forensics experts finally removed the body from the ice, they did so using clumsy pickaxes, destroying the archaeological value of the site in the process.

By now the Iceman, clothed from the waist down when initially discovered, was buck naked save for pieces of a boot on his right foot and shards of clothing strewn around the body. Even worse, his private parts were missing, perhaps stolen by one of the visitors to the site. They were never recovered.

MODERN PROBLEMS

When scientists did get around to studying him, they found a dark-skinned male between the ages of 25 and 40 who stood 5'2" tall. The Iceman surprised archaeologists with his shaved face, recently cut hair, and tattoos; experts thought that people did not "invent" shaves, haircuts, and tattoos until thousands of years later.

He also suffered from some surprisingly modern ailments. A body-scan revealed smoke-blackened lungs—probably from sitting around open fires, but definitely not from smoking—as well as hardening of the arteries and blood vessels. He also had arthritis in the neck, lower back, and hip. But he didn't die from any of them.

CAUSE OF DEATH

The fact that the Iceman's body survived so long may provide a clue about how he died. Most bodies recovered from glaciers have literally been torn to pieces by slow-moving ice. But the Iceman's wasn't. He was found in a small protective basin, 10 to 15 feet deep, that sheltered him as glaciers passed overhead. This leads archaeologists to speculate that he sought shelter in the basin when a surprise winter storm hit. "He was in a state of exhaustion perhaps as a consequence of adverse weather conditions," a team of experts theorized in *Science* magazine in 1992. "He therefore may have lain down, fallen asleep, and frozen to death." Snow covered the body, the glacier eventually flowed over it…and the body remained completely preserved and undisturbed for the next 53 centuries.

FINAL RESTING PLACE

The Iceman now resides in a freezer in Austria's Innsbruck University, kept at 98% humidity and 21°F, "the glacial temperature he had grown accustomed to over more than 5,000 years." Scientists only examine the body for 20 minutes every two weeks—anything more than that would cause the mummy to deteriorate.

About 75% of U.S. families put up a Christmas tree; 54% of the trees are artificial.

FOOD FLOPS

How can anyone in the food industry predict what people will buy, when Frankenberry Cereal and Cheez Whiz are wild successes? It's anyone's guess what America will eat...which is how they come up with clunkers like these.

LA CHOY "FRESH AND LITE" EGG ROLLS. A quick snack? Not exactly. The big, fat egg rolls took half an hour to thaw and eat, so by the time the center was hot, the shell was damp and gooey. Even the name "Fresh and Lite" was half-baked. "It sounded like a feminine hygiene product," one of the company's ad executives admitted. "And it was hard to say it was fresh anyway, because it was frozen."

MCDONALD'S MCLEAN DELUXE. In 1991, McFood scientists were ordered to come up with a burger that even health nuts could love. Their solution: to replace most of the fat with carrageenan (seaweed extract) and water to create the "91% fat free" McLean Deluxe. It was a product with no market: health-conscious eaters still avoided the Golden Arches; fast-food aficionados were revolted by the concept of a seaweed burger. After years of slow sales, McDonald's finally threw in the towel in 1996.

WINE & DINE. Acording to *Business Week* magazine, Wine & Dine was "the upscale answer to Hamburger Helper—noodles and a sauce mix bundled with a tiny bottle of Chianti. Sad to say, the labeling didn't make it clear that the Chianti in that bottle was salty cooking wine. Consumers thought they had bought a little vino for dinner. When they discovered their error, they took their wining and dining elsewhere."

I HATE PEAS. If kids won't eat peas in their natural shape, why not mash them into a paste and make them look like French fries? Answer: Because, as one kid put it, "they still taste disgusting." Consumer researcher Robert McMath summed it up: "Kids said, 'A pea is a pea is a pea....I don't like peas. In fact, I hate peas, even if they're in the shape of French fries." I Hate Beans also flopped.

None of the Beatles knew how to read music. (Paul McCartney eventually taught himself.)

MILLER CLEAR BEER. In the wake of huge publicity generated by Crystal Pepsi, Tab Clear, and other colorless soft drinks (most of which flopped), Miller came up with this clearly stupid idea. Unlike soft drinks, which are artificially colored, a beer's color is *natural*. So it's just about impossible to remove the color without destroying the flavor and body at the same time. One newspaper critic described Clear Beer as "a lager the color of 7-Up, with little head and a taste like sweetened seltzer...with the faintest touch of oily, medicinal hoppiness in the finish." Born: 1994; died: 1996.

NESTEA'S TEA WHIZ. Would you give a "yellowish, carbonated, lemon-flavored drink" a name like *Whiz*?

VIN DE CALIFORNIE. "For the first time in history, American wines will cross the sea to France!" boasted three California wine-makers in 1966. The ship might as well have sunk on the way over. Novelty shops were the only stores willing to stock "Vin de Californie" (the brand name they marketed it under)—and even there, sales were poor. "French customers approached the displays gingerly," *Newsweek* magazine reported, "almost as if they were afraid the wines might explode."

Critics considered the wine a joke. And the Californians unwittingly seemed to agree. "Vin de Californie," it turned out, is French slang for Coca-Cola.

JUMPIN' JEMS. The soft drink equivalent of the lava lamp. Introduced in 1995 by Mistic Brands, it was supposed to have "jelly balls" floating in the liquid. A major flaw: The "jelly balls" settled to the bottom of the bottle. Consumers figured the product had gone bad and wouldn't touch it. "Even *I* didn't drink it," admitted Mistic's president.

• Okay, then. A year later, the Clearly Canadian Beverage Company tried again with Orbitz. This time, the "flavored gel spheres" stayed suspended in the drink and were small enough to fit through a straw, but large enough so they "didn't look like a mistake." Reaction: "I think it's gross," one consultant told reporters. "It's like, when you drink a glass of milk, do you want to find lumps?"

REVENGE!

"Don't get mad, get even" was John F. Kennedy's motto. All of us want to get back at someone, sometime. Here are six reports we've found about people (and a rabbit) who actually did.

TRIGGER HAPPY

"Two gangsters, James Gallo and Joe Conigliaro, set about to murder a stoolpigeon, Vinny Ensuelo, alias Vinny Ba Ba. On November 1, 1973, they jumped him on Columbia Street, Brooklyn, and took him for a ride. Gallo pointed a gun at his head from the right; Conigliaro covered him from the left. The car swerved violently. The two gangsters shot each other."

As the New York *Daily News* described it:

Conigliaro, hit in the spine, was paralyzed. Every year after that Vinny Ensuelo sent wheelchair batteries to Conigliaro. A small card with the batteries always said, "Keep rolling, from your best pal, Vinny Ba Ba."

—*Remarkable Events*, by **John Train**

COMMON CENTS

"A shabbily dressed man went up to a teller yesterday at the U.S. Bank of Washington in Spokane, and asked her to validate his 60¢ parking ticket. She refused. The man asked to talk to a bank manager about the matter. The manager also refused. So 59-year-old John Barrier withdrew all the money he had on deposit—$1 million—and took it down the street to the Seafirst Bank. 'If you have $1 in a bank, or $1 million, I think they owe you the courtesy of stamping your parking ticket,' he said."

—**UPI, Feb. 21, 1989**

MASHED

In 1974, after three seasons as Col. Henry Blake on "M*A*S*H" (CBS), McLean Stevenson suddenly announced he was leaving to star in a sitcom for NBC.

The show's producers paid him back in kind. "One story around Hollywood," wrote Tom Shales in the *Washington Post*, "was that

Stevenson was so disliked on the set that Blake's death was written in to make sure there was no way he could ever come back." John Carman updated the story 20 years later in the *S.F. Chronicle:*

> To be *McLeaned* is to be blotted out fully and finally and with extreme TV prejudice.
>
> Reserved for actors who've been naughty and unappreciative, the process is named for McLean Stevenson, who wanted off M*A*S*H and saw his wish come all too true. His irate producers packed Stevenson's character, Henry Blake, into a helicopter and had it plunge from the sky. Message to McLean: You're crop dust now. You can't come home again.

LETTERS FROM HELL

"When attorney Theresa McConville sold her vacant lot in Ventura Country in 1985, a losing bidder was Reynaldo Fong, a local anesthesiologist. Fong, embittered by the loss, devised a novel form of revenge. Over ten years he took out nearly 100,000 magazine subscriptions in her name, asking in each case that the magazine bill McConville. He also sent McConville a refrigerator—C.O.D. McConville spent $50,000 to straighten out the mess."

—*Forbes* magazine, June 5, 1995

FROM THE X-(RATED) FILES

"An employee of the St. Louis Blues apparently couldn't resist a parting shot at the team after he was fired.

"On the page listing playoff records in the hockey team's media guide, between the date of the Blues' last overtime game on the road and their last overtime loss at home, the anonymous employee slipped in a crudely worded 'record' for sexual favors.

"The red-faced Blues have recalled the guide and will have to amend it, at a reported cost of $70,000."

—*L. A. Times,* Oct. 16, 1995

I'M GAME

"Near Louisville, Kentucky, a rabbit reached out of a hunter's game bag, pulled the trigger of his gun, and shot him in the foot."

—*New Yorker,* May 1947

Lake Nicaragua in Nicaragua is the only freshwater lake in the world that has sharks.

TREK WARS

As "Star Trek" creator Gene Roddenberry conceived it, the Starship Enterprise was a metaphor for an ideal world—a multiracial, multinational crew working together to achieve humanity's highest goals. In real life, however, the crew of the Enterprise was bogged down in typical 20th-century politics. Here are four examples.

CAPT. KIRK VS. EVERYBODY

William Shatner (Capt. Kirk) was originally intended to be the only star of "Star Trek." That meant he made a lot more money than everyone else—$5,000 per episode, compared to Leonard Nimoy's $1,250, and $600 to $850 for the other actors. And it meant he got what he wanted, even at other cast members' expense. In virtually every script, for example, he had more lines than any other actor. But that didn't stop him from taking other people's lines if he felt like it. As George Takei (Mr. Sulu) writes in his book *To the Stars:*

> [The script consultant] would occasionally give us an advance peek at an early draft of a script, which might contain a wonderful scene for our respective characters or even a fun line or two of dialogue.... But when the final shooting script was delivered, the eagerly awaited scene or line would now be in someone else's mouth, and invariably, it was Bill's... Even if an idea had originated with one of us, if Bill wanted it, he got it.

CAPT. KIRK VS. MR. SPOCK

Spock was conceived as a minor character, but Leonard Nimoy was so good in the role that the part kept growing. This apparently drove Shatner nuts, as J. Van Hise writes in *The History of Trek:*

> Shatner was so concerned over the situation that he counted his lines in each new script to be certain that he had more than Nimoy. If he didn't, either more were added for him at his insistence, or Nimoy's lines were cut....[One scriptwriter] witnessed the director trying to come up with an alternative way for Nimoy to react to Shatner in a scene, because for Nimoy to utter a line would have given him one line too many as far as Shatner was concerned.

U.S. mints stamp out 37 million pennies, 4.6 million nickels, 6.6 million dimes,

The rivalry started interfering with production schedules. During the first season, for example, *Life* magazine decided to shoot a photo essay on Spock's makeup. They sent a photographer to the set, and everything went smoothly until Shatner arrived. When he saw what was going on, he turned and walked away. Shortly afterward, a production assistant insisted that the photographer leave. Takei writes:

> Leonard, understandably, was livid. He got up and refused to have his makeup completed until the photographer was allowed back. Until then, he announced, he would wait in his dressing room with his makeup only half done. And with that, he exited.

For the next few hours, studio executives shuttled back and forth between Nimoy's and Shatner's dressing rooms trying to resolve the dispute. The photographer was finally allowed to finish the job, and the article appeared in *Life* as planned. By then, however, half a day's shooting had been lost.

LT. UHURA VS. NBC

Nichelle Nichols (Lt. Uhura) was the only main character who wasn't signed to a contract when she was hired. In her autobiography, *Beyond Uhura*, Nichols writes that contract talks broke down when NBC executives found out she was a black woman:

> ["Star Trek" creator Gene Roddenberry] told the network that he wanted to add a little "color" to the bridge. They assumed he was merely redecorating the set....The network men had a fit when they saw that not only was there a woman in the command crew and on the bridge, but a Black one! When they realized that Uhura's involvement would be substantial and her lines went beyond "Yes, Captain!" they furiously issued Gene an ultimatum: Get rid of her!

Roddenberry refused to fire Nichols, but couldn't get the network to hire her as a permanent cast member. So he hired her as an uncontracted "day player" for each episode. Ironically, thanks to the union wage scale, Nichols made more money than she would have under contract. "Not only did Gene get what he wanted," Nichols writes, "he made sure NBC paid—literally and dearly—for it."

An Unlikely Fan

By the end of the first season, Uhura was nearly as popular as Capt. Kirk and Mr. Spock—and got nearly as much fan mail. But

Nichols didn't know it. Studio officials had ordered that she not receive her fan mail. Near the end of the first season, a mailroom employee finally told her of the embargo. "To say I was stunned does not even begin to convey how I felt," she writes in *Beyond Uhura*.

In fact, she was so upset that she decided to quit. The following evening, however, she met Dr. Martin Luther King at an NAACP fundraiser. He turned out to be a fan of the show and urged her to stay on, arguing that "Uhura was the first non-stereotypical black character in television history"…and that *white* Americans, as well as black Americans, needed to see that character. Nichols agreed to stay and fight it out.

MR. SPOCK VS. GENE RODDENBERRY

What about the Great Idealist himself? It turns out that the creator of "Star Trek" could be just as much of a pain to work with, especially when money was involved. "My business dealings with him were always miserable," Nimoy recalled in 1994. "Gene always had an agenda—his own." One example: Early in the show's history, a Connecticut amusement park offered Nimoy $2,000 to make a personal appearance on a Saturday morning. But the only flight available was on Friday evening—which meant Nimoy had to get permission from Roddenberry to leave work a few hours early.

Rather than give Nimoy a direct answer, Roddenberry mentioned he was forming "Lincoln Enterprises," his own talent agency, and he wanted to represent Nimoy when he made public appearances. Nimoy wasn't interested; he already had an agent and didn't want someone else getting a percentage of his salary. But Roddenberry pressed the issue, as Joe Engel writes in *Gene Roddenberry: The Myth and the Man Behind Star Trek*:

> "The difference between your agent and Lincoln Enterprises," Roddenberry said, "is that Lincoln can get you off the lot at five p.m. every Friday."
>
> "Gene," Nimoy said, "I already have the job. I'm asking if you can help me out of here so I can pick up two thousand dollars this weekend."
>
> "The problem with you," Roddenberry said, "is that you have to learn to bow down and say 'Master.'"

MILLENNIUM MADNESS

There are some pretty strange goings-on associated with the millennium.
This page, excerpted from The Bathroom Reader's Guide
to the Year 2000, gives you an idea of what we mean.

WORTH WAITING FOR

The *Warsaw Voice* reports that a group called "Atrovis," in the Polish village of Niebo, expects a select group of people to be evacuated by extraterrestrials in 1999. They believe 144,000 white people and 600,000 from other races will enter eternity. The men will get new 25-year-old bodies, the women will look like 20-year-olds.

SERMON ON THE MOUNTAIN

In Cuzco, Peru, 50,000 pilgrims a year are climbing Mount Auzangate to worship an image of Christ that is painted on a rock. The image, according to the *Daily Telegraph*, was discovered in 1780—the same year the Spanish killed the last great Inca leader, Tupac Amaru II. Reportedly, the pilgrimage has become popular among Peruvians because of the widespread belief that Tupac's body will re-emerge at the site in the year 2000 to liberate his people.

JUST WAIT!

In South Korea, a "doomsday" preacher named Lee Jang-rim was sent to jail for convincing his followers—including some in the United States—that the apocalypse would occur at midnight October 28, 1992. Members sold their homes and possessions; a few even committed suicide. Many followers are still convinced. One told the *Chicago Tribune* that doomsday has only been postponed. "1999 is the end of the earth," he says. "That's for sure."

MARY, MARY

The New York Times reports that there are now so many sightings of the Virgin Mary that a newsletter called "Mary's People" is being published. People studying the visions speculate that the recent increase is connected to the approach of the year 2000.

An estimated 405,000 U.S. homes still lack indoor plumbing.

THE HONEY BUCKET

You think you got troubles? At least you're not sitting on a honey bucket. This article, by John Foley, was published in Alaska *magazine in April 1994.*

On camping trips when nature beckons, I usually seek out a tree. It goes without saying that in urban areas I find a toilet. But now I live in a place with neither trees nor toilets, and I have, to my everlasting regret, discovered the honey bucket.

Many fortunate folks from Outside are not familiar with honey buckets. When I told my mother in Iowa we had a honey bucket, she said, "Isn't that charming. Are the bees much of a nuisance?" Honey buckets, at least in these parts, do not hold honey. A honey bucket is a foot-high pail lined with a plastic bag. A child-size seat and lid are attached to the rim.

A small percentage of homes in Gambell [Alaska], have running water and thus flush toilets. The rest of the village—located on the northwestern tip of St. Lawrence Island—makes do (so to speak) with honey buckets. I took a teaching job in Gambell in mid-August. Within moments of my arrival I had to give the honey bucket a test run. Situating my 6-foot-3 frame on the low bucket was a challenge at first, but I soon mastered the technique—save for those groggy 3 a.m. visits, when my form suffers and I have a tendency to fall overboard.

My initial impulse was to put the honey bucket in the bathroom, where it belonged, by God, even if I had to brush my teeth while holding my nose. Our neighbors explained that it's best to put the bucket in the Arctic entry, as the cold cuts down the smell.

The cold has also entered my personal habits. For the first time in my adult life I don't bring reading material along when I am anticipating a sit-down visit. Nor do I linger. Some habits die hard, however, and I still find myself reaching over my shoulder to flush the honey bucket. There should be a psychological term for this tendency. Air flush, perhaps.

We adjusted to the bucket

Science fact: City dwellers have longer, thicker, denser nose hairs than country folks do.

life as well as can be expected, but some newcomers did not. Kris Lucas, another first-year teacher, had a terrible time with her honey bucket at first, primarily because it didn't have a handle.

The locals were greatly amused to see her hauling her bucket to the dump like a load of laundry; she clutched it to her chest and, for obvious reasons, threw her head back.

While Kris was suffering this indignity, her husband, Luke, was back home in Wisconsin tidying up details for his own move to Gambell. Kris decided …it would be wise marital strategy not to mention the honey bucket until he set foot on the island. Needless to say, Luke was surprised by the local plumbing. But he adjusted quickly. He had to, as he was put in charge of the honey bucket detail.

Hauling heavy buckets over soft gravel is a workout…. So we were appreciative when the principal decided to loan us the school four-wheeler once a week for honey bucket runs.

The honey bucket dump is a foul sight—not to mention smell—however you get there. Still, it's more tolerable on a weekly basis. We've designated Thursday as Honey Bucket Day and fallen into a resigned pattern.

This pattern no longer includes our wives. Amy and Kris are independent and capable women but their feminist attitudes are conspicuously absent on Honey Bucket Day, when they assume traditional roles faster than you can say "Barbara Bush." In short, they cook dinner while we haul buckets.

Luke and I have become fast friends—partly because we share this distasteful chore. It's impossible to put on airs or be standoffish when you tiptoe through a honey bucket dump with someone. As far as male-bonding activities, it ranks right up there with watching pro football.

Occasionally we get into heavy discussions during our dump run. Once we debated the etymology of "honey bucket." Luke surmised that the phrase entered the language as an ironic term, like Peacekeeper Missile or rap music. My guess is that it was a shortened form of a longer expression. This first came to mind in the pre-four-wheeler stage, when Amy would say, all too often, "Honey, go dump the bucket!" Hence, honey bucket.

PRIMETIME PROVERBS

More TV wisdom from Primetime Proverbs.

ON PRIDE
"I hate to blow my own horn, but 'Beep beep!'"
—Alex P. Keaton,
Family Ties

ON GUNS
"The intellect is a much more powerful weapon than the gun, particularly when the gun doesn't work."
—Dorian,
Blake's 7

ON LAWYERS
"Lawyers and tarts are the oldest professions in the world. And we always aim to please."
–Horace Rumpole,
Rumpole of the Bailey

ON THE BATTLE BETWEEN THE SEXES
"Did you know the male bee is nothing but the slave of the queen? And once the male has, how should I say, serviced the queen, the male dies. All in all, not a bad system."
–Phyllis Lindstrom,
The Mary Tyler Moore Show

Jules: "Roseanne, listen to this. 'Utah Housewife Stabs Husband 37 Times.'"
Roseanne: "I admire her restraint."
—*Roseanne*

ON THE MEDIA
"There's a standard formula for success in the entertainment medium—beat it to death if it succeeds."
—Ernie Kovacs,
The Ernie Kovacs Show

ON DRINKING
"Never cry over spilt milk. It could've been whiskey."
—Pappy Maverick,
Maverick

ON HOME
"A man's home is his coffin."
—Al Bundy,
Married...with Children

ON BRAVERY
"Wanna do something that's really courageous? Come on over to my mother-in-law's house and say, 'You're wrong, fatso!'"
–Buddy Sorrell,
The Dick Van Dyke Show

ON FAMILY
Maddie Hayes: "I didn't know you had a brother."
David Addison: "I never thought of him as a brother. I thought of him as Mom and Dad's science project."
—*Moonlighting*

Science fact: Goldfish remember better in cold water than in warm water.

MISS AMERICA, PART IV:
There She Is...

When you think about it, the Miss America contest is more a TV show than a pageant. Sure, we get a national figure (or figurine) out of it—but the thing that keeps it going is ratings. So just like any sitcom or talk show, it has to have a theme song. Here's how Miss America got hers.

O**N THE AIR**
After the war, the Miss America Pageant was flying high. It was oh-so-respectable, financially sound, and as popular with women as with men. Its survival was no longer in doubt.

In fact, thanks to strong media coverage, it was regarded as a national institution. Millions of Americans followed the contest in the newspapers, on the radio, and in movie newsreels. But if they wanted to watch the pageant in its entirety, they had to go to Atlantic City and view it in person. There was no other way.

Then in 1953, the fledgling American Broadcasting Company (ABC) offered $5,000 to broadcast the event over its small network of TV stations. Miss America officials seriously considered the offer, but turned it down when ABC refused to black out the broadcast in nearby Philadelphia. (The pageant had just doubled its ticket prices and was afraid too many people would stay home and watch it on TV.)

The next year, ABC upped the ante. It doubled the offer to $10,000, and lined up the Philco Television Company as a sponsor. Philco even offered to introduce a new line of "Miss America" television sets. This time pageant officials accepted. The Miss America Pageant was broadcast live on September 11, 1954; a record breaking 27 million people—39% of the viewing audience—tuned in to watch. All through the '50s, TV ratings were astronomical.

MUSIC MAN
One of the people who got caught up in the excitement was Bernie Wayne, a songwriter. He learned about the first TV broadcast in a newspaper article, and it inspired him to write a song. "Although I

---

had never seen a pageant before," he explained years later, "somehow the words and melody for the song suddenly came into mind....I just sat down in my little office, and started writing. I wrote the whole song in the space of an hour...I just tried to put myself in the place of the lucky girl—walking down the runway—an ideal, walking on air." He called his song "There She Is."

Wayne performed the song for the pageant's producer and musical director. "They loved it," he says, and told him they would use it in the pageant. Wayne phoned his mother and told her to watch for the song during the broadcast.

Then the producer called him over during final rehearsals and said they'd changed their minds—they weren't going to use the song. The reason: Bob Russell, host of the broadcast, wanted some songs *he'd* written, "This Is Miss America" and "The Spirit of Miss America," included—and he got his way. "I was brokenhearted," Wayne recalled years later....The next night I was too disappointed to go see the show. I watched it on TV from some broken-down bar."

LUCKY BREAK

"There She Is" might never have made it into the pageant, if Wayne hadn't been invited to a Park Avenue party a few months later. While performing a piano medley of his songs, he sang "There She Is." "As I sang, the place quieted down like magic. When I finished, there was such a hush I thought I'd laid an egg." Someone in the audience asked him, "Why haven't I heard this song before!"

He was Pierson Mapes, the advertising executive in charge of both the Philco account and the upcoming 1955 pageant. Mapes pressured Miss America officials to make the song a centerpiece of the broadcast—a task made all the easier by the fact that host Bob Russell did not return in 1955. Crooner Bert Parks took his place, and both Parks and "There She Is" became hits.

Still interested? We continue the story on page 257.

"Vodka" is Russian for "little water."

FAMILIAR PHRASES

More origins of everyday phrases.

IN ONE FELL SWOOP
Meaning: All at once.

Origin: Falling has nothing to do with it. *Fell* comes from the Middle English word *fel*, meaning "cruel, deadly, or ruthless" and is related to the word *felon*. The expression "one fell swoop" first appeared in *Macbeth* (Act 4, Scene iii), when Shakespeare compares the sudden death of a character to an eagle *swooping* down on some chickens and carrying them off.

HAVE YOUR WORK CUT OUT FOR YOU
Meaning: Have a difficult task ahead.

Origin: According to Christine Ammer in *Have a Nice Day—No Problem!*, the term refers to "a pattern cut from a cloth that must be then made into a garment." When the easier task of cutting out the cloth is finished, the more difficult job of sewing the garment is still left.

CALLED ON THE CARPET
Meaning: Admonished or reprimanded by a superior.

Origin: In the 19th century, carpets were prohibitively expensive, so usually, only the boss's office was carpeted. When employees were "called on the carpet," it meant the boss wanted to see them —which frequently meant they were in trouble.

SIGHT FOR SORE EYES
Meaning: Welcome sight.

Origin: According to ancient superstition, unpleasant sights could make eyes sore…and pleasant sights made sore eyes feel better.

TEN-GALLON HAT
Meaning: Big cowboy hat.

Origin: Measurements have nothing to do with it. The name comes from *sombrero galon*, which means "braided hat" in Spanish.

MORE OLYMPIC CHEATERS

*Here are four Olympians who might have cheated...and
then again, maybe they didn't. We'll never know.*

H AMMOU BOUTAYEB AND KHALID SKAH,
members of the Moroccan track team
Year: 1992

Place: Barcelona, Spain

What happened: Boutayeb fell so far behind in the 10,000-meter
event that the two front-runners, Khalid Skah and Kenya's Richard
Chelimo, were about to lap him. Rather than let them pass, Boutayeb blocked Chelimo for an entire lap before officials finally
dragged him from the track and disqualified him. But by then it was
too late—he'd allowed his teammate, Khalid Skah, to sprint past
Chelimo into first place and win the race.

Reaction: Skah's excitement was short-lived. Spectators booed
loudly and pelted him with garbage as he made his victory lap; 30
minutes later, Olympic officials disqualified him and took away his
gold medal, figuring that he and Boutayeb had been in cahoots.
Skah appealed the decision...and won: the next day the appeals
committee took the gold medal back from Chelimo and returned
it to Skah.

STELLA WALSH, Polish 100-meter runner

Years: 1932 and 1936

Places: Los Angeles and Berlin

What happened: Walsh won the gold medal in the 100-meter race
in Los Angeles and a silver medal in Berlin. But she aroused suspicions. "She ran like a man," says Roxanne Andersen, a women's
track coach in the 1930s, who also noted that at the 1936 Olympics, Walsh appeared to have a "five o'clock shadow."

Walsh's victories went unchallenged until 1980, when she was
gunned down by a man robbing a Cleveland, Ohio, discount store.
An autopsy revealed that she had a genetic condition known as
mosaicism, which gave her "traces of male *and* female genitalia," as
well as male and female chromosomes. Walsh had kept her condi-

tion secret her entire life and would probably have taken it to the grave had she not been murdered. If people had known about her condition in the 1930s, she would almost certainly have been barred from competing as a woman. "Maybe that's why she refused to room with anybody else," Andersen remarked to reporters.

Reaction: In 1991, the U.S. Women's Track and Field Committee decided not to strip Walsh of her titles, concluding that her gender identity was more complex than it seemed, and that "allegations Walsh either masqueraded as a woman or was definately a man were unfair." (Gender testing of female athletes has been standard since 1966.)

BORIS ONISCHENKO, member of the USSR pentathlon team

Year: 1976

Place: Montreal

What happened: The defending silver medalist was in the middle of the fencing competition, when the British team noticed that he scored points even when his sword didn't touch his opponent's body. Olympic officials examined his sword...and discovered it had been rigged with a "hidden push-button circuit-breaker" that enabled him to score a hit every time he pushed the button.

Reaction: Soviet officials initially protested, but later "admitted" Onischenko's guilt and apologized. "He lost many of his privileges and his career was left in ruins," says Carl Schwende, fencing director for the Montreal Games. "I heard he was working as the manager of an aquatic center in Kiev...Then I learned he was found dead at the pool. Drowning, suicide, accident? My Soviet colleagues won't talk about it."

Onischenko denied any knowledge of the rigging for the rest of his life, and no one knows if he really *was* responsible. The sword may not even have been his: "The Russians had about 20 identical-looking weapons lined up for their use," Schwende says. "A fencer is handed his mask and weapons by a coach only when his name is called....It's possible someone else rigged the weapon, but we had no proof. If we had, we would have disqualified the entire Soviet team." One theory: Onischenko was sacrificed by the Soviets to save the rest of the team. But no one will ever know.

MORE LUCKY FINDS

Here are more examples of valuable things that people have
stumbled on—including one that Uncle John found...and lost.

B URIED IN THE LIBRARY
The Find: *The Inheritance*, Louisa May Alcott's first novel

Where It Was Found: On a shelf in a Harvard University library.

The Story: The manuscript, hand-written by Alcott, represents one of the grossest oversights in Western literature: it was listed in the Harvard card catalog under "*The Inheritance*, a manuscript; Boston, 1849; 166 pages, unpublished, her first novel."

Even so, probably fewer than a dozen people even knew it existed, and it didn't occur to any of them to publish it. At least five people had checked it out since the library acquired it, and a microfilm copy was made for a scholar. But that was it—the manuscript sat virtually ignored for nearly 150 years, until Joel Myerson and Daniel Shealy, two professors researching a book on Alcott, came across it in the late 1980s. They made a Xerox copy of it, took it home, and transcribed it. In 1996, they submitted it to an agent... who began shopping it to publishers and movie studios. Estimated worth: $1 million.

MESSAGE IN A BOTTLE

The Find: The will of Daisy Singer Alexander, of the Singer sewing machine family

Where It Was Found: In a bottle on a beach near San Francisco.

The Story: In 1937, the eccentric Alexander, who lived in England, made out her will, stuffed it into a bottle, and tossed it into the Thames River in London. The will read:

> To avoid any confusion, I leave my entire estate to the lucky person who finds this bottle, and to my attorney, Barry Cohen, share and share alike—Daisy Alexander, June 20, 1937.

Almost *12 years* later, in March 1949, a unemployed man named Jack Wrum (or Wurm, depending on which version you read) was wandering along a San Francisco beach when he found the bottle. To his credit, he not only opened it and read its contents, he also took it seriously enough to find out if it was real. It was—Wrum inherited $6 million up front, and $80,000 a year in income from Alexander's Singer stock.

UNCLE JOHN'S CONFESSION

The Find: A first edition of Dr. Seuss's first book, *To Think That I Saw It on Mulberry Street*...inscribed to the mother of the boy who inspired Seuss to write it

Where It Was Found: In a farmhouse in Worcester, Vermont.

The Story: In the 1970s, Uncle John rented a woodworking shop from a woman named Phyllis Keyser. It was located next to her house, and occasionally John would wander in to chat. One day, he picked up a copy of *To Think That I Saw It on Mulberry Street* from her coffee table and noticed an inscription that read something like: "To _____, the real Marco's mother. Thanks for the inspiration. From your neighbor, Ted Geisel." Uncle John knew that Dr. Seuss's real name was Theodore Geisel and that the boy in the story was named Marco. He asked Phyllis for an explanation.

"Oh," she replied, "that's my sister. She lived next to Ted Geisel in Boston. Her son, Marco, used to make up these wild stories every day when he came home from school, and that gave Geisel the idea for the first book he ever published."

Apparently, she didn't have any idea of the book's value. Uncle John offered to check it out, but the used bookstores he talked to wouldn't touch it. "You've got to bring it to a rare book dealer," they said. Unfortunately, Uncle John dropped the ball. Keyser died a few years later, and her possessions were disposed of.

First editions of Dr. Seuss's books (as well as Dr. Seuss memorabilia) have become extremely collectible since then. And until now, most experts weren't aware that this "first of the first" edition ever existed.

So, if someone out there in Bathroom Readerland has picked it up at a garage sale, you may have something worth tens of thousands of dollars!

THE EVOLUTION OF THANKSGIVING

In "Thanksgiving Myths" (see page 95), you read about how the pilgrims ate deer, not turkey, at the first Thanksgiving celebration. So how did turkey become the food of choice? Here's more info on how Thanksgiving, as we know it, came to be.

GOING NATIONAL

As late as the 1860s, Thanksgiving was exclusively a Yankee holiday. Every Northern state celebrated it (not all on the same day), but no Southern states did. There had been several efforts to make it a national holiday—the Continental Congress tried in 1777, and George Washington proclaimed a National Day of Thanksgiving in 1789. But it never caught on, thanks to people like Thomas Jefferson, who denounced the idea as a "monarchical practice" unfit for the new republic.

Early presidents occasionally proclaimed their own days of thanksgiving to mark victories on the battlefield or other good fortune. But such occasions were one-time affairs, not annual events.

ABE STEPS IN

Then, in 1863, President Abraham Lincoln proclaimed *two* national days of Thanksgiving: one on August 6, to honor Union victories at Gettysburg and Vicksburg, and one on November 26, the last Thursday of the month, to celebrate a year "filled with the blessings of fruitful fields and healthful skies."

Lincoln didn't intend to make Thanksgiving an annual event, but when General Sherman captured Atlanta in September 1864, the president declared the last Thursday in November a day of thanksgiving for the second year in a row. And after Lincoln was assassinated, succeeding presidents turned it into a tradition in his honor. As the wounds of the Civil War healed, the popularity of the holiday grew. By the 1890s, the last Thursday in November was celebrated as Thanksgiving by nearly every state in the Union.

THE BUSINESS OF THANKSGIVING

The Pilgrims aren't responsible for making turkey the center of the Thanksgiving feast (see page 95), so who is? Business historian Thomas DiBacco believes that poultry companies deserve the credit. "There is no rhyme or reason for us to have turkey on Thanksgiving, except that business promoted it," he says, adding that poultry producers in New Jersey, Pennsylvania, and Maryland began promoting turkey as Thanksgiving food after the Civil War. Why? Because at 10¢ a pound, it was more profitable than any other bird.

Illustrators followed their lead and painted Pilgrim dinners with roast turkey on the table. Soon a brand-new "tradition" was born.

The next group of businesses to cash in on Thanksgiving were turn-of-the-century retailers, who used the holiday to jump-start Christmas sales. Newspaper ads began counting down the number of shopping days until Christmas, and in 1921, Gimbel's department store in Philadelphia came up with a retailer's tour-de-force: they held the first Thanksgiving Day parade, designed to kick off the shopping season. By 1930, department stores all over the country sponsored parades to get shoppers into their stores.

FRANKSGIVING

By the late 1930s, Thanksgiving was as much the start of the Christmas shopping season as it was a holiday in its own right. That's why retailers—still trying to dig their way out of the Great Depression—were worried in 1939. Thanksgiving was traditionally the last Thursday of the month, and since there were *five* Thursdays in that November instead of the usual four, Thanksgiving fell on the very last day of the month. That meant only 20 shopping days until Christmas. In the spring of 1939, the National Retail Dry Goods Association lobbied President Franklin Roosevelt to move Thanksgiving back one Thursday to November 23, arguing that it would boost retail sales by as much as 10%. Roosevelt agreed, and announced the change during the summer.

The decision made headlines around the country. It became a political issue as traditionalists (unaware of the day's true roots) and Republicans both condemned it. "What in the name of common sense has Christmas buying to do with it?" the Rev. Norman Vincent Peale bellowed from his pulpit. "It is questionable thinking and contrary to the meaning of Thanksgiving for the president of this great nation to tinker with a sacred religious day on the spe-cious excuse that it will help Christmas sales. The next thing we may expect Christmas to be shifted to May 1 to help the New York World's Fair of 1940."

Like the proclamations that had proceeded it, Roosevelt's Thanksgiving proclamation was only binding with federal employ-ees and in the District of Columbia—the governors of individual states had to ratify the decision for it to apply to their own states. Usually this was only a technicality...but Republican governors seized on the issue as a means of discrediting Roosevelt. As Diana Carter Applebaum writes in *Thanksgiving: An American Holiday, an American History*:

> Politician watchers...began to call November 23 the Democratic Thanksgiving and November 30 the Republican Thanksgiving Day....Colorado law required that the state observe both holidays, but Republican Governor Ralph Carr vowed to eat no turkey on the 23rd. Republican Senator Styles Bridges of New Hampshire said that he wished that while he was at it, "Mr. Roosevelt would abolish winter;" and Republican Governor Nels Hanson Smith of Wyoming commended Roosevelt for finally instituting a change "which is not imposing any additional tax on the taxpayers."

FINAL SETTLEMENT

In the end, 23 states celebrated Thanksgiving on November 23 and another 23 celebrated it on November 30, with Texas and Colora-do celebrating it on both days and the city of Minneapolis celebrat-ing it from 12:01 a.m. November 23 to 11:59 p.m. November 30. The controversy might have continued to this day if retail sales had gone up as predicted. But they didn't—some retailers even suspect-ed that the confusion caused sales to *drop*. So in May 1941, Presi-dent Roosevelt announced that, beginning in 1942, Thanksgiving would again be held on the last Thursday in November.

Several congressmen, who feared that future presidents might pull similar stunts, introduced legislation to make the change per-manent. On November 26, 1941, Roosevelt signed a compromise bill: Thanksgiving would always fall on the fourth Thursday in No-vember, whether it was the last Thursday of the month or not. (Five years out of seven, it *is* the last Thursday of the month). Thanksgiving has been celebrated on that day ever since.

DOLL DISASTERS

Some dolls, like Barbie and Cabbage Patch Kids, are enormous successes. Others seemed like good (even brilliant) ideas at the time, but they fell on their little plastic butts. Here are some "sure things" that bombed.

THE "MOST WONDERFUL STORY" DOLL
Background: In 1957, Ben Michtom, president of the Ideal Toy Company, had a brainstorm: why not sell a Jesus doll? The majority of kids in America were Christian, so he figured parents would jump at the opportunity to make playtime a religious experience. Other Ideal executives were horrified, but Michtom was convinced it was a great idea. To prove it, he took his case to a higher authority; while on vacation in Italy, he got an audience with the Pope and pitched the idea to him. The Pope gave his blessing, as did every other Christian leader Michtom consulted.
What Happened: Unfortunately for Ideal, Michtom didn't consult any parents, who probably would have told him the idea was a loser...which it turned out to be. As Sydney Stern describes the doll in *Toyland: The High-Stakes Game of the Toy Industry*:

> No one bought them because parents were horrified at the idea of undressing the Jesus doll, dragging it around, sticking it in the bathtub. Nothing sold. Ordinarily, there is a no-return policy on products already shipped. But in this case it was such a horrible mistake that Ideal took them back....It appears that what Ideal did with them was give each of its employees a doll and then ground up the rest and put them in landfills.

Jesus dolls—packaged in a box that looked like the Bible—were probably the biggest doll flop in American toy history.

THE JOEY STIVIC DOLL
Background: In 1976, Ideal came out with another product that it thought was a sure thing: the "drink-and-wet" baby Joey Stivic doll, based on Archie Bunker's grandson in TV's "All in the Family." The show was the most popular sitcom of the decade, and Ideal officials figured the hype surrounding Joey's birth (on an episode of

the show) would be as huge as when Lucille Ball had her TV baby on "I Love Lucy" in the 1950s.

What Happened: "All in the Family" was daringly realistic—the first of its kind on TV, and Ideal execs decided to be just as realistic with the Joey doll. They gave him something that few little boy dolls had in the 70s: a penis. Big mistake. America was not ready for reality-based "anatomically correct" male dolls.

CHAIRMAN MAO DOLL

Background: In 1968, a U.S. company tried to import Chairman Mao dolls into the country. The dolls—manufactured in Ireland, not China—were really a joke: they showed Mao holding a copy of his little red book in front...and a bomb behind his back. Furthermore, *Newsweek* magazine reported, "each doll comes with twelve voodoo pins, just in case anyone misses the point."

What Happened: They never got off the boat. Figuring the dolls were part of a subversive plot, the Longshoreman's Union refused to unload the shipping crates. "That's definitely Communistic!" a union member exclaimed when a U.S. Customs official opened the crate, "We'd rather lose work than handle this cargo."

"I don't believe these dolls come from Ireland," one union official told reporters. "This stuff is being pushed through by some subversives—but we're on the lookout."

THE "HAPPY TO BE ME" DOLL

Background: If Barbie were life-sized, her measurements would be 38-18-28—an outrageously impossible role model for girls. That's what prompted Cathy Meredig, a 38-year-old software designer, to develop her own doll, "Happy to Be Me," in 1989. It has measurements of 36-27-38, with "rounded tummies and hips, normal sized waists, legs, chest, neck and feet." Traditional toy manufacturers balked at selling the doll, so Meredig founded High Self-Esteem Toys and began marketing it herself.

What Happened: Happy to Be Me was the toy equivalent of boiled carrots. Grown-ups loved them, but kids overwhelmingly preferred Barbie...no matter how much their parents tried to get them to switch. Meredig's company was still in business as late as 1994, but by then the dolls were only available by mail.

Psst! 68% of gossip columnists say the best place to interview a celebrity is

ZAPPED!

Irreverent comments from the late, great Frank Zappa.

"It would be easier to pay off our national debt overnight than to neutralize the long range effects of our national stupidity."

"Remember, there's a big difference between kneeling down and bending over."

"Life is like high school with money."

"It is always advisable to become a loser if you can't become a winner."

"There will never be a nuclear war—there is too much real estate involved."

"The whole universe is a large joke. Everything in the universe are just subdivisions of this joke. So why take anything too seriously?"

"Anything played wrong twice in a row is the beginning of an arrangement."

"Seeing a psychotherapist is not a crazy idea–it's just wanting a second opinion of one's life."

"Bad facts make bad laws."

"Politics is the entertainment branch of industry."

"Thanks to our schools and political leadership, the U.S. has an international reputation as the home of 250 million people dumb enough to buy 'The Wacky Wall Walker.'"

"Stupidity has a certain charm. Ignorance does not."

"Without music to decorate it, time is just a bunch of boring production deadlines or dates by which bills must be paid."

"The only thing that seems to band all nations together is that their governments are universally bad."

[*When asked by Tipper Gore whether he feels music incites people toward deviant behavior.*] "I wrote a song about dental floss, but did anyone's teeth get cleaner?"

"People who think of music videos as an art form are probably the same people who think Cabbage Patch Dolls are a revolutionary form of soft sculpture."

THE 10 WORST SNAKES TO BE BITTEN BY

In his book, Dangerous to Man, *Roger Caras included a list of the 10 snakes he'd least like to be "trapped in a phone booth with." Here's the list, with some extra info gathered by our own herpetologists.*

1. KING COBRA

The largest poisonous snake in the world. According to many experts, it's also the most dangerous. Its venom is so powerful, it can kill an elephant...and in some known instances, it actually has. Adults measure 14 feet (longest on record is 18 feet). When angered, its hoodspring expands and it "stands" with its head 5-6 feet in the air. It's found in Southeast Asia, southern China, and India.

2. TAIPAN

A 10-footer from Australia. There's enough venom in one Taipan bite to kill 100,000 mice. Also known as the "Fierce Snake," it is normally shy and prefers to escape rather than attack. Fortunately, it lives in sparsely populated areas. A person bitten by a Taipan will die in a matter of minutes.

3. MAMBA

A black or green snake from Africa. The 10- to 14-foot black mamba, which lives among rocks and in tall grass, is the largest and most feared snake in Africa. It is the world's fastest snake (burst of speed up to 15 mph) and may be the only poisonous snake known to stalk humans. Two drops of black mamba venom can kill a person in 10 minutes. The green mamba is about half as long and spends most of its life in trees. But it's just about as deadly.

4. BUSHMASTER

The world's largest viper. Found mostly in Central America, where it occupies the abandoned burrows of other animals. Particularly dangerous because, when confronted, it attacks people rather than fleeing from them, as most snakes do. Has one-inch fangs and carries enough poison to kill several people.

5. WESTERN DIAMONDBACK RATTLER

The name comes from the diamond- or hex-shaped blotches on its skin. Measures anywhere from 3 to 8 feet. Because it's aggressive and abundant, it's the cause of more serious bites and deaths than any other snake in North America. Its poison can kill a mouse in a few seconds, and a person within an hour.

6. FER-DE-LANCE

Also known as the Terciopelo (Spanish for "velvet"), it is relatively small (about 4 feet), but especially dangerous to humans because it's nervous and quick to bite. Its venom spreads through the body and causes internal bleeding. Found in tropical areas in the Americas, such as Martinique.

7. TROPICAL RATTLESNAKE

Has a venom 10 times more potent than its cousin, the Western Rattler. This variety is found predominantly in Central and South America.

8. TIGER SNAKE

Named for the yellow stripes covering its body. Usually feeds on mice, frogs, and rats. Occasionally, this 6-footer also dines on Australians. A single dose of venom induces pain, vomiting, and circulatory collapse. Mortality rate from a bite is 40%. Considered the most dangerous reptile Down Under.

9. COMMON COBRA

Also known as the Indian Cobra. It's the kind of snake tamed by Indian snake charmers and is normally a shy hunter that eats frogs and rats. However, because it lives in populated areas, it is actually more dangerous than the King Cobra. Just one bite has enough venom to kill 30 people. It grows to 4 to 5 feet long.

10. JARRACUSSU

An aquatic snake from South America with a deadly bite. Usually, a bite from one of these water-dwellers isn't necessarily fatal. But it *will* cause blindness and tissue damage.

Australia is the only continent where poisonous snakes outnumber nonpoisonous kinds.

THE HISTORY OF THE INCOME TAX

*"In this world," Benjamin Franklin wrote in 1789, "nothing can
be said to be certain, except death and taxes." We at the BRI
have written about death once in a while, but never about
taxes. We figure it's time to make amends.*

Abraham Lincoln isn't remembered as the "Father of the
Income Tax"...but he could be. In 1862, in order to raise
money to pay for the Civil War, he signed the country's
first income tax into law.

However, under this law, only people with an income over $800
a year had to pay any tax. And only 1% of the American people
made more than $800 a year in 1862...so the government wound
up having to look elsewhere for a source of money to finance the
war (they borrowed it).

TAX CONTROVERSY

From the start, the income tax was very controversial. No one was
even sure if it was legal. The Constitution had authorized the federal government to collect taxes "to pay the debts and provide for the
common welfare of the United States"—but it didn't explicitly
state that the government had the right to levy taxes on *income*.
And as this was hotly debated, public opposition grew. The first income tax was repealed in 1872.

But it wasn't dead. By the 1890s, an overwhelming majority of
Americans supported re-establishing an income tax—as long as it
applied only to the super-rich. Farm, labor, and small-business interests promoted it as a means of taking money away from millionaires and robber barons and redistributing it for the common good.

In 1894, they succeeded in passing a 2% tax on all personal and
corporate net income over $4,000. Few Americans were in that in-
come bracket...but those who were had the incentive and resources to oppose the tax. They battled it all the way to the Supreme
Court, and in 1895 the Court declared that an income tax was
unconstitutional.

Weird coincidence: Ex-presidents Thomas Jefferson and John Adams both died on July 4, 1826.

THEODORE ROOSEVELT

Opinion was divided along party lines—Democrats and Populists supported the income tax; Republicans opposed it. But in 1908, outgoing Republican president Theodore Roosevelt broke with his party and called for both an income tax *and* an inheritance tax. He wasn't able to enact either before his term ran out, but the momentum had shifted.

In the election of 1908, America sent a pro-tax Congress and an anti-tax president—Republican William Howard Taft—to Washington. Taft tried to derail the issue by proposing a Constitutional amendment permitting the personal income tax. He figured the hurdles for such an amendment were so great that the amendment would fail and the income tax issue would go away.

But he was wrong. By February 1913, less than four years after it was introduced, 36 states had ratified the 16th Amendment to the Constitution. For the first time in U.S. history, income taxes were indisputably constitutional. On October 3, 1913, President Woodrow Wilson signed the first modern income tax into law.

POPULAR TAX?

The 1913 tax was simple—the entire tax code was only 16 pages long (compared to 9,100 pages today). The rate was 1% on income over $3,000 for a single person and $4,000 for a married person, with "super taxes" as high as 6% applied to income over $500,000. In general, the tax was popular with just about everyone…because it applied to almost no one.

The few Americans who were required to pay income taxes in 1913 paid an average of $97.88 apiece.

WEAPON OF WAR

But America's entry into World War I in 1917 changed everything. The federal budget shot up from $1 billion in 1916 to $19 billion in 1919. Faced with enormous, unprecedented expenses, the Wilson administration was forced to raise the tax rate…and to broaden the tax base to include millions of Americans who had never before paid income taxes.

To insure that the new taxes were paid promptly and in full, Wilson expanded the IRS. The agency's total number of employees mushroomed from 4,000 workers in 1913 to 21,300 in 1920.

Compared to earlier income taxes, Wilson's were pretty severe. The top tax rate, applied to income over $1 million, was 77%. These taxes revolutionized the finances of the federal government; its total tax revenue went from $344 million to *$5.4 billion*...and the percentage of government revenues collected from income taxes went from 10% to 73%.

In the 1920s, income taxes were cut five different times, but they would never again be as low as they were before the war.

WORLD WAR II

The 1930s, too, were a period of relatively low taxes. The Great Depression had wiped out the earnings of most Americans. In 1939, for example, the average blue-collar employee paid no taxes, the average doctor or lawyer paid about $25 a year, and a successful business person earning $16,000 paid about $1,000. But taxes changed once more when America began gearing up for World War II.

Like the previous "Great War," World War II was a budget buster. Government expenses rose from $9.6 billion in 1940 to $95 billion in 1945—prompting the government to raise the tax rate again (the highest bracket rose to 94%).

The tax base broadened, too. In 1939, before the war, there were 6.5 million Americans on the tax rolls; they paid about $1 billion a year. By the end of the war in 1945, 48 million Americans paid $19 billion annually. To handle this, the IRS nearly doubled in size, going from 27,000 employees in 1941 to 50,000 in 1945.

For the first time, even people with ordinary incomes had to pay taxes. As the *Chicago Times* put it, World War II transformed America's income tax "from a *class* tax to a *mass* tax."

WITHHOLDING BEGINS

Another development that came about as a result of World War II was income tax withholding, which enabled the government to collect estimated taxes every pay period, not just once a year. The federal government's cash needs were so great during the war that it couldn't wait until the end of the year, and it began withholding estimated taxes from every paycheck. Similar "pay-as-you-go" plans had been used during the Civil War and World War I, but they were abandoned. This time the change was permanent.

There was a second reason for withholding: Taxes were collected from so many new taxpayers that the IRS could no longer handle the flood of tax payments that came in on tax day. It had no choice but to spread the payments out over the entire year.

INCOME TAXES TODAY

By the end of World War II the pattern for taxation had been set: wars and other crises pushed taxes up, peace and prosperity sent them back down, although rarely to where they had been before. Today's taxes seem higher than ever, but believe it or not, when you correct for inflation they're about the same as they were in the 1960s.

On the other hand, the IRS's job *is* bigger than ever—it is now the world's largest law-enforcement agency, with more than 115,000 employees. In fiscal year 1993 it processed more than 207 million tax returns, collecting more than $586 billion in personal income taxes and $1.2 trillion in other taxes. It also paid out more than $84 billion in personal refunds, and cost taxpayers more than $7.1 billion to operate. That comes to about 60¢ for every $100 collected.

☞   ☞   ☞   ☞

TAX QUOTES

"A hand from Washington will be stretched out and placed upon every man's business; the eye of the federal inspector will be in every man's counting house. . . . The law will of necessity have inquisitorial features, it will provide penalties, it will create complicated machinery. Under it men will be haled into courts distant from their homes. Heavy fines imposed by distant and unfamiliar tribunals will constantly menace the tax payer. An army of federal inspectors, spies, and detectives will descend upon the state."
—**Virginian House Speaker Richard E. Byrd,**
predicting in 1910 what would happen if
a federal income tax became law

The average human has 50 trillion cells in their body; the average elephant, 6.5 quadrillion.

"Those citizens required to do so can well afford to devote a brief time during some one day in each year to the making out of a personal return...willingly and cheerfully."

—**The House Ways and Means Committee,
recommending passage of the landmark
1913 income-tax law**

"The hardest thing in the world to understand is income taxes."
—**Albert Einstein, 1952**

☆　☆　☆　☆

BY THE YEAR 2000...

*For decades, "experts" have been making predictions about
what the year 2000 will be like. Here are a few, from*
The Bathroom Reader's Guide to the Year 2000.

"A trip down an air street to see a neighbor may be on top of an individual flying platform; a trip to Europe by rocket may take only half an hour."

—*The New York Times,* **1967**

"Housewives [will] wash dirty dishes—right down the drain! Cheap plastic would melt in hot water." And homes will be waterproof, so "the housewife of 2000 can do her cleaning with a hose."

—*Popular Mechanics,* **1950**

"We will press a button to formulate our clothing. We will have alternatives: what color, should it give off steam, do we want it to light up, do we want it to sparkle or do we prefer a matte finish, do we want it to glow in the dark, do we want an invisible shield?"

—**Betsy Johnson,** *fashion designer*

"Men of the year 2000 could enjoy exotic extras like orgasmic earlobes, replaceable sex organs, electronic aphrodisiacs, ultrasensory intercourse, and a range of ecstasy options that would make current notions of kinkiness look sedate by comparison."

—**Howard Rheingold,** *Excursions to the Far Side
of the Mind: A Book of Memes* **(1988)**

TAKE A DRINK

The background info on three of America's favorite drinks.

MOUNTAIN DEW. Invented in the 1940s by Ally Hartman of Knoxville, it was intended as a chaser for Tennessee whiskey. The original version looked and tasted like 7-Up, but after Hartman sold the formula in 1954, a succession of new owners tinkered with it. According to one account, credit for the final version goes to William H. Jones, who bought the formula in 1961 and sold it to Pepsi three years later. "He fixed it so it had just a little more tang to it, mainly by adding citrus flavoring and caffeine," a business associate recalls. "He'd take little cups marked A, B, C and D around to high schools and factories and ask people which mixture tasted best. That's how he developed his formula."

V-8 JUICE. In 1933, W. G. Peacock founded the New England Products Company and began manufacturing spinach juice, lettuce juice, and other vegetable juices. Even though the country was in the midst of a health craze, few people wanted to drink Peacock's concoctions. So he began mixing the drinks together, hoping to find something more marketable. It took about a year, but he finally came up with a drink he called Vege-min—a combination of tomato, celery, carrot, spinach, lettuce, watercress, beet, and parsley juices. The label had a huge V for Vege-min and a large 8 listing the different juices. One day, as he gave a free sample to a grocer in Evanston, Illinois, a clerk suggested he just call the product V-8.

A&W ROOT BEER. Roy Allen made a living buying and selling hotels…until he met an old soda fountain operator who gave him a formula for root beer. "You can make a fortune with a five-cent root beer," the guy told him. It was during Prohibition when beer was illegal, so Allen decided there was a market for a root beer stand that looked like a Wild West "saloon"—including a bar and sawdust on the floor. The first stand, opened in Lodi, California, in 1919, did so well that Allen opened a second one in nearby Stockton and made one of his employees, Frank Wright, a partner. In 1922, they named the company A&W, after their own initials.

Most common place to lose the remote control: under furniture.

MOVIE RATINGS

This page is rated PG for reading by general audiences. Parental Guidance is advised.

NEW KID IN TOWN
In 1966, Jack Valenti quit his job as a senior White House aide to become president of the Motion Picture Association of America. Three weeks into his new job, he attended a meeting with studio head Jack Warner concerning some foul language in Warner Bros. upcoming film, *Who's Afraid of Virginia Woolf*.

At issue were the expressions "screw you" and "hump the hostess," which had never been heard in films before. Valenti—whose job was to protect Hollywood's image—wanted the words taken out of *Virginia Woolf*; Warner—whose job was to make money—wanted to leave them in. After three hours of arguing, Warner agreed to substitute "goddam you" for "screw you," but insisted on keeping "hump the hostess." He also agreed to include the words "Suggested for Mature Audiences" in ads promoting the film.

"As I listened to Jack Warner and his associates debate whether they should cut a 'screw' and leave in a 'hump the hostess' or vice versa," Valenti recalled years later, "it dawned on me that ...the old Production Code wasn't adequate to deal with these changes anymore."

SPEAKING IN CODE

Valenti was referring to the Motion Picture Production Code, established by Hollywood executives in 1930 to keep the government from getting involved in movie censorship. The Hollywood Code served as the official list of filmmaking dos and don'ts—complete with taboo subjects like extramarital sex—for nearly 40 years. At first, if you followed The Code, your film made it into theaters. If you didn't, your film was shut out and nobody saw it. It was that simple.

But while the Production Code remained static over the next 35 years, while world changed dramatically. In fact, it became such a ridiculous standard by which to judge films that even the censors began to ignore it. By the early 1960s, movies like the double-

---

Actor Sean Connery was once selected Scotland's "Mr. Universe."

entendre-laden James Bond films sailed through the censorship process virtually untouched, when in earlier years they would have been banned.

As the film industry's censorship powers waned, increasingly controversial films made it into the theaters. The result was the movie industry's worst nightmare—local censorship groups began to spring up all over the country. The industry challenged these groups…and lost. In April 1968, the U.S. Supreme Court handed down two rulings guaranteeing the legality of state and local censorship efforts.

LETTERS OF APPROVAL

As Valenti saw it, Hollywood had to act. If local groups began setting different standards all over the country, it would be impossible to make and market films to national audiences. Movies that were acceptable in one community would be illegal to show in others. The film industry stood to lose millions.

"It didn't take long," he recalled in 1978, "to figure out that the movies would be inundated by classification systems….We could see 200 to 300 regulating bodies across the country, each with its own ideas of what was obscene and what wasn't….So we started discussing a self-regulatory system in May 1968, and had it put together by the fall."

THE ORIGINAL CODE

After more than 100 hastily called meetings, the MPAA announced its ratings system on November 1, 1968. It included four categories:

G: *General* audiences, all ages admitted

M: *Mature* audiences, parental guidance suggested, but all ages admitted

R: Restricted, children under 16 not admitted without an accompanying parent or adult (the age was later lifted to 17)

X: No one under 17 admitted

PARENTAL GUIDANCE

Now that there was a ratings system, who would rate the films? Valenti and other Hollywood executives figured that since the ratings were designed primarily with parents in mind, parents should be the ones to rate the films. The MPAA set up a board of 13 parents to watch and issue ratings on an estimated 1,200 hours' worth of films per year. This board is still in effect today: People who serve on it are paid for their time, and for some of them, it has become a full-time career. After the board rates a film, the producer can withdraw it from release for 90 days and then re-submit it for rating, with or without re-editing.

CHANGES

• Not all the original ratings survived. When the MPAA discovered that parents mistakenly thought M was stricter than R, they changed it to GP (*General audiences, Parental guidance suggested*) …then to PG (*Parental Guidance*). When parents expressed concerns that PG had become too broad a category, they split it into PG and the stricter PG-13 (*Not recommended for children under 13*).

• The X rating posed another problem. The MPAA intended that it be used for "serious" films with adult themes, such as *Midnight Cowboy, A Clockwork Orange,* and *Medium Cool.* But when they trademarked all of the other motion picture codes in 1968, the Association either declined or forgot to trademark the X rating. This left filmmakers free to use it however they wanted. It quickly became synonymous with pornography, which made it virtually useless to the MPAA and the kiss of death to serious filmmakers. Even so, the MPAA didn't change it until 1990, when it replaced X with NC-17, "No Children Under 17"—which it trademarked.

MOVIE MISCELLANY

• How successful has the ratings system been? When it was introduced in 1968, there were more than 40 local censorship boards around the country. By 1996, there were none—the last one, in Dallas, Texas, closed up shop in 1993. The City Council of Dallas abolished it, saying that the movie industry does a better job.

• Unlike the original Motion Picture Code, the MPAA's rating system is entirely voluntary, with the exception that members agree not to release films that haven't been rated. Exhibitors are responsible for enforcement; an estimated 80% to 85% follow the guidelines and keep children out of R and NC-17 films.

In 1870, it took eight days to cross the United States by train.

IRONIC DEATHS

Here's a look at more ironic deaths.

MAJOR GENERAL JOHN SEDGWICK, *commander of the Sixth Army Corps during the Civil War*
On May 9, 1864, he was sitting under a tree making battle plans with an aide when he observed that some of his soldiers were not properly positioned for the upcoming battle.

As Sedgwick got up and started walking toward the men, a lone Confederate sniper opened fire. Rather than return fire, most of the soldiers ducked or ran for cover, which made Sedgwick laugh. "What, what men!" he told them, "Dodging for single bullets? I tell you they could not hit an elephant at this distance."

Final Irony: One of Sedgwick's aides later recounted,

> before the smile which accompanied these words had departed from his lips...there was a sharp whistle of a bullet, terminating in a dull, soft sound; and he fell slowly and heavily to the earth.

Sedgwick was killed instantly.

ALAN SIMPSON, *a U.S. airman during World War II*
In 1942, he was shot down off the coast of Sicily. He was captured and spent three years in a German prisoner-of-war camp, where he was "starved, tortured, and tossed in isolation for months at a time." According to his daughter Catherine, "He always hated the Germans for what they did to him."

Final Irony: In 1989, the 67-year-old Simpson went to London, England, for a reunion with his POW buddies. As he was crossing the street on his way to the meeting place, he was run down by a bus...filled with West German tourists.

"It took forty years, but they finally got him," his daughter was quoted as saying. "He took all the punishment they could dish out during World War II, but now they've nailed him with a bus."

Hawaii is the only U.S. state that was once a kingdom.

JEAN BAPTISTE LULLY, *orchestra conductor*

Lully liked to stamp out the beat of the music on the floor with a long, pointed staff as he conducted.

Final Irony: According to one account, "One time he missed the floor, hit his own foot, got blood poisoning from the accident, and died."

RICHARD VERSALLE, *opera tenor*

In January 1996, the 63-year-old Versalle joined the cast of New York's Metropolitan Opera House to perform in a Czech opera called *The Makropulous Case*. He played an elderly law clerk who sings about a legal case that's nearly a century old.

Final Irony: In the opening scene, Versalle climbed a 10-foot ladder to reach a file cabinet in the "law office." As he reached the top, he sang the words "You can only live so long." At that moment, he fell backward from the ladder to the stage. According to the Associated Press:

> Many of the 3,000 spectators at first thought the seemingly graceful drop from the ladder was deliberate. But admiration quickly gave way to gasps and murmurs of alarm as he lay motionless on his back with his arms outstretched.

In fact, Versalle had died from a heart attack.

JIM FIXX, *author*

Fixx, who almost single-handedly started the jogging craze of the 1970s with his 1977 bestseller *The Complete Book of Running*, ran an average of 10 miles a day. He championed its health benefits: "Research has repeatedly shown that with endurance training such as running, the heart becomes a distinctly more efficient instrument."

Final Irony: In July 1984, he had just started off on a run when he suffered a massive heart attack. An autopsy revealed that two of his arteries "were sufficiently blocked to warrant a bypass operation." He was 52.

Pierre Michelin, inventor of super-safe Michelin tires, died in a car accident.

YOU'RE MY INSPIRATION

Often, fictional characters are around long after the people who inspired them have been forgotten. Ever heard of these three people, for example?

FRANCES "FRANKIE" BAKER

Inspired: The song "Frankie and Johnny"

The Story: In 1899, when she was 22 years old, Frankie shot and killed her boyfriend, Allen (not Johnny). She pled self-defense and was acquitted. But that was just the beginning of her problems. When "Frankie and Johnny" became a popular tune, she was the talk of St. Louis. She tried to get away by moving to Omaha, then to Portland. But when *Frankie and Johnny* was released as a film in 1936, she sued the film studio for defamation of character. Ironically, she lost because she convinced jurors she was *not* a "woman of easy virtue," like the character in the film. She was committed to a mental hospital in 1950 and died two years later.

GEORGE TRAIN

Inspired: *Around the World in 80 Days*

The Story: In 1870, wealthy American businessman/eccentric George Frances Train made a highly publicized trip around the world in only 80 days—an incredible speed for that time. Two years later, Jules Verne published his acclaimed novel, but called his hero Phileas Fogg. Train, the self-described "advocate of speed," was incensed. "Verne stole my thunder," he complained. He made the round-the-world trip three more times, finally breaking his own record by completing the journey in a mere 60 days.

DENNIS PATRICK CASEY

Inspired: The poem "Casey at the Bat"

The Story: Baseball fans have long wondered about the hero in Ernest L. Thayer's 1888 poem. Who was he? Convincing evidence points to Dennis P. Casey, a popular star with the Baltimore Orioles at the time. Casey's pitching and hitting elevated the team into "First Division" in the American Association, a feat no Baltimore team had accomplished.

The word "television" means to "see at a distance."

THE MUNSTERS

Here are some things you didn't know about
TV's weirdest sitcom family.

HOW IT STARTED

In 1963, Joe Connelly and Bob Mosher were considering ideas for a new sitcom. Their 1950s hit *Leave It to Beaver,* was about to go off the air. Their 1961 sitcom *Ichabod & Me* had flopped.

Universal Pictures had recently dusted off its classic horror films —*Frankenstein, Dracula, The Mummy,* etc.—and sold them to TV. Monsters had quickly become a fad, with baby boom kids buying monster models, wallets, cards, toys, and dozens more products.

Connelly and Mosher saw a chance to bring back the Cleavers: turn them into monsters. A family of middle-class monsters in a typical suburb would make the same old sitcom plots seem new.

They were excited about the prospect, but weren't sure how the networks would react. So they assembled a crew of experienced actors—including Fred Gwynne and "Grandpa" Al Lewis (both fresh from *Car 54, Where Are You?*), and shot a 15-minute pilot episode. "It was pretty bizarre" Gwynne recalled. "They hadn't figured out the costumes or the laughs. God only knows how they ever sold it on those fifteen minutes, because it was just awful."

But they did sell it—right away. According to Norman Abbot, who directed the pilot: "We had everybody from the studio at the soundstage watching the filming. Somebody called the people from the head office and told them to come down and see it. It was wild. Jim Aubrey, [president of] CBS, bought it instantly."

INSIDE FACTS

Start and Stop

The Munsters premiered on April 30, 1964 —the same week that ABC first aired its own monster sitcom, *The Addams Family.* And it was cancelled in 1966—ironically, the same week *The Addams Family* was dumped. Which show was more popular? *The Munsters.* It ranked #18 on the list of the most popular shows of 1964-5. The

---

The first Chamber of Commerce in the U.S. was organized in 1912.

Addamses ranked 23rd. By the second season, however, the novelty of both shows had worn off, and ratings were only mediocre.

Making the Monster

• It took two hours to transform the bony 6' 5", 180-pound Fred Gwynne into Herman Munster. His face was covered with grease, balloon rubber, and yellow-green makeup (even though the show was filmed in black-and-white).

• He wore pants stuffed with foam and a shrunken jacket stuffed with foam in the shoulders and arms. The costume was so heavy and hot that he lost 10 lbs. during the first weeks of shooting.

• Gwynne's boots had 5" heels and weighed 10 lbs. They were intentionally hard to walk in, so he'd have a clumsy, "lurching" walk.

Yvonne to Be Alone

• Yvonne De Carlo's (Lily's) makeup wasn't as difficult as Gwynne's, but she hated it as much—and had five different hairdressers fired during the show's two-year run. She complained that her makeup made her look older, and even tried to paint out the grey streak that ran through her wig (the producers made her put it back in).

• She also refused to paint her own nails black, which meant she had to have fake nails glued on every day. They wouldn't stay attached; often shooting had to be suspended while De Carlo and the crew looked around the set for the nails that had fallen off.

• De Carlo didn't even want the part. "I did the show in the beginning for one reason only—I needed money at the time." Her husband, a stuntman, had been critically injured during the filming of *How the West Was Won*, and De Carlo had exhausted her savings nursing him back to health.

THE COFFIN CAPER

• Grandpa's car, the *Dragula*, was a dragster with a real coffin as a body. It wasn't easy to build. When George Barris, the car's designer, tried to buy a coffin for it, he couldn't find a funeral home that would cooperate. "They wouldn't sell one unless you were dead." Finally, Barris had someone leave an envelope full of money at a funeral home while "my guys picked up a casket and walked out with it. We literally spooked off with the casket."

The average human sheds 40 lbs. of dead skin in their lifetime.

THE 10 MOST-WANTED LOST FILMS

Only about 20% of the silent movies made between 1895 and the late 1920s (when talkies began) still survive. Many were discarded as worthless. Others, made on fragile film, have crumbled into dust. Today people are searching for—and sometimes finding—masterpieces of the silent era. In 1980, the American Film Institute (AFI) compiled this list of the 10 most historically and artistically significant "lost films." It is supplied by Gregory Lukow at AFI.

THE LIST, IN ALPHABETICAL ORDER

1. CAMILLE (1927). Norma Talmadge played the title role in one of her last triumphs. A legend of the silent screen, Talmadge watched her career all but vanish with the arrival of the "talkies." Apparently her voice did not match her image, and when audiences stopped buying tickets, the studios—which she'd helped to build—unceremoniously dropped her. Not a frame of this film (which was remade in 1937 with Greta Garbo) is known to exist.

2. CLEOPATRA (1917). This lavish half-million dollar epic featured Theda Bara, the original vamp of the silent era, as the sexy queen of the Nile. Sadly, only two of Bara's 38 films have survived. Her body of work is considered one of the lost treasures of the silent era, with *Cleopatra* the crown jewel.

3. THE DIVINE WOMAN (1928). Greta Garbo starred in 10 silent films before shifting to sound in 1930. *The Divine Woman* was her first starring role, and the only one of her films that hasn't survived. One reel was recently located in the former Soviet Union; the rest is still missing.

4. FRANKENSTEIN (1910). The first horror film (see p. 80). This version, made by Thomas Edison, has turned up in a private collection. But because the American Film Institute has no access to the film, they keep it on their list.

Sarah Josepha Hale's 1830 poem "Mary Had a Little Lamb" was inspired by a little

5. GREED (1925). Scholars and film critics consider this the Holy Grail of lost films. The original version—40 reels and 10 hours—was the masterpiece of one of film's most talented directors, Erich von Stroheim. It was released in a butchered version over von Stroheim's vociferous protests. The rest of the film was discarded. No one knows what happened to it.

6. THE KAISER, BEAST OF BERLIN (1918). Part of a series of short anti-German propaganda films made during the World War I period. Directed by and starring Rupert Julian as the Kaiser. U.S. historians are especially interested in this one.

7. LITTLE RED RIDING HOOD (1922). This was Walt Disney's first cartoon, produced six years before the introduction of Mickey Mouse in *Steamboat Willie*. Posters and a few sketches are all that remain.

8. LONDON AFTER MIDNIGHT (1927). Produced at the height of horror star Lon Chaney's short career, and hailed as a masterwork when it was released. Chaney stars as a detective who turns into a vampire at night. The false teeth he wore caused him so much pain that he was unable to keep them on for more than a few minutes at a time. Directed by Tod Browning.

9. THE ROGUE SONG (1930). Would be considered just another forgettable operetta, if it didn't contain a few non-musical scenes of Laurel and Hardy in their only known color film. It's also Laurel and Hardy's last short film. (In the '30s, they worked exclusively in features.) A three-minute segment, the original trailer, and the soundtrack (which was released as an album in 1980) are all that remain.

10. THAT ROYALE GIRL (1925). The story of an innocent girl saved from her accusers by a loving district attorney was the second film that legendary director D. W. Griffith made with W. C. Fields. Griffith was reportedly uncomfortable with the contemporary setting (he liked historical epics). However, given his status as one of the great directors of all time, and Fields's as a great comedian, film scholars would love to get another chance to see this.

FAMILIAR ORIGINS

More origins of everyday phrases.

THAT'S A LOAD OF BULL

Meaning: It's a lie or exaggeration.

Origin: It's logical to assume that this phrase started with cow-chips…but it turns out that *boule* is an Old French verb meaning "to lie."

CLAP-TRAP

Meaning: Meaningless talk; empty speech.

Origin: "Claptrap" comes from the theater. It describes any line that the playwright inserts—often knowing it's terrible—just to get applause. It's literally "a trap to catch a clap."

RED-LETTER DAY

Meaning: Special occasion or day.

Origin: As far back as the Middle Ages, Christian church calendars and almanacs had feast days, saint days, and other holy days printed in red ink; everything else was printed in black ink.

IF YOU CAN DO IT, I'LL EAT MY HAT

Meaning: I don't believe you can do it.

Origin: Why would anyone offer to eat a hat under *any* circumstances? Answer: The original hat in this expression was "hatte," an English dish that contained eggs, veal, dates, saffron, and salt. Over time, the meaning of the phrase evolved into the ridiculous proposition it *sounded* like.

MY BETTER HALF

Meaning: My spouse.

Origin: The Puritan view of people was that we're made up of two halves: a body and a soul. The soul—our spiritual side—was considered our better half. In the 16th century, the English writer Sir Philip Sidney became the first person to apply the term to the union between a married couple. By the 18th century, his use of the expression had become the most common.

Of the top 10 moneymaking Hollywood films, only *Forrest Gump* won the Best Picture Oscar.

CELEBRITY SWEEPSTAKES

Three big stars—three big products. What could go wrong with these endorsements? Try divorce, sex, and alcoholism. Here are more surefire celebrity promotions that didn't quite turn out as expected.

MADONNA
In January 1989, Pepsi agreed to pay Madonna $5 million for a two-minute commercial featuring her brand-new single, "Like a Prayer."

What they wanted: Publicity. Pepsi planned to show its "Like a Prayer" ad the night *before* the world premier of Madonna's video on MTV. So it was the first chance for Madonna fans to see her sing it. Madonna was so popular—and the deal so unusual—that Pepsi's "coup" became front-page news. They showed the ad simultaneously on all three TV networks, and in 40 countries.

What they got: A scandal. Incredibly, nobody at Pepsi previewed Madonna's video before they built their campaign around it. Their ad featured Madonna going back to her eighth birthday. But the *video* was full of sexually suggestive scenes and provocative religious symbolism—including "a scantily clad Madonna singing in front of burning crosses, suffering wounds on her hands like Jesus and kissing a saintly statue that turns into a man."

What happened: Pepsi had purposely linked its ad campaign to the video, and they were stuck with it. Fundamentalist Christians turned their wrath on the "blasphemous" soft drink company. Sensing a consumer boycott in the making, Pepsi cancelled the whole deal within 24 hours. Madonna cried all the way to the bank. "It's just what I'd expect from her," a friend said, "She doesn't have any obligations to Pepsi…and still gets to keep their money."

BURT REYNOLDS
In 1992, the Florida Department of Citrus hired Reynolds to promote Florida orange juice in a $16 million ad campaign.

What they wanted: A believable spokesperson. Reynolds was a native Floridian with a pleasant, good ol' boy image. Plus, he and his wife, actress Loni Anderson, had actually *left* Hollywood to live in the Sunshine State. "I'm kind of Mr. Florida," he told reporters modestly. "I know a lot of the growers, and I'm proud to speak for them."

What they got: "The world's ugliest and most public divorce." Anderson filed for divorce in June 1993, and nearly every detail of the split was played out in the tabloids. Most accounts blamed Reynolds for the breakup. And he didn't do much to help the situation when he admitted to the *National Enquirer* that he'd had a two-year affair with a Florida cocktail waitress.

What happened: The Citrus commission pulled the ads. "What was happening in his personal life, at the level it was being played out, overshadowed the message we were trying to communicate," a spokesman told reporters. Reynolds no longer drinks Florida orange juice, and blames the Florida Citrus commission for cashing in on his failed marriage. "They took the opportunity . . . to cash in on the P.R. from my divorce, saying I wasn't the right image for them. Yeah, like Anita Bryant is. Or Rush Limbaugh."

BRUCE WILLIS

In the mid-1980s, Willis was hired to plug Seagram's Wine Coolers for an estimated $2 to $3 million a year.

What they wanted: A macho, good-time spokesman to make their wine coolers acceptable to young male drinkers.

What they got: A huge success—albeit with some bad publicity. Seagrams' brand-new product quickly became the bestselling cooler in the country. Then, in May 1987, Willis was arrested for "scuffling" with police officers who were called to his home to break up a loud, drunken party. The charges were dropped after Willis apologized to his neighbors and promised to move away.

What happened: Seagrams stuck by its man, apparently thinking that his drunk and disorderly behavior was *good* for their product—or at least didn't hurt it.

But Willis was finally dumped in 1988 after:

1. The *National Enquirer* ran a story saying he had an alcohol problem, and

2. His wife, Demi Moore, began a public campaign against alcohol abuse.

Sure, and they can quit any time: 21% of U.S. smokers say they don't believe nicotine's addictive.

SEINFELD ON…

Comments by Jerry Seinfeld, sent to us by BRI member Ben Brand.

PAPERWEIGHTS

"Nothing compares with the paperweight as a bad gift. To me, there's no better way…to [say] to someone, 'I refused to put any thought into this at all.'…And where are these people working that papers are just blowing right off of their desks, anyway? Is their office screwed to the back of a flatbed truck going down the highway? Are they typing up in the crow's nest of a clipper ship? What do you need a paperweight for? Where's the wind coming from?"

DOCTORS

"People love to recommend their doctor to you. I don't know what they get out of it, but they really push them on you. 'He's the best. This guy's the best.' There can't be this many 'bests.' Someone's graduating at the bottom of the classes. Where are these doctors? Is someone somewhere saying to their friend, 'You should see my doctor, he's the worst. He's the absolute worst there is. Whatever you've got, it'll be worse after you see him. The man's an absolute butcher.'"

BOXING

"The simplest, stupidest sport of all. It's almost as if these two guys are just desperate to compete with each other, but they couldn't think of a sport. So they said, 'Why don't we just pound each other for forty-five minutes? Maybe someone will come watch that.'"

PLANE CRASHES

"I don't know why people always have the same reaction when they hear about a plane crash. 'Plane crash? What airline? Where was it going?' As if it makes a difference, like you're going to go, 'Oh that flight. Oh, OK, that I can understand.' Like there's some planes that are expected to crash.

"You go up to the ticket agent. 'Excuse me, this flight generally goes down quite a bit, doesn't it?'

"'Actually it does, yes. We do have another flight, but it explodes on take-off. It is, however, a snack flight.'"

New York's Central Park is almost twice as big as the entire country of Monaco.

TOY FACTS

*The BRI takes a look at random info on some
childhood (and adulthood) classics.*

NERF BALLS

After successfully inventing the game Twister (see p. 87), Reynolds Guyer decided to become a full-time toy designer. He quit his family's business and formed his own toy design firm. One of his company's first efforts was a game based on a caveman theme. It involved hiding money under foam rubber rocks and defending the loot by throwing some of the rocks at an opponent.

"Pretty soon," Guyer recalls, "we found we really enjoyed throwing the rocks. Then someone decided that the rocks were not as round as they would like, so they began shaping them, cutting them with scissors," until they were balls. Guyer soon abandoned the caveman theme entirely and focused on the balls. He made up the name "Nerfs" to communicate what he thought of as their "soft, friendly nature." Within a decade Nerf became one of the largest lines of sports/action toys on earth.

MAGIC SLATE

In the early 1920s, R. A. Watkins, owner of a small printing plant in Illinois, was approached by a man who wanted to sell him the rights to a homemade device made of waxed cardboard and tissue. You could write on it, but the messages could be easily erased by lifting up the tissue. Watkins couldn't make up his mind; he told the man to come back the next day.

In the middle of the night, Watkins's phone rang; it was the man calling from jail. He said that if Watkins would bail him out, he'd *give* Watkins the rights to the invention. The printer agreed. He wound up getting a patent for the device—which he called Magic Slate. Since then, tens of millions have been sold.

PICTIONARY

Robert Angel, a Seattle waiter, used to entertain his friends at parties by selecting a word from the dictionary, drawing it, and having them guess what it was. He didn't think about developing it into a game until Trivial Pursuit became popular. Then he spent eight months looking up 6,000 words in the dictionary (2,500 made it into the game) while a friend designed "word cards" and the board. He borrowed $35,000 to manufacture the game and started selling it to stores in Seattle out of the trunk of his car.

He got his big break when Nordstrom ordered 167 games. They didn't even have a game department. "They let us set up a table in the accessories department," Angel recalls. "If anybody glanced in our direction, we would yell at them to come and watch us play the game." Tom McGuire, a salesman at Selchow & Righter (manufacturer of Trivial Pursuit), played Pictionary at Nordstrom with his family. He was so impressed that he quit his job and began marketing it full time. By the end of 1987, over $90 million worth of Pictionary games had been sold in the United States alone.

☞   ☞   ☞   ☞

MISCELLANY

• Tonka Toys was originally called the Mound Metalcraft Company. It was renamed *Tonka* after Lake Minnetonka, which dominated the scenery around their factory.

• Mattel got its name from its two founders—Harold *Mat*son and *El*liot Handler. Handler was in the picture frame business in L.A. In 1946 he had a bunch of extra frame slats, so he and Matson built doll furniture out of them.

• Mattel was the first toy company to advertise on national TV. In 1955 they sold toy burp guns on "The Mickey Mouse Club."

• Mr. Potato Head used to come with a pipe—which bugged anti-smoking activists. "It's not only dangerous to his health," complained Surgeon General C. Everett Koop, "it also passes on the message to kids that smoking is okay." In 1987, Hasbro gave in; after 35 years of smoking, Mr. Potato Head surrendered his pipe to the Surgeon General. Koop was so pleased that he named Mr. Potato Head "Official Spokespud" for the Great Smokeout.

• World record: A game of Twister was played by 4,160 participants on May 2, 1987 at the University of Massachusetts.

MORE STRANGE LAWSUITS

Here are more real-life examples of unusual legal battles.

THE PLAINTIFF: Mary Verdev, a 73-year-old Milwaukee resident

THE DEFENDANT: St. Florian Catholic Church

THE LAWSUIT: In 1990, the church's 300-pound electronic bingo board fell on Verdev. She sued, claiming it had caused $90,000 worth of injuries. She also said that as a result of the accident, she now found herself sexually attracted to women and had begun to experience spontaneous orgasms, "sometimes in clusters."

THE VERDICT: Verdev wouldn't undergo a psychological exam ordered by the judge. He dismissed the case.

THE PLAINTIFF: Three-year-old Stacy Pevnev

THE DEFENDANT: Three-year-old Jonathan Inge

THE LAWSUIT: In February 1996, the two children were playing in the sandbox at a local park in Boston. Jonathan apparently kicked Stacy, and the parents argued heatedly. Then Stacy's mom went to court and asked that Jonathan be restrained from using the playground when Stacy was there. "Maybe it's a little emotional, maybe it's overprotective, but you do what you can," she said.

THE VERDICT: Amazingly, Superior Court Judge Charles Spurlock actually granted a temporary restraining order. Then he called the families to court and ordered them to stay separated at the playground.

THE PLAINTIFF: Richard Loritz

THE DEFENDANT: San Diego County

THE LAWSUIT: Loritz was imprisoned for three months in 1995. During that time, he says, he asked for dental floss and was refused. As a result, he developed four cavities. He sued for $2,000 in dental expenses.

THE VERDICT: The case was thrown out of court.

President Lyndon Johnson used to give electric toothbrushes with presidential seals as gifts.

THE PLAINTIFF: Sharon Silver

THE DEFENDANT: Gerald Pfeffer, her ex-husband

THE LAWSUIT: After the couple divorced in 1985, Silver moved out of state. Pfeffer stayed in their St. Paul, Minnesota, home. In 1988, the reunion committee of Silver's high school class sent an "update" questionnaire to her old address. Pfeffer filled it out and returned it. A sample of his answers:

Current occupation: "Retired on third husband's divorce settlement."

Current interests / hobbies: "Night clubbing and partying. Looking for new and wealthier husbands."

Recent outrageous / unusual / interesting experience: "Going to W. Virginia on the job and having an affair with two different guys while my third husband was in Minnesota working two jobs."

The committee printed these (and other) answers in its newsletter. Silver sued for libel; her ex-husband argued that it was all true.

THE VERDICT: After three years of litigation, the case was settled out of court for $75,000—$50,000 from Gerald, $25,000 from the Harding High School Class of 1958. "Well, I thought they were pretty good answers at the time," Pfeffer commented afterward.

THE PLAINTIFF: Kenneth Parker

THE DEFENDANT: Nevada State Prison

THE LAWSUIT: Parker was an inmate, serving 15 years for robbery. He wanted to buy two jars of chunky peanut butter from the prison canteen. (Cost: $5.) But the canteen had only one jar of chunky peanut butter. When they had to substitute a jar of creamy for the second one, Parker sued for "mental and emotional pain," asking for $5,500 and the imprisonment of a prison official.

THE VERDICT: The case went on for two years. It was finally dismissed.

THE PLAINTIFF: Jeannine Pelletier and her husband

THE DEFENDANT: Fort Kent Golf Club in Portland, Maine

THE LAWSUIT: Pelletier hit a golf ball in the spring of 1995 that bounced back and bonked her on the nose. She and her husband sued—she for physical damages, he for "loss of consortium."

THE VERDICT: The Maine Supreme Court awarded her $40,000. Her husband got zilch.

In his entire lifetime, King Louis XIV bathed three times.

CELEBRITY GOSSIP

A few random bits of gossip you've probably never heard. They're supplied by Jack Mingo, whose book The Juicy Parts *is full of great tidbits like these.*

MICK JAGGER

"About the time Mick started dating girls, his mother started selling Avon. When his parents were out, he would invite a girl to the house where they would sit at his mother's dressing table trying on her makeup. One of his dates remembers, 'He just seemed happy letting me put lipstick and mascara on him. Then he'd do the same for me. It did strike me as very strange at the time, but it was all in fun. Dating Mick was more like being with one of the girls.'"

HENRY FORD

"The automobile tycoon believed in reincarnation. Since he was born a few weeks after the battle of Gettysburg, he decided he had been a soldier killed in that battle. And later in life, he decided his niece was really the reincarnation of his mother."

W. C. FIELDS

"He didn't like to carry a lot of cash while on the road, so wherever he was, he opened a bank account. He claimed to have 700 of them in banks all over the world—including London, Paris, Sydney, and Cape Town. Usually these accounts were open under his real name, but sometimes he used odd aliases like Figley E. Whitesides, Sneed Hearn, Dr. Otis Guelpe, and (in Madrid, Spain), 'Señor Guillermo McKinley.' After his death, only about three dozen accounts were located."

MICHAEL JACKSON

• "What started him on plastic surgery? According to one report, it was because he hated the fact that he was growing up to look like his father."

• "He once met Andy Warhol and Alfred Hitchcock and thought, for some reason, that they were brothers."

• "He's been reported as saying he believes human beings can fly."

The White House was known as the White House even before it was painted white.

HARPO MARX

"In Harpo's professional debut with the Marx Brothers, he looked out at the audience…and immediately wet his pants."

WALT DISNEY

• "The animator shared an apartment with his brother Roy until Roy got married. Then Walt, feeling abandoned, decided that he (as he put it) 'needed a new roommate' and three months later, took a bride himself. His honeymoon night was spent on a train from Idaho to California; his behavior was strictly Mickey Mouse: he developed a 'toothache' and spent the entire night shining shoes in the porter's car 'to keep his mind off the pain.' "

• "Walt's famous 'trademark' signature was designed by a studio artist. He often had to insist he really *was* Walt Disney to autograph seekers who thought he was putting them on."

RICHARD NIXON

• "In first grade, his mother made a point of telling his teacher, 'Never call him Dick—I named him Richard.' Every day he wore a freshly starched white shirt with a black bow tie and knee pants, and his teacher was quoted as saying later that she could not remember him ever getting dirty."

• "He took great pains in brushing his teeth, was careful to gargle, and before he left for school asked his mother to smell his breath to make sure he would not offend anyone on the bus. He didn't like to ride the school bus, because the other children didn't smell good."

THE BEATLES & MUHAMMAD ALI

"In 1963, during their first American tour, the world-famous Beatles tried to meet heavyweight boxing champion Sonny Liston, who was going to fight Cassius Clay (later known as Muhammad Ali) for the championship in a few days. He refused to have anything to do with 'a bunch of faggots.' Instead, they met Clay. He bossed them around for the photographers, commanding them to the canvas with 'Get down, you little worms!'

"Lennon, however, got the last laugh. While Clay was talking with them, he used one of his favorite lines: 'You guys ain't as dumb as you look.' John Lennon looked him in the eye and said, 'No, but you are.' "

MUCH ADO ABOUT SNORING

*They say that if your spouse snores loudly enough to keep you awake,
one of the best things to do is lay down on the living room couch
and read until you fall asleep. Uncle John suggests saving
this chapter for just such an occasion.*

SNORE BY ANY OTHER NAME

There's an old saying: "Laugh, and the world laughs with you. Snore, and you sleep alone." But you won't *snore* alone. It's estimated that every night, as much as half the population of the world is snoring, too.

What, exactly, *is* snoring?

• When you go to sleep, the muscles that control the soft tissue in your mouth—your tongue, soft palate, uvula (the piece of flesh hanging down in the back of your mouth), tonsils, and adenoids—begins to relax.

• The deeper you sleep, the more these soft tissues relax. In some people, they actually begin to obstruct the airway. When this happens, the air that flows in and out of your mouth makes the tissues vibrate, causing the snoring sound.

WHO SNORES?

• Anyone can snore; doctors estimate that as many as 90 million Americans over the age of 18 do. But the problem is worst among people over sixty (65% of people over 60 snore), especially for males.

• For that matter, men snore more than women in just about every age group. Men have more muscles in their necks and throats than women, which means they have more to go flabby as they age.

• Girth is a factor, too. People who are overweight are three times more likely to snore than people who aren't. Why? Sleep experts point to two causes:

1. Overweight people generally have less muscle tone than people of average weight—including in their mouths. Poorly

---

According to the record books, an Englishman named Melvin Switzer is the world's loudest toned flesh flaps aroud more than toned flesh, which increases the likelihood of snoring.

2. Overweight people actually gain weight *inside* their mouths; and the more fleshy tissue in the mouth, the more likely you are to have a snore-causing obstruction.

There are also external reasons for snoring:

• Colds, allergies, nasal infections, and anything else that stops up the nose can cause snoring. Why? The sufferer has to breathe more forcefully than normal through the mouth—which increases the chance of blockage.

• People who take depressants—including alcohol and sleeping pills—snore more than people who don't, because of the relaxing effect they have on the body.

• Smoking doesn't usually cause snoring, but can aggravate the condition because it irritates the pharynx and causes mucous membranes to swell.

SNORE CURES

Quick Fixes

• Snoring is usually worst when you sleep on your back, because the soft tissue in your mouth slumps backward, blocking the airway. That's why many traditional cures aim at preventing people from sleeping on their backs. During the Revolutionary War, soldiers forced to bunk together sometimes sewed small cannonballs to the backs of the nightshirts of anyone who snored to keep them off their backs. Not much has changed—a common cure for snoring today is the "snore ball," a tennis ball in a sock that snorers fasten to the back of their pajama tops.

• Another trick that may help: raising the head of your bed four inches by placing bricks, phone books, etc., under the bed. Sleeping with more than one pillow won't do the trick. In fact, it'll probably make snoring worse by bending your body either at the neck or the waist, both of which can increase snoring. (Switching from feather to synthetic pillows can also help, if snoring is caused by allergies.)

• A preventative: Chewing two or three pieces of gum at a time may help, some sleep researchers think, by reducing flab and increasing muscle tone inside your mouth.

snorer. He has been recorded snoring as loudly as 91 decibels, more noise than is made by a

- If snoring is really serious, there are plenty of high-tech solutions. Tongue retainers and other appliances are available. Or you can try a "continuous positive air pressure" (CPAP) pump that blows a steady stream of air into your nostrils while you sleep. And if nothing else works, there's surgery: Surgeons can, for example, move your tongue forward and stitch the underlying muscle to the chin bone, so that nothing flops back into the airway during sleep.

DEADLY SNORES

- Snoring can actually be fatal. More than half of all chronic snorers over age 40 suffer from "sleep apnea." In these people, the airway becomes *totally* obstructed, cutting off the oxygen supply to their brain for as long as sixty seconds before they wake up enough to clear the obstruction. Not all sleep apnea sufferers survive. Every year, more than 2,500 of them die from cardiac arrest brought on by the condition.

- Sleep apnea may have other unfortunate side effects. It is believed to cause high blood pressure, an increased pulse, and an enlarged heart, and may also increase the risk of strokes.

- And because it disrupts the deep sleep that provides the most rest, sleep apnea also poses indirect health risks: Sufferers are often physically exhausted during the day, thus more prone to on-the-job accidents and other injuries. More than 20% of sleep apnea victims have been in car accidents caused when they fall asleep at the wheel.

LIFE SAVERS

To be fair, we should also point out that snoring can also *save* lives. This article, reported by Reuters News Service, appeared in newspapers recently:

> A London undertaker was terrified when he heard snores coming from a coffin in which 85-year-old Rose Hanover had been laid out for burial....She had collapsed and apparently died in her home. Two hours after arriving at the parlor, Mrs. Hanover began to snore, even though she had been pronounced dead by a doctor using the normal breathing and heart tests. Last night she was sitting up in a hospital bed and was reported to be much improved.

power lawnmower. (Big surprise: His wife is deaf in one ear.)

SHAKESPEARE'S INSULTS

*Shakespeare was a master at hurling off an insult or two.
Here are some of his meanest, wittiest, and cruelest.*

"The tartness of his face sours grapes."
— *Coriolanus*

"[You] leather-jerkin, crystal-button, knot-pated, agate-ring, puke-stocking, caddis-garter, smooth-tongue, Spanish pouch!"
— *Henry IV, Part 1*

"You are as a candle, the better part burnt out."
— *Henry IV, Part 2*

"He never broke any man's head but his own, and that was against a post when he was drunk."
— *Henry V*

"[Your] face is not worth sun-burning."
— *Henry V*

"You blocks, you stones, you worse than senseless things!"
— *Romeo and Juliet*

"Your horrid image doth unfix my hair."
— *Macbeth*

"His brain is as dry as the remainder biscuit after a voyage."
— *As You Like It*

"It is certain that when he makes water, his urine is con-gealed ice."
— *Measure for Measure*

"I durst not laugh, for fear of opening my lips and receiving [your] bad air."
— *Julius Caesar*

"Thy food is such as hath been belch'd on by infected lungs."
— *Pericles*

"[Your] face is Lucifer's privy-kitchen, where he doth noth-ing but roast malt-worms."
— *Henry IV, Part 2*

"He has not so much brain as ear-wax."
— *Troilus and Cressida*

"Though [he] is not naturally honest, [he] is so sometimes by chance."
— *The Winter's Tale*

"He's a most notable coward, an infinite and endless liar, an hourly promise-breaker, and the owner of no one good quality."
— *All's Well
That Ends Well*

When migrating birds fly in a "V" formation, it increases their range by as much as 70%.

MORE TAXING TRIVIA

Here are a few additional ways that income tax has shaped our culture.

H & R BLOCK

Encouraged by their mother to go into business together, Henry Bloch and his brother Richard formed the United Business Company in 1946. They planned to provide bookkeeping, management, and other services to businesses, but they spent so much time helping their customers fill out tax forms that they decided to focus on tax preparation exclusively.

• To give their business a more personal touch, they decided to name it after themselves. But rather than have customers mispronounce their name as "blotch," they changed the spelling to match the way the name is pronounced. Today, H&R Block preparers fill out one of every ten income tax returns filed with the IRS.

BOOSTING THE CREDIT CARD

In 1958, the IRS began requiring taxpayers with expense accounts to list each of their unreimbursed expenses on their tax returns. To avoid this extra record keeping, many employers issued credit cards—which itemize all purchases in the monthly billing statement—to employees with expense accounts. Result: Credit card companies reported the largest sales increases in history.

HISTORIC SWITCH

Ronald Reagan made so much money as a Hollywood actor that he ended up in the 94% tax bracket. In his autobiography *An American Life*, he revealed that the tax was instrumental in converting him from a New Deal Democrat to a conservative Republican.

"The IRS took such a big chunk of my earnings," he wrote, "that after a while I began asking myself whether it was worth it to keep on taking work. Something was wrong with a system like that. When you have to give up such a large percentage of your income in taxes, incentive to work goes down."

BATHROOM NEWS

Bits and pieces of bathroom trivia we've flushed out over the years.

WORLD NEWS

- **In Paris:** Concerned about the estimated 500,000 tons of poop that Parisian dogs deposit on city streets each year, Pierre Pascallon, Conservative member of Parliament, introduced a bill in the National Assembly requiring the installation of dog *toilets*—to be known as *canisettes*. To pay for it, he proposed that dog owners pay a graduated tax in proportion to how much their dogs weigh.

- **In Malaysia:** The government announced that it is now illegal for restaurants to substitute toilet paper as table napkins. Punishment: $80 in fines (with jail time for repeat offenders).

- **On Mt. Everest:** A state-of-the-art, $10,000 outhouse is being erected about 4 miles up the side of Mount Everest. "Until now, climbers and Sherpas have had to go off and find boulders and bushes to hide behind," a spokesman for the company doing the installation told reporters. The outhouse will help control Mt. Everest's growing waste problem. Since Sir Edmund Hillary first scaled the 29,000-foot summit in 1953, hundreds of Everest climbers have discarded tons of garbage and "other" waste—which decomposes very slowly in the frigid, low-oxygen environment.

AN HISTORIC MOMENT

What was it like to be the second person to walk on the lunar surface? Astronaut Edwin "Buzz" Aldrin, who followed Neil Armstrong moments after Armstrong made his famous first step, described the experience in an interview for British television: "I held onto the near edge of the landing gear and checked my balance and then hesitated a moment....I am the first person to wet his pants on the moon."

THE BATHROOM CRIME BLOTTER

- In 1993, Barry Lyn Stoller, a Seattle drywall installer, took some

Ex-Lax to cure his constipation…and when it didn't work, he wrote the folks at Ex-Lax demanding a refund. The company mailed him a check…with his *zip code* entered as the dollar amount. Stoller deposited the $98,002 in the bank, withdrew it a few days later…and hasn't been seen since.

• In 1994, Milton Ross was videotaped urinating into his office's coffeepot, part of an "an ongoing feud" he had with a co-worker. (Office employees had installed the video camera after noticing that their coffee tasted funny.) Ross's co-workers turned the tape over to the police…*and* the media, which broadcast it all over the world. Ross pled guilty to third-degree assault. He was sentenced to 100 hours of community service, which the judge stipulated had to be spent cleaning public restrooms.

• In October 1995, Gerald Finneran, described as "one of the world's leading authorities on Latin American debt," exploded into rage on a United Airlines flight from Buenos Aires to New York, after a flight attendant refused to serve him another drink. According to witnesses, Finneran assaulted the flight attendants, then "defecated on a serving cart, cleaned himself with the airline's first-class linens, and thus left an odor that remained in the cabin for the remaining four hours of the flight." Ordinarily, such a flight might have been diverted to a closer airport. But the president of Portugal was on board, which made a detour impossible.

PUBLIC SERVICE ANNOUNCEMENT

Do toilet seat covers really protect us against anything? According to David Feldman, in *Why Do Clocks Run Clockwise and Other Imponderables*: "Not only are venereal diseases not spread by toilet seats, but nothing else is, either. Although there was one report suggesting that the herpes virus may survive briefly in such an environment…doctors we spoke to [all said], 'There is no scientific evidence of disease transmitted from toilet seats.' "

THE FINAL FRONTIER

According to *Buzz* magazine, William Shatner, who played *Star Trek*'s Capt. Kirk, had his bathroom remodeled to resemble the bridge of the starship *Enterprise*. *Buzz* reports that he even had his toilet "custom-made in the shape of the fabled vessel."

RAMBO: THE MOVIE

*Here's the second installment of our story about the fictional
Vietnam vet who became one of the most enduring pop
icons of the 1980s. (Part I is on page 42).*

S AVED!!
First Blood, the story of Rambo, had been bouncing around
Hollywood for years when it was rescued by two film distributors who wanted to be producers. Andrew Vajna and Mario Kassar were rummaging through unused film properties at the Warner Bros. lot, looking for an action film they could sell internationally, when they stumbled on Morrell's story.

They immediately bought the movie rights. Then they hired Kirk Douglas to direct it, and picked Sylvester Stallone—whose only commercial success up to that time was *Rocky*—to star.

CHANGING THE STORY

To make the story more suitable for an action film, they changed the plot. In the novel, Rambo becomes a psychopathic killer, while the sheriff, also a veteran, is shown in a sympathetic light. For the film, however, they shifted all the sympathy to Rambo, and made the sheriff into the villain. "The portrayal of the sheriff bothered me," Morrell says. "In the novel both the police chief and Rambo had to die to show how pointless everything was.... My intent was to transpose the Vietnam war to America, whereas the film's intent was to make the audience cheer for the underdog."

PROBLEMS

Making *First Blood* quickly became difficult and expensive. Then Kirk Douglas—whom the producers were counting on to help sell the film to distributors and investors—dropped out. That left Stallone as the only well-known person connected to the film... and all of his non-*Rocky* films had been box-office disappointments. There was no reason to assume his *next* film would make money either, so no one was interested in the distribution rights. Kassar recalls, "Here I was $14 million in the red, and nothing was sold." Things were looking bad.

BREAKTHROUGH

In desperation, Vajna and Kassar spliced together 55 minutes of the unfinished film and presented it at the American Film Market convention. "Even today," the *Los Angeles Times* wrote in 1990, "distributors remember the buzz that film clip generated. Within hours, rights to *First Blood* were sold out."

First Blood's timing was perfect. The bad memories of Vietnam were fading, Ronald Reagan was in office, and the country was becoming more conservative and isolationist at the same time. The increasing threat of terrorists was making the country nervous. Morrell says. "Like Rambo, Americans felt backed into a corner by hijackers and terrorists, and they were ready to strike back, if only in fiction."

First Blood, which even Stallone feared would be a flop (he called it "the most expensive home movie ever made"), did $9 million worth of business during its opening weekend in October and went on to gross $120 million in box-office receipts worldwide.

FIRST BLOOD PART II

Two weeks after *First Blood* premiered, Vajna and Kassar decided to make a sequel—*Rambo: First Blood Part II*. In it, Rambo returns to Vietnam to obtain proof that the Vietnamese are still holding American MIAs, and ends up single-handedly liberating an entire prison camp full of U.S. soldiers. Sylvester Stallone, who wrote the script, got the idea for the plot after receiving a letter from a Virginia woman whose husband had been missing for 16 years.

First Blood Part II hit American theaters in the summer of 1985 and was an even bigger hit than the first movie: it was the third most successful launch in Hollywood history. "Sequels usually do about 60% of the original," Vajna told interviewers. "With *Rambo*, we are doing 300%, maybe 400%." By the time it finished its run, *First Blood Part II*, which cost $27 million to make, grossed more than $390 million at the box office.

POP GOES THE SYMBOL

First Blood Part II did more than just make piles of money—it turned Rambo into a household word. This was partly due to the movie, and partly due to merchandising (Rambo posters, T-shirts, action figures, collectors' knives, toy guns, toy bow-and-arrow sets, vitamins...and even Wrigley's Rambo Black Flak bubble gum, black raspberry-flavored gum shaped like shrapnel).

It was also helped along by the Reagan administration's foreign policy, the most assertive and controversial since the end of the Vietnam War. When President Reagan ordered air strikes against Libya, the London *Times* headline screamed "RAMBO JETS BOMB LIBYA"; and when Nicaraguan president Daniel Ortega made a speech at the United Nations, he urged President Reagan to remember "that Rambo exists only in the movies."

U.S. Army recruiting centers hung Rambo posters in their windows, and there was even a poster of President Reagan's head grafted onto Rambo's body. It was a bestseller.

People speculated that Rambo might become as enduring a character as James Bond. But times changed: *Rambo III*, released in 1988, was a critical and box-office flop. Vajna and Kassar's studio, Carolco Pictures, Inc., ran into financial trouble beginning in 1991 and limped along for several years before finally filing for bankruptcy in 1995.

MORE RAMBO FACTS

• Rambo got a first name in *Rambo II*—Johnny, from the song "When Johnny Comes Marching Home Again." By strange coincidence, there really was a John Rambo who fought in Vietnam. But Arthur John Rambo of Libby, Montana, didn't come back—he was killed by enemy fire in 1969.

• Morrell was earning $1,000 a month as a college professor when he sold the rights to his *First Blood* novel in 1971. His lawyer charged him $500 to revise the contract's fine print to include sequels and merchandising rights, and at the time, Morrell felt ripped off. "I told my lawyer, 'What sequels? Everyone's dead at the end of the novel. Merchandise? Who's going to bring out dolls and lunchboxes for a movie about a psychopathic killer?' He said, 'You don't understand Hollywood. They can change anything they want. They could make it into a musical.'" It was the best $500 Morrell ever spent; the contract changes earned him millions.

• How does Morrell feel about the way his anti-war novel was changed to a violent thriller? He likes it. "The *Rambo* films are marvelous special effects movies....like cartoons. When Sylvester comes down the trail with his machine gun, I laugh."

MORGAN'S SWINDLE

"Great is Mr. Morgan's power, greater in some respects even than that of presidents or kings," wrote a British journalist about financier J. P. Morgan in the late 1800s. Did the journalist know that Morgan got his start as a petty swindler?

There have been few businessmen in American history like J. P. Morgan. His bank was the most powerful in America. His financial clout was so great that after the Panic of 1893, his money helped keep the entire U.S. economy afloat. At that point, he was widely regarded as one of America's "saviours."

But when crusading reporters began to look into J. P. Morgan's career, they found that he'd gotten his start in business as a war profiteer, *ripping off* the government...and that he'd jeopardized thousands of American soldiers in order to make his first killing in the marketplace. Here's a little-known story of the great House of Morgan's business beginnings.

A CALL TO ARMS

• In May 1861, the Civil War had just begun...and the U.S. Army desperately needed rifles. It was paying top dollar to anybody who had guns to sell. So when the commander of the Union Army in St. Louis received a telegram from a man in New York offering to sell "5,000 new carbines in perfect condition" for $22 each, the commander accepted—sight unseen.

• When the rifles arrived in St. Louis, the commander found that they had a serious defect: they often misfired, blowing off soldiers' thumbs. The Army refused to pay for them.

• But 24-year-old J. P. Morgan, who was selling the guns, insisted on full payment. When he sued, the Army tried to compromise, offering $13.31 per rifle. Morgan refused to settle. The case went to court, and the judge ruled in Morgan's favor; the government was instructed to pay Morgan in full—$109,912.

• The question remained: Was it a legitimate business deal? Or had Morgan and his cronies conspired to bilk the U.S. government?

The French typing equivalent of "the quick brown fox jumped over the lazy dog" is "Take this

SUSPICIOUS FACTS

• The guns had been bought from an *army arsenal* in New York City for $3.50 apiece. They were the last of a batch that had been there since 1857, when they were condemned as "thoroughly un-serviceable, obsolete, and dangerous."

• The deal was arranged by a speculator named Simon Stevens, who knew exactly what he was buying. Court records later showed that Stevens was working for Morgan.

• After the commander agreed to buy the guns, Morgan borrowed money to purchase them—using the Army voucher as collateral for the loan. So the U.S. Army was buying its own unusable rifles—at a profit to Morgan of roughly 500% per rifle.

• Morgan never even took possession of the guns. When the loan came through, he had the defective rifles shipped directly from the New York arsenal to St. Louis.

WAS IT A CONSPIRACY?

A U.S. congressional committee investigating the arms swindle in 1862 found that Morgan had engaged in a conspiracy to defraud the U.S. government. It reported:

> The proposal actually was to sell the Government at $22 each 5,000 of its own arms, the intention being, if the offer was accepted, to obtain these arms from the Government at $3.50 each....The Government not only sold one day for $17,486 arms which it had agreed the day before to repurchase for $109,912—making a loss to the United States of $92,426—but virtually furnished the money to pay itself the $17,486 which it received.

• Morgan's case set an unfortunate precedent for the thousands of "dead horse claims" that followed, in which wartime swindlers were paid in full for putrid meat, rotting ships, flimsy tents, shoes that fell apart, and weapons that maimed the soldiers who used them.

* * * *

RANDOM THOUGHT

"I don't want a lawyer to tell me what I cannot do. I hire him to tell me how to do what I want to do."

—*J. P. Morgan*

old whiskey to the blonde judge who's smoking a cigar."

ACCIDENTAL HITS

Here are a few improbable-but-true stories that show how musicians can become stars overnight...or write hit songs without knowing it.

GET TOGETHER (1967/1969), by the Youngbloods
Background. In 1967, a group called the Youngbloods put out their first record on RCA, "Grizzly Bear." It was a modest hit. But the follow-up, a peace and love anthem called "Get Together" ("Come on people, smile on your brother / Everybody get together, try to love one another"), bombed. It reached #62 on the charts and died.

Lucky Break. Two years later, the National Conference of Christians and Jews put together a package of information for TV and radio stations to read on the air during National Brotherhood Week. They included a copy of the obscure "Get Together" in each package for the stations to use as background music

It's a Hit! People may not have paid attention to the message, but they listened to the song. Radio stations all over the country were flooded with calls asking what that record was and where they could get it. Stations began playing their copies of "Get Together," turning it into a Top 10 song that sold over 2 million copies.

HUMAN NATURE (1982), by Michael Jackson

Background. Steve Porcaro was a member of the group Toto. One day his daughter came home upset about a fight she'd had with some friends. "Why do they do that?" she asked. "It's just human nature," her father said...and then decided that was a good song title. So he went into Toto's studio and put a melody on tape, occasionally singing the line, "It's just human nature." Then he left the cassette lying around and forgot about it.

Lucky Break. Michael Jackson's producer, Quincy Jones, was looking for material to use on Jackson's new album. He asked another member of Toto, David Paitch, for some songs. Paitch went into their studio, put three tunes on a tape and sent it to Jones...who didn't care for them. But he said he loved the other song at the end of the tape.

What song? It turned out Paitch had accidentally picked up the tape on which Porcaro had recorded "Human Nature."

It's a Hit! Jones hired a lyricist to finish the song and included it on Jackson's album—called "Thriller"—which turned out to be the bestselling album in history. Porcaro earned millions for it. On top of that, the single of "Human Nature" reached #7 on its own.

HANKY PANKY (1966), by Tommy James & the Shondells

Background. In 1963, Tommy Jackson, a 16-year-old Michigan high school kid, recorded "Hanky Panky" with his band, the Shondells. It was a regional hit in Michigan, Illinois, and Indiana. Then it disappeared. A year and a half later, Jackson graduated from high school and the Shondells disbanded.

Lucky Break. Jackson was at his family's house one evening in 1965 when he got a phone call from a guy calling himself "Mad Mike" Metro.

"He said, 'I'm a deejay in Pittsburgh, and your record's number one. Can you come here?' " recalls Jackson. "I said, 'What record? Who is this? What's your name?' I thought it was one of my friends pulling my leg." But it was true. A disc jockey had found "Hanky Panky" in a 10¢ bin and started playing it on the air. Soon, every station in Pittsburgh was playing it.

It's a Hit! Jackson's old band wasn't interested in getting back together, so he flew to Pittsburgh alone and began making appearances with a new group. Meanwhile, Roulette Records released "Hanky Panky" nationally. It became the #1 song in the country, and Tommy Jackson—now known as Tommy James—became one of the biggest pop stars of the late 1960s.

OH HAPPY DAY, (1967), The Edwin Hawkins Singers

Background: Edwin Hawkins assembled the 46-piece Northern California State Youth Choir in 1967. To raise money, he picked out eight members of the choir and recorded an album in the basement of a local church. It was never intended for any audience except the limited gospel market. When they sold 600 copies they were pleased.

Lucky Break: A San Francisco rock promoter found the album in a warehouse and gave it to popular S.F. deejay, Abe "Voco" Kesh.

It's a Hit! Kesh loved it. He played it so often that it became a local hit. Then it went national and sold over a million copies.

Ramses condoms are named after Ramses II, an Egyptian pharoah who fathered 160+ children.

MISS AMERICA, PART V: The 1960s

For a brief spell during the '60s, Miss America became a political as well as cultural symbol, caught in the crossfire between forces for change that saw it as an embarrassing relic, and traditionalists who saw it as a comforting connection to the "Leave It to Beaver" years.

MIDDLE AGE

The Miss America Pageant was tremendously popular in the 1950s and early 1960s....But by the late 1960s, it began to show its age. One of the problems was that the various pageant committees had become top-heavy with stodgy Atlantic City businessmen and society matrons, who had virtually nothing in common with the young women of the sixties. After decades of innovation, the pageant officials—many of whom had run the show since the 1930s and were defensively proud of their accomplishments—had become the greatest obstacle to further change.

Out of Fashion

Pageant director Lenora Slaughter's sense of fashion was the most visible manifestation of the problem: She fought nearly every new style in clothing, hair, shoes, and swimsuits that developed in the 1960s, and banned many of them outright, including miniskirts and bikinis. The "fashions" that were permitted were so out-of-date that many were nearly impossible to find in stores, as Miss New York 1969 recounted to Frank Deford in *There She Is*:

> We spent days shopping....There weren't many of the one-piece swimsuits around—I mean, you had no choice—and the shoes with the three-inch spiked heels, they were virtually impossible to find. The clothing styles had to reach within two inches of the knee, and they just weren't selling any dresses like that....All we could do was lengthen the dresses that we bought, but the problem was that we couldn't even find dresses long enough so that when we let them down they were long enough for the pageant.

By 1969 the pageant had gone from a fashion trendsetter to "nearly a complete laughingstock," Deford writes. Contestants "quickly discovered that they were not buying a wardrobe for a pageant; they were buying one for a weeklong costume party."

WHITES ONLY

Like many American cultural institutions, the Miss America Pageant had a history of tokenism and outright racism that caught up with it during the Civil Rights movement. From the very first pageant, Native American and Puerto Rican contestants—when they were allowed to participate at all—had been shunted off to the sidelines in noncompetitive "official guest" roles. Blacks were excluded entirely, except for the 1926 pageant, when a handful of black women played slaves on the King Neptune float in the Fall Frolic.

This began to change in the mid-1950s, when the pageant quietly dropped its whites-only clause—Rule No. 7. But that only applied to the national pageant. Left to their own devices, many state pageants (at least unofficially) continued to discriminate.

A TURNING POINT

Finally in the late 1960s, the pageant began to tackle its problems. This change was partly due to the fact that Lenora Slaughter retired in 1967 after 32 years as Pageant Director, and partly to the fact that the pressures for change had become overwhelming:

• In 1967 civil rights groups threatened demonstrations to protest the fact that there were no black pageant organizers, judges, or contestants more than 10 years after the whites-only rule was abandoned. In response, the pageant agreed to institute reforms.

• A year later Pepsi, a pageant sponsor since 1957, pulled its sponsorship out of concern that the pageant had lost touch with teenagers and young adults. One Pepsi spokesman told reporters, "Miss America as run today does not represent the changing values of our society." (Pepsi's slogan at the time: "Now it's Pepsi for those who think young.")

• Beginning in 1967, the National Organization of Women (NOW) and other feminist groups organized protests at the pageant, charging that the pageant was demeaning to women, racist, and pro-war. Or as one protester put it:

It has always been a lily-white racist contest. The winner tours Vietnam entertaining the troops as a murder mascot. Where else could one find such a perfect combination of American values? Racism, militarism, and capitalism—all packaged in one "ideal" symbol: *a woman.*

The 1968 protests were the most colorful. According to Anne Marie Bivans in *Miss America: In Pursuit of the Crown,* "the feminists…marched on the Boardwalk, where they refused to speak with male reporters, chanted anti-pageant slogans, and tossed bras, girdles, makeup, and hair curlers into a 'freedom trashcan.' " Rumors also circulated that a feminist had infiltrated the pageant and would reveal herself onstage as soon as she was out of the running for the crown, but no one ever did.

The protests generated huge publicity, but after 1969 most feminist organizations backed off, as Deford explains: "The women had received so much serious attention that, practically speaking, they did not need Miss America any more. For one thing, they were beginning to get the uncomfortable feeling that they were becoming part of the show, halfway between the parade and the evening-gown competition."

And now, here it comes…the last section, on page 296.

☞　　☞　　☞　　☞

And Now for Something
Completely Different: Ping Pong

• Lawn tennis has been popular with upper-crust Englishmen for centuries, but it can't be played in the rain. That's why someone invented "table tennis" in the 1890s.

• Because it was cheaper than regular tennis, it was also more accessible, and quickly became more popular than tennis had ever been. Parker Brothers brought it to the United States in 1902.

• Thanks to the Doppler effect, which changes the sound of an object as it travels toward or away from you, the sound a table tennis ball makes when it moves away from you is different from the sound it makes when it moves toward you. Because of this, early players nicknamed the game Wick-Wack, Click-Clack, Whiff-Whaff, and Flim-Flam, before they finally settled on Ping-Pong.

MARRIED...WITH CHILDREN

*Married...With Children is one of the longest-running sitcoms in
TV history. Who created it...and how did it become popular?
Glad you asked. Here's the BRI's quick answer.*

BURNOUT
In the mid-1980s, when the Fox TV network was still in
the planning stages, Fox programming chief Garth Angier
approached Michael Moye and Ron Leavitt about creating an
"alternative" sitcom.

• The two men had written for *The Jeffersons, Happy Days, Laverne
& Shirley*, and other hits. But they were sick of "sappy" sitcoms...
and besides, no network had ever gone up against the Big Three
and survived. Why work for a surefire loser?

• Angier, however, made them an offer they couldn't refuse. "He
said, 'You can do what you want. We'll leave you alone,' " Leavitt
recalls. "It sounded lofty—an alternative network...all this freedom. It was a good incentive, even if the network was going to fold
after the first season." They accepted the job.

ENTER THE BUNDYS

• "At the time," Moye relates, "there was *The Cosby Show* and a lot
of *Cosby*-like clones where everybody was really happy and lived up
to impossibly high ideals. Ron and I felt there was an audience of
people sitting there all that time going, 'Yeah, right.' "

• So they turned that formula on its head and created the Bundys:

✔ Al was a nerdy ex-jock, a hand-in-the-pants shoe salesman
who watched too much TV and bickered constantly with his wife,
Peg, a K-mart fashion queen too proud to work outside the home
and too lazy work inside it.

✔ Their offspring were the slippery Bud (named after the
beer) and the slutty Kelly, whose high school career counselor suggested she was best qualified for a job like "logging camp toy or the
other woman"

• Picked to play Al Bundy was Ed O'Neill, who'd once been draft-
ed by the Pittsburgh Steelers and had tried out for the role of Sam

Malone in *Cheers*. Peg Bundy was played by Katey Sagal, daughter of movie producer Boris Sagal and a former backup singer for Bob Dylan, Bette Midler, and Tanya Tucker.

OPENING NIGHT

• The show premiered on Sunday, April 5, 1987…and not even the people associated with it gave it much chance for survival. "I thought we'd maybe do six episodes and that'd be the end of it," O'Neill says. But it quickly grabbed an audience no mainstream sitcom had been able to reach—young men.

• It turned out to be the sleeper hit of the network lineup. But it wasn't until a crusader named Terry Rakolta turned her attention to *Married* that it became a TV institution. One evening in January 1989, Rakolta tuned in and saw "Her Cups Runneth Over," an episode in which Al searches lingerie shops for Peg's favorite bra.

• She was "so disgusted" that she sent her young children out of the room. In the following weeks she watched more episodes, made note of who the sponsors were, and fired off letters complaining about their support of the show. "I care that there are advertisers out there paying the freight for this," she told reporters. "They're taking my dollars and putting them into soft-core pornography."

GETTING NOTICED

• At first she didn't attract much attention. Then the president of Coca-Cola wrote Rakolta personally, saying he was "professionally, and personally embarrassed" that a Coke ad appeared on the show.

• The story made the front page of *The New York Times* and was covered by *Nightline* and *Geraldo*. The result: A number of companies, including Procter & Gamble, McDonald's and Kimberly-Clark, pulled *their* ads from the show.

• *Married…With Children* toned down its act for a while, but Rakolta's strategy ultimately backfired. The controversy generated so much publicity for the show that ratings went up, and it earned more in ad revenues than ever.

• In fact, the show became so successful that the Big Three networks began dumping *Cosby*-like sitcoms in favor of blue-collar "slob-coms," such as *Roseanne* and *Grace Under Fire*. By 1995, *Married…With Children* had become the longest-running sitcom on the air, and one of the most popular shows in syndication.

GROUCHO GETS ELECTED—ACT II

Here's more from Five Star Theater, the 1933 radio show starring Groucho as Waldorf Flywheel, and Chico as his sidekick, Ravelli.

Outside. Milling crowd. Car noises.

GUARD: You guys can't come in this door. If you wanta hear the Flywheel-Maxwell political debate, you've got to go around to the main entrance.

REPORTER: But we're from the press. We want to talk to one of the candidates, Mr. Flywheel, about tomorrow's election.

GUARD: Okay, come on in. Waldorf Flywheel's in that room down the hall. First door to the right.

PHOTOGRAPHER: Thanks.

REPORTER: Funny how this man Flywheel has jumped into prominence so suddenly.

PHOTOGRAPHER: Well, when Big Boss Plunkett gets behind a candidate, he's as good as elected.. Here's the room.

Knocks.

GROUCHO: Come in.

Door opens, closes.

PHOTOGRAPHER: Good evening, Mr. Flywheel, we're from the press.

GROUCHO: Good. You can press my pants.

REPORTER: No, we're from the newspapers. We want your views on tomorrow's election.

RAVELLI (runs in): Hey boss!

GROUCHO: What's the matter, Ravelli?

RAVELLI: There's some big crowd outside. When I tried to come in here, a policeman wanted to hit me.

GROUCHO: How do you know he wanted to hit you?

RAVELLI.: Because he hit me. Whatta you gonna do about it, boss?

GROUCHO: I'm busy now, but I'll thank him later.

REPORTER: Mr. Flywheel, our paper would like to get a record of all that you've done in this town.

RAVELLI: Come on, don't bother my boss. You can get his record at the police station.

GROUCHO: Shut up, Ravelli. Reporter, I'd like to say that everything I am I owe to my great-grandfather, old Cyrus Tecumseh Flywheel. If he were alive today, the whole world would be talking about him.

REPORTER: Why, Mr. Flywheel?

GROUCHO: Well, if he were alive today, he'd be a hundred and forty years old.

REPORTER: But...

RAVELLI: Excuse me, please, Mrs. Reporter. I got-a someting important to ask my boss. Hey, Flywheel, was that hair tonic you had in the bottle on your desk?

GROUCHO: No, it was glue.

RAVELLI: Glue? (Laughs) No wonder I can't get my hat off!... Hey, here comes Big Boss Plunkett. He looks-a mad.

PLUNKETT: Flywheel!

GROUCHO: Just a minute, old boy, I want you to meet the reporters. Reporters, this is my friend and manager, Big Boss Plunkett. There are two things I want to say about Plunkett. First, he's never been in prison. And second, I don't know why.

PLUNKETT: See here...

PHOTOGRAPHER: Sorry to interrupt, but we've got to get back to the paper. And we'd like a photograph of Mr. Flywheel. Hold that smile, Mr. Flywheel. Here goes...Thank you! Goodbye!

Door shuts...followed by a knock.

PLUNKETT: Come in.

GUARD: Time for the debate.

PLUNKETT: Come on, boys . . . right through this door. This is a shortcut to the platform. Remember, Ravelli, I had a tough time getting you the job as chairman of this debate. Do you know anything about a debate?

RAVELLI: Ah-h, sure! I explain it to you. When you wanta catch de fish, you use-a debate.

GROUCHO: There you are, Plunkett. You'd have to go pretty far to find a better chairman than Ravelli. And I wish you had!

PLUNKETT: Come on!—right through this door.

Door opens, crowd is cheering, "We want Flywheel," "Hooray for Maxwell," etc.

ANNOUNCER: Ladies and gentlemen. The debate on judicial reform between Judge Herbert Maxwell and Waldorf Tecumseh Flywheel is about to begin. I now present the chairman of the meeting, Mr. Emmanuel Ravelli.

(Applause.)

RAVELLI : (in formal speaking voice): Alright, everybody...The foist guy I want to introduce is a man *everybody* is-a crazy about. A man who's good to little kids— and to big kids too... And he ain't afraid of nothin'! Ladies and gentlemen, that man is... *me!*

(Crowd claps loudly.)

Now I gonna call on Judge Maxwell.

JUDGE: Mr. Chairman, ladies and gentlemen. I was born in this city forty-eight years ago. I studied law here. I married here. And in all my forty-eight years, I...

GROUCHO: Just a minute, chairman.

RAVELLI: What you want, boss?

GROUCHO: If this guy's gonna talk only about himself, I'm going home.

JUDGE: Please, Mr. Flywheel, you'll get your chance later. Ladies and gentlemen, my candidacy is being fought by a group of men who are dishonest, grafting and meretricious!

RAVELLI: Tanks, judge. I wish you da same.

JUDGE: Wish me what?

RAVELLI: A meretricious. A meretricious and a Happy New Year!

JUDGE (furious): Mr. Chairman, will you let me go on with my speech? Fellow citizens, I...

RAVELLI (pounds gavel): At's-a all, Judge. Your time is up.

JUDGE : My time is up? Why, how long have I talked?

RAVELLI: I don't know. I haven't got a watch. You sit down. And now, people, you're gonna

hear from my boss, Mister Flywheel, the winner of this debate.

GROUCHO: Well, folks, I'm sorry my speech had to be delayed, but Maxwell insisted on talking. (Formal voice) Fellow citizens, I'm here to tell you that a vote for Flywheel means a vote for free speech, free press, free-wheeling and free cheers for the red, white and blue. (Crowd claps.)

My esteemed opponent...is all steamed up. And why? Because I broke a few promises. Well, I can make new ones just as good. And to you women in the audience, I can only say that there's one thing I'll never forget, as long as I can remember it... and that is, that the mothers of some of our greatest men were women. (Crowd claps.)

JUDGE: Flywheel, I'd like to ask a question. Is it true your organization has bought 20,000 votes to swing tomorrow's election?

GROUCHO: I'm glad you brought that up. We did buy 20,000 votes.

JUDGE: What?

GROUCHO: But don't get excited. I've got good news for you.

JUDGE: Good news?

GROUCHO: Yes, we bought five thousand more votes than we need, and we'll sell 'em to you at cost price.

Who's the new judge? For election results, turn to page 294.

"Gilligan's Island" was inspired by Daniel Defoe's Robinson Crusoe.

CELEBRITY TAX TROUBLES

It's not easy being famous, particularly if you haven't been paying your taxes properly. Here's a look at some rich and famous people who have fallen to earth with a thud, courtesy of the IRS.

WILLIE NELSON

Tax Troubles: In 1990, the IRS slapped the country singer with a bill for $32 million in delinquent taxes, penalties, and interest—one of the biggest in history—after it disallowed his heavy tax shelter investments. Nelson blamed his Price Waterhouse accountant, saying that their bad advice caused the underpayments.

What Happened: Nelson's lawyers argued that since the accountants were to blame for his troubles, he should only be required to pay the original taxes owed. The IRS ultimately agreed to charge Nelson only $9 million, and gave him three years to pay it. He raised the money by auctioning off property, signing over the rights to an album called *Who'll Buy My Memories: The IRS Tapes*, handing over the proceeds from his lawsuit with Price Waterhouse, and accepting donations from fans. "Willie is happy to be done with it," his lawyer told reporters after the last payment was made. "He has a very good relationship with the IRS now."

PRESIDENT BILL CLINTON

Tax Troubles: In December 1993, the *Washington Post* revealed that then-Governor Clinton had donated his underwear to the Salvation Army and claimed the donations as charitable deductions on his income taxes. The deductions included $1 apiece for undershorts donated in '84, $2 apiece for 3 pairs of underwear donated in '86, and $15 for a single pair of long underwear donated in '88.

What Happened: Making deductions for underwear donated to charity is perfectly legal, provided you don't claim more than the "fair market value" of the garments in your taxes. That's where Clinton ran into trouble: he claimed too large a deduction on his knickers. The actual fair market value of underwear for tax purposes is 5¢-6¢ a *pound*, even for skivvies worn by governors. (No word on whether he ever made good on the overstated deductions.)

LEONA HELMSLEY

Tax Troubles: A few years after telling an employee that "only the little people pay taxes," the hotel queen was indicted on charges that she and her husband, hotel magnate Harry Helmsley, evaded $1.2 million in income taxes by billing their business for "personal items ranging from a marble dance floor to girdles."

What Happened: Harry was eventually deemed too incompetent to stand trial because of failing health, but Leona was convicted of tax evasion in December 1989, fined $7.1 million, and sentenced to four years in federal prison. She was paroled in October 1993 and began three years of probation, which included 250 hours of community service per year.

In 1995, Helmsley's employees complained to reporters that *they* were the ones performing community service. Helmsley, they said, forced them to do the court-assigned work—wrapping gifts and stuffing envelopes for charity. "We sat around our staff dining table like field hands shucking peas," one anonymous employee complained, "but instead of shucking, we were wrapping presents in between our regular duties." The judge tacked an additional 150 hours of community service on to Helmsley's sentence.

JOE LOUIS, "THE BROWN BOMBER"

Tax Troubles: Louis was heavyweight boxing champ from 1937 to 1949, a national hero who held the title longer than any boxer in history. Like many of us, he didn't fill out his own tax forms. His manager did…and he underpaid Louis's taxes so much that by the time the champ retired in 1949, he owed more than $1.25 million. Louis was forced to come out of retirement in 1950 and try to box his way out of his IRS troubles.

What Happened: Louis fought 10 times over the next year, but never recaptured his title and never made enough money to pay off the IRS. The agency filed liens against all of his assets, and even seized the $667 he inherited from his mother when she died. But it didn't come close to paying what he owed; he had to stoop to pro-wrestling to pay the bill. This helped him settle the tax issue, although not in the way he'd expected. As *Sports Illustrated* recounted in 1985:

Sympathy for him grew as the public came to believe that the IRS had hounded the former heavyweight champion into a degrading career in wrestling. After considerable frustration, the IRS agreed in the early 1960s to limit its collections to an amount [that] did not even cover the interest on his debt.

The IRS never officially closed the books on the case, it just stopped trying to collect. As the commissioner of the IRS explained it, "We have gotten all we could possibly get from Mr. Louis, leaving him with some hope that he can live." Nearly bankrupt, Louis spent much of the 1970s working as a "greeter" at Caesar's Palace in Las Vegas. He died in 1981.

MARVIN MITCHELSON

Tax Troubles: When Mitchelson, divorce attorney to the stars and Hollywood's "Prince of Palimony," dumped a client-turned-lover, she got revenge by contacting the IRS. In 1993, he was formally indicted for filing false returns between 1983 and 1986, during which he allegedly hid more than $2 million in income.

What Happened: Mitchelson filed for bankruptcy and was convicted on charges of tax fraud, for which he was sentenced to 30 months in prison and ordered to pay more than $2 million in back taxes. "This is the second-saddest day of my life," he told the judge on the day of sentencing. "My mother's death was the first."

JERRY LEE LEWIS

Tax Troubles: The IRS nailed the '50s rock star for non-payment of back taxes in the late '70s. They seized real estate, vehicles, and other assets, but his tax bill continued to grow. By 1994, the amount due had grown to $4.1 million.

What Happened: Lewis worked out a deal to pay only $560,000, less than 15¢ on the dollar. His secret: He didn't have any money.

Lewis raised the cash through a concert tour, a record, a biography, and by temporarily opening his home in Nesbit, Mississippi, to tourists. The tours were conducted by friends or Lewis's wife and included visits to the living room, den, and piano-shaped swimming pool in back—but not the bedrooms. Price of admission: $5, not bad considering that every once in a while the tour offered something Graceland didn't—a live rock star. "At least once a week," Mrs. Lewis explained, "Jerry Lee forgets they're there and walks out in his robe or wearing jeans and a T-shirt."

UNCLE ALBERT SEZ...

Albert Einstein had a few things to say that even we bathroom readers can understand. Like these....

"If a cluttered desk is a sign of a cluttered mind, of what, then, is an *empty* desk?"

"Only two things are infinite, the universe and human stupidity, and I'm not sure about the former."

"Sometimes one pays most for things one gets for nothing."

"Problems cannot be solved at the same level of awareness that created them."

"To make a goal of comfort or happiness has never appealed to me; a system of ethics built on this basis would be sufficient only for a herd of cattle."

"Education is what remains after one has forgotten everything he learned in school."

"Common sense is the collection of prejudices acquired by age eighteen."

"When the solution is simple, God is answering."

"What does a fish know about the water in which he swims all his life?"

"Knowledge is limited. Imagination encircles the world."

"My religion consists of the humble admiration of the illimitable superior spirit who reveals himself in the slight details we are able to perceive with our frail and feeble minds."

"Peace cannot be achieved through violence, it can only be attained through understanding."

"Gravitation cannot be held responsible for two people falling in love."

"He who joyfully marches to music in rank and file has already earned my contempt. He has been given a large brain by mistake, since for him, the spinal cord would fully suffice."

"The answer is 'yes' or 'no,' depending on the interpretation."

"Nothing will benefit human health and increase the chances for the survival of life on Earth as much as the evolution to a vegetarian diet."

Believe it or not: If a man's tie is too tight, his vision gets worse.

"LIFE" AFTER DEATH

Here's an interesting question: If you make it big after you're dead, is it really you who's succeeding? After all, you—at least theoretically— don't exist anymore. Woody Allen, reflecting on this, said: "I don't want to achieve immortality through my work...I want to achieve it through not dying." Our sentiments exactly. Here are 4 examples of folks who hit it big after death. Enjoy it...while you can.

JONATHAN LARSON

In 1992, Larson wrote a musical about New York artists struggling with AIDS. He sent the script and songs to the New York Theater Workshop. The artistic director was so impressed that he spent the next four years helping Larson develop the work, called *Rent*, for the stage. It was finally scheduled to open on January 26, 1996, and would have been the biggest moment of Larson's life. But he couldn't make it—he was found dead in his apartment on January 25, a few hours after the final dress rehearsal. Cause of death: an aortic aneurysm. He was 35.

Life After Death: The show opened to rave reviews and quickly became the hottest theater ticket in town; within weeks, the New York press was printing lists of celebrities—including Woody Allen—who wanted tickets but couldn't get them. *Rent* later moved to Broadway and won the 1996 Pulitzer Prize for drama.

JOHN KENNEDY TOOLE

During the 1950s, while he was in the army, Toole wrote a novel called *A Confederacy of Dunces*. For years he tried to get it published. Finally, in 1967, Simon and Schuster expressed some interest; he was ecstatic. Unfortunately, in 1969—after Toole had spent two years on rewrites—the publisher rejected it. Toole, 31, didn't wait to see what happened next. He committed suicide.

Life After Death: Toole's mother found the manuscript among his belongings and spent the next seven years trying to get it published. In 1976, she convinced novelist Walker Percy to read it...and he convinced Louisiana State University to print 2,500 copies. An inauspicious beginning...but the novel got glowing reviews, and a major publisher picked it up. It went on to sell more than 650,000 copies and win the 1981 Pulitzer Prize for fiction.

Why did Napoleon lose at Waterloo? Among other things, he was bedridden with hemorrhoids.

OTIS REDDING

One of pop's great singers, Redding had never had a Top 10 hit, and he was determined to break into the mainstream market. So in 1967 he went to the Monterey Pop Festival and triumphantly performed with people like Janis Joplin and Jimi Hendrix. Afterward, Redding spent a week on a houseboat outside of San Francisco, "just wastin' time." He dreamed up a little pop tune called "Dock of the Bay," brought it back to Memphis, and put it on tape, planning to get back to it when he returned from a tour. Three days later, he died in a plane crash.

Life After Death: Redding's co-writer, guitarist Steve Cropper, went back into the studio and finished the record. It became the first posthumous #1 record in history.

HANK WILLIAMS

In 1952, a singer named Big Bill Lister got his first contract with a major record company. He knew country star Hank Williams, and asked if Williams had any songs he could use. To help Lister out, Hank gave him "There's a Tear in My Beer," a song he'd just written and recorded on a single acetate demo record. Lister included the tune on his album. A few months later, the 29-year-old Williams died from alcohol poisoning.

Life After Death: Lister lost track of Williams's acetate recording until 1988, when he found it while cleaning out his house. He sent it to Hank Williams, Jr. The younger Williams, now a country star in his own right, had been only three years old when his father died, so he'd never had the chance to record with him...until now. He took "There's a Tear in My Beer" into the studio, cleaned it up, and created a duet by mixing his own vocals with his father's.

Hank Jr. even made a video of "There's a Tear in My Beer." He took a film of his father singing a different song and superimposed someone else's lips onto the face. Both the song and the video became huge bestsellers, even winning the Country Music Association's Vocal Event of the Year award.

Note: Since then, other "direct from the grave" duets have been hits. Natalie Cole even won a Grammy singing with her dead father, Nat "King" Cole.

The song "You're a Grand Old Flag" was originally called "You're a Grand Old Rag."

WEIRD DOLLS

Here are a few more unusual dolls that you could have bought at your local toy store…but probably didn't.

EARRING MAGIC KEN

In 1993, Mattel decided to give Barbie's boyfriend a new look: it introduced "Earring Magic Ken" to its line of Ken dolls, complete with two-tone hair, a pink mesh shirt, a lavender "leather" vest, a plastic ring around his neck, and a single earring in one ear. "Ken's still a clean-cut guy," a Mattel spokesman explained to reporters. "He's just a little more contemporary."

Yeah, sure. "You can't look at Earring Magic Ken and *not* think gay," Chicago gay rights advocate Rick Garcia told reporters. "He's stereotypically gay—it's what you saw men wearing a few years back. And that plastic ring that Ken wears around his neck looks an awful lot like what gay men were buying at sex shops."

Retailers agreed. "We sold out in less than a month and we had to reorder them," one toy salesperson told reporters. "And it's primarily gay men who are buying them. Most customers just ask specifically for 'The Gay Ken Doll.' "

Mattel was shocked. "We gave him an earring and two-tone hair to make him look cool and hip," protested one company official, "and lavender clothing because it's a girl's second favorite color after pink."

THE J. J. ARMES DOLL

Ideal Toys had a big success with its Evel Knievel line of toys in the mid-1970s, so in 1976, they based another toy on a real-life human being—Jay J. Armes, a multimillionaire Texas private eye.

The real Armes was the James Bond of El Paso, complete with a karate blackbelt, a bomb-detecting Cadillac, a smokescreen-spewing Corvette, and a walled-in estate that he patrolled himself with a 750-pound Siberian tiger on a leash. He'd built one of the most successful detective agencies in the country, commanding fees as high as $250,000 per assignment from clients like Elvis Presley, J. Paul Getty, and Marlon Brando.

Perhaps even more interesting to the folks at Ideal was the fact that the real Armes had no hands—he had lost both of them at the age of 11 playing with dynamite blasting caps in his backyard and had worn prosthetics ever since. Most of the time he wore steel hooks, but he also had custom-made prosthetic guns that shot real bullets. Ideal figured that Armes would make a perfect action figure, and sold the J. J. Armes doll with a large suitcase full of interchangeable prosthetic machetes, magnets, suction cups, and other gadgets.

It was a flop. Ideal speculates that the doll bombed for a number of reasons: (1) kids had never heard of Armes; (2) the adventures of a real-life detective can actually be pretty boring; and (3) a lot of youngsters were spooked by the idea of pretending to be a man with hooks for hands. "Kids would find it very difficult to role-play a man with two artificial arms," one (former) Ideal executive admitted afterwards. "I don't even think you'd want to. I would be kind of squeamish about it myself."

THE PET CONGRESSMAN

Described in press reports as a "fuzzy little bow-tied lawmaker doll," it was introduced in 1992 by a Maryland businessman after he noted the similarities between his pet dog and his representatives in government. "I realized congressmen are like pets," he told interviewers. "They wet the rug, and you get mad at them. But you still elect them and keep them."

The dolls were packaged in a "dome-shaped wire cage" designed to resemble the U.S. Capitol and came with a 15-page owner's manual that explained that the pint-sized politico "expects to be entertained frequently by his owner, but will rarely offer to pick up the tab." Not surprisingly, former President Ronald Reagan bought one for his Los Angeles office. But not everyone thought the dolls were funny. One chain store refused to carry them because they were "an inappropriate way to recognize a congressman."

MARYBEL GET WELL

The hypochondriac doll from Madame Alexander. Came with crutches, a cast for her leg, bandages, pills, quarantine signs, and measles spots.

COURT TRANSQUIPS

We never imagined that court transcripts would make good bathroom reading. But that was before we read Humor in the Court *and* More Humor in the Court, *by Mary Louise Gilman, editor of the* National Shorthand Reporter. *Here are a few excerpts from these two funny volumes of "courtroom bloopers." Remember—these are actual courtroom transcripts.*

THE COURT: "Now, as we begin, I must ask you to banish all present information and prejudice from your minds, if you have any."

Q: "What is your brother-in-law's name?"
A: "Borofkin."
Q: "What's his first name?"
A: "I can't remember."
Q: "He's been your brother-in-law for years, and you can't remember his first name?"
A: "No. I tell you I'm too excited."
[Rising from the witness chair and pointing to Mr. Borofkin.] "Nathan, for God's sake, tell them your first name!"

Q: "Did you ever stay all night with this man in New York?"
A: "I refuse to answer that question."
Q: "Did you ever stay all night with this man in Chicago?"
A: "I refuse to answer that question."
Q: "Did you ever stay all night with this man in Miami?"
A: "No."

Q: "What is your name?"
A: "Ernestine McDowell."
Q: "And what is your marital status?"
A: "Fair."

Q: "Doctor, how many autopsies have you performed on dead people?"
A: "All my autopsies have been performed on dead people."

Q: "Are you married?"
A: "No, I'm divorced."
Q: "And what did your husband do before you divorced him?"
A: "A lot of things I didn't know about."

Q: "How did you happen to go to Dr. Cherney?"
A: "Well, a gal down the road had had several of her children by Dr. Cherney, and said he was really good."

Q: "Do you know how far pregnant you are right now?"
A: "I will be three months November 8th."
Q: "Apparently then, the date of conception was August 8th?"
A: "Yes."
Q: "What were you and your husband doing at that time?"

Q: "Doctor, did you say he was shot in the woods?"
A: "No, I said he was shot in the lumbar region."

Q: "Mrs. Smith, do you believe that you are emotionally unstable?"
A: "I should be."
Q: "How many times have you committed suicide?"
A: "Four times."

Q: "Were you acquainted with the deceased?"
A: "Yes, sir."
Q: "Before or after he died?"

Q: "What happened then?"
A: "He told me, he says, 'I have to kill you because you can identify me.' "
Q: "Did he kill you?"
A: "No."

Q: "Mrs. Jones, is your appearance this morning pursuant to a deposition notice which I sent to your attorney?"
A: "No. This is how I dress when I go to work."

On just one square inch of your skin, there are 20 million microscopic animals.

JESSE'S BIG NUMBERS

Uncle John's six-year-old son, Jesse, has been asking questions about numbers lately, like "What comes after a trillion?" and "What's a billion billion?" We'd never thought much about that before, but it's pretty interesting. Here's a page that Jesse will enjoy.

HOW MUCH IS A BILLION?

Depends on where you are. In the United States, 1,000 is used as a multiplier for big numbers: a million is 1,000 thousands; a billion is 1,000 millions; a trillion is 1,000 billions, and so on.

But in many other places (Britain, Spain and Latin America, for example), they use 1,000,000 (one million) as the multiplier. A million is still 1,000 thousands. But a billion is *one million* millions; a trillion is *one million billion*, and so on. Big difference.

WHAT COMES AFTER A TRILLION?

Uncle John's standard answer: a trillion and one. But there's a whole universe of numbers that most of us have never heard of which follow a million, a billion, and a trillion. Here are some, in U.S. numerical terms:

Quadrillion: 1,000 trillion
Quintillion: 1,000 quadrillion
Sextillion: 1,000 quintillion
Septillion: 1,000 sextillion
Octillion: 1,000 septillion
Nonillian: 1,000 octillion
Decillion: 1,000 nonillion
Undecillion: 1,000 decillion
Duodecillion: 1,000 undecillion

Tredecillion: 1,000 duodecillion
Quattuordecillion: 1,000 tredecillion
Quindecillion: 1,000 quattuordecillion
Sexdecillion: 1,000 quindecillion
Septendecillion: 1,000 sexdecillion
Octodecillion: 1,000 septendecillion
Novemdecillion: 1,000 octodecillion
Vigintillion: 1,000 novemdecillion

• How do these numbers look on paper? To give you a sense of scale:

Trillion: 1,000,000,000,000

Quadrillion: 1,000,000,000,000,000

Septillion: 1,000,000,000,000,000,000,000,000

Quattuordecillion:
1,000,000,000,000,000,000,000,000,000,000,000,000,000,000,000

The word "furniture" originally applied to portable military equipment.

WHAT'S THE BIGGEST NUMBER?

Theoretically, you could probably keep going forever. But practically speaking:

• According to *The Mathematics Calendar 1996*, by Theoni Pappas, the "illions" haven't really been used beyond vigintillion. Why? "Perhaps," suggests one mathematician, "most everyday phenomena can be covered by these huge numbers."

• Nonetheless, books list some bigger numbers. Among the "illions," for example, is the number *centillion*—1,000, followed by 300 zeroes, or:

1,000,000,000,000,000,000,000,000,000,000,000,000,000,000,
000,000,000,000,000,000,000,000,000,000,000,000,000,000,
000,000,000,000,000,000,000,000,000,000,000,000,000,000,
000,000,000,000,000,000,000,000,000,000,000,000,000,000,
000,000,000,000,000,000,000,000,000,000,000,000,000,000,
000,000,000,000,000,000,000,000,000,000,000,000,000,000,
000,000,000,000,000,000,000,000,000

• To deal with the "biggest number" question, one mathematician created a sort of catch-all number that has come into general use—the *googolplex*. By his reasoning, a googol is a one followed by 100 zeroes. And a googolplex is a one followed by a googol of zeroes. Presumably, we don't need any number larger than that.

HOW MUCH IS A ZILLION?

As one mathematician writes: "A zillion falls into the same category as a few, some, a lot, many. A zillion is deceiving since it ends in -illion, but it is no more specific than saying 'a tremendous amount.' "

WHERE DOES INFINITY FIT IN?

When exact numbers aren't big enough, there's always infinity, defined as "a concept of limitlessness." Or, practically speaking, a number too big for our minds to grasp or our language to describe.

When Uncle John was a kid, his sister asked: "What's bigger than infinity?" This stumped Uncle John. The answer was "infinity, +1." That sounded pretty clever, and Uncle John repeated it for years. But the truth is that since infinity goes on forever, you can't stop it at a single digit. Infinity + 1 still equals infinity.

THE MONSTER LIVES!

*When Universal Pictures coined the term "horror movie" in 1931,
it was because of this film…and Boris Karloff, the actor who brought the
monster to life. As one critic puts it: "Just as the monster of the story was
stitched together from pieces of the dead, Universal's cinematic Monster was
stitched together from the genius of Jack Pierce's makeup, James Whale's
direction, and Boris Karloff's performance. The results were so perfect
that the image of the Frankenstein monster, as seen in this classic
film, has become ingrained into the fabric of our culture."*

LUCKY BREAK

Have you ever heard of William Henry Pratt? Most people haven't. In late 1920s he was an unemployed actor, making ends meet by driving a truck for a lumber yard. In 1931, he landed a small part playing a gangster in a movie called *The Criminal Code*. It happened to premiere just as director James Whale began his search for someone to play the monster in *Frankenstein*.

A friend of Whale's saw the film, noticed Pratt, and suggested that the director take a look at him. So Whale went to see *The Criminal Code*. He was impressed with Pratt's work…but more important, he recognized that Pratt's gaunt features, exaggerated with lots of makeup, would make an excellent monster-face.

Whale drew some preliminary sketches of Pratt as the monster and showed them to Jack Pierce, head of Universal's makeup department. Then he approached Pratt about playing the part. Years later, Pratt recalled how he learned about the role:

> I'd spent 10 years in Hollywood without causing the slightest stir.
> Then one day I was sitting in the commissary at Universal, having
> lunch, and looking rather well turned out, I thought, when a man
> sent a note over to my table, asking if I'd like to audition for the
> part of a monster.

THE NAME GAME

Pratt took a screen test and got the job on the spot. But he didn't get public *acknowledgment* for the role until much later. He wasn't

---

What do pediatricians do when their kids get colds? 63% say they "let them run their course."

considered an important member of the cast, so the studio didn't even bother to list his name in the credits. Only a question mark appears next to the words "The Monster"

Within a year, however, Pratt's name would become a household word....Or at least his *stage* name would: Universal Pictures thought that "William Henry Pratt" sounded too ordinary for such an exotic monster and asked him to change it to something a little more unusual. Pratt picked a name that would be synonymous with horror for over 35 years—*Boris Karloff.*

MAKEUP

Universal put Jack Pierce, head of the studio's makeup department, in charge of creating Karloff's makeup. He prepared for the job by studying anatomy, surgery, electrodynamics, and criminology. It was this research that led to the monster's unusual flat-topped skull, as Pierce later related to *The New York Times:*

> My anatomical studies taught me that there are six ways a surgeon can cut the skull in order to take out or put in a brain. I figured that Frankenstein, who was a scientist but no practicing surgeon, would take the simplest surgical way. He would cut the top of the skull off straight across like a pot-lid, hinge it, pop the brain in, and then clamp it on tight. That is the reason I decided to make the Monster's head square and flat like a shoe box and dig that big scar across his forehead with the metal clamps holding it together.

Pierce also added a caveman-like protruding brow to suggest de-evolution, and Karoly Grosz, a Universal poster illustrator, came up with the idea of putting steel bolts in the monster's neck.

FACE FACTS

Karloff had several false teeth on the right side of his mouth; these were removed to give his already gaunt face an even more hollow appearance. This look was further accentuated when Karloff himself suggested to Pierce that his eyelids be heavily puttied with embalmers' wax, which gave the monster a sense of pathos.

The rest of the facial makeup was applied to *accent* rather than cover up Karloff's natural features, so that his face would retain its expressiveness. "We were all fascinated by the development of Karloff's face and head," Mae Clarke later recalled. "White putty on the face was toned down to a corpse-like gray. Then there was a sudden inspiration to give the face a green tint. It awed us and gave Boris and the rest of us a different feeling about the whole concept." The movie was filmed entirely in black and white (that's all there was back then) but in some prints of the film, Universal had Karloff's face tinted green by hand before they were distributed to theaters.

BODY LANGUAGE

"Karloff's face fascinated me," James Whale would recall years later. "His physique was weaker than I could wish, but that queer, penetrating personality of his, I felt, was more important than his shape, which could be easily altered." And alter it they did:

• Karloff's frame was stiffened by a five-pound spinal brace that ran up his back and steel struts in his legs.

• He also wore platform asphalt spreader's boots, which weighed twelve and a half pounds apiece.

• On top of the braces, Karloff wore padding and on top of that a thick, double-quilted suit that added tremendous bulk to his frame; its sleeves were cut short to make his arms appear longer than they really were. All in all, the braces, struts, boots, and costume weighed more than forty-eight pounds.

TEST RUN

Even after Karloff was fully made up, he wasn't sure whether the makeup was truly scary or not—would it frighten people, or just make them laugh? As he recounted years later,

> I was thinking this while practicing my walk, as I rounded a bend in the corridor and came face-to-face with this prop man. He was the first man to see the monster—I watched to study his reaction. It was quick to come. He turned white—gurgled and lunged out of sight down the corridor. Never saw him again. Poor chap, I would have liked to thank him—he was the audience that first made me *feel* like the monster.

IN THE THEATER

When Universal previewed *Frankenstein* before test audiences in

---

One ounce of gold can be beaten thin enough to cover an entire acre of ground.

Santa Monica, they noticed two important things:

1. It was Karloff's monster, not the other characters, who made the film work. This was real horror for panicked Universal execs. They'd considered Karloff unimportant and neglected to put him under contract. They quickly called his agent and signed him up. Karloff's response: "After more than 20 years of acting, for once I'll know where my next breakfast is coming from."

2. The film made people fidgety and squeamish. Rather than downplay the response, the studio decided to publicize it. They added a prologue, warning filmgoers what they were in for. Edward Van Sloan, who played Dr. Frankenstein's mentor, Dr. Waldman, told audiences:

> Mr. Carl Laemmle [head of Universal] feels it would be a little unkind to present this picture without a word of friendly warning....
> [Frankenstein] is one of the strangest stories ever told....It will thrill you,...It may shock you. It might even—horrify you! So, then, if you feel that you do not care to subject your nerves to such a strain, now is your chance to—well, we've warned you!

Theaters around the country added to the hype by posting nurses in the lobby, making free "nerve tonic" available to those who needed it, and other gimmicks. One movie house in Texas even hired a woman to sit in the empty theater and watch the film alone. But the publicity wasn't necessary—*Frankenstein* was one of the biggest hits of 1931 and went on to become one of the all-time classic Hollywood films. To this day, Boris Karloff's sensitive portrayal of the monster is the performance by which all other monster movies are measured.

GONE TO PIECES

By the late 1930s, it seemed like *Frankenstein* might finally be dying. Boris Karloff, who'd played the monster in *Frankenstein* (1931), *Bride of Frankenstein* (1935), and *Son of Frankenstein* (1939), hammered the first nail in the creature's coffin when he announced that he'd grown weary of the role. As David Skal writes in *The Monster Show*, Karloff "suspected that the monster would be increasingly relegated to the role of prop or buffoon" and didn't want to be part of it.

It didn't take long for Karloff's prediction to come true. With each new film Universal released—*Frankenstein Meets the Wolf Man* (1943), *The House of Frankenstein* (1944), and *The House of Dracula* (1945), the monster became less frightening. The studio finished the job in 1948, when it ended its Frankenstein series with *Abbott and Costello Meet Frankenstein*. Karloff agreed to help promote that film…as long as he didn't have to watch it.

KID STUFF

But even as familiarity worked against Frankenstein films, demographics were working in their favor. Thanks to the post-World War II baby boom, younger viewers were making up an increasingly large share of the movie audience. By 1958, 72% of all moviegoers were between the ages of 12 and 25.

Hollywood started making movies especially for teenagers—and they quickly found out that teenagers loved horror films. Sticking a monster, vampire, or werewolf into a film became an easy way to increase ticket sales.

Low-budget studios like American International Pictures (*I Was a Teenage Werewolf*) couldn't use Karloff's familiar monster because Universal Studios owned a copyright on *that* Frankenstein "look." But they could use the *name* Frankenstein because it was in the public domain (which means no one owns it).

And they did use it—hundreds of times. "Frankenstein" became a generic term for any manmade monster. He showed up in theaters as an alien, a sex fiend, a "demon of the atomic age," a resurrected teenage auto wreck victim, and so on; 65 years later, the Frankenstein movies keep on coming. As *The Videohound's Complete Guide to Trash Pics and Cult Flicks* says:

> Frankenstein lives in the movies better than anywhere else. With dozens of films based directly on characters from the novel, not to mention the hundreds with at least a tenuous connection to it, it may be the single most adapted work in all of cinema. No other name draws audiences so well.

Boris Karloff, the man who made Frankenstein—and horror films —a part of our culture, died in 1969. But he's been granted a weird kind of immortality. Every time a mad scientist builds a monster onscreen, it's an homage to Karloff's genius.

FRANKENSTEIN MEETS THE SPACE MONSTER

Some of these Frankenstein films are pretty watchable. Others are so bad, only a dedicated fan could even consider sitting through them. These are real movies—we didn't make them up!

1. *Frankenstein Meets the Space Monster* (1965)
NASA builds a robot named Frank and sends it into space, where it meets a space monster and goes berserk.

2. *Assignment Terror* (1971)
An alien lands on Earth, brings Frankenstein, Dracula, the Mummy, and other monsters to life, "but is thwarted by the socially aware Wolf Man."

3. *Jesse James Meets Frankenstein's Daughter* (1965)
Frankenstein's granddaughter, Maria, tries to capture Jesse James and his sidekick to turn them into monsters.

4. *I Was a Teenage Frankenstein* (1957)
A descendant of Dr. Frankenstein moves to America, where he sets up a lab and begins building monsters out of the bodies of hot rod racers killed in car accidents.

5. *Frankenhooker* (1980)
After a woman dies in a freak lawnmower accident, her mad-scientist boyfriend brings her back to life by sewing her head onto body parts taken from prostitutes on New York's 42nd Street.

6. *Frankenstein General Hospital* (1988)
Frankenstein's 12th grandson tries his experiments in the basement of a modern hospital.

7. *Frankenstein Conquers the World* (1964)
"A boy eats the radioactive heart of the Frankenstein monster and begins to grow into an ugly giant that watches Japanese teenagers do the Twist" (*The Frankenstein Movie Guide*). Japanese title: *Frankenstein vs. the Giant Crab Monster*.

Elephants can run 20 miles per hour; hummingbirds can fly 60 miles per hour.

8. *Frankenstein on Campus* (1970)
A college student plots to turn his fellow-students into monsters. "If you can sit through this tripe, go to the head of the class." (*Creature Features Movie Guide*)

9. *Frankenstein Island* (1981)
"A group of balloonists crash on a mysterious island populated by bikini-clad warrior-women descended from aliens....Frankenstein's great-great granddaughter Sheila, is around...experimenting on captives." (*Frankenstein Movie Guide*)

10. *Frankenstein Created Woman* (1966)
"Male spirit is transplanted into the body of a beautiful woman with heaving bosom, who then goes around stabbing respectable folks with a knife." (*Creature Features Movie Guide*)

11. *Frankenstein 1970* (1958)
A descendant of Dr. Frankenstein sells the TV rights to his famous ancestor's story and uses the money to build an atomic-powered Frankenstein monster. The studio thought a futuristic-sounding title would help at the box office.

12. *Frankenstein's Daughter* (1958)
Frankenstein's grandson tests a drug called *degeneral* on a teenage girl, and it "degenerates her into a bikini-clad creature running through the streets."

13. *Frankenstein '80* (1979)
Dr. Otto Frankenstein puts together a sex-crazed monster who goes on a killing spree. Lots of blood, including real surgical footage.

14. *Frankenstein's Castle of Freaks* (1973)
Using his "Electric Accumulator," Count Frankenstein brings back Goliath the caveman, Kreegin the Hunchback, and Ook the Neanderthal Man! *South Pacific* star Rossano Brazzi—"sounding like a cross between Chico Marx and Bela Lugosi"—plays the Count.

15. *Frankenstein's Great-Aunt Tillie* (1983)
Victor Jr. and his 109-year-old aunt "search for the family fortune and become involved with women's emancipation." (*The Frankenstein Movie Guide*)

Long wait: The "longest recorded interval" between the birth of twins was 136 days.

THE WORLD'S MOST FAMOUS CORPSE

More people have seen Lenin's mummy than any other mummy in history. It's a tourist attraction, a cultural artifact, and as you'll see, a political gimmick. How did this weird monument—denounced by Lenin's official historian as an "absurd idea"—come into being? Here's the full story.

L enin's tomb in Moscow's Red Square is the best-known landmark in the Soviet Union, as well as the spiritual center of Soviet political ideology. Some 150 million people have visited the mausoleum since it was first built....

There are always long lines, but you should expect to be descending the gloomy stairs into the tomb within 20-30 minutes. Without stopping, you walk around three sides of the glass case in which Lenin lies, stubbly and ashen-faced, wearing a jacket and polka-dot tie.

—*Travel Guide to the Soviet Union*

DEATH OF A LEADER

At 6:50 p.m. on January 21, 1924, Vladimir Ilyich Lenin, first leader of the Soviet Union and father of his country, suffered a stroke and died.

No one was sure how to handle it. Lenin had asked for a simple funeral. He wished to be buried next to his mother and sister in the family burial plot. But when Soviet leaders met to discuss the matter, they came up with another idea—turn the funeral into a "propaganda event" that could help legitimize the Communist regime. They decided to embalm him so he could lie in state for a while.

Then, only three days after his death, the Politburo began discussing the idea of saving the body "a little longer." Lenin's relatives balked at the idea...but Joseph Stalin insisted. As Dmitri Volkogonov writes in *Lenin: A New Biography*, Stalin "came to see [preserving Lenin's body] as the creation of a secular Bolshevik relic with huge propaganda potential." A short time later, the Politburo issued the following orders:

1. The coffin containing V. I. Lenin's corpse is to be kept in a vault which should be made accessible to visitors;

2. The vault is to be formed in the Kremlin wall on Red Square among the communal graves of the fighters of the October Revolution. A commission is being created today for the construction of a mausoleum.

A burial vault was dug along the Kremlin wall, a wooden hut was built over it to keep out the elements, and Lenin's body was placed inside following the funeral.

CORPSE OF ENGINEERS

Meanwhile, the secret police were rounding up the country's top scientists to put them to work figuring out how to embalm Lenin for eternity. A streetcar was towed into Red Square and fitted with beds, hot plates, and washbasins; it served as the terrified scientists' home for the rest of the winter.

But restoring Lenin to his former glory was not so easy. Illness had ravaged him in the final years of his life, leaving him frail-looking and emaciated. And since permanent, *lifelike* embalming had never been attempted before, research on how to accomplish such a task had to begin from scratch. In the meantime, the body continued to deteriorate.

Lenin's cadaver was packed in ice to slow the decay, and by June the scientists finally succeeded in "stabilizing" the body. By then, however, it was a mess. "In those four and a half months," historian Robert Payne writes in *The Life and Death of Lenin*, "remarkable changes had taken place: he was waxen gray, wrinkled, horribly shrunken." Nonetheless, by August 1924, Lenin's body had been cleaned up enough to put on public display.

STAYING IN SHAPE

Work on *improving* Lenin's after-death appearance would continue for more than 25 years. The task was handled by the Research Institute for "Biological Structures" (a Soviet euphemism for cadaver) and its Lenin Mausoleum Laboratory—both of which were so secret that the West did not learn of their existence until after the collapse of the Soviet Union. Part of the routine that was worked out over the years:

• To prevent Lenin from decomposing, the temperature in the mausoleum is kept at precisely 59°F. The humidity is also kept constant.

• Every Monday and Friday, the mausoleum is closed and a senior official of the institute's "body brigade" (most of whom log 20 years or more on the job before they are allowed to touch the corpse) removes Lenin's clothing and examines the cadaver for any signs of wear and tear. Any dust that has accumulated is carefully brushed away; then a special preservative ointment is applied to the skin. The corpse is then re-dressed and put back on display.

• Every 18 months, the cadaver is bathed in preservatives and injected with chemicals, which displace both water and bacteria in the cells and prevent the tissues from decomposing. Which chemicals are used in the process? Hardly anyone knows—even today, the "recipe" is as closely guarded a secret as the formula for Coca-Cola. Only the eight most senior members of the institute know the precise formula. When the process is completed, the cadaver is given a brand-new, hand-tailored suit.

KEEPING THE FAITH

As of 1996, more than five years after the collapse of the Soviet empire, Lenin's body was still on display in Red Square. Keeping the mausoleum open is no empty gesture—the corpse requires constant attention and a lot of money to keep it in good condition. But for many, it has become the political shrine that Stalin envisioned…and the Russian government fears that giving Lenin a regular burial will create a political backlash. Seventy-two years after he died, Lenin is still—literally—a political presence to be reckoned with.

MUMMIFIED FACTS

• **Wasted effort.** Soviet scientists continued perfecting their embalming techniques until the 1950s…just in time for the death of Joseph Stalin. He, too, was embalmed, then laid to rest alongside Lenin. But *that* turned out to be a waste of time. Eight years later, Nikita Khruschev ordered Stalin's body removed and buried in a more modest grave along the Kremlin wall.

A giraffe's neck has 7 vertebrae; a bird's has 14; a person's has 26.

• **Mummies for sale.** Budget cuts brought on by the collapse of the Soviet Union have forced the Research Institute for Biological Structures to make its services available to the public. The mummification process takes a full year, requires the removal of all organs, and costs around $500,000. "The precise cost depends on the condition of the body," an official explains. "But our work is the best." The $500,000, by the way, only covers the cost of the embalming—you still have to build a mausoleum with temperature and humidity controls, which the institute estimates will cost as much as $5 million...not including the cost of staffing it forever.

• **No-brainer.** In 1924, Lenin's brain was removed and handed over to the Soviet Brain Institute—an organization founded specifically to determine whether the Leader's brain was superior to other human brains. Not surprisingly, they reported in 1936 that the brain "possessed such high organization that even during Lenin's illness, it continued to function on a very high level." Alas, it was just propaganda. In 1994, the Brain Institute's director admitted that "in the anatomical structure of Lenin's brain, there is nothing sensational."

CADAVER CONSPIRACY?

Is the body on display in Lenin's Tomb really *his* body? The official word is yes. But throughout the late 1920s and 1930s, rumors spread that the embalmers had actually failed in their task. According to the story, the body in the mausoleum is a wax dummy.

This rumor is so widely accepted that the Soviet government opened an official "investigation" into the matter and invited a German doctor to participate and report his findings to the world. But the inquiry only heightened suspicions. As Payne reports, the German doctor

> was not permitted to make more than a cursory examination. He reported that he had observed frostbites on the skin, felt the cheeks, and lifted one of Lenin's arms....He inquired about the techniques and was told they were secret but would be fully revealed in three or four years' time when they had been proved effective; and nothing more was ever heard about the secret formula.

Even after the fall of Communism in Russia, no one (except for the government) knows for sure whether the corpse is real.

KNIFE-STYLES OF THE RICH AND FAMOUS

BRI member Erik Linden sent us this amazing article on plastic surgery in L.A. It's from Marie Claire *magazine, written by Sally Ogle Davis.*

At Hollywood's Oscar show, filmland's biggest night of the year, you can count on three things: tearful acceptance speeches, over-the-top gowns, and a TV audience that includes every L.A. plastic surgeon worth his or her scalpel. It's their award ceremony too. Where else can they see their carefully crafted handiwork displayed to over one billion people worldwide?

Plastic surgeon Dr. Frank Kamer, who's lifted more famous faces than the elevator at CAA—Liz Taylor, Cher, Jane Fonda, Dolly Parton, and Joan Rivers, to name a few—sits in his elegant pastel-hued clinic in Beverly Hills, smiling wryly. "They're happy their careers are going well," he says of his celebrity patients. "Whether I had something to do with that I don't know. But I think I did."

Others agree. At the bar at the Four Seasons Hotel, agents talk about the two plumped-up reasons why Demi Moore, 33, is worth a million more per picture than Julia Roberts, while the plastic surgeons at the next table prefer to focus on Demi's nose. "She had it done right after her Vanity Fair cover," said one. "Her's was the rounded kind that doesn't age well," sniffed another. "It's surprising she got as far as she did with the original."

GETTING STAR TREATMENT

Welcome to L.A....without question, the plastic surgery capital of America. Every year, four times as many breasts are enlarged in L.A. as on the entire eastern seaboard. Twice as many faces are lifted there as in New York....Los Angelenos flock to surgeons' offices...demanding "Kim Basinger's lips," "Cher's cheekbones," "Demi's breasts."

Today in L.A., you need never be fat, flat chested, or, God forbid, old....The magazines on the newsstands are chockablock with ads for liposuction artists, chemical peelers, laser surgeons, and eye debaggers, [and] hairdressers around town are experts at hiding scars....

You can't take it with you: When Empress Elizabeth of Russia died in 1762, she owned 15,000 dresses.

"It's pretty routine to us," says…the 66-year-old wife of a wealthy building contractor. She's had her neck redraped, her eyes debagged, and her upper lip chemically peeled. Only two weeks after her third face-lift, she looks 50. "We all sit around at my country club and compare doctors, prices, and pain stories like we used to discuss childbirth."

THE SECRET WORLD OF SURGERY

In the tight little world of nip-and-tuck intelligence, plastic surgeons take more oaths of secrecy than a CIA candidate. But who's done what to whom is as much grist for the Hollywood gossip mill as the weekly movie box-office returns. Dishers on divas whisper that Jessica Lange, 47, had a really terrific lift just before making *Losing Isaiah*, that 38-year-old Sharon Stone's famous frontage has been oh-so-subtly enhanced, and that 55-year-old Faye Dunaway's lift is too tight, making her look, according to one Hollywood producer, as if she has "erased her own face."

"More celebrities are having surgery than the media knows, by a mile, because if it's good you can't tell," says Dr. Kamer. There are a few holdouts in the celebrity ranks. Cybill Shepherd, 46, has so far resisted the knife; so has Meryl Streep, also 46—but don't be surprised if they succumb soon. Even the legends have gone the surgery route: Joanne Woodward, 66, and Katherine Hepburn, 88, finally bit the bullet and were lifted.

PLASTIC HISTORY

Los Angeles has been marketing eternal youth since the 1950s, thanks to Dr. Franklin Ashley, La-La Land's plastic surgery pioneer. When he opened his clinic on western L.A.'s Pico Boulevard in the early 1960s, Hollywood greats raced to his operating table. Susan Hayward came in looking like hell and went out looking like, well, Susan Hayward. Even the leathery icon John Wayne had a career-extending face-lift. (True to western code, he refused to take his boots off during the procedure.)

But it was comedienne Phyllis Diller, now 78, who changed plastic surgery in Los Angeles forever—by proving that you don't even have to start out as a Hollywood beauty to end up looking like one. The haggard hausfrau had her first face-lift by Ashley in the early 1970s, becoming a smooth-cheeked belle overnight. And, remarkably, she not only admitted it but boasted about it to the press.

Suddenly, the whole town wanted the miracle Diller treatment.

RECOVERY ZONE

Today, on tree-shaded streets all over L.A., there are unassuming houses with names like Halcyon or The Hidden Garden where bandage-swathed guests in dark glasses come to recover under the watchful eyes of private nurses. Since California law restricts patients of private surgical clinics to a stay of only 23 hours and 59 minutes, a lucrative trade flourishes in post-plastic surgery care....

Some doctors offer service even more personal. Dr. Kelly O'Neil, a dermatologist celebrated by celebs for his wrinkle-erasing chemical peels, ships recovering clients to his...five-acre ranch in Temecula. There, bandaged like mummies, they take their food through straws so as not to disturb their new, freshly smoothed faces.

BRING ON THE BOOBS

Not surprisingly, in the industry town that spawned Marilyn Monroe and houses Hugh Hefner's Playboy mansion, Boobs are BIG. And the business of enlarging them is even bigger. "We can make better breasts than God," declares Dr. Maja Ruetschi, an elegant Swiss-born surgeon....

After notorious silicone implants were banned from cosmetic surgery practice in 1992, there was a lull in the U.S. demand for breast enhancement, while die-hard wanna-haves got used to the new saline substitutes. However, surgeons expect that soon they'll be able to use Europe's most popular implant, which contains a gel that feels more natural than saline and comes with a built-in lawsuit repellent: If the jelly leaks, it's excreted by the kidneys.

"With the breast, you're talking about sexual fantasy," explains the soft-spoken Dr. Barbara Hayden. "It's as individual as the patient herself. I can give the breast a mushroom shape, or make it flatter so it's like a little trampoline. If she wants more cleavage, I can suction the sides."

ADDICTED TO PERFECTION

But having a little plastic surgery is like doing a little decorating work on your house; every improvement makes the rest look bad....

Celebrities are particularly susceptible to plastic surgery addiction, says Dr. Pam Lipkin...."These are not the world's most secure people. When you have cosmetic surgery and it goes well, there's a tremendous psychological reassurance. And when cost is no object, the more you have the more you want." Mary Tyler Moore, 59, is rumored to be a can't-stop patient. The actress has reportedly had two face-lifts, breast implants, and collagen injections.

And they're coming in younger and younger. "Melrose Place" 's Josie Bisset, 26, and 22-year-old Tiffani-Amber Thiessen of "Beverly Hills 90210" both sport bigger breasts these days. But the current junior plastic-surgery champion is Tori Spelling, 22, a continuing work-in-progress who has that what-age-is-she-anyway look that comes from too much surgery too soon. "I've worked with her several times," said a Hollywood photo editor, "and her breasts have changed twice. She's also had her nose done twice, and had cheek and chin implants." But the daddy of all plastic surgery junkies is, of course, Michael Jackson, 37, who could afford the very best but ended up with an "amputated nose." "There were a lot of people involved with that nose," one surgeon said. "One doctor would tell him 'No,' and he'd say, 'All right, I'll go somewhere else.' "...

CELEBRITY SILENCE

Yet, despite the pervasiveness of cosmetic surgery in L.A., stars still don't like to admit that their extravagant frontage is more a tribute to their surgeon's skill than God's. Some refuse comment altogether: Jane Fonda, now 58, once preached, "We should learn to love our wrinkles"—then got rid of hers and inflated her chest. Some stars have always white-lied through their neatly capped teeth: Elizabeth Taylor, 64, had admitted only to a tiny little tuck under the chin, done after she lost over 100 pounds. In fact, local surgeons say, she has had four face-lifts....

And while the rest of the country may believe that Sophia Loren, 61, came by her ageless beauty from good genes and thinking kind thoughts, Los Angelenos gossip about eye work and face-lifts done on several continents.... Michelle Pfeiffer, 39, keeps quiet about her rumored cheek implants and nose work, and there has been no peep from model Lauren Hutton, 52, who left her gap-toothed smile untouched but lifted her face some time ago. "Hairdressers everywhere have seen those scars," says one Hollywood insider. Priscilla Presley, 50, does not talk about the chemical peels she reportedly has to get of wrinkles and brown spots. Even Barbra Streisand, 54, has allegedly undergone some subtle surgical enhancement. "She still has her famous nose," says an expert. "But look at her early pictures. It's not the *same* nose."

Some celebs are only a little bit honest: Cher, 49,...owns up to her breast augmentation but says nothing about her cheek implants, tummy tuck, buttock lift, new nose, navel surgery, or liposuction. Dolly Parton, 50, admits to a face-lift but neglects to mention the silicone in her fabulous frontage and the liposuctioning of virtually every other part of her lavish anatomy....

WHAT ABOUT COMPLICATIONS?

"We don't run beauty shops," cautions Dr. Kamer. "This is not something you drop in and do on your lunch hour, whatever the advertisements claim."

More usual complications run the gamut from blood clots...to lumpy postliposuction skin...to droopy eyelids....Infections happen; so do poor healing, scarring, rejection of implants, nerve damage, rock-hard breasts, and, of course, wind-tunneled faces.

In fact, prominent botches are on display at your local theater; being rich and famous doesn't guarantee you good surgery. For every Liza Minnelli (age 50) and Susan Lucci (47), whose lifts are terrific, there's a Carol Burnett (63)—who, post-lift, looks like an entirely different person—or a Paul Hogan (56), who came up from down under for a lift. "He lost his distinctive tanned cragginess," says local surgeon. "Now he looks bland and creaseless." Another cosmetic casualty is 46-year-old actor Don Johnson, say the tongue waggers: Johnson's new eye job makes him look Oriental. "They just took away too much skin," explains another local doctor. And then there's Roy Scheider, 63, who emerged from his lift with a lop-sided face. "I think they damaged a nerve," an expert says.

No wonder Robert Redford, 59, finally showing his age from all that exposure to the Utah sun, is looking carefully before he leaps. "He's shopping around here and in Manhattan," said a Beverly Hills surgeon. "With that great face, he can't afford to take chances."

Meanwhile, it's springtime in L.A. On the streets of Beverly Hills, tanned ladies of leisure in tiny miniskirts strut their stuff.... Everything is on display. "Centuries from now," muses Dr. Novack, "when archaeologists dig up our civilization, they'll find dust, bones, and a collection of implant bags."

ACT III:
JUDGE GROUCHO

Here's the final episode of a 1933 radio show starring Groucho as newly elected Judge Waldo Flywheel, and Ravelli (Chico) as his sidekick.

BRUMMET: Well, Plunkett, Judge Flywheel owes a lot to you.

PLUNKETT: Yeah, we ran away with the election.

BRUMMET: It's lucky for you that your trial's coming up in his court.

PLUNKETT: Lucky? What do you think I got him put in office for? Judge Maxwell would've given me twenty years on this bribery charge. But with Flywheel on the bench, I ought to get off in a couple of hours.

BRUMMET: What about that lawyer you got—Ravelli? He don't look too smart to me.

PLUNKETT: Oh, Ravelli's all right. Flywheel asked me to hire him. I guess they got the whole thing worked out between them. I ain't even demandin' a jury. I'm leaving it all in Judge Flywheel's hands. Let's go in. The court-room's filling up.

BAILIFF: Hear ye, hear ye. Court is now in session. Everybody rise. His honor, Judge Flywheel.

GROUCHO: Never mind. Where's the court stenographer?

I want him to take a letter to my wife.

BAILIFF: Why, he can't do that.

GROUCHO: He can't? Better look for a new stenographer. What's the first case?

BAILIFF: It's the case of Steve Granach, charged with making too much noise in his apartment, and operating a poolroom within three hundred feet of a schoolhouse.

GROUCHO: A poolroom three hundred feet from a schoolhouse? That's a disgrace. Have them move the schoolhouse. I don't want those little kiddies walking that far. Now then, it's time I went to lunch.

BAILIFF: But Judge Flywheel, you haven't tried any cases yet.

GROUCHO: All right, bring one on. I'll try anything once.

BAILIFF: Next case is the trial of John H. Plunkett, charged with bribing public officials.

GROUCHO: Where's your lawyer, Plunkett?

RAVELLI: Here I am.

GROUCHO: Ravelli, are you the

When asked what they think is the most stressful event of the year, 20% of Americans

lawyer for the defendant?

RAVELLI: No, I'm the lawyer for this crook, Plunkett.

PLUNKETT: Say! What do you mean saying I'm a crook?

RAVELLI: Alright, alright. I didn't know it was a secret.

DISTRICT ATTORNEY: Your honor!

GROUCHO: What is it?

DISTRICT ATTORNEY: The state is prepared to proceed with the trial of John H. Plunkett. Our first witness is Leo Greenbury.

GROUCHO: Greenbury can't be a witness in this court.

DISTRICT ATTORNEY: Why not, your honor?

GROUCHO: Well, he told my wife's butcher that he didn't vote for me. The sneak!

DISTRICT ATTORNEY: I regret to say, your honor, that I consider your remark most unbecoming to a judge.

GROUCHO: What did you say?

DISTRICT ATTORNEY: I said your remark was most unbecoming to a judge.

GROUCHO: Hey, that's the sec-ond time you said that. Just for that I fine you a hundred bucks. I dare you to insult me again.

DISTRICT ATTORNEY: Oh, never mind.

GROUCHO : Oh, come on. I'll let you have this insult for fifty bucks.

RAVELLI: Come on, Plunkett, get on the witness stand, I ask you questions.

PLUNKETT: Alright, Ravelli. *(gets on stand)*

RAVELLI: How old are you?

PLUNKETT: I'm forty-five.

RAVELLI: Hey, Judge, I object.

GROUCHO: You object to your own witness's answer? On what grounds?

RAVELLI: I dunno. I couldn't think of anything else to say.

GROUCHO: Objection sustained!

DISTRICT ATTORNEY: On what grounds?

GROUCHO: I couldn't think of anything else to say either. Ravelli, proceed.

DISTRICT ATTORNEY: If your honor pleases, the state...

GROUCHO: Oh, pipe down and give somebody else a chance. You talk more than my wife. That's why I never got married.

DISTRICT ATTORNEY: The state objects, your honor. This is not a divorce case! John H. Plun-kett is charged with bribery!

GROUCHO: Bribery? Why wasn't I told about that? I don't count, do I? Oh, no. I'm just the judge here, that's all. Plunkett, I'm going to give you your choice of sentences: 10 years in Leavenworth, or 11 years in twelve-worth.

PLUNKETT: What?

GROUCHO: All right. We'll make it 5 & 10 in Woolworth.

PLUNKETT: Wait a minute, your honor. The state ain't proved that I'm guilty of bribery.

GROUCHO: The state doesn't have to. I know you're guilty.

PLUNKETT: Say, how do you know I'm guilty?

GROUCHO: Are you kidding? Don't you remember? You bribed me. That's how I became a judge.

PLUNKETT: You double-crosser!...

RAVELLI (Looking at the door): Boss, here comes Judge Maxwell.

MAXWELL: Mr. Flywheel, we have just come from the election board. Your sitting on the bench is absolutely illegal. We've just discovered that Emmanuel Ravelli voted more than once.

GROUCHO: Is that right, Ravelli? Did you vote more than once?

CHICO: Well, let me see. (*Thinking*) Mm-m. Maybe I did.

GROUCHO (Upset): Well, did you or didn't you? Think, man

RAVELLI (Still thinking): I voted one...two...three...YEP, I voted three thousand times.

☆   ☆   ☆   ☆

MORE "TRANSQUIPS"

Real courtroom conversation from Humor in the Court *and*
More Humor in the Court, *by Mary Louise Gilman.*
(see page 273 for more)

Q: Now, Mrs. Johnson, how was your first marriage terminated?
A: By death.
Q: And by whose death was it terminated?

Q: And who is this person you are speaking of?
A: My ex-widow said it.

Q: Officer, what led you to believe the defendant was under the influence?
A: Because he was argumentary and he couldn't pronunciate his words.

Literary pretensions: The TV show *The Love Boat* was based on a novel.

MISS AMERICA TODAY, PART VI

Like all social institutions, the Miss America Pageant has had to become a bit of a cultural chameleon to survive. It doesn't change drastically—it has to be true to its roots as a traditional beauty contest, after all. But when the pressure gets strong enough, it seems to creak forward. Here's an update on the state of the pageant today:

NEW AND IMPROVED

The protests of the late 1960s and early 1970s over the Miss America Pageant's alleged anti-feminist and racist attitudes launched an era of gradual change for the pageant that continues to this day. For example:

✔ In 1968, the pageant named a black clergyman to its board of directors and nominated two African American women to the hostess committee; a year later Dr. Zelma George became the pageant's first African American judge. The first African American contestant was Cheryl Brown, Miss Iowa 1970.

✔ The most crassly sexist components of the pageant (except the swimsuit contest, of course) were quietly done away with. The "Neat as a Pin Award," created in 1969 to reward $250 to the tidiest contestant, was abandoned in 1973; the Miss Congeniality Award bit the dust two years later. In 1986 the pageant abandoned the practice of publishing contestants' bust, waistline, and hip measurements.

✔ Contemporary issues were given greater attention beginning in 1974. Contestants had to answer "controversial, issue-oriented questions dealing with topics ranging from rape to prostitution." But the questions were asked offstage, away from the audience and TV cameras, to avoid the possibility of embarrassing the contestants or the pageant. The TV audience had to settle for short rehearsed issue speeches, which were made during the evening gown competition. Eventually, the pageant came up with a "platform" that the new Miss America agreed to support.

THERE HE GOES...

By the 1980s, nothing was sacred. In its endless quest for relevance and higher ratings, the pageant began leading its most sacred cows to slaughter. In 1980 it was announced that Bert Parks, who'd hosted every broadcast since 1955, was "retiring." (Pageant chairman Albert Marks later claimed that sponsors had been urging him to get rid of Bert for more than a decade.)

The move was handled shabbily—Parks learned of the firing from a reporter—and the publicity that resulted was disastrous. Miss America fans bombarded the pageant's Atlantic City headquarters with thousands of angry phone calls and letters, and "Tonight Show" host Johnny Carson, no spring chicken himself, waged an on-air campaign to have the crooner reinstated.

It didn't work. Marks stuck to his guns and replaced Parks with actor Ron Ely in 1980...then with Gary Collins in 1982...then with Regis Philbin and Kathie Lee Gifford in 1991. So far, however, no one has been able to fill Parks's shoes. (Parks made a guest appearance at the 1990 pageant—which some insiders claim was possible only because Marks had died in September 1989—but he made a lot of gaffes during the live broadcast and did not return in subsequent pageants. He died in 1992.)

There It Ain't

The axe fell again in 1982, when the Miss America Pageant failed to agree with composer Bernie Wayne on a price for using the song "There She Is" in the pageant. Wayne wanted a 15-year, $25,000 contract, but pageant officials refused, and the song was cut. As with Parks's firing, public response was negative and overwhelming...and this time it actually worked. Three years later, the pageant put "There She Is" back in the show.

THE HOLY OF HOLIES

But the biggest change of all came in 1994, when the Miss America Pageant—after suffering the lowest TV ratings in 20 years—announced that it was considering dropping the swimsuit competition altogether. This idea was hardly a new one; in fact, the swimsuit competition was as unpopular with top officials at the Miss America Pageant as with the pageant's protesters. Lenora Slaughter had spent years lobbying behind the scenes to dump the swimsuits,

---

5 most common American last names: 1. Smith 2. Johnson 3. Williams 4. Jones 5. Brown

but pressure from traditionalists and swimsuit fans had proved too great.

Now, rather than make the decision itself, the pageant left it up to viewers. And to milk the maximum amount of publicity from the event, the vote was held *during* the 1995 Miss America broadcast. Viewers could call a 900 number and cast their votes while watching the show. The vote was updated throughout the program; the final tally was to be announced toward the end of the show. Just in case the vote was in favor of axing the suits, the pageant had another "mystery" event waiting in the wings to take its place.

The mystery event wasn't needed—the suits won 60% to 40%. The live vote was the biggest pageant publicity stunt since the 1920s, and it had the desired effect: 2.1 million more people watched the broadcast in 1995 than did in 1994.

THE END?

Will the pageant survive? Maybe not as the major cultural institution that it was in the 1950s, but if the pageant's ability for reinventing itself in a crisis is any guide (and the TV ratings don't slip much further), it will probably be around for decades to come.

MISS AMERICA BEAUTY SECRETS

How do makeup artists affiliated with the Miss America Pageant keep America's beauties beautiful? Here are a few of their tricks.

Dirty hair. One of the pageant's hairstylists admits, "Dirty hair is more manageable. I can make a style fuller and stay better."

Face Putty. Used to cover up lines, scars, and pockmarks, and to create "porcelain" complexions. One makeup artist says: "I've even gone so far as to use mortician's wax mixed with the makeup."

Vaseline. Smeared on the teeth so that contestants can smile easily—even if their mouths dry up from nervousness.

Preparation H. The hemorrhoid ointment is smeared on eyelids and under the eyes. According to one makeup artist, "It smells pretty bad, but it removes puffiness."

There are ten million bricks in the Empire State Building.

MISS AMERICA SCANDALS

*The Miss America Pageant has never had a scandal big enough
to destroy it...but a bunch of middle-sized controversies have
made headlines over the years. Here are a few of the juicier
ones that we haven't already covered.*

VANESSA WILLIAMS, Miss America 1984

Scandal: It was a big deal when Williams became the first African American Miss America. And there was just as much publicity when, 10 months later, *Penthouse* magazine announced that it had obtained a series of nude pictures Williams had posed for years earlier (including photos in suggestive poses with another woman)...and was planning to publish them in its September 1984 edition. Pageant officials immediately pronounced the photos "inconsistent with the Miss America image" and gave Williams 72 hours to resign her crown.

What Happened: It was the biggest scandal ever involving a reigning Miss America. But if anything, it *boosted* Williams's career. Since 1984, she's appeared on Broadway and recorded million-selling singles and Grammy-winning albums. Ironically, she's now the most successful ex-Miss America in the history of the pageant.

VENUS RAMEY, Miss America 1944

Scandal: A few days after she won the title, Ramey, 19, revealed that she'd forged her mother's name on the contract binding her to the pageant's scheduled promotional appearances—so it was legally unenforceable. Her reason for the stunt: She wanted to negotiate her own deals directly with advertisers.

Pageant officials "invited" Ramey to New York's Waldorf-Astoria hotel, where they held her while they tried to persuade her to honor the contract. When that failed, they flew in Ramey's mother to sign the contract for real. She also refused to cooperate.

What Happened: Ramey never did honor the contract. She embarked on her own tour—which bombed. She earned only $8,500 for an entire year on the road. (By comparison, Miss America 1941 earned an estimated $150,000 during her reign.) "I wanted to get into show business," Ramey complained afterward. "I thought the

---

Chicago is *called* "The Windy City...but Blue Hill, Mass. is actually America's windiest city.

pageant would be a good entree. It is, all right—an entree into oblivion. Forever afterward, you're like a broken-down actress trying to make a comeback."

CLAIRE JAMES, *Miss California 1938*

Scandal: James made it all the way to First Runner Up, then lost out to Marilyn Meseke, Miss Ohio, when judges "disapproved of her use of mascara."

What Happened: James was furious. Her promoter, theatrical producer Earl Carroll, denounced the judges as "incompetents," and the day after the pageant called a press conference to crown James the "people's choice" for Miss America. It was a publicity stunt, but James took it seriously, often identifying herself as Miss America in commercials and in speaking tours around the country. She finally backed off after Meseke, the real Miss America, took her to court.

B. ("BILLY") DON MAGNESS, *Chairman of the Board, Miss Texas Pageant, 1970-1990*

Scandal: In September 1990, *Life* magazine alleged in an article on Magness—whose nicknames included "Mr. Miss Texas" and "God"—that, among other things, he:

- Held private swimsuit modeling sessions with Miss Texas contestants at his house.
- Made "very pointed hints" to a number of contestants over the years.
- Regularly kissed contestants on the lips.
- Telephoned contestants and asked them questions like "Wanna get nekkid?"
- Gave contestants obscene T-shirts, including one that read, "In case of rape, this side up."
- Referred to contestants as "sluts" during the *Life* magazine interview.

"While I make an attempt at appearing to be a dirty old man," Magness explained during the interview, "I make double that attempt to be sure that I'm not. Does that make sense? It's just kind of fun. You can be too clean and pure. Some of the girls just need to be dirtied up a little. It's just a continuance of their education."

The federal government owns about 20% of the land in America.

What Happened: The article quoted Miss America CEO Leonard Horn as saying Magness "has lots of elegance and class. I think B. Don really cares about these kids." But after reading the *Life* article, Horn quickly changed his tune. He ordered Texas pageant officials to investigate Magness, then threatened to keep the next Miss Texas out of the Miss America pageant unless Magness resigned.

YOLANDE BETBEZE, *Miss America 1951*

Scandal: The day after her coronation, Betbeze announced at a breakfast meeting that she would not pose in swimsuits during her reign. An earlier Miss America had taken the same stand and gotten away with it, but this time the Catalina Swimsuit Company was sponsoring the pageant, and had already booked Betbeze on a nationwide swimsuit tour.

What Happened: "The coffee cups rattled, let me tell you," Betbeze recalled years later. "The man from Catalina bathing suits stood up and fumed. He was furious. He looked at me and said, 'I'll run you off the news pages. I'll start my own contest. You'll see.' "

"I said, 'That's splendid. Good luck to you.' Anyway, he did, indeed, start the Miss USA and Miss Universe Pageants. So people can thank me—or blame me—for that."

BESS MYERSON, *Miss America 1945*

Scandal: In 1987, Myerson, then New York City's Commissioner of Cultural Affairs, was indicted for conspiracy, bribery, and fraud after she allegedly helped her boyfriend, a millionaire sewer contractor with reputed mob ties, lower his alimony payments by giving a judge's daughter a $19,000-a-year job in city government.

That was only the beginning of Myerson's legal troubles: In May 1988, she was arrested for shoplifting after she walked out of a New York department store without paying for the six bottles of nail polish, five pairs of earrings, one pair of shoes, and the flashlight batteries she'd stuffed into her purse and shopping bag. "I was leaving the store to lock my car and come back and pay for the merchandise," she explained to reporters after her arrest. Total value of the merchandise: $44.07. (Myerson was carrying $160 in cash.)

What Happened: Myerson was eventually acquitted on the alimony fixing charges, but pled guilty to shoplifting and paid a $100 fine, plus court costs.

SUSAN AKIN, *Miss America 1986*

Scandal: Within a month of her crowning, the story broke that Akin's father and grandfather had been arrested in connection with the Ku Klux Klan murders of three Mississippi civil rights workers in 1964. Neither man was convicted.

What Happened: Miss America officials didn't learn of the story until it was reported in the media, but insisted that Akin had no responsibility to disclose the family connection. Akin—who was born a month *after* the murders—admitted she was hurt by the revelations, but refused to let her family's past prevent affect her reign. "They're not Miss America," she told reporters, "I'm Miss America. …You're not going to hold it against me.…I don't even know the facts about these things because I don't want to know."

TONI GEORGIANA, *Miss New Jersey 1985*

Scandal: Shortly after Georgiana won the New Jersey title, first-runner-up Laura Bridges filed a lawsuit saying that Georgiana was actually a Pennsylvania resident, had competed twice in the Miss Pennsylvania pageant (and lost), and that she wasn't really a New Jersey student because she'd only enrolled in a single two-week education course at a state college, had not attended a single class, and had failed the course.

What Happened: New Jersey pageant officials sided with Georgiana, arguing that even if it was true, she had met minimum residency requirements set by the national pageant. Bridges lost the case.

STACY KING, *Miss Louisiana 1989*

Scandal: In 1989, the Miss Louisiana pageant director filed a protest, alleging that King was unfairly excluded from the Top 10 contestants in the national pageant because she was white and non-disabled. "It appeared that if you were black, ethnic, or had some kind of medical problem you had overcome, you stood a better chance of getting into the Top 10," he told reporters. "Two of the Top 10 were ethnic—one black and one Oriental—and there was one contestant who had a kidney transplant and another one who was deaf.…It was just awful odd the way it worked out."

What Happened: The media had fun with the "anti-politically correct" protest, but pageant officials ignored it.

EAT YOUR VITAMINS!

You've heard about vitamins since you were a little kid—but how much do you really know about them (besides the fact that they come in little pills)? Here's some food for thought, from BRI member John Dollison.

BACKGROUND. The cells in your body are constantly converting digested fats, proteins, and carbohydrates into energy, new tissue and bone cells. Unfortunately, they can't perform this task alone—they need help from certain catalyst chemicals that your body can't produce (or can't produce in sufficient quantities). You have to get these chemicals—called *vitamins*— from your food.

VITAMIN HISTORY

• Long before scientists unlocked the chemical code of vitamins, it was generally understood that eating certain foods would prevent specific diseases. One example: In the 18° century people discovered that adding citrus fruits to their diet could prevent scurvy, a disease whose symptoms included internal hemorrhaging and extreme weakness. In the 19th century, it was proven that substituting unpolished rice for polished rice would prevent beriberi, whose symptoms included paralysis and anemia.

• No one understood the relationship between these foods and the diseases they cured until 1906, when the British biochemist Frederick Hopkins proved that in addition to proteins, carbohydrates, fats, minerals, and water, foods also contained what he called "accessory factors"—substances that the body needed to convert food into chemical forms that the body could use.

• In 1911 Casimir Funk, a Polish chemist, discovered that the beriberi-preventing substance in unpolished rice was an *amine*, a type of nitrogen-containing compound. Funk understood that the amine was vital to proper body function, so he named it "vitamine" (for "vital amine").

• A year later he and Hopkins proposed the Vitamin Hypothesis of Deficiency, which theorized that the absence of a particular vitamin in the diet could lead to certain diseases. By depriving animals of different types of foods in strictly controlled experiments, scientists identified numerous other similar substances.

• But they still didn't understand their chemical makeup, so they couldn't give the proper scientific names. Instead, they just called them all vitamines, and kept them separate by assigning a different letter of the alphabet to each new substance they discovered. They soon realized that many of the vitamins weren't amines at all—but by that time, the word "vitamine" had become so popular that they couldn't change it. So they just dropped the "e."

VITAMIN BASICS

• Scientists divide vitamins into two different types: water-soluble (the B-complex vitamins and vitamin C), and fat-soluble (A, D, E, and K).

• Your body can't store water-soluble vitamins very well, so if you eat more than your RDA, or Recommended Dietary Allowance, most of them pass out of your body in your urine. That's why it's important to eat them every day.

• Fat-soluble vitamins, however, are more easily stored: Your liver tissue can store large amounts of vitamins A and D, and vitamin E is stored in body fat and reproductive organs.

KNOW YOUR VITAMINS

Vitamin A (retinol).
Sources: Animal fats and dairy products, green leafy vegetables, and carrots.
Why it's needed: Because it is a component of the pigment in the retinas of your eyes, vitamin A is necessary for good vision. It also helps keep the immune system healthy, and is necessary for the proper functioning of most organs.

Vitamin B complex (B1 [thiamine], B2 [riboflavin], B3 [niacin and niacinamide], B5 [pantothenic acid], biotin, folacin, and B12 [cobalamin]).
Sources: All meats, cereals, grains, green vegetables, dairy products, and brewer's yeast.
Why it's needed: B vitamins are necessary for healthy skin, and for the normal operation of a number of cell processes, including digestion, respiration, blood cell and bone marrow production, and metabolism. They're also needed by the nervous system.

Vitamin C (ascorbic acid).

Sources: Fresh fruits and vegetables, especially citrus fruits and tomatoes.

Why it's needed: Your body uses vitamin C to heal wounds and bone fractures; build tendons, and other tissues; and it helps you absorb iron. It's also needed for healthy teeth, gums, and blood.

Vitamin D.

Sources: Your skin produces it when exposed to sunlight; also found in eggs, butter, and fish that have fat distributed through their tissue (salmon, tuna, sardines, oysters, etc).

Why it's needed: Your body uses it to regulate its absorption of calcium and phosphorus, which makes it essential for proper bone and cartilage formation.

Vitamin E.

Sources: Green, leafy vegetables, wheat germ oil, margarine, rice.

Why it's needed: Vitamin E is one of the least understood vitamins, but it is known to be necessary for proper reproduction and prevention of muscular dystrophy in laboratory rats. It may also impair neuromuscular functions.

Vitamin K.

Sources: Not made by the body itself, but by organisms that live in our intestinal tract. Also found in yogurt, egg yolks, leafy green vegetables, and fish liver oils.

Why it's needed: Enables your body to synthesize the proteins required for the proper clotting of blood. Also helps reduce excessive menstrual flow in women.

HEALTHY HINTS

• It's a good idea to wash your vegetables before you eat them—but don't soak them. You'll lose a lot of the water-soluable vitamins (B and C) if you do.

• If you don't eat fresh vegetables within a week of buying them, you're better off buying frozen vegetables. Fresh vegetables lose their vitamins over time, and after about a week in your refrigerator they have fewer vitamins than frozen ones. And they almost always have more vitamins than canned vegetables.

JFK's PRESIDENTIAL AFFAIRS

You've heard about his liaison with Marilyn Monroe. But there's more.
A lot more. Here's some of the gossip you probably haven't heard.

BACKGROUND

Rumors of marital infidelity have plagued a number of Presidents, but perhaps none as much as John F. Kennedy.

According to books like *JFK: A Question of Character*, many of the rumors are true. While he was president, Kennedy's youth and charisma proved irresistible to scores of attractive young women who found themselves in his company—and JFK made the most of the opportunity. One member of the administration remembers: "it was a revolving door over there. A woman had to fight to get into that line."

As Traphes Bryant, a White House employee who served under the Kennedys and other first families, says, "Despite all the stories I've heard about other past presidents, I doubt we will ever have another one like Kennedy."

Here are a few of the *tamer* details that have surfaced since JFK's infidelities became public in 1977.

A LITTLE HELP FROM HIS FRIENDS

• The White House staff were directly involved in Kennedy's womanizing. Top aides such as Evelyn Lincoln, the President's personal secretary, were responsible for sneaking women in and out of the White House unobserved by Mrs. Kennedy or the press.

• According to Bryant, "there was a conspiracy of silence to protect his secrets from Jacqueline and to keep her from finding out. The newspapers would tell how First Lady Jacqueline was off on a trip, but what they didn't report was how anxious the President sometimes was to see her go. And what consternation there sometimes was when she returned unexpectedly."

• The Secret Service was also in on the act. They helped remove traces of JFK's affairs from White House bedrooms, and were responsible for ferrying Kennedy to and from "love nests" undetected during presidential trips. Charles Spaulding, one of Kennedy's closest friends, remembers one such trip when the president was staying at the Carlyle Hotel in New York. He and Kennedy traveled to their mistresses' nearby apartments via a network of underground tunnels beneath the hotel. "It was kind of a weird sight," Spaulding remembers. "Jack and I and two Secret Service men walking in these huge tunnels underneath the city streets alongside those enormous pipes, each of us carrying a flashlight. One of the Secret Service men also had this underground map and every once in a while he would say, 'We turn this way, Mr. President.'"

• On occasions when Kennedy felt he couldn't trust his Secret Service detachment with his affairs—or simply didn't want them around—he just ditched them. Once he even became separated from the Army officer carrying the "football," the briefcase containing the nation's nuclear launch codes—and went to a party unescorted. "The Russians could have bombed us to hell and back," one aide remembered, "and there would have been nothing we could have done about it."

JFK's 1,000 POINTS OF LIGHT

• JFK liked to sleep with famous women—Marilyn Monroe and actor David Niven's wife among them. According to one story, a White House staffer once asked Kennedy what he wanted for his birthday. According to another staffer's diary entry, the President "named a TV actress from California....His wish was granted."

• In addition to actresses and models, Kennedy had relationships with numerous female employees on the White House staff. He also slept with female reporters in the White House Press Pool. He even had an affair with Judith Campbell Exner, the girlfriend of a reputed mob boss Sam Giancana. And according to some accounts, the Mafia recorded the President's lovemaking sessions and used the tapes to blackmail the White House into going easy on them.

• Kennedy loved to frolic nude with girlfriends in the White House pool and let his mistresses streak through the White House corridors. Once Bryant was riding in an elevator when it stopped on the President's floor. "Just as the elevator door opened, a naked blonde office girl ran through the hall. There was nothing for me to do but get out fast, and push the button for the basement."

DANGEROUS LIAISONS

On at least one occasion, Kennedy's romances came close to destroying his presidency. Not long after being elected president, he talked his wife into hiring Pamela Turnur, a striking 23-year-old brunette with whom he was having an affair, as her press secretary. "That way [Pamela would] be right there close at hand when he wanted her," one friend remembers.

Although Jacqueline apparently knew about their relationship from the beginning and seemed to grudgingly accept it, Turnur's landlady, Mrs. Leonard Kater, did not. She waited and snapped a picture of Kennedy leaving Turnur's apartment early one morning. Determined to expose the President as a "debaucher of a girl young enough to be his daughter," Kater contacted the media and told them her story.

But luckily for JFK, the photo she took didn't actually show Kennedy's face (he was covering it with his hands)—so nobody could be sure it was really the President. When the reporters refused to cover the story, Mrs. Kater wrote a letter to the Attorney General (Bobby Kennedy)—and when that failed, she marched up and down Pennsylvania Avenue carrying a sign that said, "Do you want an adulterer in the White House?", giving away copies of her photograph. Kater was dismissed as a crackpot.

KEEPING SECRETS

No matter how hard he and the White House staff tried, Kennedy couldn't prevent his wife from finding out about his numerous affairs. Mrs. Kennedy apparently became aware of JFK's extracurricular activities soon after their marriage in 1953. And according to one close friend, she took the discovery hard. "After the first year they were together, Jackie was wandering around looking like the survivor of an airplane crash."

But as time went on she became resigned to Jack's womanizing, and even a bit cynical. Once when she discovered a pair of panties stuffed into a pillowcase on their bed, she confronted him with the evidence. One witness remembers, "She delicately held it out to her husband between thumb and forefinger—about the way you hold a worm—saying, 'Would you please shop around and see who these belong to? They're not my size.' "

HOLLYWOOD SCANDAL: 1921

A woman is found dead…a well-known celebrity is charged with murder… the whole world follows the trial. O. J. Simpson? Nope—Fatty Arbuckle. In its day, the Arbuckle trial was as big as the Simpson trial. Here's the story.

A KNOCK AT THE DOOR

On the morning of Saturday, September 10, 1921, two men from the San Francisco sheriff's office paid a visit to Roscoe "Fatty" Arbuckle, then Hollywood's most famous comedian, at his home in Los Angeles. One of the men read from an official court summons:

"You are hereby summoned to return immediately to San Francisco for questioning…you are charged with murder in the first degree."

Arbuckle, thinking the men were pulling a practical joke, let out a laugh. "And who do you suppose I killed?"

"Virginia Rappé."

Arbuckle instantly knew that this was no joke. He'd just returned from a trip to San Francisco, where he'd thrown a party over the Labor Day weekend to celebrate his new $3 million movie contract—then the largest in Hollywood history—with Paramount Pictures. A 26-year-old bit actress named Virginia Rappé had fallen ill at the party, presumably from drinking too much bootleg booze. Arbuckle had seen to it that the woman received medical attention before he returned to L.A., but now Rappé was dead—and Arbuckle had somehow been implicated in her death. Whatever doubts he may still have had about the summons vanished the following morning as he read the three-inch headlines in the *Los Angeles Examiner*:

ARBUCKLE HELD FOR MURDER!

The autopsy report showed that Rappé died from acute peritonitis, an inflammation of the abdominal lining brought on by a ruptured bladder. Why was Arbuckle a suspect in the death? Because Maude

---

A woman can detect the odor of musk—which is associated with

"Bambina" Delmont, another woman at the party, had filed a statement with San Francisco police claiming that she had seen Arbuckle drag Rappé into his bedroom against her will and assault her. As she later explained to newspaper reporters,

> I could hear Virginia kicking and screaming violently and I had to kick and batter the door before Mr. Arbuckle would let me in. I looked at the bed. There was Virginia, helpless and ravaged. When Virginia kept screaming in agony at what Mr. Arbuckle had done, he turned to me and said, 'Shut her up or I'll throw her out a window.' He then went back to his drunken party and danced while poor Virginia lay dying.

The 265 pound comedian had supposedly burst Rappés' bladder with his weight during the assault. And because the injury had gone undiagnosed and untreated, it developed into a massive abdominal infection, killing Rappé.

Pressing Charges

After Delmont's statement was filed, San Francisco District Attorney Matthew Brady had ordered Arbuckle's arrest and had issued a public statement to the press:

> The evidence in my possession shows conclusively that either a rape or an attempt to rape was perpetrated on Miss Rappé by Roscoe Arbuckle. The evidence discloses beyond question that her bladder was ruptured by the weight of the body of Arbuckle either in a rape assault or an attempt to commit rape.

FALSE WITNESS

Brady's case was based almost entirely on Delmont's police statement. And the case certainly *appeared* substantial—at least until Brady looked into Maude Delmont's background after she gave her statement. Then he discovered a police record containing more than 50 counts of bigamy, fraud, racketeering, extortion, and other crimes (including one outstanding bigamy warrant, which Brady would later use to his advantage).

WHAT REALLY HAPPENED

Brady later learned from other guests at the party that a very drunk Maude Delmont had actually been locked in a bathroom with Lowell Sherman, another party guest, during the entire time that she claimed to have witnessed Arbuckle with Rappé. She could not have seen any of the things she claimed to have seen—and if that were not bad enough, Brady later discovered that on Wednesday, September 7, Delmont had dashed off the following telegram to two different friends as Virginia Rappé lay dying at the St. Francis Hotel:

> WE HAVE ROSCOE ARBUCKLE IN A HOLE HERE
> CHANCE TO MAKE MONEY OUT OF HIM

Blind Ambition

District Attorney Brady had no case—there wasn't a shred of physical evidence to indicate that Arbuckle had committed any crime against Rappé; his only "witness" was a woman with a long criminal record; and the telegrams demonstrated clearly that Delmont's police statement was part of an attempt to blackmail Arbuckle.

Despite all this, Brady decided to bring the case to trial. Why? One theory: Brady, whom acquaintances described as a "self-serving, arrogant, ruthless man with blind ambition and a quick temper," was gearing up to run for governor of California. He probably figured that winning a murder conviction against Hollywood's biggest comedian would score points with the public.

Judge Not

Still, the case could not have gone to trial if the police judge, Sylvain Lazarus, had dismissed the case due to lack of evidence. But Judge Lazarus refused to throw it out, citing the "larger issues" surrounding the case:

> I do not find any evidence that Mr. Arbuckle either committed or attempted to commit rape. The court has been presented with the merest outline....The district attorney has presented barely enough facts to justify my holding the defendant on the charge which is here filed against him.

> But we are not trying Roscoe Arbuckle alone; we are not trying the screen celebrity who has given joy and pleasure to the entire world; we are actually, gentlemen, trying ourselves.

> We are trying our present-day morals, our present-day social conditions, our present-day looseness of thought and lack of social balance....

> I have decided to make a holding on the ground of manslaughter.

How long does it take a human's nerve impulse to reach the brain? About 8/1000 of a second.

The judge suspected Arbuckle was innocent, the district attorney *knew* Arbuckle was innocent, and yet the case still went to trial.

EXTRA!

Much like the Menendez brothers trials and the O. J. Simpson trials of the 1990s, the media—which in the 1920s consisted mostly of newspapers—had a field day with the Arbuckle trial. Unlike the Simpson trial, however, the lack of evidence in the Arbuckle trial led most newspapers to conclude that Arbuckle was innocent. *Most* papers, that is, except for those owned by media baron William Randolph Hearst. His papers loudly attacked Arbuckle's character, insinuated his guilt, and ran as many as six special editions per day to keep readers up-to-date on the latest developments in the case.

The Hearst papers published the most lurid accounts of the crime and the trial, and even stooped to publicizing totally unsubstantiated rumors about the case—the most famous of which was that Arbuckle, supposedly too impotent from booze to rape Rappé himself, had used a Coke bottle (some accounts said it was a champagne bottle) instead, causing her bladder to rupture. "Nowhere in any testimony in the court transcripts, police reports, or personal interviews did this story appear," Andy Edmonds writes in *Frame Up! The Untold Story of Roscoe "Fatty" Arbuckle*. "Everyone connected with the case vehemently denied it, yet it is the most popular story, and one of the most ugly lies, still connected with the ordeal. The fabrication haunted Roscoe throughout the remainder of his life."

GOING TO COURT

As Brady prepared his case, one of the first things he did was see to it that Maude Delmont would not be able to testify. He knew that the other witnesses would prove she had lied in her police statement. Furthermore, Delmont had changed her story so many times that Brady knew she would be caught in her own lies during cross-examination. Rather than let that happen, Brady had her arrested on an outstanding charge of bigamy. Delmont—the only person who claimed that Arbuckle had committed a crime—spent the next several months in jail, where Arbuckle's attorneys could not get at her.

THE TRIAL

The People v. Arbuckle lasted from November 14 to December 4, 1921. More than 60 witnesses were called to the stand, including 18 doctors. According to Bernard Ryan in *Great American Trials*,

> Through defense witnesses, lawyer Gavin McNab revealed Virginia Rappé's moral as well as medical history: As a young teenager, she had had five abortions in three years, at 16, she had borne an illegitimate child; since 1907, she had had a series of bladder inflammations and chronic cystitis; she liked to strip naked when she drank; the doctor who attended her in the several days before she died concluded that she had gonorrhea; when she met Arbuckle for the first time on Monday, she was pregnant and that afternoon had asked him to pay for an abortion; on Wednesday, she had asked her nurse to find an abortionist....Medical testimony proved that Virginia Rappé's bladder was cystic—one of the causes of rupture of the bladder.

Arbuckle Takes the Stand

The climax of the trial came on Monday, November 28, when Arbuckle testified in his own defense. He recounted how he had found Rappé in his bathroom vomiting into the toilet, and how he had helped her into the next room when she asked to lie down. Arbuckle testified that he spent less than 10 minutes alone with Rappé before summoning Maude Delmont, who took over and asked him to leave the room. He stood up well under cross-examination; and the final testimony, in which expert witnesses testified that the rupture of Ms. Rappé's bladder was not caused by external force, seemed to cinch the case for Arbuckle.

THE VERDICT

As the case went to the jury, both sides appeared confident of victory. But on December 4th, after 44 hours of deliberation, the jury announced that it was hopelessly deadlocked, and the judge declared a mistrial.

One juror, a woman named Helen Hubbard—whose husband was a lawyer who did business with the D.A.'s office—held out for a conviction throughout the entire deliberations.

The Second Trial

The case went to trial a second time, beginning on January 11 and lasting until February 3. The second trial was much like the first, only this time the defense introduced even more evidence concerning Ms. Rappé's shady past. But Arbuckle's lawyers, confident they would win handily, did not have Arbuckle take the stand in his defense. That was a huge mistake—this time the jury deadlocked 9-3 in favor of *conviction*.

The Third Trial

The case went to trial a third time on March 13. This time, Arbuckle's defense left nothing to chance: it provided still more evidence questioning both Rappé's physical health and her moral character, and it brought Arbuckle back to the stand to testify on his own behalf.

FINAL VERDICT

The case went to the jury on April 12, 1922. They deliberated for less than 5 minutes, then returned to court and read the following statement:

> We the jury find Roscoe Arbuckle not guilty of manslaughter.
>
> Acquittal is not enough for Roscoe Arbuckle. We feel that a great injustice has been done him. We feel also that it was only our plain duty to give him this exoneration, under the evidence, for there was not the slightest proof adduced to connect him in any way with the commission of a crime.
>
> He was manly throughout the case, and told a straightforward story on the witness stand, which we all believed.
>
> The happening at the hotel was an unfortunate affair for which Arbuckle, so the evidence shows, was in no way responsible.
>
> We wish him success....Roscoe Arbuckle is entirely innocent and free from all blame.

THE AFTERMATH

Roscoe Arbuckle was a free man, but his life was in tatters. The trials had cost him more than $750,000, wiping out nearly his entire life savings (the $3 million Paramount contract had fallen through when the scandal broke). As if that wasn't bad enough, the IRS went after him a few months later, when it seized the remainder of his estate to collect more than $100,000 in back taxes. It also obtained a court order to attach whatever wages he earned in the future until the entire tax debt was paid back.

THE HAYS OFFICE

Things got even worse for Arbuckle. Largely because of the scandal, 12 of Hollywood's top studio moguls hired William Hays, chairman of the Republican National Committee and a former postmaster general, to become America's "movie czar." His job: Keep Hollywood's image clean. His first task: Deal with Arbuckle.

Hatchet Job

Six days after Arbuckle was acquitted, the "Hays Office" (as it came to be known) banned him from the screen. The public was led to believe it was a moral issue. Actually, Hays was doing the bidding of Paramount heads Adolph Zukor and Jesse Lasky, who no longer wanted to work with Arbuckle, out of fear that he was box office poison. But they didn't take any chances; rather than risk losing Arbuckle to a competing studio, they lobbied the Hays Office to ban him from the film industry entirely.

COMEBACK

The ban was lifted eight months later, but the taint remained and Arbuckle had trouble finding work. He began work on a short subject film called *Handy Andy*, but was so hounded by reporters that he gave up on the project.

Over the next decade he appeared in stage shows, ran a Hollywood nightclub, and directed a number of films under the pseudonym William B. Goodrich (Will B. Good). But it wasn't until 1932—more than 10 years after the trials—that he had a chance to return to the screen. Studio head Jack Warner hired him to act in a film called *Hey, Pop!* It was a box office success, and Arbuckle was signed for six more films. He only completed three—*Buzzin' Around*, *Tamalio*, and *In the Dough*. The evening *In the Dough* finished shooting, Arbuckle celebrated at dinner with his wife and went home to bed. He died in his sleep at about 2:30 a.m., leaving an estate valued at less than $2,000.

LOONEY LAWS

Believe it or not, these laws are real.

In Las Vegas, Nevada, it's against the law to pawn your dentures.

In Natoma, Kansas, it's illegal to throw knives at men wearing striped suits.

It's illegal to sleep with your boots on in Tulsa, Oklahoma.

Michigan law forbids pet owners from tying their crocodiles to fire hydrants.

If you're 88 years of age or older, it's illegal for you to ride your motorcycle in Idaho Falls, Idaho.

It's against the law in Tuscumbia, Alabama, to have more than eight rabbits per city block.

It's against the law (not to mention impossible) to whistle under water in Vermont.

In Alabama, it's illegal to play dominoes on Sunday.

It's illegal to eat snakes in Kansas.

In Barber, North Carolina, it's illegal for a cat to fight a dog (or vice versa).

It's illegal to sleep with chickens in Clawson City, Michigan …and illegal to walk your elephant without a leash in Wisconsin.

The law prohibits barbers in Omaha, Nebraska, from shaving the chests of customers.

In California, it's illegal to hunt whales from your automobile. It's also against the law to use your dirty underwear as a dust rag.

In St. Louis, Missouri, it's illegal for you to drink beer out of a bucket while you're sitting on a curb.

Cotton Valley, Louisiana, law forbids cows and horses from sleeping in a bakery.

The maximum penalty for double parking in Minneapolis, Minnesota, is working on a chain gang with nothing to eat but bread and water.

For the past 150 years, Bolivia has averaged about one new government a year.

CAT FACTS

*Practically everyone in America is familiar with common cat behavior.
But a lot of us don't have any idea what's behind it. A few tidbits:*

THE INSIDE POOP

Nearly all domestic cats bury their feces—but in the wild, only timid cats do. Aggressive cats in the wild actually leave their droppings on tiny "advertising hills" that they create. This leads researchers to believe that domestic cats see themselves as submissive members of their human families and environments.

FAMILY FLAVOR

Does your cat lick its fur clean after it rubs against you? That's its way of "tasting" you—becoming familiar with the taste and scent of the people in its life.

CAT & MOUSE

Why do cats play "cat and mouse" with their victims? Experts believe it's because they're not hungry. Wild cats, who eat nothing but the food they catch, rarely, if ever, play cat and mouse.

PURR-FECT

Do cats purr because they are happy? Probably not, researchers say; even dying cats and cats in pain purr. The researchers think a cat's purr is a sign it is receptive to "social interaction."

THE BETTER TO SEE YOU WITH

Unlike human eyes, a cat's eyes have pupils that are shaped like vertical slits. These vertical slits work together with the horizontal slits of the cat's eyelid to give it greater control over how much light it allows into its eyes.

WHISKED AWAY

Because a cat's whiskers are sensitive to the slight air currents that form around solid objects (such as furniture and trees), they help it to "see" in the dark. They're especially helpful when the cat hunts at night.

A FOOD IS BORN

Sure, you've eaten the foods...but at the BRI we know that you can't really enjoy them unless you know their origins, too.

CHEX CEREALS

When William Danforth was a child, the mother of a classmate bought a bolt of gingham cloth and made checkered pants, shirts, and dresses for every member of the family. The odd clothing made such an impression that townsfolk were still talking about it decades later.

That's why, when he wanted a distinctive trademark for his Ralston Purina products, Danforth adopted a checkerboard pattern. He became so obsessed with it that he wore red-check ties, jackets, and socks to work, and even changed the company's address to Checkerboard Square. Then, in 1937, he commissioned a checkerboard breakfast cereal, Wheat Chex. Rice Chex followed in 1950, Corn Chex in 1958, and Bran Chex in 1987.

KOOL-AID

In the early part of this century, Edwin E. Perkins was president of a company called Onor-Maid, which sold more than 125 different household products

One of his products was Fruit Smack, a low-cost fruit-flavored soft drink syrup. But Fruit Smack had a problem: it was shipped in glass bottles, which were expensive and frequently broke in transit.

Perkins was considering getting rid of the drink when he noticed how popular a new powdered gelatin product, called Jell-O, was becoming. It inspired him; he decided to convert his syrup into powder form and sell it that way. He renamed the product Kool-Ade (later Kool-Aid), modeling it loosely after the company name, Onor-Maid.

RAGU SPAGHETTI SAUCE

When Giovanni and Assunta Cantisano stepped off the boat at Ellis Island at the turn of the century, they brought with them a few belongings...and a family recipe for spaghetti sauce. Giovanni opened a store selling Italian wine and foods. He thought he might be able to make a little extra money selling the family's spaghetti sauce there, too; so in 1937 he put some in mason jars and stocked his shelves with it. He never bothered to name it—he just called it *Ragú*, the Italian word for "sauce."

GOLD MEDAL FLOUR

In 1856, Cadwallader C. Washburn built an enormous new flour mill in Minneapolis, Minnesota. However, flour from harsh Minnesota wheat was dark and not very popular. So Washburn hired an engineer to design a system for separating the bran from the rest of the wheat. The result: a whiter, more desirable flour. To help shake consumer bias against Minnesota wheat flour, in 1880 Washburn entered his flour in the first Millers' International Exhibition… and won the gold medal.

HAWAIIAN PUNCH

"Hawaiian Punch was not invented in Hawaii," writes Vince Staten in *Can You Trust a Tomato in January?* "Nor was it invented by Hawaiians. It was invented in 1936 by a couple of Southern Californians, A. W. Leo and Tom Yates."

"It actually began as a soda fountain syrup. Mixed with water it was a drink, but it could also be used as an ice cream topping. By 1944 department stores were selling it in their gourmet food sections, so Leo began bottling it for consumers.…At first it was only available as a syrup. [Then] Leo brought it out in a premixed 46-oz. bottle.…It owes…its national popularity to its late-fifties TV commercials with a guy in a Hawaiian shirt offering a friend a 'Hawaiian Punch' and giving him a sock in the puss."

BROWN 'N' SERVE ROLLS

Invented accidentally by Joe Gregor, a Florida baker and volunteer firefighter. One morning the fire alarm sounded while Gregor was baking some rolls. He pulled them out of the oven before they were done, so he could go fight the fire. He intended to throw the half-baked rolls away when he got back, but he was curious to see if they were still good. He finished baking them instead.

LOG CABIN SYRUP

Invented in 1887 by a Minnesota grocer. He named it after the birthplace of his boyhood hero, Abe Lincoln.

Heavy thought: Hailstones can weigh as much as 1 1/2 lbs.

THE GRIMM PHILOSOPHY

*The Brothers Grimm are among the most famous storytellers in history.
During the 1800s, they collected such classic folk tales as Rumpelstiltskin
and Cinderella. But these weren't the Disney versions—the view of life
portrayed in Grimm tales was...well...grim. Here's an example.*

THE CAT AND THE MOUSE

A certain cat made the acquaintance of a mouse, and said so much about the great love and friendship she felt for her, that the mouse agreed that they should live and keep house together. "But we must put some food aside for winter, or we'll go hungry," said the cat; "And you, little mouse, can't venture out alone, or you'll be caught in a trap some day."

This good advice was followed, and a pot of fat was bought—but they didn't know where to put it. The cat gave it a lot of thought, and said: "I know no place where it will be safer than in the church, for no one dares take anything from there. We'll set it beneath the altar, and not touch it until we really need it."

So the pot was placed in safety, but it wasn't long before the cat had a great yearning for it, and said: "Little mouse; my cousin has brought a little son into the world, and has asked me to be godmother; he is white with brown spots, and I am to hold him over the font at the christening. Let me go out today, and you look after the house by yourself." "Yes," answered the mouse, "by all means go, and if you get anything very good to eat, think of me, I should like a drop of sweet red christening wine myself."

All this, however, was untrue; the cat had no cousin, and had not been asked to be godmother. She went straight to the church, stole to the pot of fat, began to lick at it, and licked the top of the fat off. Then she stretched herself in the sun. She didn't get home until evening. "Well, here you are again," said the mouse. "No doubt you've had a merry day." "All went well," answered the cat. "What name did they give the child?" "Top off!" said the cat quite coolly. "Top off!" cried the mouse, "What an unusual name. Is it a family name?" "What does that matter," said the cat, 'it's no worse than Crumbstealer, as your god-children are called."

Before long the cat was seized by another fit of yearning. She said to the mouse: "You must do me a favor, and once more manage the house for a day alone. I am again asked to be godmother, and, as the child has a white ring round its neck, I cannot refuse." The good mouse consented, but the cat crept to the church and devoured half the pot of fat. When she went home the mouse inquired: "And what was this child named?" "Half-done," answered the cat. "Half-done?" replied the mouse, "Why, I never heard such a name in all my life!"

The cat's mouth soon began to water again. "All good things go in threes," said she, "I am asked to stand godmother again. The child is quite black, except for its paws. This only happens once every few years; you will let me go, won't you?" "Top-off! Half-done!" mused the mouse, "they are such odd names, they make me very thoughtful." "You sit at home," said the cat, "in your dark-grey fur coat and long tail, and are filled with fancies, that's because you do not go out in the daytime."

During the cat's absence the mouse cleaned the house and put it in order, but the greedy cat entirely emptied the pot of fat. She did not return home till night. The mouse at once asked what name had been given to the third child. "It will not please you more than the others," said the cat. "He is called All-gone." "All-gone!" cried the mouse, "That's the most suspicious name of all! I have never seen it in print. All-gone; what can that mean?" She shook her head, curled up, and lay down to sleep.

After this, no one invited the cat to be godmother, but when the winter came and there was no longer any food to be found outside, the mouse said: "Come, cat, let's go to the pot of fat which we've stored up for ourselves—we shall enjoy that." "Yes," answered the cat, "you'll enjoy it as much as you'd enjoy sticking that dainty tongue of yours out of the window." They set out on their way, but when they arrived, they found that the pot of fat was empty. "Alas!" said the mouse, "now I see what has happened! You a true friend! You have devoured all when you were standing godmother. First top off, then half done, then—" "Hold your tongue," cried the cat. "One word more, and I'll eat you too." "All gone" was already on the poor mouse's lips; scarcely had she spoken it before the cat sprang on her, seized her, and swallowed her down.

Verily, that is the way of the world.

There are 250 *billion* stars in the Milky Way galaxy.

THE TV DINNER

We mentioned Swanson's TV dinners briefly in the Sixth
Bathroom Reader. *Here's the rest of the story,
submitted by BRI correspondent Jack Mingo.*

IN THE BEGINNING

Credit the Swanson brothers, Gilbert and Clarke, with inventing the TV dinner in 1951. The Swansons owned the nation's largest turkey plant in Omaha, Nebraska, and were frustrated that most Americans ate turkey only on Thanksgiving. They wanted to make turkey an everyday part of the American diet.

GONE TO POT

Their first attempt was the Swanson turkey pot pie. It was extremely popular. In fact, people started demanding more variety. The Swansons tried another approach: Inspired by popular diner "blue plate specials" in which an entire meal was served on a segmented plate, the Swansons began putting individual meal courses on segmented aluminum trays.

BALANCING ACT

In the early 50s, television was taking over America's living rooms, and Swanson decided to sponsor its own show, "Ted Mack's Family Hour." On the night of the show's premiere, Gilbert Swanson invited some friends over for a buffet dinner to celebrate. One of the guests looked around and pointed out how funny it looked for everybody to be balancing trays on their laps in front of the TV.

Swanson suddenly thought about the product his company was working on. It would be perfect for eating in front of television—and tying it into the TV craze couldn't hurt. Why not call it a TV dinner? Gilbert mentioned the idea to his brother, who suggested putting a picture of a TV on the box, with the dinner coming off the screen. In January 1952, the first Swanson's TV Dinner rolled off the line. It contained turkey with cornbread stuffing and gravy, buttered peas, and sweet potatoes in orange and butter sauce, and cost only 98¢.

When TV lost its novelty in the 1960s, Swanson redesigned the package, got rid of the picture of the TV, and downplayed the TV Dinner brand name. By 1984 it was completely off the package.

First vehicle to use inflatable rubber tires: Queen Victoria's carriage, in 1846.

CAVEAT EMPTOR

Here's a look at some recent advertising claims that prove the old adage caveat emptor—"let the buyer beware"—is still good advice.

TRIUMPH CIGARETTES

The Claim: *"Triumph Beats Merit! In a recent taste test, an amazing 60 percent said Triumph cigarettes taste as good or better than Merit!"*

The Truth: Actually, Merit beat Triumph. The results: 36% of the people surveyed said Triumph was better than Merit, but 40% said that Merit was better than Triumph. Triumph pulled ahead of Merit only when the 24% who said the two brands were equal were added to the total. That's why the ad used the words *"as good or better than Merit."*

USAIR

The Claim: *"USAir had the best on-time record of any of the seven largest airlines!"*

The Truth: USAir conveniently forgot that Pan Am, the *eighth-*largest airline, was actually rated first.

ITT CONTINENTAL BAKERIES

The Claim: *"Fresh Horizons bread contains five times as much fiber as whole wheat bread!"*

The Truth: The bread did indeed contain five times as much fiber, but the extra fiber came from *wood*...which the Federal Trade Commission dryly called "an ingredient not commonly used, nor anticipated by consumers to be commonly used, in bread."

ANACIN-3

The Claim: *"Hospitals recommend acetaminophen, the aspirin-free pain reliever in Anacin-3, more than any other pain relievers!"*

The Truth: They neglected to mention that Tylenol also contains acetaminophen...and hospitals recommend that product more than they recommend Anacin-3.

Only person in history to appear on *TV Guide's* cover 3 weeks in a row: Michael Landon.

LEVI'S 501 JEANS

The Claim: *"Ninety percent of college students say Levi's 501 jeans are 'in' on campus!"*

The Truth: Levi's cited a fall fashion survey conducted annually on 100 U.S. campuses. What they *didn't* say was that Levi's 501 jeans were the *only* blue jeans listed in the survey. Other entries included T-shirts, 1960s-style clothing, overalls, beach pants, and neon-colored clothing. So anyone who wanted to choose any type of jeans had no choice but to pick 501s.

LITTON MICROWAVE OVENS

The Claim: *"76% of independent microwave oven technicians surveyed recommended Litton!"*

The Truth: The survey included only Litton-authorized technicians "who worked on Littons and at least one other brand of microwaves. Technicians who serviced other brands, but not Littons, were excluded from the study."

* * * * *

CAR COMMERCIALS

The Claim: In 1990, Volvo aired a commercial showing a monster truck driving over several cars, including one Volvo. The roofs of the other cars were crushed; the Volvo's roof withstood the abuse.

The Truth: An onlooker videotaping the making of the commercial observed workers reinforcing the Volvo's roof with wooden planks and welded steel rods…and *cutting* the roof supports on the other cars. The man turned over his evidence to the Texas state attorney general's office; they alerted the media and threatened to sue Volvo. The company, embarrassed by the negative publicity, removed the ad from the airwaves.

The Claim: In a commercial showing Chrysler chairman Lee Iacocca speaking to the company's board of directors, Iacocca lectures, "Some things you wait for, some you don't. Minivans with air bags? You don't wait."

The Truth: Iacocca fought for years to keep the federal government from mandating airbags, even claiming that a safety engineer had once told him airbags were so dangerous that they should be used for executions.

Vincent Van Gogh was only able to sell one painting (*The Red Vineyard*) during his lifetime.

FAMOUS FOR 15 MINUTES

Here it is again—our feature based on Andy Warhol's prophetic comment that "In the future, everyone will be famous for 15 minutes." Here's how a few people have been using up their allotted quarter hour.

THE STAR: Joe "Mule" Sprinz, a professional baseball player from 1922 to 1948

THE HEADLINE: "Ouch! Blimp Ball Takes Bad Bounce"

WHAT HAPPENED: In 1939, Sprinz, 37-year-old catcher for the San Francisco Seals, caught five baseballs dropped from the Tower of the Sun (450 ft.) at the San Francisco World's Fair. The Seals' publicity agent was impressed and asked Sprinz if he'd catch a ball dropped 1,200 feet from a Goodyear Blimp, which would break the world record of 555 feet, 5 1/8 inches. "You'll become famous!" the agent promised.

Two teammates stood alongside Sprinz as the first baseball was dropped, but when they saw it break a bleacher seat…and then saw the second ball "bury itself in the ground," they backed off and let him make the third attempt by himself. "So the third one came down and I saw that one all the way. But nobody told me how fast it would be coming down," Sprinz later recalled. Traveling at a speed of 150 miles per hour, the ball bounced off Sprinz's glove and slammed into his face just below the nose, smashing his upper jaw, tearing his lips, and knocking out four teeth.

THE AFTERMATH: Sprinz spent three months in the hospital (and suffered headaches for more than five years), but recovered fully and resumed his baseball career, retiring in 1948. He never made it into the Hall of Fame…but did earn a place in the *Guinness Book of World Records* for the highest baseball catch "ever attempted." Sprinz passed away in January 1994 at the age of 91.

THE STARS: Officer Bob Geary of the San Francisco Police Department and his sidekick, Officer Brendan O'Smarty

THE HEADLINE: "Ventriloquist Vindicated in Vote"

Birds *do* fly south for the winter, but not to get warm. They do it for food.

WHAT HAPPENED: In 1992, Geary, an amateur ventriloquist, began taking "Officer Brendan O'Smarty"—a dummy dressed as a police officer—on his rounds in the city's North Beach area.

When the popular O'Smarty started to get some publicity, Geary's captain told him to leave the dummy at home; he said it made the department "look stupid."

Geary not only refused, he used $10,000 of his own money to finance an "initiative" that put the "O'Smarty issue" on the ballot in San Francisco's 1993 municipal elections. The result: Voters in overwhelmingly supported O'Smarty.

THE AFTERMATH: The pro-dummy election was reported in newspapers all over the country. O'Smarty kept his "job"…and Geary made his money back when he sold the movie rights to his story.

THE STAR: Dallas Malloy, a 16-year-old girl from Bellingham, Washington

THE HEADLINE: "Woman TKOs Boxing Association in Court …and Opponent in Ring"

WHAT HAPPENED: In 1992, Malloy set out on an amateur boxing career…but learned that the U.S. Amateur Boxing Association had a bylaw banning females from boxing in sanctioned bouts. She contacted the ACLU and together they sued, claiming that the bylaw violated Washington State's antidiscrimination laws.

Malloy won the suit, and on October 30, 1993, she squared off in the ring against 21-year-old Heather Poyner. A crowd of about 1,200 turned out to watch Malloy batter Poyner for three two-minute rounds. Malloy won in a unanimous decision. "It was great to get in the ring," she told reporters afterward. "The only thing I would change is that I would knock her out the next time. I really wanted to knock her out."

THE AFTERMATH: Malloy abandoned her career two months later. "After [the fight] I kind of lost interest," she told the Associated Press. Her boxing career lasted 14 months.

THE STAR: Andrew Martinez, a University of California, Berkeley, college sophomore

---

At one point, 74% of Pepsi drinkers said they'd switch to Coke "if it contained oat bran."

THE HEADLINE: "No Nudes Is Good Nudes? Naked Guy Nixed"

WHAT HAPPENED: In September 1992, Martinez began attending classes completely in the buff, calling his nudity a form of free speech. The university did nothing until they received numerous complaints from students and employees.

But what could they do? There weren't any university regulations banning public nudity, so the school updated its student conduct regulations to forbid indecent exposure, public nakedness, and "sexually offensive conduct." Martinez was then suspended for two weeks when he gave a nude interview to a (clothed) reporter. When he showed up nude at an administrative hearing to protest the charges, he was permanently expelled from school for failing to wear "proper attire." "I didn't think this was so controversial," Martinez told the *San Francisco Chronicle.* "I was surprised they gave me the boot."

THE AFTERMATH: Martinez became a mini-celebrity, featured in magazine and newspaper stories all over the world and appearing on several TV talk shows. His expulsion didn't stop him from waging his lone crusade. In March 1993, he was arrested near the campus for distributing free beer to the homeless while shouting the slogan, "Drink for the Revolution." He was, course, nude, and was quickly arrested for suspicion of drinking in public, for being a minor in possession of alcohol, and for resisting an officer.

THE STAR: Charlie Shaw, owner of a London, Ohio, deli shop

THE HEADLINE: "Clinton Burger Bites Back"

WHAT HAPPENED: When President Bill Clinton visited Shaw's deli in February 1994, Shaw served him a "Clinton Burger"—a beef pattie with bacon, cheese, mushrooms, onions, and a secret "Clinton sauce." Shaw and his Clinton Burger made headlines across the nation.

THE AFTERMATH: Unfortunately for Shaw, he also caught the attention of state government officials. They discovered he was operating his business while collecting disability benefits from a previous job-injury claim, a violation of state law. Authorities also discovered that he didn't have a food-service permit—which is also illegal. He was indicted on state fraud charges.

Survey result: Most males blame their partner after bad sex; most females blame themselves.

MAMA MIA!

Here's a look at five famous American mothers. You'll never guess who gave Uncle John the idea for this page.

ELIZABETH FOSTER GOOSE
Known as: Mother Goose
Background: In the 1750s, Boston printer Thomas Fleet heard his mother-in-law, Elizabeth Goose, singing nursery rhymes to her grandson—including "Hickory Dickory Dock," "Humpty Dumpty," and "Little Bo-peep." Fleet began writing them down, and in 1765 published them in a book called *Mother Goose's Melodies for Children*.

MARY HARRIS JONES
Known as: Mother Jones
Background: Mary Harris was a schoolteacher in Monroe, Michigan, in the 1850s. She married George Jones in 1861, moved to Chicago, and started a dressmaking business. But the great Chicago fire of 1871 wiped her out. Soon afterward she became active in the U.S. labor movement, and for the next 50 years traveled all over the country organizing workers in steel mills, railroads, coal mines, and the garment industry. She remained an active organizer until shortly before her death in 1930 at the age of 100.

FREDERIKA MANDELBAUM
Known as: "Marm" Mandelbaum (a.k.a. "Ma Crime")
Background: She's almost forgotten now, but Frederika Mandelbaum was one of the earliest, most famous, and most successful organized crime figures in American history. She was nicknamed "Marm," but if she were alive today, she might be known as "the Godmother." The *Encyclopedia of American Crime* describes her as "the leading criminal in America during the latter part of the 19th century."

Marm got her start as the wife of an honest dry goods store owner in New York City. She eventually took over the business and began fencing stolen property. Operating from warehouses scattered all over town, Mandelbaum bought and sold stolen property from heists up and down the East Coast. In little more than a decade she built her enterprise into one of the largest criminal organizations in the city's

---

Just a kid at heart: George Washington loved to play marbles.

history, an empire she kept afloat by paying tens of thousands of dollars in bribes to the police. She retained Howe and Hummel, one of New York's most prestigious criminal law firms, to keep herself and her friends out of jail.

She was finally caught in possession of stolen property that had been secretly marked by Pinkerton detectives (the New York D.A. thought the police were too corrupt to be trusted for the job) and was thrown in jail. A reporter later described what the detectives found when they stormed Marm's house to put her under arrest:

> It did not seem possible that so much wealth could be assembled in one spot. There seemed to be enough clothes to supply an army. There were trunks filled with precious gems and silverware. Antique furniture was stacked against a wall and bars of gold from melted jewelry settings were stacked under newspapers.

Mandelbaum and her son Julius posted $21,000 in bail the next day…and escaped to Canada with an estimated $1 million in cash. She died a free, very wealthy woman 10 years later at the age of 76.

ANNA WHISTLER

Known as: Whistler's Mother

Background: In October 1871, James Whistler decided to paint a portrait of his mother. "I want you to stand for a picture," he said. Mrs. Whistler agreed. "I stood bravely two or three days—I stood still as a statue!" she told a friend. But in the end she was too frail to stand for the long hours the portrait required. So Whistler painted her sitting down instead. Today the painting, officially called *Arrangement in Grey and Black: Portrait of the Painter's Mother,* is the second most recognizable portrait in the world…after the *Mona Lisa.*

KATE BARKER

Known as: "Ma" Barker

Background: She was the mother of Freddy, Herman, Lloyd, and "Doc"—"the Barker Brothers," four of the most famous gangsters of the 1930s. She not only *encouraged* her boys to become criminals, she actually masterminded many of their bank heists, post-office robberies and other crimes—including the kidnapping and $100,000 ransom of Brewery magnate William A. Hamm, Jr. in 1933. She and Freddy were killed in a shootout with the FBI at their Florida hideout in 1935.

THE PENCIL

Ever wonder how the pencil got its lead? We did too.

IS THERE REALLY LEAD IN A PENCIL?

Not anymore. The ancient Greeks, Romans and Egyptians used small lead disks for drawing guidelines on papyrus before writing with brushes and ink, and artists in Europe used metallic rods of lead, silver and zinc to make very light drawings centuries ago. But all that changed in 1564, when a graphite deposit was unearthed in Borrowdlae, England.

Using graphite for writing wasn't new; the Aztecs did it long before Columbus. But it was new to the Europeans. They discovered that the soft graphite—a form of carbon—made rich, dark lines. They began carving pointed "marking stones" out of it and using the stones to write with.

The problem was that the stones marked the writer's hands as much as the paper. Eventually, people figured out that they could wrap a string around the stick to keep their hands clean, unwinding the string as the graphite wore down. That was the first version of the modern pencil.

HOW THEY GET THE LEAD INTO THE PENCIL
Now, of course, the graphite comes in a wood case. But how does it get in there?

- First the graphite is ground up and mixed with fine clay. The more clay they add, the harder the lead.
- Then the mixture is forced through an "extruder" to make a long, thin rod.
- The rod is fired at a temperature of 2200° F to harden it and then treated with wax for smooth writing.
- The wood is sawed into small boards that are the length of one pencil, the width of seven pencils, and the thickness of half a pencil.
- Seven tiny grooves are cut lengthwise. Then the lead is laid into each of them, and an identical board is glued on top. A machine cuts the boards into seven individual pencils.
- Last step: They're painted with non-toxic paint.

An adult crocodile exerts a force of 1,540 lbs. between its jaws. Humans exert 40-80 lbs.

THE DEATH OF JIM MORRISON

*Did Jim Morrison really leave the land of the living in 1971...
or did he just slip out of the limelight? From* It's a
Conspiracy! *by the National Insecurity Council.*

The Deceased: Jim Morrison, the lead singer of the Doors,
one of the most popular rock bands of the 1960s.

How He Died: In the summer of 1971, Morrison and his
girlfriend, Pamela Courson, went to Paris on vacation. On July 5,
Courson allegedly found him dead in the bathtub. Two days later,
he was buried in a quiet service attended by five close friends. The
official cause of death was listed as a heart attack. He was 27.

SUSPICIOUS FACTS
• Nobody but Courson ever saw Morrison's dead body; neither
Morrison's friends nor his family were given the opportunity to
view it. After Morrison died, Courson asked Bill Siddons, the
Doors' road manager, to come to Paris. He said that when he arrived on July 6, he "was met at the flat by Pamela, a sealed coffin,
and a signed death certificate." He never saw Morrison's body.

• When asked the name of the doctor who signed the death certificate, Siddons said he didn't know, and Courson said she didn't remember. Moreover, according to *No One Here Gets Out Alive*, a
1980 biography of Morrison, "There was no police report, no doctor present. No autopsy had been conducted."

• When Courson filed the death certificate at the U.S. Embassy on
July 7, the day of the funeral, she claimed there were no living relatives—which meant that since there was no one to be notified,
Morrison could be buried quickly. In fact, Jim's family lived in Arlington, Virginia.

• Morrison's friends kept the story of his death a secret for almost a
week. Siddons told his story to the media six days after Morrison
died, two days after the funeral. Beyond noting that Morrison had
died of "natural causes," Siddons had no more to add.

It's Auto-matic: 40% of American couples first discuss marriage in a car.

POSSIBLE CONCLUSIONS

• **Morrison is really dead.** His friends say they hushed up his death to protect his privacy. A statement prepared for the public said, "The initial news of his death and funeral was kept quiet...to avoid all the notoriety and circus-like atmosphere that surrounded the deaths of such other rock personalities as Janis Joplin and Jimmy Hendrix."

• **Morrison is hiding out.** At the time of his death, Morrison's life was a mess. He had been convicted on two counts of profanity and indecent exposure in Miami and faced a jail sentence if his appeal failed; he faced a possible 10-year sentence after being busted by the FBI for being drunk and disorderly on an airplane; and more than *twenty* paternity suits were pending against him.

Morrison was sick of his life as a rock star and had been saying so for years. He said he wanted to start over anonymously, so he could just write. With Courson's help, he could easily have faked his own death to give himself a fresh start.

For years, Courson had urged Morrison to quit the band and develop himself as a poet.

She, or someone else, started a rumor that Morrison may have visited a Paris hangout earlier in the evening and obtained some heroin. That, mixed with alcohol, is what supposedly killed him. Yet for all the drugs he ingested, no friends ever mentioned heroin, and Morrison was afraid of needles.

The absence of an autopsy and police report is very suspicious, and the lie about his parents and the quick "burial" forestalled any further inquiries. A doctor could have been bribed to fake a death certificate.

Finally, Morrison had repeatedly talked about Paris. According to one close friend of the singer, "he thought it was a place where he could be himself and not have people hounding him and making a circus out of his life, making him something he wasn't."

RECOMMENDED READING

All of the quotes in this chapter are from *No One Here Gets Out Alive*, by Jerry Hopkins and Danny Sugerman (Warner Books, 1980).

New Hampshire allows boys to be married at 14 and girls at 13—with parental permission.

GIVE YOURSELF SOME CREDIT

*Did you use a credit card to buy this book? Credit cards are a way of
life to Americans. In fact, you could argue that those little pieces of
plastic are actually the backbone of the American economy.
How's that for a scary thought?...And they haven't
even been around that long. Here is a brief history.*

BACKGROUND. By the 1950s gasoline companies, department stores and major hotels had developed their own credit cards—small pieces of cardboard or metal plates they gave their best customers to use instead of cash (allowing holders to pay for purchases at the end of the month). But these early cards were different than the ones we use today—they were only accepted at the business that had issued them.

THE FIRST SUPPER

That all changed in one night in 1950, when businessman Robert X. McNamara finished his dinner in a posh New York restaurant— and realized that he didn't have enough cash to pay for the meal. His wife had to drive across town to pay for it, which embarrassed him deeply. But it also gave him an idea: why not issue a "diners' card" that people could use to pay for meals when they were short of cash?

McNamara proposed his idea to a number of restaurants around town. In exchange for honoring his new "Diners Club" card, he would pay for the meal of anyone who presented the card. Diners Club would absorb the risk of non-payment; the restaurant got the money even if the cardholder was a deadbeat. How the card made its money: it paid the restaurants 90-95¢ on the dollar, billed the cardholder $1.00, and kept the difference in the form of a "discount." The restaurants balked at this arrangement at first, but McNamara convinced them that people with cards would spend more money—and more often—than people without them. By the end of the year he had signed up 27 New York restaurants and 200 cardholders. The age of the credit card as we know it had begun.

Feeling hungry? The average supermarket stocks 12,341 different items.

CREDIT CARD FACTS

• The average American holds 2.9 Visas or MasterCards; even so, credit card companies send out more than 1 billion new credit card offers every year.

• Why do merchants like credit cards? On average, consumers spend 23% more money when they pay with credit cards than when they pay cash.

• Had you signed up for Sears' Discover card when it premiered in 1986, you would have been entitled to meal discounts at Denny's restaurants and 50% off psychiatric exams.

• Today more than 31 million of the 211 million Visa and Master-card cards in circulation are "affinity cards"—cards that donate a portion of each purchase to the charity shown on the card. One popular version, the Elvis card, features a picture of the King on it. (Elvis is dead, so the bank gets to keep most of the money; even so, the card has more than 10,000 subscribers.) One of the least popular: the Muscular Dystrophy Association Card, which has a picture of Jerry Lewis on it. It bombed so badly that it was taken off the market.

• It's illegal now, but credit card companies used to mail credit cards to people who hadn't even applied for them. It wasn't always good business: In 1966, five Chicago banks banded together and mailed 5 million credit cards to people who hadn't asked for them. But "the banks had been less than cautious in assembling their mailing lists. Some families received 15 cards. Dead people and babies got cards. A dachshund named Alice was sent not one but four cards, one of which arrived with the promise that Alice would be welcomed as a 'preferred customer' at many of Chicago's finest restaurants."

• In 1972, Walter Cavanagh and a friend bet a dinner to see who could accumulate the most credit cards. Eight years later he won the bet—and broke the world record—by applying for and getting 1,003 credit cards, weighing 34 pounds and entitling him to $1.25 million in credit. He's still applying for credit cards, and has set a goal of 10,000 cards.

• In 1987, aspiring moviemaker Robert Townsend paid for his first film, *Hollywood Shuffle,* by charging $100,000 on his fifteen personal credit cards. Luckily, the movie made enough money for him to pay back the money.

The Danish flag, used since the 13th century, is the oldest unchanged national flag in existence.

COLORS

Colors have a lot more impact on our daily lives than you might think. Here are some things researchers have found out about people and color.

BLUE

• Blue has a tranquilizing effect on people. Bridges are often painted blue to discourage suicide attempts. And according to one report: "When schoolroom walls were changed from orange and white to blue, students' blood pressure levels dropped and their behavior and learning comprehension soared."

• Researchers say blue is the #1 color for women's sweaters, because women think men like it. (They're right; it's U.S. men's favorite color.)

RED

• Red is a stimulant that can cause "restlessness and insomnia" if it's used in bedrooms.

• According to marketing studies, red makes people oblivious to how much time is passing. That's why it's "the color of choice for bars and casinos."

• Women tend to prefer blue-toned reds, while men like yellowish reds. Businesses keep this in mind. For example: the Ford Mustang, which is targeted to men, is orange-red (called "Arrest-me" red at Ford); the Probe, targeted to women, is offered in more blue-red shades.

GREEN

• Because it reminds people of fields and foliage, green makes us feel secure. Researchers say it's a good color for bedrooms; and green kitchens reportedly make cooks more creative.

• Studies show that "people working in green environments get less stomachaches than people in areas where other colors predominate."

YELLOW

• It's the color most likely to stop traffic...or sell a house.

• But yellow also represents "caution or temporariness—so car rental agencies and taxis use it, but not banks."

• Too much yellow makes people anxious. "Babies cry more and temperamental people explode more in yellow rooms."

America's favorite colors— #1: Blue. Then red, green, white, pink, purple and orange.

MISS PIGGY

Porcine words of wisdom from America's favorite Pig.

DIET TIPS

"Never eat anything at one sitting that you can't lift."

"Always use one of the new—and far more reliable—elastic measuring tapes to check on your waistline."

ARTICHOKES

"These things are just plain annoying...after all the trouble you go to, you get about as much actual 'food' out of eating an artichoke as you would from licking thirty or forty postage stamps. Have the shrimp cocktail instead."

PERFUME

"Perfume is a subject dear to my heart. I have so many favourites: Arome de Grenouille, Okéfénokée, Eau Contraire, Fume de Ma Tante, Blast du Past, Kermes, Je suis Swell, and Attention S'il Vous Plait, to name but a few."

TIPPING

"There are several ways of calculating the tip after a meal. I find that the best is to divide the bill by the height of the waiter. Thus, a bill of $12.00 brought by a six foot waiter calls for a $2.00 tip."

TRAVEL TIPS

"If you're traveling alone, beware of seatmates who, by way of starting a conversation, make remarks like, 'I just have to talk to someone—my teeth are spying on me' or 'Did you know that squirrels are the devil's oven mitts?' "

"Public telephones in Europe are like our pinball machines. They are primarily a form of entertainment and a test of skill rather than a means of communication."

HOTELS

"Generally speaking, the length and grandness of a hotel's name are an exact opposite reflection of its quality. Thus the Hotel Central will prove to be a clean, pleasant place in a good part of town, and the Hotel Royal Majestic-Fantastic will be a fleabag next to a topless bowling alley."

HATS

"Someone you like is wearing an ugly hat, and she asks you to give her your honest opinion of it: 'What a lovely chapeau! But if I may make one teensy suggestion? If it blows off, don't chase it.' "

MUMMY'S THE WORD

Mummies are as much a part of Ameican pop culture as they are a part of Ancient Egyptian culture. But how much do you know about them?

R AG TIME
As long as there have been people in Egypt, there have been mummies—not necessarily *man-made* mummies, but mummies nonetheless. The extreme conditions of the desert environment guaranteed that any corpse exposed to the elements for more than a day or two dried out completely, a process that halted decomposition in its tracks.

The ancient Egyptian culture that arose on the banks of the Nile River believed very strongly in preserving human bodies, which they believed were as necessary a part of the afterlife as they were a part of daily life. The formula was simple: no body, no afterlife—you couldn't have one without the other. The only problem: as Egyptian civilization advanced and burial tombs became increasingly elaborate, they also became more insulated from the very elements—high temperatures and dry air—that made natural preservation possible in the first place.

The result was that a new science emerged: artificial mummification. From 3,100 B.C. to 649 A.D. the ancient Egyptians deliberately mummified the bodies of their dead, using methods that became more sophisticated and successful over time.

MUMMY SECRETS

Scientists have yet to unlock all of the secrets of Egyptian mummification, but they have a pretty good idea of how the process worked:

• When a king or other high official died, the embalmers slit open the body and removed nearly all the organs, which they preserved separately in special ceremonial jars. A few of the important organs, like the heart and kidneys, were left in place. The Egyptians apparently thought the brain was useless and in most cases they shredded it with small hooks inserted through the nostrils, pulled it out the nose using tiny spoons, and then threw it away.)

• Next, the embalmers packed the body in oil of cedar (similar to turpentine) and natron, a special mineral with a high salt content. The chemicals slowly dried the body out, a process that took from 40 to 70 days.

• The body was now compeletely dried out and "preserved," but the process invariably left it shrunken and wrinkled like a prune, so the next step was to stuff mouth, nose, chest cavities, etc., with sawdust, pottery, cloth, and other items to fill it out and make it look more human. In many cases the eyes were removed and artificial ones put in their place.

• Then the embalmers doused the body with a water-proofing substance similar to tar, which protected the dried body from moisture. In fact, the word mummy comes from the Persian word *mumiai*, which means "pitch" or "asphalt," and was originally used to describe the preservatives themselves, not the corpse that had been preserved.

• Finally, the body was carefully wrapped in narrow strips of linen and a funerary mask resembling the deceased was placed on the head. Afterwards it was placed in a large coffin that was also carved and painted to look like the deceased, and the coffin was placed in a tomb outfitted with the everyday items that the deceased would need in the afterlife.

THE MUMMY GLUT

Pharaohs weren't the only ancient Egyptians who were mummified—nearly anyone in Egyptian society who could afford it had it done. The result: By the end of the Late Period of Ancient Egypt in the seventh century A.D., the country contained an estimated 500 million mummies, far more than anyone knew what to do with. They were too numerous to count, too disconnected from modern Egyptian life to have any sacred spiritual value, and in most cases were thought to be too insignificant to be worthy of study. Egyptians from the 1100s onward thought of them as more of a natural resource than as the bodies of distant relatives, and treated them as such.

Well into the 19th century, mummies were used as a major fuel source for locomotives of the Egyptian railroad, which bought them by the ton (or graveyard). They were cheaper than wood and burned very well.

For more than 400 years, mummies were one of Egypt's largest export industries, and the supply was so plentiful that by 1600 you could buy a pound of mummy powder in Scotland for about 8 shillings. As early as 1100 A.D., Arabs and Christians ground them up for use as medicine, which was often rubbed into wounds, mixed into food, or stirred into tea.

By the 1600s, the medicinal use of mummies began to decline, as many doctors began to question the practice. "Not only does this wretched drug do no good to the sick," the French surgeon Ambrose Paré wrote in his medical journal, "…but it causes them great pain in their stomach, gives them evil smelling breath, and brings on serious vomiting which is more likely to stir up the blood and worsen hemorrhaging than to stop it." He recommended using mummies as fish bait.

By the 1800s, mummies were imported only as curiosities, where it was fashionable to unwrap them during dinner parties.

Mummies were also one of the first sources of recycled paper: During one 19th-century rag shortage (in the days when paper was made from *cloth* fibers, not wood fibers), one Canadian paper manufacturer literally imported Egyptian mummies as a source of raw materials: he unwrapped the cloth and made it into sturdy brown paper, which he sold to butchers and grocers for use as a food wrap. The scheme died out after only a few months, when employees in charge of unwrapping them began coming down with with cholera.

Note: What happened when the supply of mummies became scarce? A grisly "instant mummy" industry sprang up in which fresh corpses of criminals and beggars were hastily embalmed and sold as real mummies.)

MUMMY FACTS

• Scientists in South America have discovered mummies from the ancient civilization of Chinchorros that are more than 7,800 years old—nearly twice as old as the oldest Egyptian mummy. And, just as in Egypt, the mummies are plentiful there. "Every time we dug in the garden or dug to add a section to our house, we found bodies," one elderly South American woman told *Discover* magazine. "But I got used to it. We'd throw their bones out on a hill, and the dogs would take them away."

Among many other things, Thomas Jefferson is the inventor of the calendar clock.

- The average Egyptian mummy contains more than 20 layers of cloth that, laid end-to-end, would be more than four football fields long.

- In 1977, an Egyptian scientist discovered that the mummy of Pharaoh Ramses II, more than 3,000 years old, was infested with beetles. So they sent it to France for treatment, complete with an Egyptian passport describing his occupation as "King, deceased."

- What's the quickest way to tell if an Egyptian mummy still has its brains? Shake the skull—if it rattles, the brain is still in there.

- The Egyptians were also fond of mummifying animals. To date, scientists have discovered the preserved remains of bulls, cats, baboons, birds, crocodiles, fish, scorpions, insects…even wild dogs. One tomb contained the remains of more than one *million* mummified birds.

- Some mummies have been discovered in coffins containing chicken bones. Some scientists believe the bones have special religious meaning, but (no kidding) other experts theorize that the bones are actually leftover garbage from the embalmer's lunch.

* * * * * *

CELEBRITY MUMMIES

Jeremy Bentham and his "Auto Icon." Bentham was a famous 19th-century English philosopher. When he died in 1932, he left instructions with a surgeon friend that his body be beheaded, mummified, dressed in his everyday clothes, and propped up in a chair, and that a wax head be placed on his neck to give the corpse a more realistic appearance. He further instructed that his real head also be mummified and placed at his feet, and that the whole arrangement be put on public display. The corpse and its head(s) can still be seen at University College in London, where they sit in a glass case specially built for that purpose.

Vladimir Lenin. When the Soviet leader died on January 21, 1924, the Communist Party assembled a team of top embalmers to preserve his corpse for all eternity. Unlike the embalming processes of the ancient Egyptians, which prevented decomposition by removing body fluids, the Soviets *replaced* cell fluids with liquids that inhibited deterioration. (For more info, see p. 284.)

A column of air 1 inch square and 600 miles high weighs about 15 pounds.

A SLICE OF LIFE

A slice of the history of the most popular "ethnic" food in America.

ORIGIN. The ancient Greeks invented pizza. The most accomplished bakers of the ancient world, they made a variety of breads topped with spices, herbs, and vegetables. Their first pizza was designed as a kind of "edible plate," with the thick crust around the edge serving as a handle.

How did pizza become Italian? The Greeks occupied part of Italy for 6 centuries; one of their legacies is the popularity of pizza there.

TOMATOES

• Early pizzas featured cheese, herbs, vegetables, and fish or meat—but no tomatoes. Tomatoes, a New World food, didn't reach Italy until the mid-1500s—and weren't popular until the late 19th century because people believed they were poisonous.

• In 1889 pizza maker Raffaele Esposito added tomatoes to pizza for the first time. The reason: He wanted to make a pizza for Italian Queen Margherita in the colors of the Italian flag—red, white, and green—and needed something red to go with white mozzarella cheese and green basil.

PIZZA IN THE U.S.

• The first American pizzeria was opened in New York in 1905. By the early 1920s, family-run pizzerias were popping up all over the American Northeast...but it was still considered an exotic food.

• American G.I.s returning from Italy after World War II made pizza popular throughout the U.S. But it wasn't until the '60s that it became a fad...and a movie may have been responsible. In the controversial 1961 film *Splendor in the Grass*, Warren Beatty asks a waitress, "Hey, what is pizza?" The waitress takes him "out back," introducing him to pizza and a bit more.

• Today Americans eat more than 30 million slices of pizza per day—or 350 slices a second—and spend as much as $25 billion a year on pizza.

• Pepperoni is the most popular pizza topping nationwide; anchovies are the least favorite.

THE GODZILLA QUIZ

Here's a multiple-choice quiz to find out how much you know about filmdom's most famous dinosaur. (Answers start on p. 507.)

1 Godzilla first lumbered out of the ocean in a 1954 film titled *Gojira*. The dino-monster was awakened from a million-year
♦ slumber by A-bomb testing underseas and went on a rampage, destroying Tokyo, wreaking havoc with his radioactive breath. In 1956, the movie was brought to the U.S. as *Godzilla, King of Monsters* ("Makes King Kong Look Like a Midget!"). How did they adapt it for American audiences?

  A) They made it seem as though Godzilla was fighting for the U.S. during World War II.

  B) They inserted footage of Godzilla destroying New York City and Washington, D.C. as well.

  C) They added Raymond Burr, casting him as a hospitalized reporter who remembers the whole incident as a flashback.

2. The first Japanese sequel to *Gojira* was made in 1955. But when this flick finally made it to the U.S. in 1959, it didn't mention Godzilla in the title. What was it called, and why?

  A) *The Monster vs. the Maiden*; the studio tried to make it sexier.

  B) *The Rockin' Monster*; rock 'n' roll movies were hot.

  C) *Gigantis*; it was illegal to use the name Godzilla.

3. In the 1964 flick, *Godzilla Vs. Megalon*, Godzilla saves the world from the Seatopians, an evil alien race that plans to take over using two secret weapons—Gaigan and Megalon. How would you describe this evil pair?

  A) A King Kong-like ape and a giant poisonous frog.

  B) A giant cockroach and a robot with a buzz saw in his stomach.

  C) A giant pickle and a Richard Nixon look-alike.

4. *Godzilla vs. the Thing* was released in 1964. What Thing did Godzilla fight?

  A) A giant rabbit.

  B) A giant moth.

  C) A giant spider.

Breakfast treat: In Colonial America, kids ate popcorn with cream and sugar for breakfast.

5. How did Godzilla celebrate his 20th anniversary in 1974?

A) He fought a Godzilla robot from outer space.

B) He saved the world from a giant alien grasshopper.

C) He made an appearance on the Johnny Carson Show.

6. *Godzilla on Monster Island* was released in 1971. The plot: Earth is invaded again. This time it's giant cockroaches from outer space, using monsters to do their dirty work. They've got Gaigan (the monster in *Godzilla Vs. Megalon*) and Ghidrah. Who's Ghidrah?

A) Godzilla's mother-in-law.

B) A giant anteater.

C) A three-headed dragon.

7. In 1972, a scientist discovers a growing mass in a polluted lake. He wonders if it's a giant tadpole...but no! It's a new monster named Hedora! What will Godzilla be fighting this time?

A) The Smog Monster—a 400-foot blob of garbage.

B) The Phlegm Monster—a 2-ton ball of mucus.

C) The Sludge Monster—A 60-foot-wide hunk of waste.

8. In *Godzilla's Revenge*, released in 1969, Godzilla returns for what purpose?

A) To settle a score with another monster named Gorgo.

B) To show a little kid how to fight bullies.

C) To get revenge on Raymond Burr.

9. In the 1966 epic, *Godzilla vs. the Sea Monster*, Godzilla fights for the Free World against Red Bamboo, an evil totalitarian group. Their secret weapon is Ebirah. Who is he?

A) A hypnotist who can brainwash Godzilla.

B) A mechanical jellyfish.

C) A giant lobster.

10. In 1969, Godzilla reappeared with Minya. What was special about this new monster?

A) It was Godzilla's mother.

B) It was Godzilla's cousin.

C) It was Godzilla's son.

THE WORLD'S MOST POPULAR TWINS

To most people, all twins are fascinating.
Here are three sets of twins who are famous as well.

C HANG AND ENG BUNKER
Claim to Fame: The original "Siamese twins."
Background: Chang and Eng—"left" and "right" in Thai—
were born at Meklong, Siam (Thailand) on May 11, 1811, permanently attached at the chest by a fleshy band of skin. They were discovered by an American sea captain who put them on display in Europe and America—where P.T. Barnum bought out their contract.

The Bunkers became world-famous as "Siamese twins." They managed to live relatively normal lives, becoming American citizens, marrying (unattached) sisters Adelaide and Sarah Yates in 1864, and
somehow fathering 22 children between them. They spent their entire lives looking for a doctor who'd guarantee they'd both survive an
operation to separate them, but never found one. They died hours
apart in 1874.

Gossip: Chang and Eng hated each other—and fought constantly.
According to an 1874 article in the *Philadelphia Medical Times*, "Eng
was very good-natured, Chang cross and irritable….Chang drank pretty heavily—at times getting drunk; but Eng never drank. They often
quarrelled; and, of course, under the circumstances their quarrels were
bitter. They sometimes came to blows, and on one occasion came under the jurisdiction of the courts."

ESTHER PAULINE AND PAULINE FRIEDMAN

Claim to Fame: The most popular advice columnists in America.
Background: Esther Pauline (Eppie) and Pauline Esther (Popo) Fried-
man were born 17 minutes apart on July 4th, 1918, in Sioux City,
Iowa. They were inseparable throughout their youth; they dressed
identically, double-dated, slept in the same bed until their wedding
nights, and married on the same day in a double wedding.

Eppie got her start as Ann Landers in 1955 when she entered and
won a *Chicago Sun-Times* contest to succeed the original Ann Land-

---

Not yet, Mom: 23% of men between 35 and 39 live with their parents.

ers. In the first weeks of the column, Eppie mailed some of the Landers column's letters to California, where Popo apparently helped answer them. But when the *Sun-Times* editors found out about it, they prohibited her from sending any more letters out of the office. The twins had to stop working together.

A few weeks later, Popo walked into the office of the *San Francisco Chronicle* and complained about the paper's advice columnist. The editor gave her a stack of past columns, and told her to fill in her own answers. She did—and the editor hired her the next day. Popo chose Abigail Van Buren as her pen name (from President Martin Van Buren), and her column became Dear Abby.

Gossip: When Eppie found out about her sister's column, she was furious. "I got into this work first," she told a reporter. "She saw what a great time I was having. And she got into it. I felt it was mine, something that I did. It was a serious problem." They didn't speak to each other for 8 years, but eventually buried the hatchet.

JOAN AND JANE BOYD
Claim to Fame: TV's first "Doublemint Twins."
Background: In 1959, the 21-year-old sisters were singing advertising jingles at CBS radio. One day they were asked if they wanted to audition to be the first live Doublemint twins. (Wrigley's Gum had used illustrated twins since the '20s.) They were taken to meet the boss—P.K. Wrigley—who hired them on the spot. That was the only time they ever saw him.

The girls became American icons and made Doublemint the #1 gum. But the magic ended in 1963, when Wrigley learned that Joan—recently married—was pregnant...and fired them. (Their contract prohibited pregnancy, even within marriage.) Since then there have been more than 20 different sets of Doublemint twins—but none as popular as the originals.

Gossip: Wrigley never gave the twins free gum—even though fans were always walking up to them and asking for it. "We never got a free pack of chewing gum in our lives," Jane remembers. "So we'd buy our own gum to give to people on the street." They were also never allowed to chew gum in their commercials. According to Joan, "We were told that Mr. Wrigley had said, 'I never want to see gum in the mouths of the Doublemint Twins. My girls do not chew gum on-camera.'"

THE SINGING CHIPMUNKS

*Alvin, Simon, and Theodore are the most famous chipmunks
in the world. This mini-biography was taken from* Behind
the Hits, *by Bob Shannon and John Javna.*

THE WITCH DOCTOR

In 1957, a 38-year-old songwriter named Ross Bagdasarian
(stage name: David Seville) was sitting in his study when an
idea for a new song came to him.

"I looked up from my desk and saw a book called *Duel with the
Witch Doctor*," he recalled. "All the teenage records seemed to have
one thing in common back then—you couldn't understand any of
the lyrics. So I decided to create a 'Witch Doctor' who would give
advice to the lovelorn in his own language—a kind of qualified
gibberish."

Bagdasarian quickly wrote and recorded the song...but was
stumped about what kind of voice to use for the witch doctor
(Whose advice consisted of : "Oo-ee, Oo-ah-ah, Ting-tang, Walla-
walla Bing-bang.")

FINDING A VOICE

One day Bagdasarian was fooling around with a tape recorder, playing with the speeds. He sang into the machine while it was running
at half-speed...and then played it back at full-speed. The result: It
sounded like he'd swallowed helium...or played a 45-rpm record at
78 rpm. It was exactly the voice he'd been looking for. (Note: Remember this was 1957; today's sophisticated recording equipment
hadn't been invented yet.)

Bagdasarian brought his finished tape to Liberty Records. "They
flipped," he said. Before 24 hours had elapsed, "The Witch Doctor"
was on its way to record stores. And within weeks it was the #1
song in the nation. In all, it sold about 1.5 million copies.

THE SINGING CHIPMUNKS

A year later, Liberty Records found itself in financial trouble. So
they asked Bagdasarian to come up with another song like "The

---

According to astronaut Neil Armstrong, the moon's surface is "fine and powdery."

Witch Doctor." He agreed to try.

He decided to turn the Witch Doctor's voice into several different characters. As his son recalls: "He didn't know whether to make them into hippos or elephants or beetles or what. He came up with the idea of chipmunks when he was driving in Yosemite National Park and this chipmunk almost dared him and his huge car to drive past. My dad was so taken with their audacious behavior that he decided to make these three singing characters chipmunks. He named them after three executives at Liberty Records. (Alvin: Al Bennett, the label president; Simon: Si Waronker, vice-chairman of the label; Theodore: Ted Keep, Liberty's chief recording engineer.)

"Then he took the song he'd written, 'The Chipmunk Song,' to Liberty and the president, Alvin's namesake, said, 'We need hits, not chipmunks.' My dad said, 'You have nothing to lose, why don't you put it out?' In the next seven weeks they sold 4.5 million records."

Ultimately, the first Chipmunk record sold more than 7 million copies; At the time, it was the fastest-selling record in history.

LIFE AFTER DEATH

The Chipmunks outlived Bagdasarian. He died in 1972 of a heart attack; eleven years later, in 1983, the Chipmunks emerged as stars of their own Saturday morning TV cartoon show. Today they rank as three of the most lucrative characters ever created in a pop song.

• • • •

THE "PURPLE PEOPLE EATER"

In 1958, a friend of actor/singer Sheb Wooley's told him a riddle he'd heard from his kid: "What flies, has one horn, has one eye, and eats people?" The answer: "A one-eyed, one-horned people eater." Wooley thought it was funny, and wrote a song based on it.

A short time later, he met with the president of MGM Records to decide on his next record. Wooley played every song he'd written, but there was nothing the guy liked. "You got anything else?" the president asked. "Well, yeah," Wooley said, "one more thing— but it's nothing you'd want to hear." The president insisted, so Wooley reluctantly played him "Purple People Eater." Three weeks later it was the #1 song in the country.

Lobbyist's leverage: The average freshman U.S. Senator enters office $266,073 in debt.

MYTH AMERICA

Some of the stories we recognize as Americans myths today were taught as history for many years. This one, about the "father of our country," was reverentially passed down for more than 150 years.

MYTH: Young George Washington chopped down a cherry tree. When his father found it and asked who was responsible, George stepped forward and said, "I cannot tell a lie, father—I did." The elder Washington was so moved by George's honesty that he didn't punish his son.

BACKGROUND: It's hard to believe today, but as late as the 1950s, this tale was still being taught in school as fact. It first appeared in a biography of Washington written by Parson Mason Locke Weems, called *The Life of George Washington with Curious Anecdotes: Equally Honorable to Himself and Exemplary to His Young Countrymen.* Here's the original version of the story:

> "George," cried his father, "do you know who killed this beautiful little cherry tree yonder in the garden?" This was a tough question: and George staggered under it for a moment; but quickly recovered himself: and looking at his father, with the sweet face of youth brightened with the inexpressible charm of all-conquering truth, he bravely cried out, "I can't tell a lie, Pa; you know I can't tell a lie, I did it with my hatchet." — "Run to my arms, you dearest boy," cried his father in transports, "run to my arms; glad am I, George, that you killed my tree: for you have paid me for it a thousand fold. Such an act of heroism in my son is more worth than a thousand trees, though blossomed with silver, and their fruits of purest gold."

THE TRUTH: Weems made it up. The book was first published in 1800—and was a huge best-seller in its time—but the story about the cherry tree didn't show up until the fifth edition, in 1806. Weems's only supporting documentation was his own statement that the tale was "too true to be doubted."

Weems didn't claim to be much of an historian to begin with; he was just capitalizing on an obvious market. "There's a great deal of money lying in the bones of old George," he reportedly told his publisher.

THE MONA LISA

It's the most famous painting in the world—even Uncle John has heard of it. But what else do you know about this mysterious lady?

BACKGROUND. Sometime between 1501 and 1506—no one is sure exactly when—Leonardo da Vinci, the great Renaissance artist, scientist, and thinker, painted his masterpiece "La Joconde," better known as the Mona Lisa. Hardly anything is known about the painting. Da Vinci kept extensive records on many of his *other* paintings, but none on the Mona Lisa. He never once mentioned it in any of his notebooks, and never made any preliminary studies of it.

However, historians believe the painting was one of Leonardo's favorites. Unlike most of his other paintings, which he painted on commission and turned over to their owners as soon as they were finished, da Vinci kept the Mona Lisa for more than 15 years—and still had it in his possession when he died in 1519.

WHO'S THAT GIRL?

No one knows who really modeled for the Mona Lisa—but some of the popular candidates are:

• **Mona Lisa Gherardini,** wife of Francesco del Giocondo, a Florentine silk merchant. After da Vinci's death, Gherardini was so widely believed to have been the model for the painting that it was named after her. But art historians now doubt she was the model, because the source of this rumor was Giorgio Vasari, da Vinci's biographer—who never even saw the painting in person.

• **Another Noblewoman** da Vinci knew—or perhaps a composite painting of two or more of them.

• **No one.** Some historians think the painting was a *finzione* or "feigning"—a fictional woman not based on any particular person.

• **Himself.** The painting is a feminine self-portrait. This theory is strange but surprisingly plausible. In 1987, computer scientists at AT&T Bell Laboratories took da Vinci's 1518 Self-Portrait, reversed the image (it faces right, not left like the Mona Lisa), enlarged it to the same scale, and juxtaposed it against the Mona Lisa, the similarities were too striking to be accidental...or so they say.

MONA LISA FACTS

• The Mona Lisa is considered one of the most important paintings of the Renaissance period—but King Francis I of France, who took possession of the painting after da Vinci died, hung it in the palace bathroom.

• Napoleon, on the other hand, was a big fan of the painting; he called it "The Sphinx of the Occident" and kept it in his bedroom.

• Why is Mona Lisa wearing such a strange smile? Some art historians suspect that this most famous feature may actually be the work of clumsy restorers who tried to touch up the painting centuries ago. Da Vinci may have intended her to wear a much more ordinary expression. Dozens of other theories have been proposed to explain the strange grin, including that Mona Lisa has just lost a child, has asthma or bad teeth, or is really a young man. Sigmund Freud theorized that da Vinci painted the smile that way because it reminded him of his mother.

• Mona Lisa may be "in the family way." According to writer Seymour Reit, "the lady is definitely pregnant, as shown by the slightly swollen hands and face, and her 'self-satisfied' expression." Other historians disagree—they think that Mona Lisa is just chubby.

THE THEFT

• According to a 1952 Paris study, there are at least 72 excellent 16th- and 17th- century replicas and reproductions of the Mona Lisa in existence—leading conspiracy theorists to speculate that the painting in the Louvre is itself a replica.

• One of the most interesting forgery theories has to do with a theft of the painting that occurred in 1911. On August 21 of that year, the Mona Lisa vanished from the Louvre in what was probably the biggest art heist of the century. French authorities conducted a massive investigation, but were unable to locate the painting. Two years later, an Italian carpenter named Vincenzo Perugia was caught trying to sell the masterpiece to an Italian museum.

The official story is that Perugia wanted to return the work to Italy, da Vinci's (and his) birthplace...But Seymour Reit, author of *The Day They Stole The Mona Lisa*, theorizes that the plot was the work of Marqués Eduardo de Valfierno, a nobleman who made his living selling forged masterpieces to unsuspecting millionaires. He wanted to do the same with the Mona Lisa—but knew that no one would buy a forgery of such a famous painting unless the original were stolen from the Louvre first. So De Valfierno paid a forger to paint half a dozen fakes, and then hired Perugia to steal the real Mona Lisa.

Reit argues that De Valfierno had no plans for the original masterpiece—he didn't want to sell it or even own it himself—and was only interested in selling his forgeries. He never even bothered to collect the original from Perugia, who hid it in the false bottom of a dirty steamer trunk for more than two years waiting for De Valfierno to come and get it. But he never did, so Perugia finally gave up and tried to sell the Mona Lisa to an Italian museum. As soon as he handed over the painting, he was arrested and the painting was returned to France. Perugia was tried and convicted for the theft, but spent only 7 months in prison for his crime. De Valfierno was never tried.

PROTECTING THE PAINTING

• The Mona Lisa isn't painted on canvas—it's painted on a wood panel made from poplar. This makes it extremely fragile, since changes in the moisture content of the wood can cause it to expand and shrink, which cracks the paint.

• Because of this, the Louvre goes to great lengths to protect the Mona Lisa from the elements—and from vandals. Since 1974 the painting has been stored in a bulletproof, climate-controlled box called a *vitrine* that keeps the painting permanently at 68° Fahrenheit and at 50-50% humidity.

• Once a year, the painting is removed from its protective case and given a checkup. The process takes about an hour and requires almost 30 curators, restorers, laboratory technicians, and maintenance workers.

• Despite nearly 500 years of accumulated dust, dirt, and grime, the risks associated with cleaning the masterpiece are so great that the museum refuses to do it—even though the filth has changed the appearance of the painting dramatically. Pierre Rosenberg, the Louvre's curator, says: "If we saw the Mona Lisa as da Vinci painted it, we would not recognize it....Da Vinci actually painted with bright, vivid colors, not the subdued tones that are visible today." But he's adamant about leaving the painting in its present state. "The Mona Lisa is such a sacrosanct image that to touch it would create a national scandal."

THE MERRY-GO-ROUND

Wow! Here's more fascinating, but useless,
information—a B.R.I. specialty. This batch was
contributed by B.R.I. member Jack Mingo.

The carousel

The name *carousel* originated with a popular 12th-century Arabian horseman's game called *carosellos*, or "little wars." The rules were simple: teams rode in circles throwing perfume-filled clay balls from one rider to another. If a ball of perfume broke, the team lost. Their penalty: they carried the smell of defeat with them for days after.

The game was brought to Europe by knights returning from the Crusades, and it evolved into elaborate, colorful tourneys called *carrousels*.

Making the Rounds. In the 17th century, the French developed a device to help young nobles train for carrousels. It featured legless wooden horses attached to a center pole. As the center pole turned (powered by real horses, mules, or people), the nobles on their wooden steeds would try to spear hanging rings with their lances. (This later evolved into the "catching the brass ring" tradition.) The carousel device gradually evolved into a popular form of entertainment. The peasants rode on barrellike horses; the nobles rode in elaborate chariots and boats.

The Machine Age. In the first half of ther 19th century, carousels became popular all over Europe and the U.S. (where they were advertised as healthful devices that improved blood circulation). But until the 1860s, they were still dependent on horses and mules for power. That finally changed when Frederick Savage, an English engineer, designed a portable steam engine which could turn as many as four rows of horses on a 48-foot diameter wheel. Later, Savage also patented designs for the overhead camshafts and gears that moved the wooden horses up and down. This new type of carousel was called a "round-about" ...and eventually became known as a "merry-go-round."

If you keep your goldfish in a dark room, they'll turn white.

DEFINITIONS

In previous Bathroom Readers we've included some uncommon words, and their meanings, to help build weak vocabularies. Here's another batch.

Ambivert: A person who's half introvert and half extrovert.

Backclipping: Shortening a longer word into a smaller one, like *chrysanthemum* to *mum*.

Boomer: A male kangaroo.

Callipygian: Having shapely buttocks.

Chad: The little circles of paper your hole-punch makes.

Furfurrate: What dandruff does when it falls from your scalp.

Genuglyphics: Painting or decorating a person's knees to make them more erotic.

Hypocorism: Baby talk.

Infix: A word placed inside another word to change its meaning, as in fan-f-----tastic.

Izzard: The name of the letter "z."

Kith: Your friends.

Lecanoscopy: The act of hypnotizing yourself by staring into a sink filled with water.

Liveware: People who work with computer software and hardware.

Nidus: A place where bacteria multiplies

Otorhinolaryngologist: An ear, nose, and throat doctor.

Otoplasty: A surgical procedure to fix ears that stick out.

Pandiculate: To yawn.

Paradog: A military dog that's been trained to parachute out of airplanes.

Paranymph: The bridesmaid or best man at a wedding.

Pica: A desire to eat non-foods (like dirt).

Pilomotor reaction: What your hair does when it stands on end.

Pip: What an unhatched chick does to break through its eggshell.

Pullet: A female chicken one year old or younger.

Puwo: An animal that's half poodle and half wolf.

Taresthesia: The tingling sensation you get when your foot falls asleep.

Tautonym: A word consisting of two identical parts, like *tutu*.

Ucalegon: A neighbor whose house is burning down.

Zoonoses: Diseases humans can get from animals.

OL' BLOOD 'N' GUTS

General George Patton was famous for his one-liners
as he was for his military victories in World War II.

"In war, just as in loving, you've got to keep on shoving."

"To be a successful soldier you must know history....What you must know is how man reacts. Weapons change but man who uses them changes not at all. To win battles you do not beat weapons—you beat the soul of the enemy man."

"Wars may be fought with weapons, but they are won by men. It is the spirit of the men who follow and of the man who leads that gains the victory."

"The most vital quality a soldier can possess is self-confidence, utter, complete, and bumptious."

"Never tell people *how* to do things. Tell them *what* to do and they will surprise you with their ingenuity."

"A pint of sweat will save a gallon of blood."

"Untutored courage is useless in the face of educated bullets."

"Take calculated risks. That is quite different from being rash."

"A piece of spaghetti or a military unit can only be led from the front end."

"Use steamroller strategy; that is, make up your mind on the course and direction of action, and stick to it. But in tactics, do not steamroller. Attack weakness. Hold them by the nose and kick them in the pants."

"There's one thing you men can say when it's all over and you're home once more. You can thank God that twenty years from now when you're sitting by the fireside with your grandson on your knee, and he asks you what you did in the war, you won't have to shift him to the other knee, cough and say, 'I shoveled crap in Louisiana.' "

Tax Break: 75% of Americans get a refund from the IRS.

WHAT IS HYPNOTISM?

You are getting sleepy…sleepy…you will do anything we tell you. Now listen carefully: When you leave the bathroom, you will experience an irresistible urge to give everyone you know copies of Uncle John's Ultimate Bathroom Reader. *Do you understand? Good. When you emerge from the bathroom, you won't remember anything we've said. Now resume reading.*

BACKGROUND. The history of hypnotism—drawing someone into an "altered state of consciousness" in which they are more susceptible to suggestion than when fully conscious—dates back thousands of years and is as old as sorcery, medicine, and witchcraft. The first person in modern times to study it was Franz Mesmer, an 18th-century Viennese physician. In 1775 he devised the theory that a person could transmit "universal forces," known as *animal magnetism*, to other people.

Critics derisively named this practice "Mesmerism," and chased him out of Vienna for practicing witchcraft. He then resettled in Paris, where a royal commission dismissed Mesmerism's "cures" as the product of his patients' imaginations.

Viewed as a crackpot science by the entire medical establishment, Mesmerism might have died out, except for one thing: anesthesia hadn't been invented yet, and physicians were desperately looking for something to kill the pain in surgical procedures. Mesmer himself had performed surgery using mesmerism as anesthesia as early as 1778, and other doctors soon began trying it.

One of the most successful was John Elliotson, a London surgeon who used it successfully on thousands of patients—but at great personal cost: he was booted out of his professorship and became a laughing stock of English medical society. John Elsdaile, a medical officer with the East India Company, had better luck: he performed hundreds of operations, including amputations, "painlessly and with few fatalities" using mesmerism. At about the same time another English physician experimenting with the procedure, James Braid, renamed it "hypnosis" after Hypnos, the Greco-Roman god of sleep.

In the 1880s Sigmund Freud visited France and decided to experiment with hypnosis in the fledgling field of psychology. He used it to treat neurotic disorders by helping patients remember events in their past that they had either forgotten or repressed. But as he developed his method of psychoanalysis, he lost interest in hypnosis and eventually dumped it entirely.

Despite Freud's rejection, hypnotism continued to grow in popularity. By the mid-1950s the British and American Medical Associations had approved its use. Although hypnotism is seldom used as an anesthetic in surgery today—except in combination with pain-killing drugs—it is widely used to prepare patients for anesthesia; ease the pain of childbirth; lower blood pressure; combat headaches; ease the fear associated with dentist appointments; and a variety of other applications. More than 15,000 physicians, dentists, and psychologists currently incorporate hypnotherapy into their practices.

BENEFITS
According to *US News and World Report*, as many as 94% of hospital patients who are hypnotized as part of their therapy "get some benefit" from it. Some examples cited by the magazine:

• "Cancer patients can undergo chemotherapy without the usual nausea if they are first hypnotized."

• "Burn patients recover faster and with less medication if they are hypnotized within two hours of receiving their burns and told they will heal quickly and painlessly. Researchers think hypnotherapy gives them the ability to will the release of anti-inflammatory substances that limit the damage."

• "J. Michael Drever, a cosmetic surgeon, finds that postsurgical hypnotic suggestions can see his patients through breast reconstructions and tummy tucks with less bleeding, fewer complications and quicker recovery."

NONBELIEVERS
One of hypnotism's most outspoken critics is Las Vegas performer "The Amazing Kreskin," who dismisses it as "just a figment of the imagination." Kreskin worked as a hypnotherapist under the supervision of a New Jersey psychologist in the 1960s. But he ultimately became a skeptic: "Anything I ever did with a patient who was supposedly under hypnosis I was able to do without putting them in the slightest trance—by persuading them, encouraging them, threatening them, browbeating them or just giving them an awful

lot of confidence....All that's happening is what Alfred Hitchcock does every time he terrifies you and changes the surface of your skin with goosebumps. You're using your imagination."

HYPNOSIS FACTS

• It is impossible to hypnotize someone against their wishes.

• A hypnotized person, even when they appear to be asleep or in a trance, is physiologically awake at all times. Unlike sleepwalkers, their brain waves are identical to those of a person who's fully awake.

• A hypnotized person is always completely aware of his or her surroundings—although they can be instructed to ignore surrounding events, which creates the appearance of being unaware of their surroundings.

ANOTHER FORM OF HYPNOSIS?

Here's some background on America's most pervasive credit cards:

American Express. Formed by American Express in 1958 to complement its lucrative travelers check business. According to *American Heritage* magazine, "American Express came to dominate the field partly because it could cover the credit it was extending with the float from its traveler's checks, which are, after all, a form of interest-free loan from consumers to American Express."

Visa. California's Bank of America began issuing its BankAmericard in 1958. At first it was intended to be used at stores near Bank of America branches, but it was so profitable that the bank licensed banks all over the country to issue it. However, other banks hated issuing a card with B of A's name on it. So in 1977 the card's name was changed to *Visa.*

MasterCard. Originally named Master Charge, the card was formed in 1968 by Wells Fargo Bank and 77 other banks, who wanted to end BankAmericard's dominance of the credit card business. They succeeded: thanks to mergers with other credit cards, it became the biggest bank card within a year. Can you remember why it changed its name to MasterCard in 1979? According to company president Russell Hogg, they wanted to shed the card's "blue collar" image.

WESTERN NICKAMES

Wild Bill…Black Bart…Billy the Kid…Butch and Sundance. Western heroes had colorful nicknames—but they weren't all as complimentary as they sound. Here's some info on a few of the names.

James Butler **"Wild Bill" Hickok.** Had a long nose and a protruding lip, and was originally nicknamed "Duck Bill."

William "Bat" Masterson. The famous sheriff of Ford County, Kansas, hit more lawbreakers over the head with his cane than he shot with his gun, and earned the nickname "Bat."

Robert LeRoy "Butch Cassidy" Parker. As a teenager, Parker idolized a criminal named Mike Cassidy, and eventually began using his friend's last name as an alias. He picked up the name "Butch" while working in a Rock Springs, Wyoming butcher shop.

Harry "The Sundance Kid" Longabaugh. As a teenager during the 1880s, Longabaugh spent 1-1/2 years in the Sundance Jail in Wyoming, serving out a sentence for horse stealing.

William "Billy The Kid" Bonney. Looked like a kid.

Henry "Billy The Kid" McCarty. Looked like a goat.

John "Doc" Holliday. A professional dentist by trade. He only became a gunslinger and professional gambler after a bout with tuberculosis forced him to move west in search of a drier climate. Even at the height of his criminal career, he practiced dentistry part-time. Holliday's girlfriend was a prostitute named "Big Nose" Kate Elder.

Charles E. "Black Bart" Boles. Came up with the name himself. He became a stagecoach robber by accident. Originally a schoolteacher in northern California's gold country, Boles had a friend who was a Wells Fargo stagecoach driver and decided to play a trick on him. One day in 1875, he covered his face with a scarf, found a stick about the size of a pistol, and jumped out in front of the coach hoping to scare his friend. To his surprise, the driver threw down the strongbox and rode off before Boles could tell him it was only a joke. Opening the strongbox, Boles discovered a fortune in gold coins and bullion. Realizing there was more money in stick-ups than there was in education, Boles quit his teaching job and began holding up stagecoaches full time. He robbed 28 stagecoaches between 1875 and 1883.

After each robbery, he penned a small poem and left it behind in the empty strongbox where he knew investigators would find it. He always signed it "Black Bart, Po-8." One read: "Blame me not for what I've done, I don't deserve your curses/and if for some cause I must be hung/Let it be for my verses." Boles was eventually caught and sentenced to 4 years in San Quentin prison, but returned to stagecoach robbing within a few weeks of his release. This time Wells Fargo detectives cut a deal with Boles behind the scene: according to legend, they offered Boles a lifelong pension of $200 a month in exchange for his agreement to give up crime. Whether or not the story is true, the robberies stopped immediately.

...And now, folks, we'd like you to meet the dumbest train robber in the West.

Al Jennings, a successful Oklahoma lawyer in the early 1890s, and his brother Frank, also a lawyer, gave up their chosen profession and began second career: sticking up trains—or at least trying to.

In 1897 they tried to rob a mail car on a Santa Fe train, but the conductor chased them away. Two weeks later the brothers tried to stop another train by blocking the track with railroad ties, but the train steamed right through the barrier. In another robbery attempt, they tried to dynamite open two safes, but only succeeded in blowing up the boxcar the safes were on.

The law eventually caught up with them; Frank got 5 years in prison and Al was sentenced to life in prison, but President Theodore Roosevelt granted him a "full citizenship" pardon in 1907.

Jennings returned to his law practice, and eventually ran for county attorney under the slogan, "When I was a train robber I was a good train robber, and if you choose me, I will be a good prosecuting attorney." He lost. In 1914 he ran for governor of Oklahoma (this time his slogan was "It takes the same sort of nerve to be an honest governor as to rob a train or bank") and lost that too.

There are 7 spikes in the Statue of Liberty's crown.

CONTROVERSIAL CHARACTERS

Honestly—what kind of political trouble could Mighty Mouse or Barbie get into? Well, as weird as it sounds, times are so volatile that even a cartoon mouse can be accused of being a bad influence.

The Character: Mighty Mouse

Controversy: Did Mighty Mouse snort cocaine on April 23, 1988, in the TV cartoon show, *Mighty Mouse: the New Adventures*?

The Fight: In 1988 a Tupelo, Mississippi, watchdog group called the American Family Association (AFA) complained to CBS about a scene in a *Mighty Mouse: The New Adventure* cartoon. Reverend Donald Wildmon, head of the AFA, described the scene as follows: "Mighty Mouse is down in the dumps, and he reaches in his cape, pulls out a substance and sniffs it through his nostrils, and from that point on in the cartoon he is his normal self." Wildmon charged that the substance Mighty Mouse "snorted" was cocaine.

Reaction: CBS producer Ralph Bakshi, who was responsible for the cartoon, angrily rejected the accusation: "This is Nazism and McCarthyism all over again. I don't advocate drugs—that's death. I'm a cartoonist, an artist, not a pornographer. Who are these people anyway? Why does anybody listen to them?" According to Bakshi, Mighty Mouse was actually sniffing crushed flowers he had placed in his pocket during an earlier scene. According to the CBS version of the story, Mighty Mouse was sad because the female character he was attracted to did not love him. So he took out the flowers she'd given him in the earlier scene and sniffed them.

The Characters: Popeye the Sailor and Olive Oyl

Controversy: Should Popeye and Olive take a pro-choice stand on abortion?

The Fight: In July 1992 Bobby London, the artist who wrote and drew the syndicated *Popeye* comic strip for King Features, decided "to show these old cartoon characters coping with the modern world." He submitted a strip with the following plot:

* Olive Oyl receives a baby Bluto doll in the mail and doesn't want to keep it.

* She and Popeye get into an argument about what to do with it. Olive Oyl tells Popeye that she wants to "send the baby back to its maker."

* Two priests happen to be walking by and hear the argument. They mistakenly assume that Olive Oyl is talking about having an abortion and try to persuade her not to do it. When that fails, the priests try to get passers-by to help. Olive Oyl tells them that "she can do what she wants to do, because it's her life."

Reaction: King Features fired London and withdrew the strip before it was published.

The Character: Mattel's Barbie doll

The Controversy: Does Barbie promote the "radical agenda" of environmentalism?

The Fight: In the wake of Earth Day 1990, Mattel decided to promote its new line of Barbie dolls with the "Barbie Summit," an all-expenses-paid gathering of children who had submitted winning suggestions on how to improve the world. In the commercial announcing the contest, Barbie asked viewers how they would help make the world a better place—and offered a seemingly innocuous suggestion: "We could keep the trees from falling, keep the eagles soaring," she said.

But the Oregon Lands Commission, an anti-environmentalist lobbying group, was outraged with the ad. They claimed it was exposing children to "the preservationist's radical agenda." "We want to wake up corporate American to the fact that powerful, monied groups are at work shutting down the engines of this country and they are doing it in the name of environmentalism," the commission's spokesperson claimed. The commission organized a boycott, telling its 61,000 members that buying Barbie dolls "would help stop timber harvesting."

Reaction: Mattel went ahead with the promotion, which was a success. "We kind of thought," explained a Mattel spokesperson, "how can anybody criticize a program that is designed to give children a voice in a world they are going to inherit?"

Financial Whiz: Rock star Mick Jagger went to the London School of Economics for 2 years.

HERE'S JOHNNY...

Quips from the archetypal late-night talk show host, Johnny Carson.

"I now believe in reincarnation. Tonight's monologue is going to come back as a dog."

"The only absolute rule is: Never lose control of the show."

[On Jimmy Carter] "I think he rented his family. I don't believe Lillian is his mother. I don't believe Billy is his brother. They're all from Central Casting."

"[Rona Barrett] doesn't need a steak knife. Rona cuts her food with her tongue."

"I like my work and I hope you do, too—but if you don't, I really couldn't care less. Take me or leave me—but don't bug me."

"The difference between divorce and legal separation is that a legal separation gives a husband time to hide his money."

"Never use a big word when a little filthy one will do."

"I don't know where my creativity comes from, and I don't want to know."

"The best things in life are free. And the cheesiest things in life are free with a paid subscription to *Sports Illustrated*."

"The worst gift is a fruitcake. There is only one fruitcake in the entire world, and people keep sending it to each other."

"The difference between love and lust is that lust never costs over two hundred dollars."

"Married men live longer than single men. But married men are a lot more willing to die."

"Anytime four New Yorkers get into a cab together without arguing, a bank robbery has just taken place."

"Thanksgiving is an emotional holiday. People travel thousands of miles to be with people they only see once a year. And then discover once a year is way too often."

WHO IS MONTY PYTHON?

The English comedy troupe, "Monty Python's Flying Circus," has been defunct for years. But their TV show is still one of the funniest ever made.

HOW "MONTY PYTHON" MET

In the mid-'60s, David Frost—one of England's most popular TV stars—began work on a new series called "The Frost Reports." The staff of young writers he hired included Michael Pa-lin and Terry Jones (who'd performed together since college), John Cleese and Graham Chapman (who'd toured together in Cambridge University's comedy revue), and Eric Idle, a Cambridge student. It was the first time the five of them had worked together.

When Frost's show folded in 1966, they went their separate ways, but they sometimes met and discussed the possibility of doing a program together. When Terry Gilliam (an American friend of John Cleese's) moved to England, he became part of the group. Cleese helped get him a job in the BBC.

THEIR TV DEBUT

In 1969 BBC comedy producer Barry Took tried to team Palin and Cleese in their own show. But they refused to do it unless all six of the group were hired. Took decided they'd complement each other as performers and went along with it. The BBC didn't trust them... but Took insisted.

The BBC had been running a religious program late on Sunday nights, and no one was watching it...so the network decided to replace it with entertainment. That was how "Monty Python's Flying Circus" got on the air.

On Oct. 5, 1969, anyone who tuned in for religion would have seen John Cleese instead, announcing, "And now for something completely different." At first, Monty Python was on so late that almost no one saw it. But eventually it attracted a huge following.

THE U.S. DEBUT

American audiences didn't see the "Flying Circus" until years after its British debut. The first U.S. appearance was a group visit to the

"Tonight Show," hosted that night by Joey Bishop. The audience had no idea what was going on and didn't find them amusing. But in 1974 Public Broadcasting Station KERA in Dallas picked up the British series. It quickly became one of PBS's most popular imports.

THE NAME

The group came up with a number of names before deciding on "Monty Python's Flying Circus" They almost used:
1. "A Horse, a Spoon, and a Basin"
2. "The Toad Elevating Moment"
3. "Bunn, Wackett, Buzzard, Stubble and Boot" (an imaginary soccer team's forward line)
4. "Owl Stretching Time"
5. "Gwen Dibley's Flying Circus" (Gwen was Michael Palin's music teacher when he was eleven). Soon Monty Python—a name they made up—replaced Gwen Dibley. At first the BBC rejected the troupe's crazy name, but when the Pythons threatened to change their name every week, the network relented.

THE DIALOGUE

A few samples of Python humor.

Graham Chapman: "I think TV's killed real entertainment. In the old days we used to make our own fun. At Christmas parties I used to strike myself on the head repeatedly with blunt instruments while crooning. (sings) *'Only make believe, I love you,* (hits himself on head with bricks). *Only make believe that you love me,* (hits himself). *Others find peace of mind . . .'* "

Railroad Passenger (who thinks he's been let off at the wrong stop): "I wish to make a complaint."
Porter: "I don't have to do this, you know."
Passenger "I beg your pardon?"
Porter: "I'm a qualified brain surgeon. I only do this because I like being my own boss."
Passenger: "Er, excuse me, this is irrelevant, isn't it?"
Porter: "Oh yeah, it's not easy to pad these out to thirty minutes."

Narrator: "It was a day like any other and Mr. and Mrs. Samuel Brainsample were a perfectly ordinary couple, leading perfectly ordinary lives—the sort of people to whom nothing extraordinary

The Red Sea is the world's warmest sea.

ever happened, and not the kind of people to be the centre of one of the most astounding incidents in the history of mankind . . . So let's forget about them and follow instead the destiny of this man (camera pans to businessman in bowler hat and pinstripe suit)... Harold Potter, gardener, and tax official, first victim of Creatures from another Planet."

Candy maker: "We use only the finest baby frogs, dew picked and flown from Iraq, cleansed in finest quality spring water, lightly killed, and then sealed in succulent Swiss quintuple smooth treble cream milk chocolate envelope and lovingly frosted with glucose."

Government Hygiene Inspector: "That's as may be, but it's still a frog."

Narrator: "Dinsdale was a gentleman. And what's more, he knew how to treat a female impersonator."

• • •

BATHROOM ETIQUETTE

In the Middle Ages, it was considered sufficient to step "an arrow's flight" distance into the gardens before doing what had to be done. Royalty apparently even thought this unnecessary—one English noble was appalled to find that the visiting king and retinue defecated wherever they chose throughout his castle—and during a conversation with a young noblewoman, he was surprised to hear tinkling water and watch a puddle spreading across his floor beneath her long dress.

Though officially banned as early as 1395 in Paris, it was a centuries-long practice throughout Europe to empty bedpans from high windows into the street. Oft-ignored etiquette demanded that they first shout the classic warning "Gardez l'eau!" In Edinburgh you could hire a guide to walk ahead of you and shout "Haud your hand!" to people in the windows above.

One of history's earliest etiquette books, penned by Erasmus of Rotterdam (1465-1536), laid down several laws about behavior concerning bodily functions. "It is impolite," he wrote, "to greet someone who is urinating or defecating." He then advises the person in need of "breaking wind" to "let a cough hide the explosive sound...Follow the law: replace farts with coughs."

There are more plastic flamingos in America than real ones.

THE WHOLE TOOTH

Some info to give you a little historical perspective when you're brushing your teeth.

TOOTH BRUSHES. People have been cleaning their teeth for thousands of years, but the implements they used weren't much like toothbrushes. Many cultures used "chew sticks," pencil-sized twigs with one end frayed into soft bristles; they've been found in Egyptian tombs dating back to 3,000 B.C.

The first toothbrush to resemble modern ones originated in China around 1498. The bristles were plucked from hogs and were set into handles of bone or bamboo. But animal hair is porous and water-absorbent, which makes it a breeding ground for bacteria; so brushing often did more harm than good. Nevertheless, by the 19th century, hogshair brushes were the standard for people who brushed.

Toothbrushing didn't become widely popular in the U.S. until the late 1930s. Two reasons for its spread: with the invention of nylon bristles by DuPont chemists in 1938, Americans finally had a hygienic substitute for hogshair; and every soldier who fought in World War II was instructed in oral hygiene and issued a brush—when the war ended they brought the habit home to their families.

TOOTHPASTE. History's first recorded toothpaste was an Egyptian mixture of ground pumice and strong wine. But the early Romans brushed their teeth with human urine...and also used it as a mouthwash. Actually, urine was an active component in toothpastes and mouthwashes until well into the 18th century—the ammonia it contains gave them strong cleansing power.

Fluoridated toothpaste came about as the result of a discovery made in Naples, Italy in 1802, when local dentists noticed yellowish-brown spots on their patients' teeth—but no cavities. Subsequent examination revealed that high levels of fluoride in the water caused the spots *and* prevented tooth decay, and that less fluoride protected teeth without causing the spots. It took a while for the discovery to be implemented; the first U.S. fluoridated water tests didn't take place until 1915, and Crest, the first toothpaste with fluoride in it ("Look, Ma...") didn't hit stores until 1956.

Poll results: U.S. bartenders say they hear more complaints about work than any other subject.

10 CANDY BARS YOU'LL NEVER EAT

These tasty tidbits about candy bars that are gone for good come from Dr.
Ray Broekel, chocolate and candy bar historian and publisher of
Candy Bar Gazebo, *a newsletter on old and new candy bars.*

T
HE AIR MAIL BAR. Introduced in 1930 to honor the first airmail flight in the U.S.—in 1918, from Washington, D.C. to New York City. Ironically, the first flight never made it to New York. After takeoff, the pilot noticed someone had forgotten to fill the fuel tank. Then he got lost over Maryland and had to land in a cow pasture. The Air Mail candy bar had a similar fate.

FAT EMMA. In the early1920s the Pendergast Candy Company in Minneapolis introduced a candy bar with a nougat center. They planned to call it the *Emma* bar. But when it wound up twice as thick as expected (they accidentally put too much egg white in the mixture), they changed the name to Fat Emma. Later, Frank Mars copied the idea to create the Milky Way bar.

THE SAL-LE-DANDE BAR. The first candy bar named after a stripper—Sally Rand, whose "fan dance" at the 1933-34 Chicago World's Fair in shocked and tititlated the nation. In the '60s another stripper bar was available briefly: the Gypsy bar, named after Gypsy Rose Lee.

THE RED GRANGE BAR. Endorsed by Red Grange, the most popular football player of his day. After starring at the University of Illinois, he joined the Chicago Bears in 1925 and helped keep the National Football League in business. Unfortunately, he couldn't do the same for his candy bar.

THE VEGETABLE SANDWICH BAR. One of the weirdest "health" bars ever made, this 1920s vegetable concoction contained cabbage, celery, peppers, and tomatoes. Its makers claimed it aided digestion and "will not constipate."

The average American throws out 1,905 lbs. of garbage every year.

THE ZEP CANDY BAR. "Sky-High Quality." One of several candy bars that capitalized on the popularity of "lighter-than-air" dirigibles in the 1930s. This one featured a sketch of a Graf Zeppelin on the wrapper. It was taken off the market after the Hindenburg exploded in 1937.

THE CHICKEN DINNER BAR. One of the bestselling bars you've never heard of. It was introduced in the 1920s and remained on the market for about 50 years. The original wrapper featured a picture of a roasted chicken on a dinner plate—a bizarre way of suggesting it was a nourishing meal and encouraging consumers to associate it with prosperity ("a chicken in every pot"). The manufacturer, Sperry Candy Co., even dispatched a fleet of Model A trucks disguised as giant sheet-metal chickens to deliver the candy to stores. Several years after the bar's debut, Sperry dropped the chicken from the wrapper. But it kept the name.

THE BIG-HEARTED "AL" BAR. George Williamson, owner of the Williamson Candy Company, was a good Democrat and a good friend of New York Governor Al Smith, Democratic nominee for president in 1928. Smith lost in a landslide to Herbert Hoover, and his candy bar soon followed.

THE SEVEN UP CANDY BAR. Got its name from having seven connected pieces, each with a different center. The bar came out in the 1930s, before the 7-Up Bottling Company began producing its soft drink—so the Trudeau Candy Company owned the trademark rights to the name. Eventually the 7-Up Bottling Company bought the bar and retired it, so they had exclusive use of the name no matter how it was spelled—*Seven Up* or *7-Up*.

THE "IT" BAR. The #1 female sex symbol of the silent movie era was Clara Bow—known as the "It Girl." (She had that special quality her movie studio called "It.") In 1927, the McDonald Candy Company of Salt Lake City tried cashing in on her popularity with a candy bar featuring her face on the wrapper. It did well for a few years, then disappeared along with Bow. (She wasn't able to make the switch to talkies, because although she was lovely to look at, her Brooklyn accent made her impossible to listen to.)

Also Gone: The Betsy Ross bar, the Lindy (for Charles Lindbergh), Amos 'n' Andy, Poor Prune, Vita Sert, and Doctor's Orders.

THE CURSE OF KING TUT

*After Tutankhamen's tomb was unearthed in 1922, a number of
people associated with the discovery died mysterious deaths.
Was it coincidence...or was it a curse?*

BACKGROUND: King Tutankhamen reigned from about
1334 to 1325 B.C., at the height of ancient Egypt's glory.
The "boy king" was only about 9 when he was crowned, and
died mysteriously at the age of 18 or 19. He was buried beside other
pharaohs in the Valley of the Kings, near the Nile River at Luxor,
the capital of ancient Egypt.

THE DISCOVERY

King Tutankhamen's tomb remained undisturbed for more than
three thousand years until it was unearthed in November, 1922 by
Howard Carter, an amateur archeologist commissioned by the English nobleman Lord Carnarvon to find it. Carter's discovery was due
largely to luck; having exhausted a number of other leads, he finally
decided to dig in a rocky patch of ground between the tombs of
three other pharaohs. Three feet under the soil he found the first of
a series of 16 steps, which led down to a sealed stone door. Mark-
ings on the door confirmed that it was a royal tomb. Realizing what
he had discovered, Carter ordered the steps buried again, and wired
Lord Carnarvon in London to join him.

Three weeks later Carnarvon arrived and digging resumed. The
first stone door was opened, revealing a 30-foot-long passage way
leading to a second stone door. Carter opened the second door and,
peeking into the darkness with the light of a single candle, was
greeted by an amazing sight—two entire rooms stuffed with priceless gold artifacts that had not seen the light of day for more than
30 centuries. The room was so crammed with statues, chariots, furniture, and other objects that it took two full months to catalog and
remove items in the first room alone. Tutankhamen's body lay in a
solid gold coffin in the next room; the gold coffin was itself encased
inside three other coffins, which rested inside a huge golden shrine
that took up nearly the entire room.

The discovery of the site was hailed as "the greatest find in the annals of archeology." Unlike other tombs, Tutankhamen's was almost completely undisturbed by graverobbers; its hundreds of artifacts provided a glimpse of ancient Egyptian cultural life that had never been seen before.

THE CURSE

But unearthing the treasures may have been a dangerous move—soon after the Tut discovery was announced, rumors about a curse on his tomb's defilers began to circulate. They weren't taken seriously—until Lord Carnarvon came down with a mysterious fever and died.

The curse gained credibility when word came from Lord Carnarvon's home in England at 1:50 a.m.—the exact moment of Lord Carnarvon's death—that his favorite dog had suddenly collapsed and died. And at *precisely* the same moment, Cairo was plunged into darkness, due to an unexplainable power failure.

Other Deaths: Over the next several years, a series of people associated with the Tut excavation died unexpectedly, often under mysterious circumstances. The dead in 1923 alone included Lord Carnarvon's brother, Col. Aubrey Herbert; Cairo archaeologist Achmed Kamal, and American Egyptologist William Henry Goodyear.

• The following year, British radiologist Archibald Reed died on his way to Luxor, where he planned to x-ray Tut's still-unopened coffin. Oxford archeologist Hugh Eveyln-White, who had dug in the necropolis at Thebes, also died in 1924.

• Edouard Neville, Carter's teacher, as well as George Jay-Gould, Carnarvon's friend, papyrus expert Bernard Greenfell, American Egyptologist Aaron Ember, and the nurse who attended to Lord Carnarvon, all died in 1926. Ember's death was particularly spooky—he was attempting to rescue from his burning house a manuscript he had worked on for years: The Egyptian Book of the Dead.

• In 1929, Lord Carnarvon's wife, Lady Almina, died, as did John Maxwell, the Earl's friend and executor, and Carter's secretary, Richard Bethell, who was found dead in bed, apparently from circulatory failure, at the age of 35.

THE AFTERMATH

Fallout from the rumors of the curse continued for years, as did the string of mysterious deaths.

• As accounts of the deaths circulated, hysteria spread. In England, hundreds of people shipped everything they had that waseven remotely Egyptian to the British Museum—including an arm from a mummy.

• The popularity of the curse legend led to a series of classic horror films: "The Mummy" (1932), starring Boris Karloff, and "The Mummy's Hand" (1940) and three sequels starring Lon Chaney, Jr.—"The Mummy's Tomb" (1942), "The Mummy's Ghost" and "The Mummy's Curse" (both 1944).

LAST WORDS

• Was the curse for real? Many prominent people insisted that it wasn't; they argued that the mortality rates of people associated with the Tutankhamen discovery and other finds were no higher than that of the general public. Dr. Gamal Mehrez, Director-General of the Egyptian Museum in Cairo, disputed the curse in an interview made several years after the discovery of Tut's tomb. "All my life," he said, "I have had to deal with pharaonic tombs and mummies. I am surely the best proof that it is all coincidence." Four weeks later he dropped dead of circulatory failure, as workers were moving Tutankhamen's gold mask for transport to London.

• For what it's worth, Lord Carnarvon's son, the sixth Earl of Carnarvon, accepts the curse at face value. Shortly after the fifth Earl's burial, a woman claiming psychic powers appeared at Highclere Castle and warned the sixth Earl, "Don't go near your father's grave! It will bring you bad luck!" The wary Earl heeded the crone's advice, and never visited the grave. In 1977 he told an NBC interviewer that he "neither believed nor disbelieved" the curse—but added that he would "not accept a million pounds to enter the tomb of Tutankhamen."

Profound Thought: "It's a question of whether we're going to go forward with the future, or past to the back." —*Dan Quayle*

According to experts, "Elvis" is the most popular name for pet King snakes.

THE LAST LAUGH: EPITAPHS

In the second Bathroom Reader, *we included some unusual epitaphs sent to us by B.R.I. members. Here's a bunch we've gotten since then.*

Seen in Medway, MA:
In Memory of Peter Daniels, 1688-1746:
Beneath this stone, a lump of clay,
Lies Uncle Peter Daniels,
Who too early in the month of May
Took off his winter flannels.

Seen in Ribbesford, England:
Anna Wallace
The children of Israel wanted bread,
And the Lord he sent them manna.
Old clerk Wallace wanted a wife,
And the Devil sent him Anna.

Seen in Westminster Abbey:
John Gay
Life is a joke, and all things show it;
I thought so once and now I know it.

Seen in Death Valley, CA:
May Preston
Here lies the body of fat May Preston
Who's now moved to heaven
To relieve the congestion.

Seen in Falkirk, England:
Jimmy Wyatt
At rest beneath this slab of stone
Lies Stingy Jimmy Wyatt;
He died one morning just at ten
And saved a dinner by it.

Seen in Thanet, England:
Against his will, here lies George Hill
Who from a cliff, fell down quite stiff.
When it happened is not known,
Therefore not mentioned on this stone.

Seen in Shutesbury, MA:
To the Four Husbands Of Miss Ivy Saunders
Here lies my husbands, One, Two, Three,
Dumb as men could ever be.
As for my fourth, well, praise be God,
He bides for a little above the sod.
Alex, Ben and Sandy were the first three's names,
And to make things tidy I'll add his—James.

Canada is the second largest country on Earth.

LIMERICKS

*Limericks have been around since the 1700s. Here are
some that readers have sent us over the years.*

There once was a spinster
from Wheeling,
Endowed with such
delicate feeling,
That she thought any chair
Should not have its legs bare,
So, she kept her eyes fixed
on the ceiling.

There was a young lady
of Kent,
Who always said just what
she meant;
People said, "she's a dear—
So unique—so sincere—"
But they shunned her by
common consent.

There once was a pious
young priest,
Who lived almost wholly
on yeast;
"For," he said, "it is plain
We must all rise again,
And I want to get started
at least."

I sat next to the Duchess
at tea,
Distressed as a person
could be.
Her rumblings abdominal
Were simply phenomenal—
And everyone thought
it was me!

A rocket explorer
named Wright
Once traveled much faster
than light.
He set out one day
In a relative way,
And returned
on the previous night.

There once was an old man
of Boolong
Who frightened the birds
with his song.
It wasn't the words
Which astonished the birds
But the horrible
dooble ontong.

A classical scholar
from Flint
Developed a
curious squint.
With her left-handed eye
She could scan the whole sky
While the other was reading
small print.

There was a young girl
from Detroit
Who at kissing was
very adroit;
She could pucker her lips
Into total eclipse,
Or open them out
like a quoit.

It's impossible to drown in quicksand—the sand in the water actually helps you float.

SECRETS OF DISNEYLAND

Well, they're not really secrets—more like gossip. But most people don't know much about the history and operations of the original mega-theme park. And it's pretty interesting stuff.

INSPIRATION

A couple of Walt Disney's top animators were real train buffs. They got Uncle Walt interested in the hobby and he set up a miniature steam railroad that circled his house and gardens (note: *Bathroom Reader #2*, p. 62), big enough to ride. After several train-theme parties, Walt got the idea that if his friends got such a kick from this one ride, maybe a whole amusement park would lure vacationers visiting Hollywood to star-gaze.

HOW WALT GOT THE MONEY

Walt proposed the idea to his brother Roy, the Disney stockholders, and their bankers...but they rejected it. In fact, they thought he was nuts. (In those days, amusement parks were sleazy places full of carnival side-shows, rip-off games, and cheap mechanical rides.)

So Disney was on his own. He went on a relentless search for financing. He sold his Palm Springs home and cashed in his $100,000 life insurance policy to finance his research. He lined up corporate sponsors, who were willing to pay for exhibits and restaurants in exchange for name recognition.

But the turning point came when he made a deal with ABC-TV. At the time ABC, a relatively new network, was a distant third in the ratings. It was desperate for the high-quality, high name-recognition programming Disney could provide. But Disney had already turned down offers from other networks. Why should he join forces with a loser like ABC? The answer: financing for his amusement park. In exchange for doing the show, Disney received a substantial sum of money and ABC agreed to call the show "Disneyland," virtually making the weekly show a one-hour commercial for the park. But perhaps more important, later, in an "unrelated" deal,

---

Death is sweet? Alexander the Great was reportedly buried in a vat of honey.

ABC purchased a 34% interest in Disneyland, Inc., the company set up to build the park.

When Roy saw the package Walt had put together, he changed his mind and hopped on the Disneyland bandwagon. In 1954, ground was broken in an Anaheim orange grove.

OPENING DAY

In the wake of its enormous success, people have forgotten that Disneyland's opening day was a disaster. Nearly 33,000 people—twice as many as the number invited—packed the park with the help of forged tickets and surreptitiously placed ladders. Not all the rides were operational, and the restaurants ran out of food after a few hours. In some parts of the park, concrete and asphalt hadn't hardened properly, and women walked out of their high-heel shoes.

Also, there had been a plumber's strike during construction, and there weren't enough drinking fountains. The press thought it was a ploy to get visitors to purchase soft drinks. What they didn't know was that, in order to be ready for opening day, Walt had to choose between installing toilets or drinking fountains.

Thanks to nationwide TV coverage emceed by Ronald Reagan, the entire country learned of the mess. The next day's newspaper headlines read, "Walt's Dream A Nightmare"—and Disney seemed to agree: for the rest of his life he referred to opening day as "Black Sunday."

LAND OF ILLUSIONS

When Uncle Walt bought the property for Disneyland in Anaheim in the early 1950s, he couldn't afford to buy all the land he wanted. So, in order to fit everything in, he used movie makers' tricks to make everything look bigger.

One trick was to use things that are familiar, but make them smaller than normal. Unless you look carefully and measure with your eyes, you'll assume, for instance, that the Disneyland train is normal size. It isn't. It is built to 5/8 scale. Many of the Disney buildings use the same trick, but that's just the beginning.

If you look carefully at some of the Disney buildings, especially those on Main Street, you'll notice there's something a little odd about them. They are not only smaller than normal, but their second and third stories are smaller still. This is known in art and in movie making as "forced perspective." By tapering the upper stories, the designers fool your eye into believing that they are bigger and taller than they really are.

This is done especially skillfully on Sleeping Beauty's Castle, even to the point that the bricks get smaller and smaller with each level.

In making Disney World this was less of a problem, because by that time the company could afford to buy an area bigger than most cities. It used many of the same tricks, but on an even bigger scale.

DISNEYLAND DEATHS

According to an article in *Egg* magazine, at least 53 people have died at Disneyland. According to *Egg*:

• The first Disney death was apparently a suicide: In 1964, after an argument with his girlfriend, a passenger on the Matterhorn stood up on the ride and was catapulted onto the tracks when his car came to a sudden stop. He never regained consciousness, and died four days later.

• The Matterhorn killed again in 1984, when a 48-year-old woman fell out of the ride and was struck by the following car. (For the rest of the day the Matterhorn was closed due to "technical difficulties.")

• Two people have been killed in accidents in Tomorrowland's "PeopleMover" ride, two others drowned in the river surrounding Tom Sawyer's Island. Another person was run down by the Monorail when he tried to sneak into the park without paying; and a park employee was crushed by a moving wall in the "America Sings" attraction.

• The park's first homicide occurred in 1981, when a man was stabbed after touching another man's girlfriend. (Disneyland was found negligent in the death and fined $600,000 after a park nurse neglected to call paramedics—and instead had the victim driven to the hospital in a park van.)

• Not all of the accidents happen inside the park: in 1968, 44 people were killed in two separate helicopter accidents traveling between Disneyland and Los Angeles International Airport; and in 1987 a teenage male was killed during a gunfight in the parking lot.

ORIGIN OF THE "BIG THREE" NETWORKS

They're a big part of your life...but we'll bet you don't know how they got there. Let's correct that.

THE NATIONAL BROADCASTING COMPANY (NBC)
NBC is the oldest of the "Big 3" American broadcasting networks. It was founded on September 13, 1926, by the Radio Corporation of America (RCA), the world's largest radio manufacturer, because they feared poor quality radio broadcasting was hurting sales.

Spurred on by RCA president David Sarnoff, NBC quickly became the most potent force in radio. The demand for programming was so high that within a year NBC split its radio operations into two divisions—the Red and Blue networks. The two continued broadcasting side by side until 1943, when the U.S. Government forced NBC to sell off the Blue network in an antitrust suit.

Meanwhile, RCA was experimenting with television (which Sarnoff called "the art of distant seeing"). In 1931 NBC built its first television transmitter, on top of the Empire State Building. Although development of TV was subsequently slowed by the Depression, regular TV service was started by NBC in 1939...and the first TV network broadcast ever was on January 11, 1940, from NBC in New York City to a GE-owned station in Schenectady, New York.

Because America was putting its resources into the war effort from 1941 to 1945, NBC couldn't begin regular network TV broadcasts until 1945.

RCA was the sole owner of NBC until 1985, when GE—an original partner in 1926—bought RCA for $6.8 billion.

THE COLUMBIA BROADCASTING SYSTEM (CBS)

In the 1920s, Arthur Judson was a talent agent whose clients included the New York Philharmonic. When NBC pioneered TV broadcasting in 1926, Judson cut a deal with them to broadcast several of his clients—but NBC reneged on its promise.

Judson was so angry that he started his own radio broadcasting network. He called it the United Independent Broadcasters, and began signing up independent radio stations around the country.

Judson was too broke to run the company alone, so he joined forces with the Columbia Phonograph and Records Co. and changed the network's name to the Columbia Phonograph Broadcasting System. It initially provided 10 hours of programming per week to 16 affiliates. But CPBS was losing money, and Columbia Phonograph pulled out. They sold their shares to Jerome Louchheim, a wealthy Philidelphia builder, who renamed CPBS the Columbia Broadcasting System. He, in turn, sold out to William S. Paley for $400,000 in 1929. Paley (whose father, owner of the Congress Cigar Co., was one of CBS's largest advertisers) turned the ailing network around almost overnight. By 1932 CBS was earning more than $3 million a year in profits—and in 1939 it was doing so well that it bought its former owner, Columbia Phonograph and Records.

THE AMERICAN BROADCASTING SYSTEM (ABC)

When the U.S. government forced NBC to sell off its Blue network in 1943, Lifesaver candy manufacturer Edward J. Noble bought it for $8 million and renamed it the American Broadcasting Company. Ten years later, ABC merged with United Paramont Theaters—a chain of movie theaters the government had forced Paramount Pictures to sell—and went into TV broadcasting.

A perpetual "weak sister" to its larger rivals, ABC remained a second-rate network until 1954, when its gavel-to-gavel coverage of the U.S. Senate's Army-McCarthy hearings made broadcasting history...and gave them newfound respectability.

ABC remained much smaller than its rivals, but made up for its lack of money and affiliate stations by producing more innovative TV shows than CBS and NBC. Some of its groundbreaking shows: "Disneyland," "The Mickey Mouse Club," and "Batman." ABC also revolutionized sports coverage with shows like "Monday Night Football," "Wide World of Sports," and its coverage of the Olympics. The network used the profits generated from sports and miniseries shows to strengthen its news and prime-time programming—and in 1975 its overall ratings shot ahead of its rivals for the first time. It has been on equal footing ever since.

A strong bolt of lightning can contain as much as 100 million volts of electricity.

MALCOLM X SPEAKS

Malcolm X was one of the most controversial—and significant—figures in recent American history.

"You're not supposed to be so blind with patriotism that you can't face reality. Wrong is wrong, no matter who does it or who says it."

"It's easy to become a satellite today without even being aware of it. This country can seduce God. Yes, it has that seductive power—the power of dollarism."

"I for one believe that if you give people a thorough understanding of what confronts them and the basic causes that produce it, they'll create their own program, and when the people create a program, you get action."

"I believe in the brotherhood of man, all men, but I don't believe in brotherhood with anybody who doesn't want brotherhood with me. I believe in treating people right, but I'm not going to waste my time trying to treat somebody right who doesn't know how to return that treatment."

"Power never takes a back step—only in the face of more power."

"Nobody can give you freedom. Nobody can give you equality or justice or anything. If you are a man, you take it."

"After you get your freedom, your enemy will respect you."

"You cannot seperate peace from freedom, because no one can be at peace until he has his freedom."

"Truth is on the side of the oppressed."

"Learn to see...listen...and think for yourself."

"The colleges and universities in the American education system are skillfully used to miseducate."

"There shouldn't be bars. Behind bars, a man never reforms. He will never forget. He will never get completely over the memory of the bars."

Survey Results: 70% of high school students try cigarettes, but only 13% smoke regularly.

"MADAM, I'M ADAM"

A palindrome is a word or phrase that spells the same thing backward and forward. Here are the best that B.R.I. members have sent us. Try your own. If you come up with a good one, send it to us and we'll publish it in the next edition.

TWO-WORD PHRASES

No, Son.

Sue us!

Pots nonstop.

Dump mud.

Go, dog!

Stack cats.

Worm row.

Party trap.

LONGER PHRASES

Wonder if Sununu's fired now.

Never odd or even.

Ed is on no side.

Step on no pets.

Rise to vote, sir!

Naomi, did I moan?

"Desserts," I stressed.

Spit Q-Tips.

Roy, am I mayor?

A car, a man, a maraca.

Are we not drawn onward, we few, drawn onward to new era?

A man, a plan, a canal… Panama!

Live not on evil.

If I had a Hi-Fi…

A slut nixes sex in Tulsa.

Put Eliot's toilet up.

Pull up, Bob, pull up!

Pa's a sap.

Ma is as selfless as I am.

NONSENSE PHRASES

Did mom poop? Mom did.

We panic in a pew.

Yawn a more Roman way.

Mr. Owl ate my metal worm.

There are no words in the English language that rhyme with purple.

IT LOSES SOMETHING IN TRANSLATION...

Have you ever thought that you were communicating brilliantly, only to find out other people thought you were speaking nonsense? That's a particularly easy mistake when you're speaking a foreign language. A few classic examples:

BUT HE'S NOT SQUEEZING THEM

When President Jimmy Carter arrived in Poland in 1977, he made a brief speech to press and officials. But his interpreter delivered a slightly different speech. Carter said he had "left the United States that day." His interpreter said he'd "abandoned" it. Carter referred to the Poles' "desires for the future." His interpreter translated this as "lusts for the future." And, finally, the interpreter explained to the crowd: "The president says he is pleased to be here in Poland grasping your private parts."

LOOKING FOR PROTECTION

Shannon, Ireland (UPI) — "A young Russian couple caused an embarrassing mix-up at Shannon Airport when they were mistaken for political defectors.

"The pair, on a technical stopover on the Havana-Moscow Aeroflot route, approached a counter at the big Shannon duty-free store Monday. In halting English, the man asked for "protection," according to an airport spokesman.

"He was quickly whisked away for questioning by Immigration authorities. But after 20 minutes, officials determined it was not political protection he was after, but sexual protection. He just wanted to buy some condoms."

MORE BIRTH CONTROL

In one campaign to introduce its ball-point pens to Mexico, the Parker Pen Co. used the slogan "It won't leak in your pocket and embarrass you." The company's translators mistakenly used the verb *embarazar*, which sounds like "to embarrass" but actually means "to become pregnant." The ad appeared to suggest that the pen could control unwanted pregnancies.

New Mexico is the only state named after a country.

CULTURAL THAI'S

"Thais still talk about President Lyndon Johnson's visit in the mid-'60s, when, seated next to King Bhumibol Adulyadej on national television, the lanky Texan hitched his foot up over his thigh and pointed his shoe directly at the king—a common obscene gesture in that country. It didn't relieve tensions when, on the same telecast, the American president gave the Thai queen a big "hi, honey" hug. Solemn tradition in Thailand demands that nobody touches the queen."

—*Washington Post*

COMIC DELIVERY

According to Roger Axtell, in his book *Do's and Taboos of Hosting International Visitors*, a high-ranking insurance company executive visiting Japan in the 1980s delivered a speech that began with a joke. It went over well...but later on he learned that it was translated something like this:

> American businessman is beginning speech with thing called joke. I am not certain why, but all American businessmen believe it necessary to start speech with joke. [Pause] He is telling joke now, but frankly you would not understand it, so I won't translate it. He thinks I am telling you joke now. [Pause] Polite thing to do when he finishes is to laugh. [Pause] He is getting close. [Pause] Now!

"The audience not only laughed," Axtell says, "but in typical generous Japanese style, they stood and applauded as well. After the speech, not realizing what had transpired, the American remembered going to the translator and saying, 'I've been giving speeches in this country for several years and you are the first translator who knows how to tell a good joke.' "

WHAT A GUY!

When the Perdue Chicken Co. translated its slogan—"It takes a tough man to make a tender chicken" —into Spanish, they ended up with "It takes a hard (sexually aroused) man to make a chicken affectionate."

Florence Nightingale carried a pet owl in her pocket wherever she traveled.

DEMOCRACY IN ACTION

"It's the worst form of government," said Mark Twain, "except for every other form of government." Here's a B.R.I. election report on the sillier —or is that just "human"?—side of government "by the people."

ABSENTEE BALLOTS
A *report from* Parade *magazine, January 2, 1994.*

"What if they held an election and no one voted? It happened in Centerville, Miss....Denny James looked like a sure thing for the board of aldermen—he was the only candidate. But no one voted for him. State law says a candidate must get at least one vote before being declared the winner of an election.

"The moral of the story: Don't take anything for granted. Everyone in town assumed the neighbors would be voting. When the polls closed early, even James—who worked late that day—was shut out. But another election was held, and James got 45 votes."

MAKING AN ASS OF VOTERS

In 1936, Kenneth Simmons, mayor of Milton, Washington, placed a candidate named Boston Curtis on the ballot for the Republican precinct committee. Curtis ran as a "dark horse"...and although he gave no speeches and made no promises, he won.

The victory made national news, because Curtis was a mule; his hoof prints were even imprinted on the filing notice. Simmons later claimed he'd sponsored the mule's candidacy "to show how careless many voters are."

MAN STOPS FOR BURRITO—ALTERS HISTORY

ASHFORD, CONN.— "Robert Brady was driving through town last month and decided to stop at a convenience store for a burrito. Next door, in front of Town Hall, he saw a sign that read, 'Vote Today.'

"For a lark, the former Ashford resident—who was still registered

---

California is the first state to send two women to the U.S. Senate at the same time.

to vote here—strolled into the Town Hall and voted 'Yes' in what turned out to be a referendum on the town budget. He later learned that the $5 million budget had passed by a single vote. 'Hey, I changed the course of history, all for a burrito,' Brady said, laughing."

—*Hartford Courant*, July 15, 1991

PLANNED OBSOLESCENCE

"In 1978, William Smith, of Waukegan, Illinois, was elected Lake County auditor. But in a referendum on the same ballot, voters abolished the position of auditor altogether. 'I feel like I've gone off a diving board and suddenly found the pool was empty,' Smith said."

—*The Emperor Who Ate the Bible*

HEADS, YOU SERVE

In 1975, Lib Tufarolo and Miles Nelson ran for mayor of Clyde Hill, Washington. Tufarolo got 576 votes; so did Nelson.

"The law says that in case of a tie you decide the election by lot," the local superintendent of elections informed them. Then he suggested they flip a coin. Tufarolo was outraged. "It's just ridiculous. I don't think that's how the people would want it done," he said. But Nelson, who'd spent a total of $5 on his campaign (which was $5 more than Tufarolo had spent), disagreed. He called it "the least offensive method" of settling the issue.

Tufarolo won the toss and became mayor. The Associated Press noted that "the community of 3,200 appears indifferent."

—**Fenton and Fowler's**
More Best & Worst & Most Unusual

DEAD MEN CAST NO VOTES

U.S. voters have occasionally elected dead men to office. Usually the candidate dies after being nominated, and it's too late to remove the name from the ballot and nominate someone who's alive. But at least once—in 1868—a corpse was actually nominated... and elected. The "elected official" was the last remains of Rep. Thaddeus Stevens, of Lancaster County, Pennsylvania. His supporters did it as a tribute.

MYTH AMERICA

Do you think all cowboys in the Old West looked like John Wayne?
Here's some info about at least one important difference.

THE MYTH
All the cowboys in the American West were white.

BACKGROUND
Most of what Americans "know" about the Wild West comes from movies, TV, and popular authors. For years, these media have portrayed the Old West as virtually lily-white.

For example: Seven of the top ten television shows of the 1958-1959 season were Westerns: *Gunsmoke, Wagon Train, Have Gun Will Travel, The Rifleman, Maverick, Tales of Wells Fargo,* and *Wyatt Earp.* All of them featured all-white regular casts.

Hollywood even went so far as to cast white actors to play the parts of real-life black cowboys, as in the 1951 film *Tomahawk.* The film featured Jim Beckwourth, a legendary black frontiersman... but the part was played by Jack Oakie, a white actor.

THE TRUTH
Nearly one in three cowboys in the American West were black, with the ratio higher in some states. Oklahoma, for example, saw thirty all-black towns spring up between 1890 and 1910, and 26 of the first 44 settlers of Los Angeles were black.

In fact, many of the most celebrated American cowboys were black, including:

• **Bill Pickett,** a rodeo star who toured under the name Will Pickett the Dusty Demon. He was a huge rodeo star in the early 1900s (Will Rogers was one of his early assistants) and starred in several silent films. He also invented the sport of "bulldogging"—wrestling a bull to the ground by its horns—although his preferred method, biting the bull's lip as he threw it to the ground, never caught on with other rodeo stars.

• **Nat Love,** also known as "Deadwood Dick," was a unique character who got his start as a cowboy in Dodge City at the age of 15

Good news? Marriages lasting more than 13 years are more likely to end in death than divorce.

and went on to become a rodeo star. A friend of the famous law-man Bat Masterson, Love boasted of having 14 bullet wounds, and was famous for an incident in a Mexican bar in which he ordered drinks for his horse.

• **Cherokee Bill,** an Indian scout and notorious outlaw who in his day was as well known as Billy the Kid. His luck was just about as bad as Kid's was, too: his run-ins with the law resulted in his being hanged one month shy of his 20th birthday.

• **Mary Fields,** better known as Stagecoach Mary, a "strapping 6-footer who never shied from a shootout. A fearless mail carrier while in her 60s, she spent much of her final years in a Cascade, Montana, saloon playing cards with the boys."

• **Isom Dart,** a former slave who became famous as a rodeo clown, cattle rustler, prospector, and broncobuster.

* * * * *

BLACK WESTERNS

Hollywood has, on occasion, featured blacks in Westerns, but the depictions have rarely been historically accurate. The '30s and '40s saw a spate of cowboy 'race' films, including *Bronze Buckaroo* and *Harlem Rides the Range*; the '60s saw some racially relevant West-erns like *Major Dundee* and *The Professionals*…and the "blaxploita-tion" wave of the '70s even resulted in some patronizing black Westerns, the worst of which was probably *The Legend of Nigger Charlie*.

In the 1980s it became common to cast blacks in Westerns without referring to their race in the film, but it wasn't until the 1990s—when independent black filmmakers began directing their own Westerns—that films like Mario Van Peebles's *Posse* (1993) began to feature blacks as they really were in the West, a develop-ment that has been lauded by filmmakers, historians, and sociolo-gists alike. "It's so important that the West be pictured as it was, not some lily-white John Wayne adventure story," says William Loren Katz, author of *The Black West* and *Black People Who Made the Old West*. "Books make it seem like, after the Civil War, blacks went home and went to sleep and didn't wake up until Martin Lu-ther King. A whole heritage has been lost to generation after gen-eration of schoolchildren, black and white."

INSIDE "JEOPARDY!"

"If I had a TV in my bathroom," writes B.R.I. member J. Haines, "I'd be a regular "Jeopardy!" watcher. Unfortunately, I don't. How about a few pages on the program, so I can still think about 'Jeopardy!' in the john?" Okay, J.—here's some info from The Jeopardy! Book, by Alex Trebek.

ORIGIN. In 1963 Merv Griffin and his wife, Juliann, were on a flight to New York when they began discussing game shows. Griffin describes the conversation:

"After the quiz show scandals of the late fifties, the networks were leery of shows where contestants answered questions for money....I mentioned how much I liked the old quiz shows, but reminded her that the scandals had created credibility problems for producers.

" 'So,' Juliann joked, 'Why not just give them the answers to start with?' She was kidding, but the thought struck me between the eyes. She said to me, '79 Wistful Vista.' And I replied, 'What's *Fibber McGee and Molly's* address?' " "Jeopardy" 's format was born.

THE SHOW GOES ON

As soon as the plane landed in New York, Griffin began working on the show. "I decided to create separate categories of answers, such as History, Literature, Motion Pictures. Put the categories in columns and assign dollar values to each square. That was it. One big board with ten categories and ten answers in each category. We called the game 'What's the Question?' and had a game board built to show to NBC."

The Name. "During the development process, I showed our efforts to network executive Ed Vane, who commented, 'I like what I see, but the game needs more Jeopardies,' " or portions of the game where the players risk losing it all. "I didn't hear another word he said after that. All I could think of was the name: goodbye 'What's the Question?,' hello 'Jeopardy!' "

Showtime. At first, NBC executives disliked the show. During the final sales presentation to the network, NBC head Mort Werner played the game with Merv Griffin acting as host. Halfway through the game Werner threw up his hands and shouted, "I didn't get one question right; it's too hard." But before he could reject the show out of hand, one of his assistants leaned over and whispered, "Buy it." Werner bought it. (His young assistant, a man named Grant Tinker, eventually became head of NBC himself).

THE HOSTS

• **Art Fleming.** The first "Jeopardy!" host was an announcer Merv Griffin had seen on a TWA commercial. Fleming hosted the program for more than 12 years, ultimately appearing on 2,858 shows between 1964 and 1979.

• **Alex Trebek.** Trebek took over when the show was revived in 1984. Earlier that year Chuck Wollery, host of "Wheel of Fortune" (another Merv Griffin game show) became ill. The producer needed a replacement host to tape the program. So he called Alex Trebek, who was emceeing a game show called "Battlestars." Trebek agreed to fill in, and did so well that he was hired to host the new "Jeopardy!"

ANSWERS & QUESTIONS

• How do they come up with their questions?

A research staff of 12 writers drafts the questions and provides at least two sources verifying the information.

Then the show's editorial associate producer edits the questions and assigns dollar amounts.

The questions are then sent back to a different researcher, who verifies them again.

From there the questions are given to the show's producer, who can ask for even further verification.

Then on game day Alex Trebek reviews the questions himself.

• In the show's 20 seasons, nearly 300,000 questions—61 per episode—have been through this review process.

CONTESTANTS

Where do they get the contestants?

Every year 250,000 people apply for an audition, either through the station that broadcasts the show in their area, or by contacting the show itself.

Only 15,000 are chosen for the initial screening exam, and only 1,500 qualify to become contestants.

Only 500 actually make it on the air.

UNEXPECTED ENCOUNTERS

"East is east, and west is west, and never the twain shall meet." When we were kids, that seemed to make sense—except the 'twain' part. That wasn't even a word, as far as we knew. Anyway, here are some examples of people you'd never expect to see together:

CHARLIE CHAPLIN & MAHATMA GANDHI

When: 1931, in London.

Who: Chaplin, the "Little Tramp," was the world's most famous comedian. Gandhi, a tiny figure in a loincloth, was one of the world most revered political and religious leaders.

What Happened: As they posed for photographers, Chaplin tried to figure out what to say. In his autobiography, he writes about his terror: "The room was suddenly attacked by flashbulbs from the camera as we sat on the sofa. Now came that uneasy, terrifying moment when I should say something astutely intelligent upon a subject I know little about...I knew I had to start the ball rolling, that it was not up to the Mahatma to tell me how much he enjoyed my last film...I doubted he had ever even seen a film." He finally got up the courage, and the two men politely exchanged political views. Then Chaplin stayed and watched Gandhi at his prayers.

GORGEOUS GEORGE & MUHAMMAD ALI

When: 1961, at a radio studio in Las Vegas.

Who: Gorgeous George, with his permed blonde hair and purple robes, was one of TV wrestling's original superstars. He sold out arenas wherever he played, and was named Mr. Televison in 1949; but by 1961 his career was almost over. Cassius Clay (aka Muhammad Ali) was a young boxer who'd just turned pro.

What Happened: In 1961 George made a wrestling appearance in Las Vegas. To promote it, he went on a local radio show, shouting "I am the greatest!" As it happened, the other guest on the program was a young Cassius Clay, who was so impressed with George's theatrics that he went to the wrestling match that evening. The place was packed. "That's when I decided I'd never been shy about talking," Ali remembers, "but if I talked even more, there was no

---

Americans say microwave ovens are the best recent change in their lives, infomercials the worst.

telling how much money people would pay to see me."

NICHELLE NICHOLS & MARTIN LUTHER KING, JR.

When: 1967, at a party.

Who: King was America's greatest civil rights leader, and the recipient of the Nobel Peace Prize. Nichols was playing Lt. Uhura in *Star Trek*'s first (low-rated) season. She was considering quitting the show because Paramount wouldn't give her a contract.

What Happened: According to one source: "A friend came up to Nichols at a party and said someone wanted to meet her. She expected a gushing Trekkie… but when she turned around, she was looking at Martin Luther King…who actually *was* a fan. He said he'd heard she was considering leaving *Star Trek*, and urged her not to; she was too important a role model for blacks—and the only black woman on TV with real authority. 'Do you realize that you're fourth in command on the *Enterprise?*' he asked. Nichols didn't. The next day she checked and found he was right…. She stayed with the show and finally got her contract the next season."

HARPO MARX & GEORGE BERNARD SHAW

When: 1931, at the Villa Gallanon in the south of France.

Who: Shaw was "the most important British playright since Shakespeare." Marx was part of the world's most popular slapstick team.

What Happened: Here's how Harpo described the meeting in his autobiography: "I went down the cliff to the little sheltered cove we used for nude bathing, took off my clothes, and went for a swim. I came out of the water and stretched out on a towel to sunbathe ….I was startled out of my doze in the sun by a man's voice, blaring from the top of the cliff. 'Halloo! Halloo! Is there nobody home?'

"I wrapped the towel around myself and scrambled up the cliff to see who it was. It was a tall, skinny, red-faced old geezer with a beard, decked out in a sporty cap and knicker suit. There was a lady with him. 'Who the devil are you?' I told him I was Harpo Marx. 'Ah, yes, of course,' he said. He held out his hand. 'I'm Bernard Shaw,' he said. Instead of shaking hands with me, he made a sudden lunge for my towel and snatched it away, and exposed me naked to the world. 'And this,' he said, 'is Mrs. Shaw.' From the moment I met him, I had nothing to hide from George Bernard Shaw." They became good friends.

BLOTTO, LOOPED, FRIED

Most people know what sloshed, loaded and looped mean: being drunk, of course. But there are plenty of other words that mean the same thing. Here's a list of America's favorites that appear in I Hear America Talking.

(The words are followed by the year they came into use.)

Stiff (1737)

Fuzzy (1770)

Half Shaved (1818)

Bent (1833)

Slewed (1834)

Stinking (1837)

Screwed (1838)

Lushy (1840)

Pixilated (1850)

Swizzled (1850)

Whipped (1851)

Tanglefooted (1860)

Spiffed (1860)

Frazzled (1870)

Squiffy (1874)

Boiled (1886)

Paralyzed (1888)

Pickled (1890)

Woozy (1897)

Pifflicated (1900)

Ginned (1900)

Ossified (1901)

Petrified (1903)

Tanked (1905)

Blotto (1905)

Shellacked (1905)

Jingled (1908)

Piped (1912)

Plastered (1912)

Gassed (1915)

Hooted (1915)

Have A Snoot Full (1918)

Jugged (1919)

Canned (1920)

Juiced (1920)

Fried (1920)

Buried (1920)

Potted (1922)

Dead To The World (1926)

Crocked (1927)

Busted (1928)

Rum-dum (1931)

Bombed (1940)

Feeling No Pain (1940)

Swacked (1941)

Sloshed (1950)

Boxed (1950)

Clobbered (1951)

Crashed (1950s)

Zonked (1950s)

A BREED APART

Ever wonder why a Dachshund is so long and skinny—or why Great Danes are so tall? The answer: They were bred with a specific purpose in mind. Here are the stories behind the names and appearances of some of the world's most popular breeds of dogs.

BASSET HOUNDS. The name comes from the French adjective *bas,* which means "low thing." Originally bred to hunt rabbits, raccoons, and other small mammals. Their short legs make them relatively slow runners, but they're especially adept at chasing prey through thickets.

BULLDOGS. According to legend, in 1209 A.D. Lord William Earl Warren of Stamford, England, was looking out onto his meadow and saw two dogs fighting a bull. He so admired their courage that he gave the meadow to the townspeople—on the condition that they begin holding annual dog-bull fights. Over the next 600 years, bullbaiting became a popular sport, and the bulldog breed evolved along with it. Like pit-bulls, bulldogs were originally bred to be fearless and vicious. But in 1835, bullbaiting was banned in England. Bulldog lovers used breeding techniques to eliminate their viciousness, making them acceptable house pets.

COCKER SPANIELS. A member of the *Spanyell* family of dogs that dates back to the 14th century. Their small size made them ideal for hunting woodcocks, earning them the name *cockers,* which eventually became *cocking spaniels,* then *cocker spaniels.*

FRENCH POODLES. Actually bred in 15th-century Germany as hunting dogs. The name "poodle" comes from the German word *pudel,* which means puddle or splash. The reason: They're good swimmers and were often used to retrieve game from ponds, etc.

GREAT DANES. Got their name from the French, who thought they were Danish. They weren't: they were actually from Germany, where they were bred large enough to tackle and kill wild boars.

It takes 12 bees their entire lifetime to make a tablespoon of honey.

ROTTWEILERS. When soldiers of ancient Rome went into battle, they had no way of bringing enough fresh meat with them to last the entire campaign. So they brought cattle—and Rottweiler dogs to herd them. In 700 A.D., the local duke in an area of Germany the Romans had once occupied commissioned a Catholic church to be built near the ruins of some Roman baths. Because the baths had red tile roofs, the Duke issued instructions to build at "das Rote Wil,"—the red tiles. Later the area became known as the town of Rottweil, and the breed of dogs the Romans had left behind were called Rottweilers.

GREYHOUNDS. One of the oldest breeds of dogs; dating back as far as ancient Egypt (where they were a favorite pet of the pharoahs). Tomb paintings nearly 5,000 years old depict them hunting wild goats, deer, and other animals. According to one theory they're actually named after the Greeks, taking their name from the word *Graius*, which means Grecian or Greek.

DACHSHUNDS. Although the name is derived from the German words *dachs* (badger) and *hund* (dog), dachshunds have been used to hunt animals as large as wild boars. Their long bodies make them ideal for chasing badgers and rabbits through their tunnels.

BLOODHOUNDS. The bloodhound's unrivaled sense of smell has made it one of the most popular hunting dogs in history. Dog experts believe it dates back several hundred years B.C. and was first used as a hunting dog in and around Constantinople. Its skills were so valuable that it became known as a royal, or "blooded" hound, and was a favorite pet of aristocrats.

PEKINGESE. Came from imperial China, where the purest breeds were reserved for members of the royal family. The dogs were so precious that when British troops sacked the Imperial Palace in 1860, most of the pets were destroyed by their owners...who preferred killing them to surrendering them to the enemy. However one woman—the Emperor's aunt—committed suicide before she killed her dogs, and the British found 5 of them hiding behind a curtain in her quarters. The dogs were brought back to England, and one was presented to Queen Victoria. She fell in love with it, and the breed immediately became popular.

Pop singer Michael Jackson collects mannequins.

THE STORY OF WALL STREET

Why is Wall Street the financial center in the U.S.? For that matter, why is it even called Wall Street? Glad you asked that question.

HISTORY. In the early 1600s, the southern tip of Manhattan Island was a Dutch settlement known as New Amsterdam. In 1653, the governor of the colony decided the best way to protect his thriving trading post from Indians and the British was to build a wall from the Hudson River to the East River.

However, the wall did little to deter the British. They attacked by ship in 1664, easily overwhelmed the Dutch, and renamed the city New York. Thirty years later, they tore down the wall and used it for firewood.

NAME. The dirt road that ran alongside the wall was—naturally enough—known as Wall Street. When the wall was destroyed, the road became a main thoroughfare in New York.

MAIN INDUSTRY. Wall Street has been a commercial center ever since the British took over.

• They immediately set up a number of "exchanges"—open, shed-like buildings used for trading commodities like furs, molasses, and tobacco—on Wall Street.

• About 100 years later the first stocks and bonds were sold on the street. At the end of the Revolutionary war the Colonies were so deeply in debt that the first Congress of the U.S. issued $80 million in bonds (government IOUs). Stocks were added two years later, when Alexander Hamilton (then Secretary of the Treasury) established the nation's first bank, the Bank of the United States, and offered shares to the public.

The New York Exchange. Stocks and bonds soon became a booming business, and in 1792 a group of 24 brokers decided to create an informal exchange to specialize in these "paper transactions."

Amusing stat: Ohio has 22 roller coasters—the most of any state.

They signed a document known as the "Buttonwood Agreement" (named after the tree on Wall Street where the group met), in which they agreed to trade only among themselves and to charge customers a minimum 25% commission. These men are considered the original members of the New York Stock Exchange.

• When conditions on the street got too crowded, the exchange moved into a coffeehouse, then rented a room at 40 Wall Street. New members were required to pay an initiation fee of not less than $25; the amount varied, depending on the location of their seat in the room. This is how traders came to buy "a seat on the exchange."

• By 1848, the prestigious New York Stock Exchange and Board had absorbed all other exchanges on Wall Street and was conducting business in an orderly and unexciting manner: the chairman called the name of each stock twice a day and any trading was completed before moving on.

The American Exchange. Meanwhile, those who couldn't afford to become members continued to trade on the street after-hours, and became known as "curb brokers." For this army of opportunists, the action was in stocks considered too speculative by members of "The Big Board"—especially railroads and mining companies created after the discovery of gold in California.

• By the late 1890s, some of the brokers on "The Curb Exchange" could afford to rent offices in nearby buildings. Telephone clerks took orders and shouted them out the window to the brokers below, who wore loud checkered jackets and hats, from bright green derbies to pith helmets, so their clerks could spot them in the crowded street. When the shouting got out of hand, a system of hand signals (some of which are still used today) was developed to pass on price and volume information.

• This entire scene moved indoors in 1921. And in 1953, the New York Curb Exchange, its name since 1928, became the American Stock Exchange, the second largest exchange on Wall Street.

Miscellany. The term "broker" comes from the french *brochier*, meaning someone who broaches, or breaks, a wine keg. It was originally used to refer to entrepreneurs who bought wine by the barrel, "broke it open," and sold it by the cup.

To avoid being trapped in a burning building, Hans Christian Anderson always carried a rope.

SENATE FIGHTS

You've heard of floor fights in Congress...but you probably never imagined the kind where people get bloody noses and pull guns on each other. In a few instances, that's exactly what's happened.

FOOTE VS. BENTON

Background: Senator Henry Foote of Mississippi had a reputation as a hothead and a fighter; he'd been injured in no less than three duels. His temper reached legendary proportions on April 17, 1850, when he drew a pistol on Thomas Hart Benton of Missouri in the Senate chamber.

What Happened: Benton had just finished delivering a stinging attack on Foote's recently-deceased mentor, former Vice President John C. Calhoun of South Carolina. Suddenly Foote leaped to his feet and denounced Benton as a coward. When Benton advanced toward the offending senator, Foote retreated and pulled a pistol from his coat. Benton replied: "I have no pistols. Let him fire. Stand out of the way. Let the assassin fire."

Result: Chaos ensued. Finally, Senator Daniel Dickinson of New York took Foote's pistol away. Foote was later reprimanded for his behavior but no other charges were pressed.

BROOKS VS. SUMNER

Background: Civil War tensions boiled over in Congress on May 22, 1856, when South Carolina Representative Preston Brooks brutally attacked and injured Massachusetts Senator Charles Sumner with a cane. The incident followed a heated address by the anti-slavery Sumner, who had specifically attacked Brooks's relative, Senator Andrew Butler of South Carolina.

What Happened: When the Senate adjourned, Brooks approached Sumner—who was sitting at his desk—and began striking him on the head with a cane. Sumner was trapped. To avoid the blows, he tried to rise from his bolted-down desk. His effort was so great that he literally ripped the screws from the floor.

Result: Sumner was so badly injured that he spent the next three years recovering. Efforts to punish Brooks—who became a hero in the South—were unsuccessful. He died shortly after the attack.

More than $1 billion worth of candy is sold in the U.S. during the Halloween season.

TILLMAN VS. McLAURIN

Background: On February 28, 1902, the Senate was debating a bill relating to government aid for the Philippines.

What Happened: Senator Benjamin Tillman of South Carolina charged that "improper influences" had influenced his colleague, John McLaurin—also from South Carolina—to change his vote on the legislation. When McLaurin heard Tillman's charges, he ran back to the Senate chambers "pale with anger" and accused Tillman of lying. Tillman lunged at McLaurin and punched him in the eye. McLaurin came back with a blow to Tillman's nose.

Result: A doorkeeper and several senators intervened and the gallery was immediately cleared. Later that day, both were suspended for six days for "disorderly conduct." The fight eventually led to Senate Rule 19, which says "no Senator in debate shall, directly or indirectly, by any form of words impute to another Senator or to other Senators any conduct or motive unworthy or unbecoming a Senator."

ENGLE VS. THE FILIBUSTER

Background: On June 10, 1964, one of the most dramatic votes in Senate history took place. Democratic Senator Clair Engle of California, terminally ill with a brain tumor, cast a vote from his wheelchair that led to the passage of the Civil Rights Act of 1964.

A Southern filibuster had stalled the bill on the floor of the Senate. Ending the filibuster required a two-thirds majority, and it looked like the Democrats were one vote short.

What Happened: "Then came the moment few had expected," *The New York Times* reported. "Seconds before his name was called, Senator Clair Engle of California was pushed into the chamber in a wheelchair. He was smiling slightly. 'Mr. Engle,' the clerk called. There was a long silence. Senator Engle, recuperating from two brain operations, tried to speak. He could not. Finally he raised his left arm, as though trying to point toward his eyes. He nodded his head, signaling that he was voting 'aye.' He was wheeled out of the chamber minutes later and taken by ambulance back to his home."

Result: The resolution passed by one vote. Nine days later, on June 19, 1964, the Senate passed the final version of the Civil Rights Act, again with Engle's vote. A month later, "Congressman Fireball"—as Engle had once been called—died at the age of 52.

STATE YOUR NAME

You know the names of all 50 states…but do you know where even one of them comes from? Since you're not about to get up and go anywhere right now, here's a chance to learn.

ALABAMA. Possibly from the Creek Indian word *alibamo*, meaning "we stay here."

ALASKA. From the Aleutian word *alakshak*, which means "great lands," or "land that is not an island."

ARIZONA. Taken either from the Pima Indian words *ali shonak*, meaning "little spring," or from the Aztec word *arizuma*, meaning "silver-bearing."

ARKANSAS. The French somehow coined it from the name of the Siouan *Quapaw* tribe.

CALIFORNIA. According to one theory, Spanish settlers named it after a Utopian society described in a popular 16th-century novel called *Serged de Esplandian*.

COLORADO. Means "red" in Spanish. The name was originally applied to the Colorado River, whose waters are reddish with canyon clay.

CONNECTICUT. Taken from the Mohican word *kuenihtekot*, which means "long river place."

DELAWARE. Named after Lord De La Warr, a governor of Virginia. Originally used only to name the Delaware River.

FLORIDA. Explorer Ponce de Leon named the state "Pascua Florida"—"flowery Easter"—on Easter Sunday in 1513.

GEORGIA. Named after King George II of England, who chartered the colony in 1732.

HAWAII. An English adaptation of the native word *owhyhee*, which means "homeland."

IDAHO. Possibly taken from the Kiowa Apache word for the Comanche Indians.

Survey Results: 56% of high school seniors try alcohol before the 8th grade.

ILLINOIS: The French bastardization of the Algonquin word *illini*, which means "men."

INDIANA: Named by English-speaking settlers because the territory was full of Indians.

IOWA: The Sioux word for "beautiful land," or "one who puts to sleep."

KANSAS: Taken from the Sioux word for "south wind people," their name for anyone who lived south of Sioux territory.

KENTUCKY: Possibly derived from the Indian word *kan-tuk-kee*, meaning "dark and bloody ground," or *kan-tuc-kec*, "land of green reeds," or *ken-take*, meaning "meadowland."

LOUISIANA: Named after French King Louis XIV.

MAINE: The Old French word for "province."

MARYLAND: Named after Queen Henrietta Maria, wife of English King George I.

MASSACHUSETTS: Named after the Massachusetts Indian tribe. Means "large hill place."

MICHIGAN: Most likely from the Chippewa word for "great water," *micigama*.

MINNESOTA: From the Sioux word for "sky tinted" or "muddy water."

MISSISSIPPI: Most likely taken from the Chippewa words *mici* ("great") and *zibi* ("river").

MISSOURI: From the Algonquin word for "muddy water."

MONTANA: Taken from the Latin word for "mountainous."

NEBRASKA: From the Otos Indian word for "broad water."

NEVADA: Means "snow-clad" in Spanish.

NEW HAMPSHIRE: Captain John Mason, one of the original colonists, named it after his English home county of Hampshire.

NEW JERSEY. Named after the English Isle of Jersey.

There are 635,013,559,600 different possible hands in bridge.

NEW MEXICO. The Spanish name for the territory north of the Rio Grande.

NEW YORK. Named after the Duke of York and Albany.

NORTH AND SOUTH CAROLINA. From the Latin name *Carolus*; named in honor of King Charles I of England.

NORTH AND SOUTH DAKOTA. Taken from the Sioux word for "friend" or "ally."

OHIO. Means "great," "fine," or "good river" in Iriquois.

OKLAHOMA. The Choctaw word for "red man."

OREGON. Possibly derived from *Ouaricon-sint*, the French name for the Wisconsin River.

PENNSYLVANIA. Named after William Penn, Sr., the father of the colony's founder, William Penn. Means "Penn's woods."

RHODE ISLAND. Named "Roode Eylandt" (Red Island) because of its red clay.

TENNESSEE. Named after the Cherokee *tanasi* villages along the banks of the Little Tennessee River.

TEXAS. Derived from the Caddo Indian word for "friend" or "ally."

UTAH. Means "upper" or "higher," and was originally the name that Navajos called the Shoshone tribe.

VERMONT. A combination of the French words *vert* ("green") and *mont* ("mountain").

VIRGINIA AND WEST VIRGINIA. Named after Queen Elizabeth I of England, the "virgin" queen, by Sir Walter Raleigh in 1584.

WASHINGTON. Named in tribute to George Washington.

WISCONSIN. Taken from the Chippewa word for "grassy place."

WYOMING. Derived from the Algonquin word for "large prairie place."

A scallop has 35 eyes—all of them blue.

WHO WERE HARLEY & DAVIDSON?

They're two of the best-known names in America. But who were they?

The first motorcycle was developed by Gottlieb Daimler, one of the founders of Daimler-Benz (maker of the Mercedes Benz) in Germany in 1885. Ten years later two German brothers, Hildebrand and Alois Wolfmuller, began manufacturing motorcycles to sell to the public.

In 1901 news of the Wolfmullers' motorcycles reached Milwaukee, Wisconsin. Four young friends—21-year-old William Harley and the Davidson brothers, William, Walter, and Arthur—decided to build a small engine in the Davidsons' backyard and attach it to one of their bicycles. Legend has it that the engine was made from household castoffs, including a carburetor made of a tomato can.

After working out the bugs on their prototype, they built three more motorized bicycles in 1903 and began riding them around town. Their bikes were simple but reliable—one of them ultimately racked up 100,000 miles. People began asking if they were for sale.

The Harley-Davidson Motorcycle Company legally incorporated in 1909. More than 150 U.S. manufacturers eventually followed suit, but Harley-Davidson has outlasted them all. It's now the only American motorcycle company and sells more than 50,000 motorcycles a year.

THE HARLEY IMAGE

In the mid-1980s, Harley's "rough rider" image began hurting sales. So the company took steps to change it. They encouraged Harley execs to wear white or red shirts to biker rallies to dispel the notion that Harley riders wear only black. They formed the Harley Owner's Group (H.O.G.) and the "Ladies of Harley" club to offset outlaw biker clubs. And they licensed the Harley name and logo to $100 million worth of products as diverse as wine coolers, cologne, and removable tattoos for women. Still, the company prefers customers with permanent Harley tattoos: "If you can persuade the customer to tattoo your name on their chest," one company executive admits, "they probably will not switch brands."

FAMOUS TRIALS: THE WITCHES OF SALEM

Here's a bit of American history we're all familiar with…but know almost nothing about. The BRI wants to change that, because we don't want witch trials—or witch hunts—in our era. After all, someone just might decide that reading in the bathroom is a sign of demonic possession.

BACKGROUND. The trouble at Salem, Massachusetts began with two young girls acting oddly. It exploded into one of the strangest cases of mass hysteria in American history. In the 6-month period between March and September 1692, 27 people were convicted on witchcraft charges; 20 were executed, and more than 100 other people were in prison awaiting trial.

CHILD'S PLAY

In March, 1992, 9-year-old Betty Parris and her cousin Abigail Williams, 12, were experimenting with a fortune-telling trick they'd learned from Tituba, the Parris family's West Indian slave. To find out what kind of men they'd marry when they grew up, they put an egg white in a glass…and then studied the shape it made in the glass.

But instead of glimpsing their future husbands, the girls saw an image that appeared to be "in the likeness of a coffin." The apparition shocked them…and over the next few days they exhibited behavior that witnesses described as "foolish, ridiculous speeches," "odd postures," "distempers," and "fits."

Reverend Samuel Parris was startled by his daughter's condition and took her to see William Griggs, the family doctor. Griggs couldn't find out what was wrong with the girl, but he suspected the problem had supernatural origins. He told Mr. Parris that he thought the girl had fallen victim to "the Evil Hand"—witchcraft.

The family tried to keep Betty's condition a secret, but rumors began spreading almost immediately—and within two months at least 8 other girls began exhibiting similar forms of bizarre behavior.

THE PARANOIA GROWS

The citizens of Salem Village demanded that the authorities take action. The local officials subjected the young girls to intense questioning, and soon the girls began naming names. The first three women they accused of witchcraft were Tituba, and two other women from Salem Village, Sarah Good and Sarah Osborne.

The three women were arrested and imprisoned for questioning. A few weeks later two more suspects, Martha Cory and Rebecca Nurse, were arrested on similar charges. And at the end of April a sixth person—the Reverend George Burroughs, a minister that Abigail Williams identified as the leader of the witches—was arrested and imprisoned. The girls continued to name names. By the middle of May, more than 100 people had been arrested for witchcraft.

THE TRIALS

On May 14, 1692, the newly appointed governor, Sir William Phips, arrived from England. He immediately set up a special court, the Court of Oyer and Terminer, to hear the witchcraft trials that were clogging the colonial legal system.

• The first case heard was that against Bridget Bishop. She was quickly found guilty of witchcraft, sentenced to death, and then hung on June 10.

• On June 19 the court met a second time, and in a single day heard the cases of five accused women, found them all guilty, and sentenced them to death. They were hung on July 19.

• On August 5 the court heard 6 more cases, and sentenced all 6 women to death. One woman, Elizabeth Proctor, was spared because she was pregnant—and the authorities didn't want to kill an innocent life along with a guilty one. The remaining 5 women were executed on August 19.

• 6 more people were sentenced to death in early September (Only 4 were executed: one person was reprieved, and another woman managed to escape from prison with the help of friends). The remaining sentences were carried out on September 22.

• On September 17th, the court handed down 9 more death sentences. (This time 5 of the accused "confessed" in exchange for a commutation of the death sentence and were not hung.) The remaining 4 were hung on September 22.

• Two days later the trials claimed their last victim when Giles Cory, an accused wizard, was executed by "pressing" (he was slowly crushed to death under heavy weights) after he refused to enter a plea.

REVERSAL OF FORTUNE

By now the hysteria surrounding the witch trials was at its peak. 19 accused "witches" had been hung, about 50 had "confessed" in exchange for lenient treatment; more than 100 people accused of witchcraft were under arrest and awaiting trial—and another 200 people had been accused of witchcraft but had not yet been arrested. Despite all this, the afflicted girls were still exhibiting bizarre behavior. But public opinion began to turn against the trials. Community leaders began to publicly question the methods that the courts used to convict suspected witches. The accused were denied access to defense counsel, and were tried in chains before jurors who had been chosen from church membership lists.

The integrity of the girls then came under question. Some of the adults even charged that they were faking their illnesses and accusing innocent people for the fun of it. One colonist even testified later that one of the bewitched girls had bragged to him that "she did it for sport."

As the number of accused persons grew into the hundreds, fears of falling victim to witchcraft were replaced by an even greater fear: that of being falsely accused of witchcraft. The growing opposition to the proceedings came from all segments of society: common people, ministers, etc.—even from the Court itself.

THE AFTERMATH

Once the tide had turned against the Salem Witchcraft Trials, many of the participants themselves began having second thoughts. Many of the jurors admitted their errors, witnesses recanted their testimony, and one judge on the court of Oyer and Terminer, Samuel Sewall, publicly admitted his error on the steps of the Old South Church in 1697. The Massachusetts legislature made amends as well; in 1711 it reversed all of the convictions issued by the Court of Oyer and Terminer (and did it a second time in 1957), and made financial restitution to the relatives of the executed, "the whole amounting unto five hundred seventy eight pounds and twelve shillings."

What's an ermine? A weasel whose coat has turned white for the winter.

THE COOLEST MOVIE LINES EVER

*Here's an entry inspired by the Captain of Cool,
Gene Sculatti, and his book* Too Cool.

THE WILD ONE
Girl to Brando: "Hey Johnny, what are you rebelling against?"
Brando: "Whaddaya got?"

THE KILLERS
Claude Akens: "You said Johnny North died. How'd he die?"
Clu Gulager: "Questions . . . he asked one too many."

HIGH SCHOOL CONFIDENTIAL
(*Teenage interpretation of Queen Isabella's reaction to Columbus*)
"Christy, what is this jazz you puttin' down 'bout our planet being round? Everybody's hip that it's square!"

THE COURT JESTER
Mildred Natwick: "The pellet with the poison's in the flagon with the dragon. The chalice from the palace holds the brew that is true."
Danny Kaye: "What about the vessel with the pestle?"

OCEANS 11 (*To doc examining X-Rays*)
"So tell me, doc. Is it the big casino?"

I WAS A TEENAGE FRANKENSTEIN
"I know you have a civil tongue in your head. I sewed it there myself."

THE BIG CARNIVAL
"I've met some hard-boiled eggs in my time, but you—you're 20 minutes."

MIDNIGHT RUN
Dennis Farina (*to henchman*): "I want this guy taken out and I want him taken out fast. You and that other dummy better start gettin' more personally involved in your work, or I'm gonna stab you through the heart with a f----- pencil. You understand?"
Henchman: "You got it, Jimmy."

THE SWEET SMELL OF SUCCESS
(*Hustler Tony Curtis, about to go into action*) "Watch me make a hundred-yard run with no legs."

GOODFELLAS
"I'm an average nobody. I get to live the rest of my life like a schnook."

---

5 most persuasive words in the English language: *discover, easy, guarantee, health,* and *results.*

THREE MEMORABLE SALES PROMOTIONS

Companies are always trying to get our attention—and our money—with catchy slogans, free stuff, discounts, and so on. But occasionally a promotion stands out for ineptitude...or cleverness. Here are three examples.

A PENNY SAVED

The Company: *Reader's Digest*

The Promotion: For years the *Digest* solicited subscriptions with a letter that began, "An ancient Persian poet once said, 'If thou hast two pennies, spend one for bread and the other to buy hyacinths for the soul...' " In 1956, someone decided to give it a new twist by including two pennies with each letter. The point: People could keep one, and send the other back with their subscription order to get the "soul-satisfying" *Digest*.

What Happened: The magazine planned to send out 50 million letters, which meant they needed 100 million coins—enough to deplete the entire New York area of pennies. The U.S. Mint intervened, forcing *Reader's Digest* to make quick arrangements to ship in 60 million more pennies from all over the country. Then, when the company finally got all the pennies it needed, it stored them all in one room—and the floor collapsed under the weight. In the end, though, it was worth the effort—the promo drew a record number of responses.

HOOVERGATE

The Company: Hoover Europe, England's most prestigious manufacturer of vacuum cleaners.

The Promotion: In 1992 Hoover tried to put a little life into the British vacuum market by offering an incredible deal: Any customer who bought at least 100 British pounds' (about $150) worth of Hoover merchandise got two free round-trip plane tickets to a European destination. Customers who bought 250 pounds' worth ($375) qualified for two tickets to either New York or Orlando, Florida.

What Happened: It was one of the biggest marketing fiascos in history. Customers realized the obvious—vacuum cleaners are cheaper than airline tickets—and snapped up every available Hoover. An estimated 200,000 customers—roughly 1 in every 300 people in Great Britain and Ireland—claimed they qualified for free flights.

The company sold so many vacuums that the factory switched to a 7-day work week to meet the demand—which made it, as one obeserver noted, "a classic case of mispricing a promotion so that the more products the company sold, the more money it lost." The promotion caused such a run on airline tickets that Hoover had to charter entire planes to meet the demand.

The promotion cost the company $48.8 million more than it expected—and cost 3 top executives their jobs. The parent company, Maytag, had to take a $10.5 million loss in the first quarter of 1993.

NORTH TO ALASKA

The Company: Quaker Oats.

The Promotion: Quaker was the long-time sponsor of "Sergeant Preston of the Yukon," a popular kids' TV series. In 1955, they decided to create a tie-in between the show and some cereals that weren't selling too well—Quaker Puffed Rice and Quaker Puffed Wheat. Their ad agency came up with an unusual plan: Buy up a parcel of land on the Yukon River in Alaska, then subdivide it into 21 million one-inch-square parcels and give away a real deed to one of the parcels in each box of cereal.

What Happened: According to *Getting it Right the Second Time*, "[Quaker's ad exec] and a company lawyer flew to Dawson, Alaska, selected a 19.11-acre plot of ice on the Yukon River from the air, and bought it for $10,000. [The ad man] wanted to go home, but the Quaker lawyer insisted on investigating the land close up by boat. As it turned out, the boat developed a leak in the middle of the half-frozen river, and the passengers were forced to jump overboard. They paddled back to shore, only to find they'd missed their dogsled connection back to the airstrip. As darkness fell, the Quaker contingent was forced to walk six miles in subzero weather to meet the aircraft and go home."

Was it worth the aggravation? Quaker thought so. They sold more than 21 million boxes of Puffed Rice/ Wheat; and it has been cited as one of the 3 most successful cereal promotions ever.

Joe Louis was the world heavyweight boxing champ for 11 years and 252 days.

THE DEATH OF WARREN G. HARDING

Did Warren Harding die of a heart attack or a poisoned relationship? This examination of the question is from It's a Conspiracy!, *by the National Insecurity Council.*

The Deceased: Warren G. Harding, 29th president of the United States (1921-1923)

How He Died: In the summer of 1923, President Harding was visiting Vancouver when he became gravely ill. He was rushed to San Francisco and seemed to recover. But then, on August 2, 1923, he suddenly died of a heart attack. *The New York Times* reported: "Mrs. Harding was reading to the President, when utterly without warning, a slight shudder passed through his frame; he collapsed....A stroke of apoplexy was the cause of his death."

Although initial newspaper accounts didn't mention it, the White House physician, General Sawyer, was probably in the room as well when the president died.

SUSPICIOUS FACTS
Warren and the Duchess

• Harding owed his political success to his ambitious wife, Florence (nicknamed "the Duchess"). But his marriage wasn't a happy one; he strayed often. During the 1920 campaign, for example, the Republican National Committee paid a former lover of Harding's $20,000 for incriminating letters, paid her $2,000 a month for her silence, and sent her to Europe to keep her away from reporters.

• Harding had a child by Nan Britten, the daughter of a friend. In fact, they had regular trysts in a large White House closet.

• According to former Treasury agent Gaston Means, who worked for Mrs. Harding, the president's wife despised her husband for his affairs and his ingratitude. In his bestselling book about Harding's death, Means reported that when the president's wife found out Harding had fathered Britten's baby, she got hysterical and vowed revenge. "I made him, I made him president!" she raved. When she confronted her husband, there was a nasty scene. He roared that he had never loved her, was sick of the whole presidential charade, and wanted to live with Britten and his child.

After Harding's Death

• To everyone's surprise, Mrs. Harding refused to allow either an autopsy or a death mask.

• The *New York World* reported: "There will be no death mask made of President Harding....Although it is the usual custom, when a Chief Executive dies, to have a mask made that his features may be preserved for posterity, Mrs. Harding demurred."

• About a year later, while the president's widow was visiting General Sawyer, the former White House physician unexpectedly died in his sleep.

• According to the account in *The New York Times*: "General Sawyer's death was almost identical with the manner of death of the late Warren G. Harding when General Sawyer was with the President in San Francisco. Mrs. Harding was at White Oaks Farm (Sawyer's home) when General Sawyer was found dead. Members of his family had no intimation of the seriousness of the General's condition up to the moment he expired."

POSSIBLE CONCLUSIONS

• **Harding really did have a heart attack.** His administration was riddled with scandals, and people were calling for his impeachment. The president, who'd previously had 5 nervous breakdowns, was said to be despondent. He may have succumbed to the stress.

• **Harding was poisoned by his wife.** If Harding was really ready to give up his political career and marriage, then the Duchess may have poisoned him either to avoid disgrace or to exact revenge. She may have tried first in Vancouver; when Harding didn't die, the attempt was dismissed as food poisoning. Five days later, in San Francisco, she may have succeeded.

Refusing a death mask and an autopsy is consistent with this scenario. (Poison victims sometimes die with horrible grimaces.)

Sawyer's death is either a remarkable coincidence or proof of Mrs. Harding's guilt. Even if he wasn't involved in killing the president, as a physician Sawyer may have guessed what had happened and helped to cover it up. Mrs. Harding could have poisoned him to keep her secret safe.

THE HONEYMOONERS

*When TV critics are asked to pick the best sitcom in history, many select
Jackie Gleason's 1955 one-season wonder, "The Honeymooners." Here are
some facts about that classic program from* Cult TV, *by John Javna.*

HOW IT STARTED

In the early days of TV, the three networks were CBS,
NBC...and Dumont. This third network was founded in
1946 by the Allen Dumont Laboratories and limped along for nine
years before finally disappearing in 1955. Its main contribution to
television history was making Jackie Gleason a star.

In 1950 Gleason wasn't welcome on the major networks—he'd
done poorly as star of NBC's sitcom *The Life of Riley* the previous
season, and network executives were wary of his excessive lifestyle.
But on Dumont, he flourished. As host of its 1950 variety show,
"Cavalcade of Stars"—performing his own comedy sketches as well
as emceeing—he was a smash. His first two shows attracted a large
audience and got rave reviews.

For the third one, Gleason wanted to come up with something
special. So he invented a husband/wife comedy sketch based on his
childhood environment. "I knew a thousand couples like these in
Brooklyn," Gleason said. "It was like the loudmouth husband...
with the wife who's a hell of a lot smarter than [him]. My neighborhood was filled with them."

His writers wanted to call the skit "The Beast," but Gleason
didn't like it. The husband might be a windbag, Gleason said, but
he wasn't an animal—he and his wife really loved each other. So
the writers suggested "The Lovers"—which was close, but not right.
Finally, Gleason came up with "The Honeymooners."

The sketch, which featured Jackie as bus driver Ralph Kramden
and Pert Kelton as his wife, Alice, was only on for a few minutes.
But it elicited an enormous response from viewers. In fact, it was so
popular that it became a regular feature on Gleason's show. Gleason added two neighbor characters: sewer worker Ed Norton and
his wife, Trixie.

When Gleason moved to CBS in 1952, he brought "The Honeymooners" with him, and in 1955 it became a series. Thirty-nine episodes aired. Although it was a popular program, Gleason didn't

want to continue it. He preferred variety shows, where "The Honeymooners" periodically surfaced. The last "Honeymooners" special aired in 1978. Gleason unveiled 75 "lost episodes" in the 1980s.

INSIDE FACTS

Belly Laughs. Gleason never rehearsed, and generally didn't need to because he had a photographic memory—one look at the script and he had it down. Nonetheless, he occasionally forgot his lines, which was a potential disaster in the days of live TV. When he did forget, Gleason would pat his stomach—a sign for someone else to think of something…quick. Once Alice snapped, "If you get any bigger, gas bag, you'll just float away." That wasn't in the script.

Another time, Gleason forgot to make an entrance. Art Carney (Ed Norton), who was onstage at the time, calmly went to the icebox, pulled out an orange, and began peeling it until Gleason realized his mistake.

On one evening Art Carney showed up for a performance completely plastered. Gleason, who'd memorized Carney's part as well as his own, did the whole show by asking a sitting (and incoherent) Carney yes or no questions.

Heeere's Alice. Pert Kelton, the first actress to play Alice Kramden on the show, fell ill with a heart condition and could not continue in the role when Gleason moved to CBS. When another actress, Audrey Meadows, was asked if she knew anyone who could play the part of Alice, she said, "Me." Gleason turned her down because she was too pretty. That made her want the part more. She sent Gleason photos of herself as a "frumpy" housewife, and Gleason triumphantly announced he'd found the right actress—not realizing she was the same woman he'd already rejected.

You Can Do Better. Joyce Randolph played Ed Norton's wife, Trixie. But Randolph's mother didn't like her daughter playing the part—she thought Joyce "could do better than marrying a sewer worker."

Ice Cold. One of the few pieces in the Kramdens' living room was an old-fashioned icebox. A refrigerator company once offered to sponsor "The Honeymooners" if Gleason would replace it with a refrigerator. He refused.

In 1992 former Panamanian pres. Noriega's wife was arrested in Miami for shoplifting buttons.

ONE-HIT WONDERS

*You're listening to the radio, and you hear this great (or terrible) song by
a new group. It rockets all the way to #1 and sells 5 million copies...but
then you never hear anything by the artists again. They're one-hit
wonders—part of a pop music phenomenon no one can explain.
Here are a few case studies for B.R.I. members to ponder.*

T**he Artist:** The Monotones
The Song: "The Book of Love" (1958, #5)
The Story: In 1955 six kids from Newark, New Jersey,
formed a doo-wop band called The Monotones. One day a member
of the group was looking at the sheet music for a song called "Book
of Love," when he heard a Pepsodent toothpaste commercial on
the radio: "You'll wonder where the yellow went, when you brush
your teeth with Pepsodent." It inspired him to write: "Oh I wonder,
wonder who...who wrote the book of love."

He and the group turned it into a song. "It was a joke to us," he
explains. But when a rival group wanted to record it, The Monotones quickly made a demo and sold it to a record company. It became a rock classic and a Top 10 hit. Unfortunately, The Monotones didn't bother putting out a follow-up record until 3 months
after "Book of Love" peaked. By then, their fans had moved on.

The Artist: David Soul
The Song: "Don't Give Up On Us, Baby" (1977, #1)
The Story: David Solberg dropped out of college in the 1960s to
become a folk singer. He decided he needed a gimmick to get attention, so he wrote a song called "The Covered Man"—which he
sang while wearing a ski mask. The stunt got him on "The Merv
Griffin Show" more than 20 times, but he still couldn't sell any
records. Solberg (now renamed Soul) did, however, get enough exposure to land a starring role on the TV show "Starsky & Hutch."
The program's popularity encouraged him to try music again. He
released "Don't Give Up On Us Baby" in 1977. It hit #1...but
none of his follow-ups made it into the Top 40. He gave up recording about the same time "Starsky & Hutch" went off the air.

---

5 most popular garden veggies: tomatoes, peppers, onions, cucumbers, and beans.

The Artist: Steam

The Song: "Na-Na, Hey, Hey, Tell Him Goodbye" (1969, #1)

The Story: In 1969 a singer named Gary DeCarlo recorded his first single for Mercury Records. Then he went back to the studio to record a throwaway "flip side"—something so bad no disc jockey would accidentally play it instead of the "A" side.

A few friends were at the studio that night; they suggested a tune they'd performed in a band in 1961. It was called "Kiss Him Goodbye," and it was perfect for the "B" side of the record...except that it had no chorus. No problem—they made one up on the spot, with "na-nas" instead of lyrics. They described it as "an embarrassing record...an insult."

But to the band's horror, Mercury thought it was great and decided to release it as a single. No one wanted to be identified with the record, so it was credited to "Steam."

"Na-Na" sold more than a million copies, but DeCarlo wouldn't make another Steam record. Mercury got a different group to do the follow-ups, but the best they could come up with was "I've Gotta Make You Love Me," which reached #46 on the charts in 1970.

The Artist: Zager and Evans

The Song: "In the Year 2525 (Exordium & Terminus)" (1969, #1)

The Story: In 1968 Denny Zager and Rick Evans were playing folk music in a motel lounge in Lincoln, Nebraska. One of their most popular songs was "In the Year 2525," an up-tempo apocalyptic vision Evans had written four years earlier. They decided to record it. For $500, they got recording studio time and 1,000 copies of their single—which they sold to local record stores and passed out to Nebraska radio stations.

Zager and Evans were delighted when the song began getting airplay in Lincoln...and flabbergasted when it drew the attention of a hotshot management firm in Los Angeles. An executive with the firm flew to Lincoln and signed Zager and Evans to a personal contract; then he signed them to a recording contract with RCA.

A few weeks later, "In the Year 2525" was released nationally ....and a few weeks after that, it was #1 in America. However, Denny Zager had never really liked the song and wasn't interested in doing any more tunes in the same style. None of the pair's subsequent records even made it into the Top 100.

WILDE ABOUT OSCAR

*Wit and wisdom from Oscar Wilde, one of the 19th century's
most popular—and controversial—writers.*

"The only way to get rid of temptation is to yield to it."

"It is better to have a permanent income than to be fascinating."

"The soul is born old but grows young. That is the comedy of life. And the body is born young and grows old. That is life's tragedy."

"Seriousness is the only refuge of the shallow."

"Children begin by loving their parents. After a time they judge them. Rarely, if ever, do they forgive them."

"There's no sin…except stupidity."

"Experience is the name everyone gives to their mistakes."

"Formerly we used to canonize our heroes. The modern method is to vulgarize them. Cheap editions of great books may be delightful, but cheap editions of great men are absolutely detestable."

"All women become like their mothers. That is their tragedy. No man does. That's his."

"Society often forgives the criminal; it never forgives the dreamer."

"It is better to be beautiful than to be good, but it is better to be good than to be ugly."

"The only portraits in which one believes are portraits where there is very little of the sitter and a very great deal of the artist."

"The youth of America is their oldest tradition. It has been going on now for three hundred years."

"One should always play fairly—when one has the winning cards."

"Discontent is the first step in the progress of a man or a nation."

"The well-bred contradict other people. The wise contradict themselves."

The three best-known western names in China: Jesus Christ, Richard Nixon, and Elvis Presley.

CHILDHOOD WISDOM

Quotes from classic children's books.

"We are all made of the same stuff, remember, we of the Jungle, and you of the City. The same substance composes us—the tree overhead, the stone beneath us, the bird, the beast, the star—we are all one, all moving to the same end....Bird and beast and stone and star—we are all one, all one—Child and serpent, star and stone—all one."
—The Hamadryad, *Mary Poppins*

"If I can fool a bug, I can fool a man. People are not as smart as bugs."
—Charlotte, *Charlotte's Web*

"Money is a nuisance. We'd all be much better off if it had never been invented. What does money matter, as long as we all are happy?"
—Dr. Doolittle, *Dr. Doolittle*

"Winter will pass, the days will lengthen, the ice will melt in the pasture pond. The song sparrow will return and sing, the frogs will awake, the warm wind will blow again. All these sights and sounds and smells will be yours to enjoy, Wilbur—this lovely world, these precious days."
—Charlotte, *Charlotte's Web*

"Don't be angry after you've been afraid. That's the worst kind of cowardice."
—Billy the Troophorse, *The Jungle Books*

"Time flies, and one begins to grow old. This autumn I'll be ten, and then I guess I'll have seen my best days."
—Pippi Longstocking, *Pippi Goes on Board*

Are you lonesome tonight? In a recent survey, 1% of Americans said they have no friends.

LEFT-HANDED FACTS

Here's some info for lefties. Why devote two whole pages to the subject?
Okay, okay. We admit it—Uncle John is left-handed.

LEFT-HANDED STATS
• Lefties make up about 5-15% of the general population—but 15-30% of all patients in mental institutions.

• They're more prone to allergies, insomnia, migranes, schizophrenia and a host of other things than right-handers. They're also three times more likely than righties to become alcoholics. Why? Some scientists speculate the right hemisphere of the brain—the side left-handers use the most—has a lower tolerance for alcohol than the left side. Others think the stress of living in a right-handed world is responsible.

• Lefties are also more likely to be on the extreme ends of the intelligence scale than the general population: a higher proportion of mentally retarded people *and* people with I.Q.s over 140 are lefties.

LEFT OUT OF SCIENCE
• For centuries science was biased against southpaws. In the 1870s, for example, Italian psychiatrist Cesare Lombroso published *The Delinquent Male*, in which he asserted that left-handed men were psychological "degenerates" and prone to violence. (A few years later he published *The Delinquent Female*, in which he made the same claims about women.)

• This theory existed even as late as the 1940s, when psychiatrist Abram Blau wrote that left-handedness "is nothing more than an expression of infantile negativism and falls into the same category as…general perverseness." He speculated that lefties didn't get enough attention from their mothers.

LEFT-HANDED TRADITIONS
• Why do we throw salt over our left shoulders for good luck? To throw it into the eyes of the Devil, who of course, lurks behind us to our left.

• In many traditional Muslim cultures, it is extremely impolite to touch food with your left hand. Reason: Muslims eat from communal bowls using their right hand; their left hand is used to perform "unclean" tasks such as wiping themselves after going the bathroom. Hindus have a similar custom: they use their right hand exclusively when touching themselves above the waist, and use only the left hand to touch themselves below the waist.

• What did traditional Christians believe was going to happen on Judgement Day? According to custom, God blesses the saved with his right hand—and casts sinners out of Heaven with his left.

• Other traditional mis-beliefs:

> * If you have a ringing in your left ear, someone is cursing you. If your right ear rings, someone is praising you.

> * If your left eye twitches, you're going to see an enemy. If the right twitches, you're going to see a friend.

> * If you get out of bed with your left foot first, you're going to have a bad day.

> * If your left palm itches, you're going to owe someone money. If your right palm does, you're going to make some money.

LEFT-HANDED MISCELLANY

• Why are lefties called "southpaws"? In the late 1890s, most baseball parks were laid out with the pitcher facing west and the batter facing east (so the sun wouldn't be in his eyes). That meant left-handed pitchers threw with the arm that faced south. So Chicago sportswriter Charles Seymour began calling them "southpaws."

• Right-handed bias: Some Native American tribes strapped their children's left arms to the mother's cradleboard, which caused most infants to become predominantly right-handed. The Kaffirs of South Africa acheived similar results by burying the left hands of left-handed children in the burning desert sand.

• The next time you see a coat of arms, check to see if it has a stripe running diagonally across it. Most stripes are called *bends* and run from the top left to the bottom right. A stripe that runs from the bottom left to the top right, is called a "left-handed" bend or a *bend sinister*—and means the bearer was a bastard.

THE MYTH-ADVENTURES OF THOMAS EDISON

Most Americans believe that Thomas Edison invented the light bulb. He didn't. In fact, although he was a great inventor, there are a number of myths we commonly believe about Edison. Let's puncture a few.

THE MYTH: Edison was the father of electric light.

THE TRUTH: Electric lighting had been made practical decades before Edison began his famous research. Although incandescent light (the kind that's made by charging a wire filament until it glows white hot with energy) had not yet been perfected, by the 1870s *arc* lighting (light that's created when a spark "arcs" across two highly charged electric rods) was already in use in lighthouses and in the street lamps of some major cities.

The only problem was, they used too much energy and generated too much light (300 times as much as the household gas lights of the day) to be practical in homes. A less powerful source of light was needed.

THE MYTH: Edison invented the incandescent light bulb.

THE TRUTH: Incandescent light bulbs had been around as a laboratory curiosity since 1823, and the first incandescent bulb was patented by Joseph Swan, an English inventor, in 1845.

By the time Edison began experimenting with light bulbs in 1878, scientists around the world had already spent 55 years trying to perfect them. Edison wasn't trying to invent the light bulb; he was trying to find a long-lasting *filament* that would make the light bulb practical for the first time.

Incandescent light bulbs operate on the principle of electrically heating a tiny filament until it glows white hot with energy, creating light in the process. The main problem at the time: most substances either melted or burned up when heated to such a high temperature, causing the bulb to burn out after only a few seconds.

Vacuum bulbs, which had some of their air removed, solved part of the problem; by reducing the amount of oxygen in the bulb, they lengthened the time it took for the filament to burn up. Even so, in 1878 even the best bulbs only only lasted a short time…and *that's* where Edison came in.

THE MYTH: He perfected the incandescent bulb by himself.

THE TRUTH: He failed on his own, and had to bring in experts. Edison thought the secret to building a better light bulb was to design a switch inside the bulb that would function like a heater thermostat, turning off the electricity when the filament got too hot, and turning it on again as soon as the filament cooled off—a process that would take only a fraction of a second.

Edison thought (and announced) that he could develop the switch in a few weeks—but he guessed wrong. It didn't work at all.

More a scientific tinkerer than a scientist, his strategy had always been to blindly build prototype after prototype. He ignored work that other researchers had done and, as a result, often unwittingly repeated their failed experiments. That's what happened with the light bulb. After a month of trying on his own, he threw in the towel and hired Francis Upton, a Princeton physicist, to help him.

As soon as Upton signed on, he had the lab's researchers study old patents, electrical journals, and the work of competing inventors to see what progress they had made. He also shifted the focus of the work from testing prototypes to methodically experimenting with raw materials (in order to understand their scientific properties and see which ones made the best filaments). Without this important shift in strategy, Edison's lab might never have developed a practical bulb at all…and certainly would have fallen behind competing labs.

THE MYTH: Edison made his critical breakthrough on October 21, 1879—known for many years as "Electric Light Day"—when he kept a light bulb lit for more than 40 hours.

THE TRUTH: The story is a fake. According to lab notes, nothing important happened on October 21—and it took another full year to produce a 40-hour bulb. The October 21 date was made up in late December 1879—by a newspaper reporter who needed a good story for the Christmas season.

The founding fathers' name for the American Revolution was "The War with Britain."

REEFER MADNESS

After being widely cultivated for 10,000 years, marijuana was suddenly outlawed in America in 1937. Was it because it was a threat to the American public—or only to certain business interests?

For thousands of years, hemp (*cannabis sativa*) has been one of the most useful plants known to man. Its strong, stringy fibers make durable rope and can be woven into anything from sails to shirts; its pithy centers, or "hurds," make excellent paper; its seeds, high in protein and oil, have been pressed for lighting and lubricating oils and pulped into animal feed; and extracts of its leaves have provided a wide range of medicines and tonics.

HEMP & AMERICA

• Hemp also has a notable place in American history:

Washington and Jefferson grew it.

Our first flags were likely made of hemp cloth.

The first and second drafts of the Declaration of Independence were written on paper made from Dutch hemp.

When the pioneers went west, their wagons were covered with hemp canvas (the word "canvas" comes from *canabacius*, hemp cloth).

The first Levis sold to prospectors were sturdy hemp coveralls.

Abraham Lincoln's wife, Mary Todd, came from the richest hemp-growing family in Kentucky.

• After the Civil War, however, hemp production in the States declined steeply. Without slave labor, hemp became too expensive to process. Besides, cotton ginned by machines was cheaper. Still, hemp fabric remained the second most common cloth in America.

• The plant's by-products remained popular well into this century. Maple sugar combined with hashish (a resin from hemp leaves) was sold over the counter and in Sears Roebuck catalogs as a harmless candy. Hemp rope was a mainstay of the navy. Two thousand tons of hemp seed were sold annually as birdfeed. The pharmaceutical industry used hemp extracts in hundreds of potions and vigorously fought attempts to restrict hemp production. And virtually all good paints and varnishes were made from hemp-seed oil and/or linseed oil.

WHAT HAPPENED

• In the 1920s and '30s, the American public became increasingly concerned about drug addiction—especially to morphine and a "miracle drug" that had been introduced by the Bayer Company in 1898 under the brand name "Heroin." By the mid-1920s, there were 200,000 heroin addicts in the U.S. alone.

• Most Americans were unaware that smoking hemp leaves was intoxicating; however, until William Randolph Hearst launched a campaign of sensational stories that linked "the killer weed" to jazz musicians, "crazed minorities," and unspeakable crimes. Hearst's papers featured headlines like:

MARIJUANA MAKES FIENDS OF BOYS IN 30 DAYS:
HASHEESH [SIC] GOADS USERS TO BLOOD-LUST
NEW DOPE LURE, MARIJUANA, HAS MANY VICTIMS

• In 1930, Hearst was joined in his crusade against hemp by Harry J. Anslinger, commissioner of the newly organized Federal Bureau of Narcotics (FBN). Hearst often quoted Anslinger in his newspaper stories, printing sensational comments like: "If the hideous monster Frankenstein came face to face with the monster marijuana he would drop dead of fright."

• Not everyone shared their opinion. In 1930, the U.S. government formed the Siler Commission to study marijuana smoking by off-duty servicemen in Panama. The commission found no lasting effects and recommended that no criminal penalties apply to its use.

• Nonetheless, Hearst and Anslinger's anti-hemp campaign had results. By 1931, twenty-nine states had prohibited marijuana use for nonmedical purposes. In 1937, after two years of secret hearings— and based largely on Anslinger's testimony—Congress passed the Marijuana Tax Act, which essentially outlawed marijuana in America.

• Because Congress wasn't sure that it was constitutional to ban hemp outright, it taxed the plant prohibitively instead. Hemp

---

The original Gotham City was a mythical English town whose residents were extremely stupid.

growers had to register with the government; sellers and buyers had to fill out cumbersome paperwork; and, of course, it was a federal crime not to comply.

• For selling an ounce or less of marijuana to an unregistered person, the federal tax was $100. (To give some sense of how prohibitive the tax was, "legitimate" marijuana was selling for $2 a pound at the time. In 1992 dollars, the federal tax would be roughly $2,000 per ounce.)

• The Marijuana Tax Act effectively destroyed all legitimate commercial cultivation of hemp. Limited medical use was permitted, but as hemp derivatives became prohibitively expensive for doctors and pharmacists, they turned to chemically derived drugs instead. All other nonmedical uses, from rope to industrial lubricants, were taxed out of existence.

• With most of their markets gone, farmers stopped growing hemp, and the legitimate industry disappeared. Ironically, though, hemp continued to grow wild all over the country, and its "illegitimate" use was little affected by Congress.

WAS IT A CONSPIRACY?

Was a viable hemp industry forced out of existence because it was a threat to people's health or because it was a threat to a few large businesses that would profit from banning it?

THE HEARST CONSPIRACY

• Hemp was outlawed just as a new technology would have made hemp paper far cheaper than wood-pulp paper.

• Traditionally, hemp fiber had to be separated from the stalk by hand, and the cost of labor made this method uncompetitive. But in 1937—the year that hemp was outlawed, the *decorticator* machine was invented; it could process as much as 3 tons of hemp an hour and produced higher-quality fibers with less loss of fiber than wood-based pulp. According to some scientists, hemp would have been able to undercut competing products overnight. Enthusiastic about the new technology, *Popular Mechanics* predicted that hemp would become America's first "billion-dollar crop." The magazine pointed out that "10,000 acres devoted to hemp will produce as much paper as 40,000 acres of average [forest] pulp land."

- According to Jack Herer, an expert on the "hemp conspiracy," Hearst, the du Ponts, and other "industrial barons and financiers knew that machinery to cut, bale, decorticate (separate fiber from the stalk) and process hemp into paper was becoming available in the mid-1930s." (*The Emperor Wears No Clothes*)

- Hearst, one of the promoters of the anti-hemp hysteria, had a vested interest in protecting the pulp industry. Hearst owned enormous timber acreage; competition from hemp paper might have driven the Hearst paper-manufacturing division out of business and caused the value of his acreage to plummet. (ibid.)

- Herer suggests that Hearst slanted the news in his papers to protect his pulp investments. "In the 1920s and '30s," he writes, "Hearst's newspaper chain led the deliberate...yellow journalism campaign to have marijuana outlawed. From 1916 to 1937, as an example, the story of a car accident in which a marijuana cigarette was found would dominate the headlines for weeks, while alcohol-related car accidents (which outnumbered marijuana-related accidents by more than 1,000 to 1) made only the back pages." (ibid.)

- Herer says that Hearst was even responsible for popularizing the term "marijuana" in American culture. In fact, he suggests, popularizing the word was a key strategy of Hearst's efforts: "The first step [in creating hysteria] was to introduce the element of fear of the unknown by using a word that no one had ever heard of before...'marijuana.'" (ibid.)

THE DU PONT CONSPIRACY

- The Du Pont Company also had an interest in the pulp industry. At this time, it was in the process of patenting a new sulfuric acid process for producing wood-pulp paper. According to the company's own records, wood-pulp products ultimately accounted for more than 80% of all of Du Pont's railroad car loadings for the next 50 years. (ibid.)

- But Du Pont had even more reasons to be concerned about hemp. In the 1930s, the company was making drastic changes in its business strategy. Traditionally a manufacturer of military explosives, Du Pont realized after the end of World War I that developing peacetime uses for artificial fibers and plastics would be more profitable in the long run. So it began pouring millions of dollars into research—which resulted in the development of such synthetic fibers as rayon and nylon.

Two years before the prohibitive hemp tax, Du Pont developed a new synthetic fiber, nylon, that was an ideal substitute for hemp rope.

The year after the hemp tax, Du Pont was able to bring another "miracle" synthetic fabric onto the market—rayon. Rayon, which became widely used for clothing, was a direct competitor to hemp cloth.

"Congress and the Treasury Department were assured, through secret testimony given by Du Pont, that hemp-seed oil could be replaced with synthetic petrochemical oils made principally by Du Pont." These oils were used in paints and other products. (ibid.)

• The millions spent on these products, as well as the hundreds of millions in expected profits from them, could have been wiped out if the newly affordable hemp products were allowed onto the market. So, according to Herer, Du Pont worked with Hearst to eliminate hemp.

• Du Pont's point-man was none other than Harry Anslinger, the commissioner of the FBN. Anslinger was appointed to the FBN by Treasury Secretary Andrew Mellon, who was also chairman of the Mellon Bank, Du Pont's chief financial backer. But Anslinger's relationship to Mellon wasn't just political; he was also married to Mellon's niece.

• Anslinger apparently used his political clout to sway congressional opinion on the hemp tax. According to Herer, the American Medical Association (AMA) tried to argue for the medical benefits of hemp. But after AMA officials testified to Congress, "they were quickly denounced by Anslinger and the entire congressional committee, and curtly excused."

FOOTNOTES

• Five years after the hemp tax was imposed, when Japanese seizure of Philippine hemp caused a wartime shortage of rope, the government reversed itself. Overnight, the U.S. government urged hemp cultivation once again and created a stirring movie called "Hemp for Victory"—then, just as quickly, it recriminalized hemp after the shortage had passed.

• While U.S. hemp was temporarily legal, however, it saved the

Cincinnati was so famous for its hog industry in the 1830s that it was nicknamed "Porkopolis."

life of a young pilot named George Bush, who was forced to bail out of his burning airplane after a battle over the Pacific. At the time, he didn't know that:

- Parts of his aircraft engine were lubricated with hemp-seed oil.

- 100% of his life-saving parachute webbing was made from U.S.-grown cannabis hemp.

- Virtually all the rigging and ropes of the ship that rescued him were made of cannabis hemp.

- The fire hoses on the ship were woven from cannabis hemp.

Ironically, President Bush consistently opposed decriminalizing hemp grown in the United States.

- Does the hemp conspiracy continue? In March 1992, Robert Bonner, the chief of the Drug Enforcement Agency, effectively rejected a petition to permit doctors to prescribe marijuana for patients as medication for chronic pain. Bonner said: "Beyond doubt the claims that marijuana is medicine are false, dangerous and cruel." But, according to a federal administrative law judge, Francis Young, "the record clearly shows that marijuana has been accepted as capable of relieving the distress of great numbers of very ill people and doing so with safety under medical supervision." (*The New York Times*)

RECOMMENDED READING

- This article was excerpted from *It's A Conspiracy*, by the National Insecurity Council (as are others in the book—see p. 2). It's highly recommended by the BRI. In fact, some of the BRI members worked on it, so it's just as much fun to read.

- If you'd like a copy (and we know you would), send a check for $10 to *Conspiracy*, EarthWorks Press, PO Box 1117, Ashland, Oregon 97520. Or ask for it at your local bookstore.

FIRST REPORTS

Over the years, we've collected "First Reports"—newspaper articles that gave readers their first glimpse of something that eventually became important in some way. Here are a few examples.

SPACED OUT

Most people don't know it was one incident—and one short newspaper story—that started the UFO craze. Here's the story, sent out over the AP wire from the Pendleton East Oregonian *on June 25, 1947.*

Pendleton, Ore. June 25 (AP)—"Nine bright saucer-like objects flying at 'incredible speed' at 10,000 feet altitude were reported here today by Kenneth Arnold, a Boise, Idaho, pilot who said he could not hazard a guess as to what they were.

"Arnold, a United States Forest Service employee engaged in searching for a missing plane, said he sighted the mysterious objects yesterday at three p.m. They were flying between Mount Rainier and Mount Adams, in Washington State, he said, and appeared to weave in and out of formation. Arnold said that he clocked and estimated their speed at 1200 miles an hour.

"Enquiries at Yakima last night brought only blank stares, he said, but he added he talked today with an unidentified man from Ukiah, south of here, who said he had seen similar objects over the mountains near Ukiah yesterday.

" 'It seems impossible,' Arnold said, 'but there it is.' "

This story was picked up by papers all over the world. At that moment, according to the UFO Encyclopedia, *"the age of flying saucers began."*

THE XEROX MACHINE

When this article appeared in 1948, Xerox was still known as the Haloid Company.

Rochester, N.Y. Oct. 23—"A revolutionary process of inkless printing has been developed that might completely change all the operations of the printing and publishing industry. This was announced yesterday by Joseph C. Wilson, presidential the Haloid Company of Rochester, New York.

"Known as 'Xerography,' this basic addition to the graphic arts reproduces pictures and text at the speed of 1,200 feet a

---

In case you were wondering: The little flap in the back of your throat is called a *uvula*.

minute, on any kind of surface.

"Although there is no immediate prospect of applying the method to general photography, the process will be available within about six months for copying uses. Wilson said it will be in the form of a compact Xerocopying machine for reproducing letters, documents, and line work...

"Looking farther ahead, he said he foresaw incorporating the entire process in a portable Xerocamera. 'With such a camera, the picture taker can snap the shutter and within a few seconds pull out a finished Xeroprint. If he doesn't like the picture, he can discard it and try again, using the same Xeroplate.' "

DEAR ABBY

Dear Abby's first column appeared in the San Francisco Chronicle *on January 9, 1956. She answered 4 letters. Here's one of them.*

"**Dear Abby:** Maybe you can suggest something to help my sister. She is married to a real heel. He is 6' 3" and weighs 240 and she is 5' and weighs 106. He has a terrible temper and frequently knocks the daylights out of her. —L.L.

"**Dear L.L.:** I admit your sister is no physical match for her heavyweight husband, but I've seen smaller gals flatten out bigger guys than this with just one look. If your sister has been letting this walrus slap her around frequently, maybe she likes it. Stay out of their family battles, Chum."

INTRODUCING THE CD

This article appeared in the New York Times, *March 18, 1983*

"Five years ago, the electronics industry brought out the videodisk, heralded as the future of home entertainment systems. This month, the digital compact disk audio system will make its way into American homes, making similar promises. But marketers of the audiodisk play down the kinship, with good cause; sales of videodisks have been dismal. The compact audiodisk system, meanwhile, is expected to replace stereo turntables and albums as the industry standard within the decade.

"Some question whether the audiodisk will succeed. Players now cost $800-$900, and disks are $16-20 each, far too expensive for a popular market.

"Even if prices come down ...some analysts doubt whether consumers will be willing to sacrifice substantial investments in turntables and stacks of traditional recordings."

Women have Adam's apples, too. Men's are larger to accommodate longer vocal cords.

COLORS

More on the way colors have a lot more impact on our daily lives. Here are additional things researchers have found out about people and color.

PINK

• Studies show that people almost always believe "pastries from a pink box taste better than from any other color box."

• People are willing to pay more for personal services (e.g., haircuts) performed by people wearing pink.

• Men believe pink products do the best job, but don't want to be seen buying them. If they think someone's watching, they'll choose something brown or blue.

ORANGE

• A quick attention-getter, it communicates informality.

• When it's used on a product, it "loudly proclaims that the product is for everyone."

PALE BLUE

• Pale blue can actually make people feel cooler. Designers often use it in places where men work, "because men feel 5° warmer than a woman in the same room temperature."

•Blue inhibits the desire to eat; in fact, researchers say "people tend to eat less from blue plates."

• Because blue is associated with eating less, marketers use it to sell products like club soda, skim milk, and cottage cheese.

BROWN

• Researchers say a brown suit "a symbol of informality that invites people to open up." It's recommended for reporters and marriage counselors.

GRAY

• Your eye processes gray more easily than any other color.

• Even so, people often become prejudiced against it, especially in areas with a bleak climate.

BRONZE

• This metallic hue gets a negative response. Researchers say it's "useful when rejection is desired."

GREEN

It's used to sell vegetables and chewing gum. But people avoid using it to sell meat, because it reminds consumers of mold.

Red is rarely used on ice cream packages, because it reminds people of heat.

MYTH-PRONUNCIATION

It's surprising how many of our words are references to gods that we've never heard of. Here are some of the characters in Greek and Roman mythology we refer to daily.

Cereal: named after Ceres, the Roman goddess of grain and agriculture.

Atlas: One of the Greek Titans banished by Zeus when they sided with his son against him. Atlas was condemned to carry the world on his shoulders. That scene was popular with early map-makers, who regularly put it on the covers of their books of maps. The books themselves eventually became known as atlases.

Panic: Named after the Greek god Pan, who was believed to howl and shriek in the middle of the night. Greeks who heard these noises often *panicked*.

Hygiene: Inspired by Hygeia, the Greek goddess that brings good health.

Panacea: The Roman goddess that cures diseases.

Tantalize: Tantalus was a Greek God who was punished by the other gods. He was forced to stand in a pool of water up to his chin, but when he lowered his head to drink, the water receded just out of reach. The same was true with food: whenever he reached to pick a piece of fruit from a tree, the wind blew them just out of reach. The *tantalizing* food filled him with desire, but was complete-ly unobtainable.

Siren: The Greeks believed the Sirens were women who called to passing sailors with their beautiful singing voices. Sailors couldn't resist them; in fact, men were driven mad by the songs, and dashed their ships on the nearby rocks in their frenzy to get closer.

Helium: This element, found in the gaseous atmosphere of the sun, is named after Helios, the Greek god of the sun.

Iridescent: Named after Iris, the Greek goddess of the rainbow.

Slow Learner: President Woodrow Wilson couldn't read until he was 11 years old.

Erotic: Named after Eros, the Greek god of...you guessed it: love.

Brownie: These cousins of the Girl Scouts are named after the Celtic *brownies,* small, brown-cloaked fairies that perform household chores while the family sleeps.

Aphrodisiac: named after Aphrodite, the Greek goddess of love. Her specialty: stirring up feelings of desire among the other gods.

Ghouls: From the Arabic word *ghul,* which was an evil spirit that robbed tombs and ate corpses. Today the name is given to anyone with an unhealthy interest in the deceased.

Lethargy: Named after the mythical Greek river of forgetfulness, *Lethe*.

Aegis: Originally the name of the shield of Zeus; today anything that's protected by someone else is said to be under its aegis.

Money: Named after Juno Moneta, the Roman goddess of money.

SPACE-FILLER: MONEY FACTS

• Ancient Sparta had a creative way of preventing capital flight: they made their coins so large and heavy that it was almost impossible to take them out of the country.

• The British Pound Sterling, originally composed of 240 silver pennies, really did weigh a pound.

• The Greek word *drachma* originally meant "handful."

• Why were gold and silver so widely used in coins? They were rare, valuable, and didn't deteriorate or rust. They were also pretty to look at—which historians say was no small consideration.

• U.S. law requires that the words "liberty," "United States of America," "E Pluribus Unum," and "In God We Trust" be inscribed on all coins.

• Biggest and smallest coins in history: the 1644 Swedish *ten-daler* coin (43.4 pounds), and the 1740 Nepalese silver *quarter-dam* (1/14,000 of an ounce).

• Biggest and smallest bills in history: the 14th-century Chinese *one-kwan* note (9 by 13 inches) and the 1917 Rumanian *ten-bani* note (1-1/2 square inches).

THE GOODYEAR BLIMP

No major sporting event is complete without it. In fact, it's probably the best-known lighter-than-air ship ever (except maybe the Hindenburg, which is famous for blowing up). Here's the story of the Goodyear blimp.

I n 1909 Charles Goodyear, a hardware merchant from Connecticut, saw that rubber had tremendous commercial potential—but only if it could be made less sticky and would hold a shape better than it already did.

So he obtained a large quantity of latex, and tried mixing it with everything in his desk, cellar, and pantry—including witch hazel, ink, and cream cheese—with no luck. One day he tried mixing rubber with sulfur. Then, while working on something else, he accidentally knocked the sulfurized rubber mixture onto a hot stove. He found that the rubber had changed form; it was no longer sticky and snapped back to its original shape when stretched. He named the process *Vulcanizing* after Vulcan, the Roman god of fire.

THE GOODYEAR COMPANY

Goodyear didn't get rich from his discovery—he died penniless in 1860. But when Frank A. Seiberling started a rubber company in Akron, Ohio in 1898, he decided to name it after the inventor. It's likely he hoped to profit from the confusion created by having a name similar to another Akron rubber company, B.F. Goodrich.

Goodyear's first products were bicycle and horse carriage tires, rubber pads for horseshoes, rubber bands, and poker chips. The company produced its first auto tires in 1901, airplane tires in 1909, and, using a Scottish process for rubberized fabric, the skins for airplanes in 1910. (This was back when airplanes were based on kite designs and made mostly of wood and cloth.)

The same rubberized fabric turned out to be useful for lighter-than-air craft, and Goodyear flew its first dirigible in 1922.

THE MILITARY CONNECTION

The military used Goodyear blimps for observation and reconnaissance during World War I and World War II. After World War II, Goodyear bought five of its blimps back from the armed forces.

The distance between a Boeing 747's wing tips is longer than the Wright Brothers' first flight.

It painted them and began using them for promotional purposes. But the company's executives didn't see the value of having blimps. In 1958, they tried to ground the airships permanently, to save the operating and maintenance expenses.

The plan was stalled at the last minute by a plea from Goodyear's publicity director, Robert Lane. To demonstrate the blimps' worth to the company, he scheduled a six-month marathon tour that sent the airship *Mayflower* barnstorming the Eastern Seaboard. It generated so much favorable press that the executives were convinced to keep it.

The blimps' first TV coverage was an Orange Bowl game in the mid-1960s. Now they're used in about 90 televised events a year. Goodyear doesn't charge TV networks; the publicity generated makes the free service worthwhile.

BLIMP FACTS

• Each blimp is equipped with a crew of 23, consisting of 5 pilots, 17 support members who work on rotating schedules, and one public relations representative. The blimps cruise at a speed of 45-50 miles per hour (max 65 mph unless there's a really good wind).

• Each blimp can carry 9 passengers along with the crew. The seats have no seatbelts.

• The camera operator shoots from the passenger compartment through an open window from about 1200 feet up, where he or she can see everything, read a scoreboard, and hear the roar of a crowd. The hardest sport for the pilots to film is golf, because they have to be careful not to disturb a golfer's shot with engine noise or by casting a sudden shadow over the green.

• If punctured, the worst that will happen is that the blimp will slowly lose altitude. Good thing, too, since the company reports that a blimp is shot at in the air abut 20 times a year.

• Each blimp is 192 feet long, 59 feet high, and holds 202,700 cubic feet of helium. The helium does leak out, like a balloon, and has to be "topped off" every four months or so.

• The word *blimp* is credited to Lt. A. D. Cunningham of Britain's Royal Navy Air Service. In 1915, he whimsically flicked his thumb against the inflated wall of an airship and imitated the sound it made: "Blimp!"

GO ASK ALICE

*Alice In Wonderland and Through the Looking Glass aren't
just for kids. They're great reading for grown-ups, too.
Especially in the bathroom. Here are some sample quotes.*

"**D**ear, dear! How queer everything is today! I wonder if
I've been changed in the night? Let me think: was I the
same when I got up this morning? I almost think I can
remember feeling a little different. But if I'm not the same, the
next questions is, 'Who *am* I?' Ah, that's the puzzle!"
—Alice, *Alice in Wonderland*

"Cheshire Puss," began Alice, "would you tell me, please, which
way I ought to go from here?"

"That depends a good deal on where you want to get to," said
the Cat.

"I don't much care where—" said Alice.

"Then it doesn't matter which way you go," said the Cat.

"—so long as I get *somewhere*," Alice added as an explanation.

"Oh, you're sure to do that," said the Cat, "if only you walk long
enough."

—*Alice in Wonderland*

Alice laughed. "There's no use in trying," she said. "One can't believe impossible things."

"I daresay you haven't had much practice," said the Queen.
"When I was your age, I always did it for half-an-hour a day. Why,
sometimes I've believed as many as six impossible things before
breakfast."

—*Through the Looking Glass*

"You should say what you mean," said the March Hare.

"I do," Alice hastily replied; "at least—I mean what I say—that's
the same thing, you know."

"Not the same thing a bit!" said the Hatter. "Why, you might

Before he was nicknamed "Stonewall," Thomas Jackson was known as "Fool Tom."

just as well say that 'I see what I eat' is the same as 'I eat what I see'!"

"You might as well say," added the March Hare, "that 'I like what I get' is the same thing as 'I get what I like'!"

"You might just as well say," added the Dormouse, "that 'I breathe when I sleep' is the same thing as 'I sleep when I breathe'!"

"It *is* the same thing with you," said the Hatter.

—*Alice in Wonderland*

"It's no use going back to yesterday, because I was a different person then."

—Alice, *Alice in Wonderland*

"Be what you would seem to be—or, if you would like it put more simply—Never imagine yourself not to be otherwise than what it might appear to others that what you were or might have been was not otherwise than what you had been would have appeared to them to be otherwise."

—The Duchess, *Alice in Wonderland*

"Take some more tea," the March Hare said to Alice, very earnestly.

"I've had nothing yet," Alice replied in an offended tone: "So I can't take more."

"You mean you can't take less," said the hatter: "It's very easy to take *more* than nothing."

—*Alice in Wonderland*

"If everybody minded their own business," the Duchess said in a hoarse growl, "the world would go round a deal faster than it does."

"Which would not be an advantage," said Alice. "Just think what work it would make with the day and night! You see, the earth takes twenty-four hours to turn round on its axis—"

"Talking of axes," said the Duchess, "chop off her head!"

—*Alice in Wonderland*

Note to Mother Goose: The London Bridge has never fallen down.

ENGLISH / JAPANESE WORDS

Purists in the Land of the Rising Sun don't like it, but the Japanese language is becoming more Americanized. A number of words that commonly appear in Japanese pop culture have been loosely adapted from English. Here are some of the words, written phonetically. See if you can tell what they mean. Answers are at the bottom of the page.

1. Biiru	13. Kappu	25. Kado
2. Terebi	14. Bata	26. Pointo
3. Nyusu	15. Sekkusu	27. Makudonarudo
4. Supotsu	16. Bitami	28. Sungurasu
5. Basu	17. Dezain	29. Sunobbari
6. Rajio	18. Pantsu	30. Caresu
7. Gasu	19. Supu	31. Weta
8. Hoteru	20. Dorama	32. Tawa
9. Resutoran	21. Sosu	33. Sumato
10. Sabisu	22. Burausu	34. Boru
11. Memba	23. Sutecchi	35. Gorufu
12. Peji	24. Bonasu	36. Sumoggu

ANSWERS

1. beer; 2. TV; 3. news; 4. sports; 5. bus; 6. radio; 7. gas; 8. hotel; 9. restaurant; 10. service; 11. member; 12. page; 13. cup; 14. butter; 15. sex; 16. vitamin; 17. design; 18. pants; 19. soup; 20. drama; 21. sauce; 22. blouse; 23. stitch; 24. bonus; 25. card; 26. point; 27. McDonald's; 28. sunglasses; 29. snobbery; 30. caress; 31. waiter; 32. tower; 33. smart; 34. ball; 35. golf; 36. smog

---

Malaysians wash their babies in beer to protect them from disease.

OOPS!

Everyone's amused by tales of outrageous blunders—probably because it's comforting to know that someone's screwing up even worse that we are. So here's an ego-building page from the BRI. Go ahead and feel superior for a few minutes.

A PUBLISHING BOMB

"In 1978 Random House issued a cookbook that contained a potentially lethal mistake. *Woman's Day Crockery Cuisine* offered a recipe for caramel slices that inadvertently left out one simple ingredient—water. It was soon discovered that if the recipe was followed exactly, a can of condensed milk called for in the book could explode. Random House had to recall 10,000 copies of the book" to correct the potentially lethal recipe.

—From *The Blunder Book*, by M.L. Ginsberg

TAKE THAT!

"In 1941 the British warship *Trinidad* sighted a German destroyer and fired a torpedo at it. The icy Arctic waters apparently affected the torpedo's steering mechanism—it began to curve in a slow arc. As the crew watched in horror, it continued curving slowly around until it was speeding right back at them at forty knots. The *Trinidad*'s torpedo slammed into the *Trinidad* and caused so much damage that it put the warship out of action for the rest of the war. "

—From *The Emperor Who Ate the Bible*, by Scott Morris

SOLID PLANNING

"In 1974 the Nigerian government decided to initiate a 'Third National Nigerian Development Plan,' intended to bring the country in a single leap into line with most developed Western nations.

"The planners calculated that to build the new roads, airfields, and military buildings which the plan required would call for some 20 million tons of cement. This was duly ordered and shipped by freighters from all over the world, to be unloaded at Lagos docks.

"Unfortunately, the Nigerian planners had not considered the fact that the docks were only capable of handling two thousand tons a day. Working every day, it would have taken 27 years to un-load just the ships that were at one point waiting at sea off Lagos. These contained a third of the world's supply of cement—much of it showing its fine quality by setting in the hold of the freighters."

—From *David Frost's Book of the World's Worst Decisions*

CALLING ALL CARS

In 1977, carmakers actually recalled more vehicles than they pro-duced. 9.3 million cars were made in America that year; 10.4 mil-lion were recalled.

RAISING THE DEAD

"A mixup at a company that makes compact disks resulted in rock music with lines like 'God told me to skin you alive' being shipped to radio stations labeled as religious music.

"The Southern Baptist Radio-TV Commission, which markets a weekly religious radio program called *Powerline*, is calling more than 1,200 radio stations across the country to warn them that some CDs it sent out for religious broadcasts are mislabeled.

"The CDs are supposed to contain inspirational talks and music. They are actually the alternative rock band Dead Kennedys' album, 'Fresh Fruit for Rotting Vegetables.'"

—Reported in the *Chicago Tribune*, June 22, 1993

HAPPY BIRTHDAY

"Festivities marking the centennial of organized soccer in Hereford, England, were canceled abruptly when officials discovered the league was only 90 years old."

—From *News of the Weird*

USING HIS HEAD

"On May 26, 1993, Texas Rangers outfielder Jose Canseco went back for a fly ball hit by Carlos Martinez of the Cleveland Indians. It missed his glove, bounced off his head, and ricocheted into the stands for a home run. 'I thought I had it,' Canseco explained later. 'Now I'll be on ESPN for a month.'"

—The *San Francisco Chronicle*

A restaurant in Mississippi called *Hello, I'm...Jello* served over 400 dishes made from Jell-O.

BARNUM'S
HISTORY LESSON

*P.T. Barnum said, "There's a sucker born every minute"...then he proved it
with his side shows and circuses. He also wrote about it. In a book called
Humbugs of the World, published in 1866, he delightedly catalogued
some of the great hoaxes in history. This excerpt was one of his favorites.
It took place in 1667 in France, when an ambassador from Persia
arrived at the pampered court of Louis XIV.*

THE AMBASSADOR ARRIVES

It was announced formally, one morning, to Louis XIV, that
His Most Serene Excellency, Riza Bey, with an interminable
tail of titles, hangers-on and equipages, had reached the port of
Marseilles to lay before the great "King of the Franks" brotherly
congratulations and gorgeous presents from his own illustrious master,
the Shah of Persia.

The ambassador and his suite were lodged in sumptuous apartments
in the Tuileries, under the care and guidance of King Louis's
own assistant majordomo and a guard of courtiers and regiments of
Royal Swiss. Banqueting and music filled up the first evening; and
the next day His Majesty sent the Duc de Richelieu to announce
that he would receive them on the third evening at Versailles.

THE AMBASSADOR IS WELCOMED

Meanwhile the most extensive preparations were made for the audience;
when the time arrived, the entire Gallery of Mirrors was
crowded with the beauty, the chivalry, the wit, taste, and intellect
of France at that dazzling period. Louis the Great himself never appeared
to finer advantage. His royal countenance was lighted up
with pride and satisfaction as the Envoy of the haughty Oriental
king approached the splendid throne on which he sat. As he descended
a step to meet him, the Persian envoy bent the knee, and
with uncovered head presented the credentials of his mission.

A grand ball and supper concluded this night of splendour, and
Riza Bey was launched at the French court; every member of the illustrious
court tried to outdo his peers with the value of the books,
pictures, gems, etc. which they heaped upon the illustrious Persian.

"The more outrageous a subject can get, the more I like it." —Alfred Hitchcock

The latter gentleman very quietly smoked his pipe and lounged on his divan before company—and diligently packed up the goods when he and his jolly companions were left alone. The presents of the Shah had not yet arrived, but were daily expected, and from time to time the olive-coloured suite was diminished by the departure of one of the number with his chest on a special mission to England, Austria, or other European powers. In the meantime, the Bey was feted in all directions...and it was whispered that the fair ones of the court were, from the first, eager to bestow their favours.

THE AMBASSADOR'S PLANS

The King favoured his Persian pet with numerous personal interviews, at which, in broken French, the Envoy unfolded the most imposing of schemes of conquest and commerce that his master was willing to share with his great brother of France. At one of these téte-à-tétes, the magnificent Riza Bey, upon whom the King had already conferred his own portrait set in diamonds, and other gifts worth several millions of francs, placed in the Royal hand several fragments of opal and turquoise said to have been found near the Caspian sea, which teemed with limitless treasures of the same kind, and which the Shah of Persia proposed to divide with France for the honour of her alliance. The King was enchanted.

THE AMBASSADOR DISAPPEARS

At length, word was sent to Versailles that the gifts from the Shah had come, and a day was appointed for their presentation. The day arrived, and the Hall of Audience was again thrown open. All was jubilee; the King and the court waited, but no Persian—no Riza Bey—and no presents from the Shah!

That morning three men had left the Tuileries at daylight with a bag and a bundle, never to return. They were Riza Bey and his last bodyguards; the bag and the bundle were the smallest in bulk but the most precious in value of a month's plunder. The turquoises and opals bestowed upon the King turned out, on close inspection, to be a new and very ingenious variety of coloured glass.

Of course, a hue and cry was raised—but totally in vain. It was afterward believed that a noted barber and suspected bandit, who had once really travelled in Persia, was the perpetrator of this pretty joke. But no one was sure—no one ever heard from him again.

SANDBURGERS

*Thoughts from Carl Sandburg, one of America's
most celebrated poets and authors.*

"Even those who have read books on manners are sometimes a pain in the neck."

"Put all your eggs in one basket and watch the basket."

"Everybody talks about the weather and nobody does anything about it."

"Blessed are they who expect nothing for they shall not be disappointed."

"Those who fear they may cast pearls before swine are often lacking in pearls."

"May you live to eat the hen that scratches on your grave."

"A lawyer is a man who gets two other men to take off their clothes and then he runs away with them."

"Six feet of earth make us all one size."

"I want money in order to buy the time to get the things that money will not buy."

"Many kiss the hands they wish to see cut off."

"Time is the storyteller you can't shut up…"

"We asked the cyclone to go around our barn but it didn't hear us."

"Someday they'll give a war and nobody will come."

"Who swindles himself more deeply than the one saying, 'I am holier than thou?' "

"There are dreams stronger than death. Men and women die holding these dreams."

"If there is a bedbug in a hotel when I arrive he looks at the register for my room number."

"Why is the bribe-taker convicted so often and the bribe-giver so seldom?"

"Liberty is when you are free to do what you want to do and the police never arrest you if they know who you are and you got the right ticket."

After the birth: New parents spend about 50% more on health care, and 34% less on alcohol.

SCRATCH 'N' SNIFF

*No, this is not a scratch 'n' sniff page—it's about
the scratch 'n' sniff phenomenon.*

BACKGROUND. For years advertisers understood that scents can help sell products, but they couldn't find a way to include smells in printed advertisements. The first attempt came in the '50s, when newspaper companies tried printing with scented ink. The experiment flopped—either the smells dissipated rapidly, or they mixed with the newspaper's smell, spoiling the effect.

In 1969 the 3-M Corp. and National Cash Register Co. (NCR) each developed a way to impregnate printed advertisements with fragrances. They called the technique "microencapsulation," because it literally sealed the smells in the surface of the ad until the consumer released them by scratching the page. For the first time in history, products as diverse as bananas, bourbon, shaving cream, dill pickles, pine trees—and, of course, perfume, could be advertised using their scents.

HOW IT WORKS

• The printing company takes a product like perfume or food, and extracts its aromatic oils.

• The oils are mixed with water, which breaks them up into tiny droplets—an average of 1 million drops per square inch.

• The droplets are sprayed onto paper or some other surface, and are covered with a layer of plastic resin or gum arabic.

• The scent remains fresh beneath the resin until someone scratches the surface. This bursts the layer of resin or gum that holds the droplets, and the smell escapes.

SCRATCH 'N' SNIFF FACTS

• Scratch 'n' sniff pages and scented pages aren't just novelties; they're big business. According to a study commissioned by Ralph Lauren Fragrances, 76% of women who buy new perfumes are introduced to the fragrances through scented inserts in magazines.

• On average, scented pages cost twice as much as "scent-free" ads.

• A lot of people hate perfume strips, despite their popularity with

---

Albert Einstein slept 10 hours a night.

perfume and ad companies. In fact, they can actually make sensitive people ill. In June 1991, a man wrote to *The New Yorker* complaining that "A very noxious and pervacious [sic] odor invaded this house with the mail today. Much to our surprise, it came from the arriving copy of *The New Yorker*....I am an elderly asthmatic, allergic to perfume, and although I have retched occasionally at some material in *The New Yorker*, I have never vomited on it before." As a result of his and other complaints, many magazines now offer scented and unscented editions.

• Another problem was that magazines were running more and more ads with perfume strips. Magazines got so smelly that perfume companies had to limit the number that could appear—and the post office itself began regulating scented inserts.

WEIRD USES

• In 1989 the English National Opera produced a scratch 'n' sniff version of Prokofiev's "Love For Three Oranges." Audience members received a special "fragrance panel" at the beginning of the play, along with instructions telling them when to sniff. The card even contained a scent for an unpleasant character named Farfarello, who has "bad breath and emits gasses." His smell was supposed to be "a cross between bad eggs and body odor," but the stench was so overpowering that it made the entire fragrance panel stink. In later performances of the play, his scent was left out.

• In 1990 the rock group Swamp Zombies released *Scratch and Sniff Car Crash*, an album whose cover smelled like burnt rubber. Weird inspiration: the band members got the idea after two of them narrowly escaped serious injury in automobile accidents.

• In 1989 the RJ Reynolds Tobacco company test-marketed Chelsea cigarets, a brand targeted at women. Its major selling point: the smokes were rolled in a paper that gave off a sweet smell when it burned. They promoted the brand with scratch 'n' sniff newspaper ads showing off the scented papers. The ads smelled great—but cigaret sales stank, and the brand was dropped.

• In 1989 BEI Defense Systems, a Dallas missile manufacturer, ran a scratch 'n' sniff ad in *Armed Forces Journal* touting the company's "extraordinarily lethal" Flechette rocket. The ad smelled like cordite (the explosive contained in the warhead), an aroma the company called "the smell of victory."

Q: Is a coin more likely to come up "heads" or "tails"? A: Tails; the "heads" side is heavier.

BY GEORGE!

Wisdom from our first president, George Washington.

"Associate with men of good quality if you esteem your own reputation; for it is better to be alone than in bad company."

"Discipline is the soul of an army. It makes small numbers formidable, procures success to the weak, and esteem to all."

"Cursing and swearing is a vice so mean and low that every person of sense and character detests and despises it."

"Let us rise to a standard to which the wise and honest can repair."

"I have always given it as my decided opinion that…everyone had a right to form and adopt whatever government they liked best to live under themselves."

"It is only after time has been given for cool and deliberate reflection that the real voice of the people can be known."

"To be prepared for war is one of the most effectual means of preserving peace."

"A great and lasting war can never be supported on [patriotism] alone. It must be aided by a prospect of interest, or some reward."

"Few men have virtue to withstand the highest bidder."

"Do not conceive that fine clothes make fine men, any more that fine feathers make fine birds."

"In a free and republican government, you cannot restrain the voice of the multitude."

"The preservation of the sacred fire of liberty, and the destiny of the republican model of government, are…staked, on the experiment entrusted to the hands of the American people."

"Our cruel and unrelenting enemy leaves us only the choice of brave resistance, or the most abject submission. We have, therefore, to resolve to conquer or die."

"It is well I die hard, but I am not afraid to go."

If you bury a traffic ticket, it will decompose in about 4 weeks.

BY GEORGE, TOO

Words of wisdom from George Carlin, one of America's most popular wise guys.

"Energy experts have announced the development of a new fuel made from human brain tissue. It's called assohol."

"I think I am. Therefore, I am...I think."

"The only good thing to come from religion is the music."

"When I was real small I heard about this thing called the decline of civilization... and I decided that it was something I would like to become involved in."

"I hope that someday a Pope chooses the name Shorty."

"If God really made everything, I'd say he had a quality control problem."

"People are okay taken two or three at a time. Beyond that number they tend to choose up sides and wear armbands."

"I am not a complete vegetarian. I eat only animals that have died in their sleep."

"If you want to really test a faith healer, tell him you want a smaller shoe size."

"Remember: dishonesty is the second best policy."

"I wonder why prostitution is illegal. Why should it be illegal to sell something that's perfectly legal to give away?"

"I say live and let live. Anyone who can't accept that should be executed."

"Just when I found the meaning of life, they changed it."

"I never thought I'd grow old. I always thought it was something that would happen to the other guy."

"Scientists announced today that they have discovered a cure for apathy. However, they claim no one has shown the slightest bit of interest in it."

"I don't mind a little government regulation, but requiring people to wear helmets during intercourse is going too far."

Cracker Jacks has given away more than 16 million toys since 1912.

WHAT IS SPAM?

Everybody's tried it and hardly anyone says they like it...but 30% of all American households have a can on hand. So how much do you know about Spam? How much do you want to know? Not much, probably. Too bad—we're going to tell you about it, anyway.

MAKING A SILK PURSE OUT OF A SOW'S EAR
It's a question as timeless as the pork-packing industry itself: Once you've removed all the choice meat from the carcass of a pig, what do you do with all the pig parts nobody wants?

That's the question the folks at the George A. Hormel Company faced in 1937. Their solution: Take the *parts* that nobody wants and make it into a *loaf* nobody wants. Jack Mingo describes the historic moment in his book *How the Cadillac Got Its Fins:*

> Seeing thousands of pounds of pork shoulders piling up in the Hormel coolers in 1937 gave one of the company's executives an idea: Why not chop the meat up, add some spices and meat from other parts of the pig, and form it into small hamlike loaves? Put it in a can and fill the excess space with gelatin from the pig's leftover skin and bones—you could probably keep the meat edible for months without refrigeration. They tried it. It worked. Hormel's Spiced Ham quickly found a niche in the market. It was inexpensive, savory, convenient, and it didn't need refrigeration.

PORCINE PLAGIARISM

But pig parts were piling up just as high at other pork packers, and as soon as they saw Hormel's solution they began selling their own pig loafs. Afraid of being lost in the sow shuffle, Hormel offered a $100 prize to anyone who could come up with a brand name that would make its pork product stand out from imitators. The winner: A brother of one of the Hormel employees, who suggested turning "Spiced Ham" into *Spam*.

PIGS AT WAR

Described by one writer as "a pink brick of meat encased in a gela-

---

People drink coffee in every state...but Hawaii is the only one that *grows* it.

tinous coating," Spam seems pretty gross to folks who aren't used to it (and even to plenty who are). It probably wouldn't have become popular if it hadn't been for World War II.

Because it was cheap, portable, and didn't need refrigeration, Spam was an ideal product to send into battle with U.S. GIs. It became such a common sight in mess halls (where it earned the nickname "the ham that didn't pass its physical") that many GIs swore they'd never eat the stuff again. Even General Dwight Eisenhower complained about too much Spam in army messes.

THEIR SECRET SHAME

American G.I.s *said* they hated Spam, but evidence suggests otherwise. Forced to eat canned pork over a period of several years, millions of soldiers developed a taste for it, and when they returned home they brought it with them. Spam sales shot up in supermarkets after the war.

Laugh if you want (even Hormel calls it "the Rodney Dangerfield of luncheon meat—it don't get no respect"), but Spam is still immensely popular: Americans consume 3.8 cans of it every second, or 122 million cans a year. That gives Spam a 75% share of the canned-meat market.

SPAM FACTS

• More than 5 billion cans of Spam have been sold around the world since the product was invented in 1937. "Nowhere," says Carolyn Wyman in her book *I'm a Spam Fan*, "is Spam more prized than in South Korea, where black-market Spam regularly flows from U.S. military bases and locally produced knockoffs, such as Lospam, abound. In fact, young Korean men are just as likely to show up at the house of a woman they are courting with a nine-can gift pack of Spam as wine or chocolate."

• Spam may have helped defeat Hitler. Nikita Khruschev, himself a war veteran, credited a U.S. Army shipment of Spam with keeping Russian troops alive during WWII. "We had lost our most fertile, food-bearing lands," he wrote in *Khruschev Remembers*, "Without Spam, we wouldn't have been able to feed our army."

• Spam isn't as gross as legend would have you believe. There aren't any lips, eyes, or other pig nasties in it—just pork shoulder, ham, salt, sugar, and sodium nitrate.

TEST YOUR "BEVERLY HILLBILLIES" I.Q.

Come on in, set a spell. Take a little quiz about a man named Jed....
(See Answers, beginning on p. 507)

1. How did Paul Henning, the creator of "The Beverly Hillbillies," get the idea for the show?

A) He based the story on his own experience of moving from the Ozarks to California with his hillbilly uncle. (The character Jethro is loosely autobiographical.)

B) He was touring a Civil War site while on vacation with his wife and mother-in-law.

C) Someone told him the story of Ned Klamper, a Texas sharecropper who struck oil blowing up a tree stump, and moved to Las Vegas with his family. Henning changed the names and locations so that he wouldn't have to pay for the story.

2. What was planned as the original location for the show?

A) New York

B) Beverly Hills—Henning wanted a wealthy town with the word "hills" in it...and Beverly Hills fit the bill perfectly.

C) Riyadh, Saudi Arabia—Henning originally conceived of the show as the "Arabian Hillbillies." According to the original storyline, Jed strikes it rich and moves to the Middle East so that he can learn the oil business from a greedy Saudi prince. He brings Granny (originally conceived as a Bible-thumping, anti-Arab bigot) with him; she would have had run-ins with merchants, camel dealers, etc. But protests from the Saudi royal family forced Henning to move the location to California and remake the greedy prince into Milburn Drysdale, head of the Commerce Bank.

3. Granny was the last character cast, and Irene Ryan was a long shot for the part from the get-go. Who almost got her part?

A) A real live hillbilly—but she was illiterate and couldn't read the script.

From 1950-71, buying or displaying a Chinese stamp was considered "trading with the enemy."

B) Actress Bea Benaderet—but her boobs were too big for the part. She went on to play Cousin Pearl in *The Beverly Hillbillies* and later had her own show, *Petticoat Junction*.

C) Both of the above.

D) None of the above—There was no "Granny" character called for in the original story, but Irene Ryan, wife of Filmways chairman Jack Ryan, had just completed an acting class and was itching to try out her training. She badgered her husband for a full 9 months for a part in one of his shows, but he refused to give her one...until she threatened him with divorce, that is. He finally gave in and ordered that the character be created for *The Beverly Hillbillies*. Why that show? He was convinced the series would bomb.

4. Why was Raymond Bailey so believable in his role as Milburn Drysdale, the Clampett's banker (and jerk) who lives next door to them and manages their family fortune?

A) He really was a banker.

B) He really was a jerk.

C) Trained as a classical Shakespearean performer by Lawrence Olivier, Bailey was one of the greatest actors of his time. The other members of the *Hillbillies* called him "the human chameleon" and boasted that he could have played Granny if he had wanted to.

5. Donna Douglas, who played Elly May, was as friendly in real life as she was on the show, but she was downcast and moody when she returned from vacation to film the 1966 season. Why?

A) She was bitten by a wild racoon during a camping trip and had to endure more than a dozen painful rabies shots into her abdomen. The experience traumatized her so much so that she didn't want to work with animals anymore. But studio officials insisted...and for a while she was depressed because she had to work with them.

B) She fell in love with Elvis Presley while filming a movie with him in the off-season...but he didn't return her feelings.

C) Eager to cash in on her affinity with "critters," Douglas wanted to form her own "Elly May" pet food company...but studio officials vetoed the idea and she spent the entire 1966 season in a funk.

6. How well did the show fare with critics and the public?

A) The critics loved the show's traditional family values (Jed took care of Granny, and Elly May and Jethro lived at home until they married)…but the public hated it.

B) The critics hated it—even so, the public loved it.

C) The critics *and* the public loved it, especially Ryan's portrayal of Grannie—she became known as "the backwoods Bette Davis."

7. At first, Buddy Ebsen didn't want the part of Jed. Why?

A) He'd already played too many hillbillies and was afraid of being typecast as a hayseed.

B) He hated hats, especially the ratty old one he wore on the show.

C) He'd lost the part of the Tin Woodsman in the 1939 film *The Wizard of Oz* (and almost lost his life after the poisonous silver makeup infected his eyes and lungs and forced him to drop out of the film), and never got over it. He was trying to drum up support for a sequel. He took the part of Jed after the Oz project collapsed.

8. What did the owners of the Bel-Air mansion used in the series think of the show?

A) They loved it—after the show became popular they sold the estate for 10 times what they had paid for it.

B) They hated it—the house became a sort of West Coast Graceland, with fans of the show hounding them day and night.

C) They never saw it—the house was owned by Ravi Shankar, the famous guru and mentor to the Beatles. He didn't own a TV.

9. What ill-fated celebrity had a part in the show as a typist in the Commerce Bank's secretarial pool?

A) Janis Joplin

B) Sharon Tate

C) Christine Jorgenson

10. What was Granny Clampett's real name on the show?

A) Elvira Clampett

B) Daisy May Moses

C) Nadene Peckinpah

Brazilian fans are so rowdy that many of the country's sports fields are surrounded by moats.

DISASTER FILMS

Some films, like The Poseidon Adventure *and* The Towering Inferno, *are about disasters. Other films* are *disasters. Take these losers, for example:*

ISHTAR (1987)

Description: Dustin Hoffman and Warren Beatty starred as inept singer-songwriters who travel to the Middle East looking for work.

Dollars and Sense: Budgeted at $27.5 million, *Ishtar* wound up costing $45 million...and losing $37.3 million.

Wretched Excess: Director Elaine May decided the desert's natural sand dunes didn't look authentic—so workers spent nearly 10 days scraping away the dunes to make the desert flat. *Ishtar's* crew spent days looking for a suitable animal to play a blind camel. They found the perfect camel, but when they came back to pick it up, the owner had eaten it. Dustin Hoffman and Warren Beatty each received $6 million—roughly the cost for filming the entire film *Platoon.*

The Critics Speak: "It's interesting only in the way that a traffic accident is interesting." —Roger Ebert

INCHON (1982)

Description: A 140-minute epic about General Douglas MacArthur's military excursion into Korea. Bankrolled by Reverend Sun Myung Moon, who shipped the entire cast and crew to South Korea to film on location.

Dollars and Sense: "They wasted tremendous amounts of money in every way imaginable," said one crew member. "Always in cash. I got the feeling they were trying to make the film cost as much as possible." The film ultimately cost $48 million...and *lost* $48 million, making it the biggest bomb of the 1980s.

Wretched Excess: At first *Inchon* was dismissed as just another weirdo cult project, but then Moon began to sign big names to the project, including Jacqueline Bisset, Ben Gazzara...and Sir Laurence Olivier as General Douglas MacArthur. "People ask me why I'm playing in this picture," Olivier told a critic. "The answer is simple: Money, dear boy." He was paid $1.25 million for the part

...and later sued for an additional $1 million in overtime when the film ran months behind schedule. Terence Young received $1.8 million to direct.

Cast and crew waited for two months for their equipment to clear customs—at a cost of $200,000 a day!

A typical day of shooting featured a fleet of ships, six fighter bombers, and a bagpipe marching band. The film's opening was hyped with "The *Inchon* Million Dollar Sweepstakes." Prizes included a Rolls Royce, paid vacations to Korea, MacArthur-style sunglasses and "50,000 beautifully illustrated *Inchon* souvenir books."

The Critics Speak: "Quite possibly the worst movie ever made...stupefyingly incompetent." —Peter Rainer, *LA Herald Examiner*; "A larger bomb than any dropped during the Korean police action."—*Variety*

HEAVEN'S GATE (1981)

Description: Written and directed by Michael Cimino, whose *Deerhunter* had won Oscars for best director and best film the previous year . Kris Kristofferson starred as an idealistic Harvard graduate who became a U.S. marshall in the Wyoming territory.

Dollars and Sense: Studio executives put Cimino's girlfriend in charge of controlling expenses; he wound up spending nearly $200,000 a day. Originally budgeted at $7.8 million, the film cost $44 million to make. It lost over $34.5 million.

Wretched Excess: Harvard refused to let Cimino shoot the film's prologue on their campus, so for an additional $4 million, the director took his crew and cast to England and shot the scene at Oxford. In the final version, it was less than 10 minutes of the film.

They picked Glacier National Park as their ideal location, then painted acres of unspoiled grassland there with green and yellow paint to make it look more "natural." Two hundred extras were hired for a roller skating scene, given a cassette with their skating music, and sent home for six months to practice.

The Critics Speak: "*Heaven's Gate* fails so completely," Vincent Canby wrote in *The New York Times*, "that you might suspect Mr. Cimino sold his soul to the Devil to obtain the success of *The Deer Hunter,* and the Devil has just come around to collect."

In case you were wondering: The average rhino's horn grows at a rate of 3 inches per year.

AUNT ERMA SEZ...

Thoughts from Erma Bombeck, who was one of America's wittiest dispensers of common sense.

"A child develops individuality long before he develops taste."

"Never go to a doctor whose office plants have died."

"The bad times I can handle. It's the good times that drive me crazy. When is the other shoe going to drop?"

"My mother phones daily to ask, 'Did you just try to reach me?' When I reply 'No,' she adds, 'So, if you're not too busy, call me while I'm still alive,' and hangs up."

"There are few certainties when you travel. One of them is that the moment you arrive in a foreign country, the American dollar will fall like a stone."

"I firmly believe kids don't want your understanding. They want your trust, your compassion, your blinding love and your car keys, but you try to understand them and you're in big trouble."

"To my way of thinking, the American family started to decline when parents began to communicate with their children. When we began to 'rap,' 'feed into one another,' and encourage our kids to 'let things hang out' that mother didn't know about and would rather not."

"If a man watches three football games in a row, he should be declared legally dead."

"It seems rather incongruous that in a society of supersophisticated communication, we often suffer from a shortage of listeners."

"I will never engage in a winter sport with an ambulance parked at the bottom of the hill."

"When you look like your passport photo, it's time to go home."

"Guilt is a gift that keeps on giving."

If a pack-a-day smoker inhaled a week's worth of nicotine all at once, he would die instantly.

NAME YOUR POISON

Here are the stories of how two popular alcoholic drinks got their names.

DRAMBUIE

Originally the personal liqueur of Prince Charles Edward (history's "Bonnie Prince Charlie"), who tried to overthrow King George II (1727-1760) in 1745. His Scottish troops made it to within 80 miles of London, but they were ultimately beaten back and Charles was driven into hiding. In 1760 a member of the Mackinnon clan helped the prince escape to France. Charles was so grateful that he presented the man with the secret formula for his personal liqueur, which he called *an dram budheach*—which is Gaelic for "the drink that satisfies." The Mackinnons kept the drink to themselves for nearly a century and a half, but in 1906 Malcolm Mackinnon began selling it to the public under the shortened name Drambuie.

Historical Note: The recipe for Drambuie remains a family secret as closely held as the recipe for Coca-Cola—only a handful of Mackinnons know the recipe; to this day they mix the secret formula themselves.

CHAMPAGNE

Accidentally invented by Dom Perignon, a 17th-century monk in the Champagne region of France. Technically speaking, he didn't invent champagne—he invented *corks*, which he stuffed into the bottles of wine produced at his abbey in place of traditional cloth rag stoppers.

The cloth allowed carbon dioxide that formed during fermentation to escape, but the corks didn't—they were airtight and caused bubbles to form in the wine. Amazingly, Dom Perignon thought the bubbles were a sign of poor quality—and devoted his entire life to removing them, but he never succeeded.

Louis XIV took such a liking to champagne that he began drinking it exclusively. Thanks to his patronage, by the 1700s champagne was a staple of French cuisine.

BAD HAIR DAYS

*Think you've ever had a bad hair day? Just be glad
you never had one like these folks.*

B ACKGROUND
"One kind of day that everyone dreads is the widely known
and feared *bad hair day*," wrote columnist William Safire
when a reader asked him about the term. Safire speculated that it
started with comedian Gary Shandling. "Irritated with his coverage
in *Us* magazine, Shandling (who used to begin his routine with 'Is
my hair all right?') told the *Seattle Times* in January 1991: 'I was at
a celebrity screening of *Misery* and they made up a quote for me.
They said I told them I was having a *bad hair* day. They didn't even
talk to me.' "

A month later the phrase appeared in the *L.A.Times*, then the
Toronto Star ("Was Robert DeNiro caught in a crosswind, or was he
just having a bad hair day?"), and now it's a part of our lexicon.

SIX *REAL* BAD HAIR DAYS

1. Michael Jackson

In February 1984, Jackson and his brothers were filming a $1.5 mil-
lion commercial for Pepsi-Cola in which he walked down a stair-
case as a pyrotechnic display went off behind him. They shot the
scene four times, but according to *Time* magazine, "The effect was
not quite right for Director Bob Giraldi....He asked the singer to
move more slowly and ordered the fireworks 'heated up' a bit. The
combination proved volatile: On the fiery fifth take...sparks from a
smoke bomb ignited Jackson's hair, sending the singer to the hospital with second- and third-degree burns on his scalp.

2. Albert Anastasia

Anastasia was head of the Mangano crime family, one of the infamous "five families" of the New York mafia. On the morning of
October 25, 1957, he went for a haircut at the Park Sheraton Hotel. While his bodyguard parked the car, Anastasia sat down in the
barber chair and fell asleep. Minutes later, two men wearing scarves
over their faces walked up to him, drew their guns, and opened fire.
Anastasia jumped out of the chair and tried to attack the gunmen,
but he was too badly wounded and collapsed dead on the floor.

A blue whale's sound can be heard from more than 500 miles away.

3. Hans Steininger

Steineger was a 16th-century Austrian man famous for having the longest beard in the world. In September 1567, he tripped on his beard as he was climbing the stairs to the council chamber of Brunn, Austria. He fell down the stairs and died.

4. Hans Hoffman

In 1993, Hoffman, a 31-year-old vagrant, robbed a Rotterdam (Netherlands) bank of $15,000, telling the teller he needed the money to get a haircut and buy a piece of cheese. A few hours later he showed up at the Rotterdam police department, surrendered, and handed over a bag full of cash. Police counted the money and it was all there—minus the price of a haircut and a piece of cheese.

5. King Louis VII of France

King Louis had a beard when he married Eleanor of Aquitaine in 1137, but when he shaved it off, Eleanor thought he looked ugly without it and insisted he grow it back. Louis refused—so she left him and married King Henry II of England. However, Louis refused to give back Aquitaine, Eleanor's ancestral lands, which had became part of France when the couple got married. King Henry declared war. "The War of the Whiskers" lasted 301 years, until peace was finally signed in 1453.

6. President Bill Clinton

In May 1993, President Clinton received a $200 haircut on Air Force One. The only problem: At the time, Air Force One was parked on the tarmac, and according to a Federal Aviation Administration official, the trim shut down two of LAX's four runways for 56 minutes. The scene generated so much bad publicity that the hair stylist, Christophe, held a press conference to deny that Clinton was as smug, self-important, or stylish as the incident suggested.

"I am not saying this in a negative way," he told reporters, "but from what you can see, do you really think that Hillary or Bill Clinton, are very concerned about their appearance?"

The whole thing may have been the work of a political trickster. Subsequent checks of the records at LAX showed that the haircut had actually caused no problems. Runways were not shut down, and no planes were kept waiting.

A GAGGLE OF GEESE

*You've used the terms a "pack" of wolves and a "flock" of sheep...
here are some animal terms you probably haven't even heard of:*

MAMMALS

A shrewdness or troop of apes (also monkeys)

A pace of asses

A cete of badgers

A sloth of bears

A colony of beavers

A singular of boars

A clouder of cats

A brood of chickens

A rag of colts

A cowardice of curs

A gang of elk

A business of ferrets

A skulk or troop of foxes

A trip of goats

A drift of hogs

A troop of kangaroos

A kindle of kittens

A leap of leopards

A nest of mice

A barren of mules

A string of ponies

A nest of rabbits

A crash of rhinoceroses

A bevy of roebucks

A dray of squirrels

A sounder of swine

A pod or gam of whales

BIRDS

A murder of crows

A dole or piteousness of doves

A paddling of duck (swimming)

A raft of duck (in the water, but *not* swimming)

A team of ducks (in the air)

A charm of finches

A gaggle of geese (on the ground)

A skein of geese (in the air)

A siege of herons

A deceit of lapwings

An exaltation or bevy of larks

A parliament of owls

A covey of quail

An ostentation of peacocks

A nye or covey of pheasants (on the ground)

A bouquet of pheasants (taking to the air)

An unkindness of ravens

A murmuration of sandpipers

A rafter of turkeys

A descent of woodpeckers

INSECTS

An army of caterpillars

A business of flies

A cluster of grasshoppers

A plague or swarm of locusts

OTHER

A shoal of bass

A clutch of eggs

A bed of snakes

A knot of toads

A bale of turtles

A nest of vipers

The world's rarest matchbook, issued after Lindbergh's Atlantic flight, is worth over $4,000.

THE NUMBERS GAME

This is a tough game—very few people can solve more than a few of these equations on the first try. But don't look at the answers in the back of the book right away. People often come up with them later, when their minds are relaxed. And you can work on this page for a number of "sittings." It was sent to us by BRI member Peter Wing. Answers start on page 507.

INSTRUCTIONS

Each equation contains the initials of words that will make it a correct statement. Your job is to finish the missing words. For example: 26 = L. of the A. would be 26 = *Letters of the Alphabet*. Good luck.

1. 7 = W. of the A. W.
2. 1001 = A. N.
3. 12 = S. of the Z.
4. 54 = C. in a D. (with the J.)
5. 9 = P. in the S. S.
6. 88 = P. K.
7. 13 = S. on the A. F.
8. 32 = D. F. at which W. F.
9. 90 = D. in a R. A.
10. 99 = B. of B. on the W.
11. 18 = H. on a G. C.
12. 8 = S. on a S. S.
13. 3 = B. M. (S. H. T. R.)
14. 4 = Q. in a G.
15. 1 = W. on a U.
16. 5 = D. in a Z. C.
17. 24 = H. in a D.
18. 57 = H. V.
19. 11 = P. on a F. T.

20. 1000 = W. that a P. is W.
21. 29 = D. in F. in a L. Y.
22. 64 = S. on a C.
23. 40 = D. and N. of the G. F.
24. 2 = T. T.
25. 76 = T. in a B. P.
26. 8 = G. T. in a L. B. C.
27. 101 = D.
28. 23 = S.
29. 4 = H. a J. G. F.
30. 16 = M. on a D. M. C.
31. 12 = D. of C.
32. 5 = G. L.
33. 7 = D. S.
34. 2.5 = C. in a T. A. F.
35. 1, 2, 3 = S. Y. O. at the O. B. G.
36. 3 = M. in a T.
37. 13 = B. D.

33% of Americans say being 1 hour late still counts as being "fashionably late."

DEAR ABBY

A few thoughts from one of America's all-time favorite advisors, Abigail Van Buren.

"If you want a place in the sun, you have to put up with a few blisters."

"Some people are more turned on by money than they are by love. In one respect they are alike. They're both wonderful as long as they last."

"If you are looking for a kindly, well-to-do older gentleman who is no longer interested in sex, take out an ad in the *Wall Street Journal*."

Dear Abby: My wife sleeps nude. Then she showers, goes into the kitchen and fixes breakfast—still in the nude. We're newlyweds and have no kids, so I suppose there's nothing wrong with it. What do you think?
Dear Rex: It's all right with me, but tell her to put on an apron when she's frying bacon.

"The best index to a person's character is how he treats people who can't do him any good, and how he treats people who can't fight back."

Dear Abby: I have always wanted to have my family history traced, but I can't afford to spend a lot of money on it. Any suggestions?
Dear Sam: Yes. Run for public office.

"Wisdom doesn't automatically come with old age. Nothing does—except wrinkles. It's true, some wines improve with age. But only if the grapes were good in the first place."

"It is almost impossible to throw dirt on someone without getting a little on yourself."

Dear Abby: What factor do you think is the most essential if a woman is to have a lasting marriage?
Dear Dotty: A lasting husband.

"I have long suspected that more people are sleeping apart because of snoring than are sleeping together for all the other reasons combined."

"People who fight fire with fire usually end up with ashes."

THE FLYING NUN

If you had to pick the most ridiculous sitcom premise in history, what would it be? Our choice is "The Flying Nun." How did they come up with such a stupid idea?...And why did Sally Field take the role? Here are the answers.

NUN-SENSE

It was one of the most improbable sitcom plots in American television history: Elsie Ethrington, an American teenager, gives up her life as a beach bunny and enters a Puerto Rican nunnery called the Convent San Tanco, where she is ordained as Sister Bertrille. Weighing only 90 pounds, she discovers that wearing her order's bulky coronet (nun's hat) on windy days enables her to fly, a skill she uses to get into and out of trouble (and fight crime).

Sure, the concept was ridiculous, but the show was one of the surprise hits of the 1967 TV season. More important, it gave a needed boost to the acting career of 19-year-old actress Sally Field, who had just finished work on the "Gidget" TV series.

YOU'RE MY INSPIRATION(S)

• Believe it or not, "The Flying Nun" was inspired by a real-life incident involving a small nun, a big hat, and high winds.

• In 1955, author Tere Rios recalled a trip she had made to France. "I saw a little Sister of Charity in her big white bonnet nearly blown off her feet in Paris," she recalls. It gave her the idea for *The Fifteenth Pelican,* a book about a flying nun that became the inspiration for the TV series.

• The show was also inspired by "Bewitched," a successful TV series about a friendly witch with magic powers, and "I Dream of Jeanie," a show about a magical genie who marries an astronaut. "Bewitched" creator Harry Ackerman thought a similar show about a nun would be a hit, but he worried that giving a nun magical powers would be too controversial. So he stuck with *The Fifteenth Pelican*'s original premise and gave the nun special powers, brought on by high winds, her coronet, and the laws of aerodynamics, instead of magic ones.

SHE'D HAVE NUN OF IT

• The show might never have made it onto the air if "Gidget," another of Ackerman's shows, hadn't bitten the dust in 1965. Ackerman knew that Sally Field, the show's 19-year-old star, had talent, and he wanted to find another series for her.

• The only problem: Field wanted to quit TV. When "Gidget" failed, she took it to heart. As *TV Guide* put it, "Sally came away with the feeling that she was somehow responsible for Gidget's flop and no one would tell her why....She left the studio 'feeling defeated'... and embarked on a movie career, determined that TV should never darken her door again."

• Field's first stab at a movie career bombed as badly as "Gidget." She tried out for the part of daughter Elaine Robinson in *The Graduate*...but Katherine Ross got the part. Then she tried out for the role of Neely in *Valley of the Dolls*...but lost it to Patty Duke.

• All of a sudden, another TV series didn't look so bad. "It was presumptuous to think I could step into movies," Field later recalled. " 'Idiot,' I told myself, 'you're not Liz Taylor!' 'The Flying Nun' would give me time to learn and still keep me in the public eye. So—I changed my mind." (Studio executives cemented the deal by raising her $450-a-week "Gidget" salary to $4,000 a week.)

CATHOLIC CONTROVERSIES

• Studio executives were worried about potential Catholic objections to "The Flying Nun" and went to great lengths to see that the Church was not offended. They gave special sneak previews of the pilot episode to high Church officials all over the country, hoping to enlist their support for the show. "We just wanted to be sure the Catholic community dug it," one of the show's promoters told *TV Guide* in 1968.

But their concerns were unfounded: Catholic Church officials loved the show. They saw it as a much-needed recruiting film for nuns, whose numbers had been in decline since Vatican II.

"The show is positioning nuns as human beings," an official with the National Catholic Office for Radio and Television said. "Only the studio, the agencies and the sponsors were worried. I guess they thought Catholics might stop buying toothpaste."

FIVE PET FADS

*An informal study by the BRI has shown that many bathroom readers
are also pet aficionados. Uncle John himself keeps a piranha
in his bathtub. And he's trying to convince Mrs. Uncle
John to keep a fainting goat in the bedroom.*

AQUARIUMS

Fish tanks were popular in the U.S. as far back as the early 1800s, but for the most part only the wealthy had them. The reason: Water quickly became deprived of oxygen, and fish died unless the water was constantly changed. No one wanted to take on that responsibility...unless they could afford to pay someone to do it for them.

It wasn't until 1850 that Robert Warington, a chemist, announced to the world that he'd kept a pet fish alive for a year in a tank without changing the water. His secret: He added plants to the tank, which replenished the oxygen supply. His contribution was so significant that the first aquariums were known as Warrington [sic] cases.

Not long afterward, British naturalist Philip Gosse published *The Aquarium*, a how-to book that quickly became a bestseller. Soon, American and British fish lovers had made aquarium keeping one of the largest and most popular pet fads in the world.

COLLIES

For centuries, Collies were common in the Scottish Lowlands, but virtually unknown everywhere else in the world. A working dog used to guard the large flocks of sheep that roamed the area, the Collie might still be uncommon today if it hadn't been for Queen Victoria. She happened to notice some of the dogs outside of Balmoral Castle and was so charmed with them that she brought a few back to London. The British upper classes, quick to take a royal hint, made the Collie one of the most popular breeds in the country...and eventually in the world.

THE MAKECH BEETLE

A short-lived fad of the 1960s, the "makech" was a gilded and stone-encrusted living beetle that was attached to a pin by a thin gold chain. The wearer attached the pin to their shirt, and let the beetle walk over their shoulder and neck. Phyllis Diller wore a makech emblazoned with gold lace and white seed pearls. "How else," she asked at the time, "am I going to get ten men standing around looking at my chest?" Not everyone liked the fad. "A makech's appeal is primarily to the screwball fringe," said a customs agent in charge of breaking up illegal beetle-smuggling rings. "It takes some kind of nut to wear a bug."

PIRANHAS

Another weird pet craze of the 1960s was the piranha. Enterprising pet store owners skirted laws banning importation and possession of the meat-eating fishes, claiming they were actually friendly pets, not the flesh-eating meanies they were reputed to be. "We got very attached to ours," one owner told reporters about her aquatic carnivore. "He had a personality that most tropical fish don't seem to have." But state and federal officials held the line—to date it is still illegal to import or own a piranha. According to one biologist with the California Fish and Game Department, "Piranhas eat people."

FAINTING GOATS

Fainting goats aren't much different from normal goats...except that they have a genetic trait that causes them to stiffen up and fall over when someone (usually the owner or the owner's friends) frightens them. Fainting faddists rank their pets' "skill" on a scale of one to six, with "six being the highest, meaning they lock up most of the time and fall over," says Kathy Majewski, founder of The American Tennessee Fainting Goat Association (TATFGA).

First observed in Tennessee in the 1800s, the goats were nearly driven extinct by coyotes, who (for obvious reasons) preferred them to regular goats. But TATFGA was formed to save them.

The group boasts more than 200 members, but not everyone thinks their motives are pure. "To raise animals with an abnormality for use as entertainment is sick," says Lisa Landres of the Tennessee Humane Society. "The whole phenomenon is mind-boggling." She may not have to worry, though—the fad may die out on its own because it gets increasingly harder to scare the goats once they get to know you...which defeats the purpose of owning them in the first place.

THE STORY OF LAS VEGAS

Have you ever wondered how Las Vegas became the gambling capital of the world? Here's the story:

NAME. "Las Vegas" means "the meadows" or "the fertile plains" in Spanish. The city acquired this name in the early 1800s, when it was a peaceful rest stop on the Old Spanish Trail.

HISTORY. Ironically, the Mormans were the first to settle Las Vegas, in 1855. They built the first church, first fort, and first school in Nevada, only to abandon them three years later. Pioneers were still using the site as a watering hole and, as one missionary noted, few could be induced to attend the church. "Only one man attended," he wrote. "The rest of them were gambling and swearing at their camps."

Las Vegas didn't become a real town until almost 50 years later. Because of its central location and ample water supply, the railroad decided it would make an ideal stop on the transcontinental train line. They bought the land and, one scorching hot day in 1905, auctioned it off to 1,200 eager settlers. A few days later, the town appeared: a haphazard assortment of canvas tent saloons, gambling clubs and drinking parlors that quickly established the city's character and reputation.

Despite prohibitionist protests, Las Vegas maintained its early emphasis on night life and continued to flourish throughout the 1920s. "Such places as the Red Rooster, the Blue Goose, the Owl, and Pair-o-Dice were temporarily inconvenienced from time to time by raids from federal agents," writes one local historian. "But they were, of course, as safe as a church from local interference."

In 1931, the Nevada state legislature enacted two well-publicized "reforms": They liberalized divorce laws, changing residency requirements from 6 months to 6 weeks, and officially legalized gambling. Now Las Vegas had two unique attractions. While the rest of the country was suffering through the Great Depression, Las Vegas casinos made a killing catering to the workers constructing nearby Boulder Dam, as well as the 230,000 tourists who came to see it. (Las Vegas also became a significant divorce center after movie star Clark Gable's wife, Rhea, chose it as the place to divorce him.)

The first full-fledged resort, the plush El Rancho Vegas, was built in 1940. Another (the New Frontier) followed, and the notorious Vegas "strip" was established. A military base and a magnesium plant were installed nearby in the early 1940s, and both brought more people to the area and kept the town prosperous through World War II. By 1970 more than half of Nevada's entire population lived in Las Vegas.

MAIN INDUSTRY. Las Vegas as we know it today might never have been born if it weren't for gangster Ben "Bugsy" Siegal. Wanted for murder in New York, Siegal was sent out West to set up a booking service for the mob and became obsessed with the idea of creating a "glittering gambling mecca in the desert." He borrowed $6 million in mob money and constructed the Flamingo Hotel, a lavish olive-green castle surrounded by a 40-acre garden that was planted literally overnight in imported soil brought in by truck.

Unfortunately for Bugsy, the Flamingo was initially a bust. To top it off, the mob found out he'd been skimming profits. They had him killed in 1947. But business at the Flamingo picked up, and over the next few years Mafia-owned resort casinos sprang up all along Highway 91, the Las Vegas "strip."

According to *The Encyclopedia of American Crime*, for example:
- Meyer Lansky put up much of the money for the Thunderbird.
- The Desert Inn was owned by the head of the Cleveland mob.
- The Dunes "was a goldmine" for the New England mob.
- The Sahara "was launched by the Chicago mob."

"Despite the huge profits," the *Encyclopedia* adds, "by the mid-'50s the mob had started selling off its properties to individuals and corporations. In the 1960s billionaire Howard Hughes started buying one casino after another. In the early 1970s the mob's interest in Vegas was reportedly at a low point, but by the close of the decade, many observers concluded, mobsters were returning to the scene."

Claim to Fame: Grand Rapids, Michigan was the first city to fluoridate its water supply.

GREETINGS FROM OZ

The Wizard of Oz, by Frank Baum, is on the BRI's list of recommended bathroom reading for adults. Here are a few random quotes taken from it.

O N COURAGE
"There is no living thing that is not afraid when it faces danger. True courage is in facing danger when you are afraid. "

—**The Wizard**

ON MONEY

"Money in Oz!...Did you suppose we are so vulgar as to use money here? If we used money to buy things, instead of love and kindness and the desires to please one another, then we should be no better than the rest of the world....Fortunately, money is not known in the Land of Oz at all. We have no rich, no poor: for what one wishes, the others all try to give him in order to make him happy, and no one in all of Oz cares to have more than he can use."

—**The Tin Woodsman**

ON EXPERIENCE

"Can't you give me brains?" asked the Scarecrow.

"You don't need them, [said the Wizard]. You are learning something every day. A baby has brains, but it doesn't know much. Experience is the only thing that brings knowledge, and the longer you are on earth, the more experience you are sure to get."

ON THE VALUE OF BRAINS

"I realize at present that I'm only an imitation of a man, and I assure you that it is an uncomfortable feeling to know that one is a fool. It seems to me that a body is only a machine for brains to direct, and those who have no brains themselves are liable to be directed by the brains of others."

THE BEST THING IN THE WORLD

"Brains are not the best thing in the world," said the Tin Woodsman.

"Have you any?" enquired the Scarecrow.

"No, my head is quite empty," answered the Tin Woodsman. "But once I had brains, and a heart also; so, having tried them both, I should much rather have a heart...for brains do not make one happy, and happiness is the best thing in the world."

*   *   *   *

...And Now, Back to the World of Facts & Stats

• There are an estimated 5,000 foreign languages spoken throughout the world today—and nearly 100% of them have a dictionary translating them into English.

• The largest encylopedia of all time was a 16th-century Chinese encyclopedia; it was 22,937 volumes.

• Do you know what "unabridged" means when it refers to English dictionaries? It doesn't mean the work contains all the words in the English language; it just means that it contains all the words listed in earlier editions.

• The world's first Mongolian-English dictionary was published in 1953.

• What language has the most words? Mandarin Chinese, which has an estimated 800,000 words. English is believed to rank second.

• In English dictionaries, the letter "T" has the most entries.

• Few English dictionaries agree on which word is the longest in the language. Two contenders:

> *floccipaucinihilipilification* (OED), "the action of estimating as worthless."

> *pneumonoultramicroscopicsilicovolcanoconiosis* (Webster's Third International), "a lung disease common to miners."

• Many dictionaries do agree on the longest word *in common use:* it's *disproportionableness.*

• The oldest word in the English language that still resembles its earliest form is *land*, which is descended from *landa*, the Old Celtic word for "heath." It predates the Roman Empire (founded in 200 B.C.) by many hundreds of years.

DUBIOUS ACHIEVERS

Here are some of the stranger people
listed in the Guiness Book of World Records:

Randy Ober, Bentonville, Arkansas
Achievement: Spit a wad of tobacco 47 feet, 7 inches in 1982.

Joe Ponder, Love Valley, North Carolina
Achievement: Lifted a 606-pound pumpkin 18 inches off the ground with his teeth in 1985.

Neil Sullivan, Birmingham, England
Achievement: Carried a large bag of "household coal" 34 miles on May 24, 1986. It took him 12 hours and 45 minutes.

Travis Johnson, Elsberry, Missouri
Achievement: Held 9 baseballs in his hand "without any adhesives" in 1989.

David Beattie and Adrian Simons, London, England
Achievement: Rode up and down escalators at the Top Shop in London for 101 hours in 1989. Estimated distance of travel: 133.19 miles.

Pieter van Loggerenberg, Hoedspruit, South Africa
Achievement: Played the accordion for 85 hours during a wildlife festival in 1987.

Michel Lotito, Grenoble, France
Achievement: Has been eating metal and glass since 1959; currently he eats more than 2 pounds of metal every day. Since 1966 he has eaten 10 bicycles, a supermarket food cart, 7 televisions, 6 chandeliers, a coffin, and a Cessna airplane.

"Country" Bill White, Killeen, Texas
Achievement: Buried alive in a coffin, more than 6 feet underground, for 341 days in July 1981. Only connection to the outside world: a 4-inch tube used for feeding and breathing.

Trap 40 fireflies in a jar and they'll generate enough light for you to read by.

King Taufa'ahau, Tonga
Achievement: World's fattest king; weighed 462 pounds in 1976.

Alfred West
Achievement: Split a human hair into 17 different pieces "on eight different occasions."

Remy Bricka, Paris, France
Achievement: In 1988, using 13-foot-long floating "skis," he "walked" across the Atlantic Ocean from Tenerife, Spain, to Trinidad (a distance of 3,502 miles). The trip took 60 days.

Steve Urner, Tehachapi, California
Acheivement: Threw a dried, "100% organic" cow chip more than 266 feet on August 4, 1981.

N. Ravi, Tamil Nadu, India
Acheivement: Stood on one foot for 34 hours in 1982.

"Hercules" John Massis, Oostakker, Belgium
Achievement: Used teeth to stop a helicopter from taking off, 1979.

Zolilio Diaz, Spain
Achievement: Rolled a hoop from Mieres to Madrid, Spain, and back—a distance of more than 600 miles. It took him 18 days.

Nine employees of the Bruntsfield Bedding Centre, Scotland.
Achievement: Pushed a wheeled hospital bed 3,233 miles between June 21 and July 26, 1979.

Fred Jipp, New York City, New York
Achievement: Most illegal marriages: Between 1949 and 1981, using over 50 aliases, married 104 women in 27 states and 14 foreign countries. Sentenced to 34 years in prison and fined $336,000.

Octavio Guillen and **Adriana Martinez,** Mexico City, Mexico
Acheivement: Longest engagement: 67 years. They finally tied the knot in 1969. Both were age 82.

Sisters Jill Bradbury and Chris Humpish, London, England
Achievement: Made a bed (2 sheets, 1 undersheet, 1 blanket, 1 pillow, and a bedspread) in 19 seconds flat on October 8, 1985.

THE DUKE

*Some people call John Wayne an American hero, others call him a
Neanderthal right-winger. Neither side really knows much about him,
but the B.R.I. does. Here are some facts about the Duke.*

As a boy, Wayne learned to handle a gun by shooting rattle-
snakes while his father plowed the land. But, according to
one biographer, the experience gave Wayne nightmares of
"slithering, disembodied snake heads coming at him. [He] often
awoke in a cold sweat in the middle of the night—but he kept these
fears to himself."

After finishing high school, Wayne tried to get into the U.S. Naval
Academy...but was turned down. In later years, referring to the
Academy's rejection, Wayne claimed "I'd probably be a retired admiral by now." (However, during World War II, he received an ex-
emption for being the father of four children.)

Wayne created his tough-guy image only because he didn't think he
could act. Later in his career he explained to *The New York Times*:
"When I started, I knew I was no actor and I went to work on this
Wayne thing. It was as deliberate a projection as you'll ever see. I
figured I needed a gimmick, so I dreamed up the drawl, the squint,
and a way of moving meant to suggest that I wasn't looking for trouble but would just as soon throw a bottle at your head as not. I practiced in front of a mirror."

After attending Governor Ronald Reagan's inauguration in 1971,
the Duke spotted a group of Vietnam War protesters waving Viet-
cong flags. Enraged, he charged into the crowd screaming, "You
dirty no–good bastards," and punching wildly. Police intervened,
and the scuffle quickly ended; however, the next day, one of the
protesters filed a complaint with the local police, claiming Wayne
had disturbed the peace. Police refused to prosecute.

Wayne died in 1979. His funeral was held at 5 a.m., and his body
was buried in an unmarked grave to prevent fans from mobbing the
burial site. Four fresh "decoy" graves were also dug to prevent anyone from positively identifying the real one.

VIVE LA DIFFERENCE!

Researchers say that males and females are naturally different from one another in a number of unexpected ways. Here are a few of the things they've found out.

Women are more likely to smile than men when delivering bad news.

Infant girls as young as 2 and 3 years old maintain eye contact with adults nearly twice as long as infant boys do.

At the age of 4 months, infant girls can distinguish between photographs of people they know and don't know; most boys can't.

Did you have a nightmare last night? Women are twice as likely as men to say they did.

In households that have them, males control the TV remote control 55% of the time; women have control 34% of the time.

Doctors consider men obese when 25% of their body is composed of fat, and women obese when 30% is fat.

Boys fight more than girls do. The difference begins at about age two.

Fifty-nine percent of females— but only 4% of males—say they didn't enjoy the first time they had sex.

The average male brain is 14 percent larger than the average female brain.

Seventy-one percent of car-accident victims are male; only 29% are female.

On average, a man's skin ages 10 years slower than a woman's does.

In the year following a divorce, the average woman's standard of living falls 73%; the man's standard of living actually *rises* by 43%.

Male snow skiers are more likely to fall on their faces; female skiers are more likely to fall on their backs.

In one recent study, 36% of husbands surveyed said their wife "is like a god." Only 19% of women said the same thing about their husbands.

Women cry about five times as much as men; a male hormone may actually suppress tears.

Americans spend over $1.5 billion on toothpaste (and $680 million on mouthwash) every year.

IT'S IN THE CARDS

Do you like to play poker?…gin rummy?…bridge…or (in the bathroom) solitaire? Then maybe we can interest you in reading a couple of pages on the origin of playing cards.

HISTORY

Origin. The first playing cards are believed to have come from the Mamelukes, people of mixed Turkish and Mongolian blood who ruled Egypt from 1250 to 1517. Like today's standard playing cards, the Mamelukes' deck had 52 cards and four suits (swords, polo sticks, cups, and coins), with three face cards and 10 numbered cards per suit. Mameluke decks did not include queens or jacks; they used "Deputy Kings" and "Second," or "Under-Deputy Kings" instead.

European Popularity. In the mid-1300s the cards were introduced to Europe, where they spawned a gaming craze similar to the Monopoly or Trivial Pursuit fads of the 20th century. Historians measure their popularity not by how many times people wrote about them (cards received little or no mention) or by the number of decks that survive (few did), but by the number of cities that *banned* them. Paris was one of the first: it outlawed card-playing among "working men" in 1377. Other cities soon followed, and by the mid-1400s anti-card sentiments reached a fervor. During one public demonstration in Nuremburg, led by the Catholic priest and saint John Capistran (better known by his Spanish name, San Juan Capistrano), more than 40,000 decks of cards, tens of thousands of dice, and 3,000 backgammon boards were burned in a public bonfire. None of the attempts to eliminate card-playing were successful; in fact, cards are one of only a few items of the 12th century that survive almost unchanged to this day.

THAT SUITS ME FINE

• The four modern suits—hearts, clubs, spades, and diamonds—originated in France around 1480, at a time when card makers were beginning to mass produce decks for the first time.

• The simple single-color designs were easier to paint using stencils and cheaper to produce than the more elaborate designs that had been popular in the past.

• Not all today's cards use diamonds, hearts, spades, and clubs as suit symbols. Traditional German cards use hearts, leaves, acorns, and bells; Swiss cards use roses, shields, acorns, and bells; and Italian cards use swords, batons, cups, and coins.

CARD FACTS

• For more than 500 years, playing cards were much larger than today's versions and didn't have the *indices* (the numbers, letters, and suit marks on the top left corners) that let you read the cards in a tightly held hand. Card players either had to hold their cards in both hands to read them (which made them easy for other players to see), or else had to memorize them and then play with none of the cards showing. In the mid-19th century card makers began adding the indices in decks called "squeezers" (which let you hold the cards closely together).

• It was in "squeezer" decks that the jacks became a part of the deck. Earlier they had been called knaves, which, like kings, started with the letter "K." To avoid the confusion of having two types of cards with the letter "K," card makers changed *knaves* to *jacks* (a slang term for the knaves already) and used the letter "J" instead.

• The first face cards were elaborately painted, full-length portraits. While beautiful, they posed a serious disadvantage: when they were dealt upside down, novice players tended to turn them right-side-up—telling experienced players how many face cards were in their hand. Card makers corrected this in the 19th century, when they began making decks with "double-ended" face cards.

• The joker is the youngest—and the only American—card in the deck. It was added in the mid-19th century, where it was the highest-value card in an American game called Euchre. From there it gained popularity as a "wild" card in poker and other games.

• In November 1742 an Englishman named Edmond Hoyle published a rule book on the popular game of Whist. The book was so successful that dozens of writers plagiarized it, even using the name "Hoyle's" in the pirate editions. Today's "Hoyle's" rule books are descendants of the *plagiarized* versions, not the original.

• The word "ace" is derived from the Latin word *as*, which means the "smallest unit of coinage."

ACCIDENTAL DISCOVERIES

*Not all scientific progress is the product of systematic experimentation.
A number of important modern discoveries have been a matter of chance—
which means you should keep your eyes and ears open, even while you're
just sitting there on the john. You never know what might happen.*

The Discovery: Insulin

How It Happened: In 1889 Joseph von Mering and Oscar
Minkowski, two German scientists, were trying to understand more about the digestive system. As part of their experiments, they removed the pancreas from a living dog to see what
role the organ plays in digestion.

The next day a laboratory assistant noticed an extraordinary
number of flies buzzing around the dog's urine. Von Mering and
Minkowski examined the urine to see why...and were surprised to
discover that it contained a high concentration of sugar. This indicated that the pancreas plays a role in removing sugar from the
bloodstream.

Legacy: Von Mering and Minkowski were never able to isolate the
chemical that produced this effect, but their discovery enabled
John J. R. MacLeod and Frederick Banting, two American researchers, to develop insulin extracts from horse and pig pancreases
and to pioneer their use as a treatment for diabetes in 1921.

The Discovery: Photography

How It Happened: The *camera obscura*, designed by Leonardo da
Vinci in the early 1500s and perfected in 1573 by E. Danti, was a
workable camera. It was widely used in the early 1800s—but not
for taking photographs. The reason: the technology for photos
didn't exist. People used the camera for tracing images instead,
placing transparent paper over its glass plate.

In the 1830s, French artist L. J. M. Daguerre began experimenting with ways of recording a camera's images on light-sensitive
photographic plates. By 1838 he'd made some progress; using silver-coated sheets of copper, he found a way to capture an image.

Aztec emperor Montezuma had a nephew, Cuitlahac, whose name meant "plenty of excrement."

However, the image was so faint that it was barely visible. He tried dozens of substances to see if they'd darken it...but nothing worked. Frustrated, Daguerre put the photographic plate away in a cabinet filled with chemicals and moved on to other projects.

A few days later, Daguerre took the plate out. To his astonishment, the plate had mysteriously darkened; now the image was perfectly visible. One of the chemicals in the cabinet was almost certainly responsible...but which one?

He devised a method to find out. Each day he removed one chemical from the cabinet and put a fresh photographic plate in. If the plate still darkened overnight, the chemical would be disqualified. If it didn't, he'd know he'd found the chemical he was looking for. It seemed like a good idea, but even after *all* the chemicals had been removed, the plate continued to darken. Daguerre wondered why. Then, examining the cabinet closely, he noticed a few drops of mercury that had spilled from a broken thermometer onto one of the shelves.

Legacy: Later experiments with mercury vapor proved that this substance was responsible. The daguerrotype's worldwide popularity paved the way for the development of photography.

The Discovery: Safety glass
How It Happened: In 1903 Edouard Benedictus, a French chemist, was experimenting in his lab when he dropped an empty glass flask on the floor. It shattered, but remained in the shape of a flask. Benedictus was bewildered. When he examined the flask more closely, he discovered that the inside was coated with a film residue of cellulose nitrate, a chemical he'd been working with earlier. The film had held the glass together.

Not long afterward, Benedictus read a newspaper article about a girl who had been badly injured by flying glass in a car accident. He thought back to the glass flask in his lab and realized that coating automobile windshields, as the inside of the flask had been coated, would make them less dangerous.

Legacy: Variations of the safety glass he produced—a layer of plastic sandwiched by two layers of glass—are still used in automobiles today.

NO RESPECT

Words to forget from comedian Rodney Dangerfield.

"We sleep in separate rooms, we have dinner apart, we take separate vacations—we're doing everything we can to keep our marriage together."

"I told my psychiatrist that everyone hates me. He said I was being ridiculous—everyone hasn't met me yet."

"If it weren't for pickpockets, I'd have no sex life at all."

"I once asked my father if things were bad for him during the Depression. He said the first six months were bad, then he got used to me."

"My wife and I were happy for twenty years. Then we met."

"It's a good thing you're wearing a mustache. It breaks up the monotony of your face."

"My wife's an earth sign. I'm a water sign. Together we make mud."

"I don't get no respect. No respect at all. Every time I get into an elevator the operator says the same thing: 'Basement?' No respect. When I was a kid we played hide-and-seek. They wouldn't even look for me. The other day I was standing in front of a big apartment house. The doorman asked me to get him a cab....I bought a used car—I found my wife's dress in the back seat."

"Last week I told my wife a man is like wine, he gets better with age. She locked me in the cellar."

"Always look out for Number One and be careful not to step in Number Two."

"I broke up with my psychiatrist. I told him I had suicidal tendencies. He told me from now on I had to pay in advance."

MOOO: Most cows give more milk when they listen to music.

THE BERMUDA TRIANGLE

*It's as famous as UFOs, as fascinating as the Abominable Snowman,
as mysterious as the lost city of Atlantis. But is it real?*

BACKGROUND

The next time you're looking at a map of the world, trace your finger from Key West, Florida, to Puerto Rico; from Puerto Rico to the island of Bermuda; and from there back to Florida. The 140,000-square-mile patch of ocean you've just outlined is the Bermuda Triangle. In the past 50 years, more than 100 ships and planes have disappeared there. That may sound like a lot, but it's actually about standard for a busy stretch of ocean.

"Besides," says Larry Kuche, author of *The Bermuda Triangle Mystery Solved,* "hundreds of planes and ships pass safely through the so-called triangle every day....It is no more logical to try to find a common cause for all the disappearances in the triangle than to try to find one cause for all the automobile accidents in Arizona."

Experts agree that the only real mystery about the Bermuda Triangle is why everyone thinks it's so mysterious.

THE DISAPPEARANCE THAT STARTED IT ALL

The "Lost Squadron." On December 15, 1945, Flight 19, a group of 5 U.S. Navy Avenger planes carrying 14 men, took off from the Fort Lauderdale Naval Air Station at 2 p.m. for a three-hour training mission off the Florida coast. Everything went well until about 3:40 p.m., when Lt. Charles C. Taylor, the leader of Flight 19, radioed back to Fort Lauderdale that both of his compasses had malfunctioned and that he was lost. "I am over land, but it's broken," he reported to base. "I am sure I'm in the Keys, but I don't know how far down and I don't know how to get to Fort Lauderdale." Shortly afterward he broke in with an eerier transmission: "We cannot see land....We can't be sure of any direction—even the ocean doesn't look as it should."

Over the next few hours, the tower heard numerous static-filled transmissions between the five planes. The last transmission came at 6:00 p.m., when a Coast Guard plane heard Taylor radio his colleagues: "All planes close up tight...will have to ditch unless land-

---

fall. When the first plane drops to 10 gallons we all go down to-gether." That was his last transmission—that evening all five planes disappeared without a trace.

A few hours later, a search plane with a crew of 13 took off for the last reported position of the flight…and was never seen again. No wreckage or oil slick from any of the planes was ever found, prompting the Naval Board of Inquiry to observe that the planes "had disappeared as if they had flown to Mars."

A MYTH IS BORN

The Lost Squadron would probably be forgotten today if it hadn't been for a single news story published on September 16, 1950. An Associated Press reporter named E. V. W. Jones decided to occupy his time on a slow day by writing a story about the Lost Squadron and other ships and planes that had disappeared into the Atlantic Ocean off the Florida coast.

Dozens of newspapers around the country picked it up…and for some reason, it captured people's imaginations. Over the next few years the story was reprinted in tabloids, pulp magazines, pseudo-science journals, and "unexplained mysteries" books.

IT GETS A NAME

In 1964, Vincent Gaddis, another journalist, gave the story its *name*. He wrote an article in *Argosy* magazine called "The Deadly Bermuda Triangle" and listed dozens of ships that had disappeared there over the centuries, starting with the *Rosalie* (which disap-peared in 1840) and ending with the yacht *Conne-mara IV* (which vanished in 1956). He also offered an explanation for the disap-pearances, speculating that they were caused by "a space-time con-tinua [that] may exist around us on the earth, inter-penetrating our known world," a pseudo-scientific way of suggesting that the planes and ships had disappeared into a third dimension.

Interest in the Bermuda Triangle hit a high point in 1974, when Charles Berlitz (grandson of the founder of Berlitz language schools) authored *The Bermuda Triangle: An Incredible Saga of Un-explained Disappearances*. Without presenting a shred of real evi-dence, he suggested the disappearances were caused by electromag-netic impulses generated by a 400-foot-tall pyramid at the bottom of the ocean. The book shot to the top of the bestseller list, inspiring scores of copycat books, TV specials, and movies that kept the Bermuda Triangle myth alive for another generation.

DEBUNKING THE MYTH

Is there anything to the Bermuda Triangle theory? The U.S. government doesn't think so—the Coast Guard doesn't even bother to keep complete statistics on the incidents there and attributes the disappearances to the strong currents and violent weather patterns.

And, in 1985, an air-traffic controller named John Myhre came up with a plausible theory about the Lost Squadron's strange fate. A few years earlier he had been flipping through a book on the subject, when he came across a more complete record of the last radio communications between the five planes. Myhre was a pilot and had logged many hours flying off the coast of Florida. "When I ran across a more accurate version of Taylor's last transmissions," Myhre recounts, "I realized what had happened....The lead plane radioed that he was lost over the Florida Keys. Then he said he was over a single island and there was no land visible in any direction." Myhre believes the island Lt. Taylor reported "had to be Walker's Cay," an island that is not part of the Florida Keys:

> I've flown over it dozens of times and it's the only one of the hundreds of islands around Florida that's by itself out of sight of other land. And it's northwest of the Abacos, which, in fact, look very much like the Keys when you fly over them. Clearly if he thought he was in the Keys, he thought he could reach mainland by flying northeast. But if he was in the Abacos, a northeast course would just take him farther over the ocean.

* * * * *

MOVIE NOTE

The original Lost Squadron story became so embellished with new "facts" (Taylor's last words were reported to have been "I know where I am now...Don't come after me!...They look like they're from outer space!"), that filmmaker Stephen Spielberg included the Lost Squadron in a scene in *Close Encounters of the Third Kind*. The crew reappears on board the mother spaceship after being missing in action for decades.

A: Nobody knows for sure where they're buried.

MORE EPITAPHS

More unusual epitaphs and tombstone rhymes from our
wandering B.R.I. tombstoneologists

Seen in Oxfordshire, England:
**Here lies the body of John
Eldred,**
At least he will be here when
he is dead.
But now at this time, he is
alive,
The 14th of August, 1765.

Seen in Plymouth, Mass.:
Richard Lawton
Here lie the bones of Richard
Lawton,
Whose death, alas! was
strangely brought on.
Trying his corns one day to
mow off,
His razor slipped and cut
his toe off.
His toe, or rather, what it
grew to,
An inflammation quickly
flew to.
Which took, Alas! to mortify-
ing,
And was the cause of Richard's
dying.

Seen in Luton, England:
Thomas Proctor
Here lies the body of Thomas
Proctor,
Who lived and died without a
doctor.

Seen in Shrewsbury, England:
**Here lies the body of Martha
Dias,**
Who was always uneasy, and
not over-pious;
She lived to the age of three
score and ten,
And gave to the worms what
she refused to the men.

Seen in Marshfield, Vt.:
**Here lies the body of William
Jay,**
Who died maintaining his
right of way;
He was right, dead right, as he
sped along,
But he's just as dead as if he'd
been wrong.

Seen in Lee, Mass.:
**In Memory of Mrs. Alpha
White, Weight 309 lbs.**
Open wide ye heavenly gates
That lead to the heavenly
shore;
Our father suffered in passing
through
And Mother weighs much
more.

Seen in Putman, Conn.:
Phineas G. Wright
Going, But Know Not Where

It took 14 years to build the Brooklyn Bridge.

FAMILIAR MELODIES

*These songs are so familiar that it's a little surprising to realize people wrote
them. But they did, and these stories are part of their legacy.*

DIXIE
Written in 1859 by Daniel Decatur Emmett for a "black-
face" minstrel show. Ironically, though his song became the
anthem of the South, Emmett was a northerner who detested the
Confederacy. When he found out the song was going to be sung
at Confederate President Jefferson Davis's inauguration, he told
friends "If I had known to what use they were going to put my song,
I'll be damned if I'd have written it."

HERE COMES THE BRIDE
Composer Richard Wagner wrote the "Bridal Chorus" in 1848 for
his opera *Lohengrin*. He used it to score a scene in which the hero
and his new bride undress on their wedding night and prepare to
consummate their marriage. It was first used as a bridal march in
1858, when Princess Victoria (daughter of England's Queen Victoria) married Prince Frederick William of Prussia. Interestingly, because of the sexual nature of the original opera scene, some religions object to using the song in wedding ceremonies.

CHOPSTICKS
In 1877, 16-year-old Euphemia Allen, a British girl, published
"Chopsticks" under the pseudonym Arthur de Lulli. Included with
the sheet music were instructions telling the pianist to play the
song "with both hands turned sideways, the little fingers lowest, so
that the movement of the hands imitates the chopping from which
this waltz gets its name." Allen never wrote another song.

TAPS
As late as 1862, the U.S. military used a song called "Extinguish
Lights" to officially end the day. General Daniel Butterfield disliked
the song…so he decided to compose a new one to replace it. He
couldn't play the bugle, so he composed by whistling notes to his
butler, who'd play them back for Butterfield to evaluate. They went
through dozens of tunes before he got one he liked.

THE "WILD THING" STORY

"Wild Thing" is one of those ridiculously catchy tunes you can't forget.
It's been a hit in three different decades and performed by some of the
greatest—and some of the most forgettable—artists. This tale of how it
was written comes from Behind the Hits *by Bob Shannon.*

AN OPPORTUNITY

In 1966 Chip Taylor—actor Jon Voight's brother—was a songwriter working for a music publisher in New York City. One day he got a phone call from a friend who was producing a record by a group called Jordan Christopher and the Wild Ones. The friend explained that the songs he was supposed to use on the album weren't good enough. He wondered if Taylor had "something different, something unique."

Taylor said he'd work on it and send something over.

"It was around one o'clock when I spoke to my friend," Taylor recalls. "I was planning to go into the studio at five o'clock, so between that time and five, I had to figure out what I was gonna do. I didn't come up with anything until around four o'clock…and then I started to get this little riff on the guitar."

IMPROVISING AT THE STUDIO

It was almost 5:00, so Taylor headed for the recording studio. He says: "Between my office and the studio, which was about four blocks, I was humming this crazy little thing, 'Wild Thing, you make my heart sing,' and just had this groove going.

"I got to the studio and I asked the engineer just to let the tape roll, and I told him not to stop me, I was gonna do this nonsense thing and see what came out. I basically had the chorus already, so I just sang it over and over again, and every once in a while I stopped and said some things. What came out was exactly what you've heard on records.

"The next morning, I listened to this [terrible song]. I said, 'All right, send it over to my friend'—because I promised I'd send something over to him—[but] don't let anybody else hear this demo. I was really embarrassed."

THE FIRST VERSION

Eventually, Jordan Christopher and the Wild Ones did make the first recording of "Wild Thing."

"But they did it very differently, with horns," Taylor explains, "and they changed the rhythm and stuff like that. I didn't think it [was very] good, and I was kind of glad that it wasn't a hit. I was glad they recorded it, but I was a little embarrassed anyway."

IT'S A HIT

The music publisher Taylor worked for had a deal with a music company in England—they had to send everything they published to the British company. Taylor was horrified. "I asked them not to send it over," he says, "but somehow it was included with the other material they sent."

To his surprise, a few months later "Wild Thing," by a little-known group called the Troggs (from the word "troglodytes"), hit #2 in England and #1 in the U.S. Even more surprising to Taylor, it later became a rock classic, recorded by everyone from Jimi Hendrix to X. Taylor himself got in on the fun in 1967 when he produced a "Wild Thing" satire performed by "Senator Bobby," a Robert Kennedy soundalike. Even *that* version was a Top 20 hit.

FOR THE RECORD

• How did the Troggs pick "Wild Thing"?

Taylor says: "The story I hear is that when they were presented the package to choose what songs to do, they were given a stack of about fifty tapes. They just kept listening to them until they got to 'Wild Thing,' and decided they wanted to do it."

The leader of the Troggs, Reg Presley, tells a different tale. He recalls that their manager picked the song—and that he couldn't stand it. "I looked at the lyrics—'Wild thing, you make my heart sing...You make everything groovy'...and they seemed so corny and I thought, 'Oh God, what are they doing to us?' "

• The ocarina solo on the Troggs' record was copied from Taylor's demo tape. But it was originally played on someone's hands, not an instrument. Taylor explains: "While the engineer, Ron Johnson, was playing the tape back in the studio, I heard him playing this little thing on his hands. I said to him, 'Go on out and do that in the middle part.' If you play my demo against the Troggs' record, you'll see it's almost exactly the same."

Look out below: An average of 14 people jump off of the Golden Gate Bridge every year.

STRANGE LAWSUITS

Are we turning into a litigious society? Judge for yourself: Here are a few more real-life examples of peculiar legal battles.

THE PLAINTIFF: 27-year-old Scott Abrams.
THE DEFENDANTS: The owners and managers of an apartment building.
THE LAWSUIT: During an electrical storm in 1991, Abrams was sitting on the ledge of the apartment-building roof with his feet in a puddle of water. He was hit by lightning and suffered a cardiac arrest; fortunately, he was revived by a rescue squad. But in 1993 he filed a $2 million lawsuit charging the defendants with negligence. His reason: "They should have provided signs and brighter paint."
VERDICT: Unknown

THE PLAINTIFF: Dimitri K. Sleem, a 38-year-old Yale graduate.
THE DEFENDANT: Yale University.
THE LAWSUIT: In April 1993, an old college friend called Sleem to read him the entry listed under his name in the 1993 Yale alumni directory. It said: "I have come to terms with my homosexuality and the reality of AIDS in my life. I am at peace."
  Sleem—who didn't have AIDS, wasn't gay, and was married with 4 children—filed a $5 million libel suit against Yale.
VERDICT: Unknown. Meanwhile, another lawsuit was brewing: Yale hired a handwriting expert to find out who submitted the false statement.

THE PLAINTIFF: Ella B., a customer of the Friendly Food Mart outside of Anderson, S.C.
THE DEFENDANT: The Friendly Food Mart.
THE LAWSUIT: Ms. B. regularly played the video poker game at the food mart, where the store customarily gave 25¢ for each replay earned on the machine. Ms. B. claimed that one day in 1993 she won 999,999 replays worth $249,999.75. The store said the score was the result of a machine malfunction, and refused to pay. Ms. B.

filed suit to recover the amount.

THE VERDICT: Unknown

THE PLAINTIFF: Widow of Walter Hughes, who died in 1991.
THE DEFENDANTS: McVicker's Chapel on the Hill and Kevin Robinson, Hughes's son-in-law and former director of the Longview, Washington funeral home.
THE LAWSUIT: Mrs. Hughes sued the funeral home when she learned that it had buried her husband without his favorite cowboy hat.
VERDICT: She was awarded $101,000 in damages.

THE PLAINTIFF: Seven patrons of Charley Brown's, a Concord, California restaurant.
THE DEFENDANT: The restaurant.
THE LAWSUIT: In 1992, the restaurant hired an actor to stage a mock robbery as part of a dinner show called "The Suspect's Dinner Theater." The actor, dressed as a masked gunman, burst into the restaurant shouting "All you m------, hit the floor!" Dinner guests, thinking the robbery was real, cowered under their tables while the man shouted threats and fired several blank rounds from his .45-caliber pistol. (One patron, an investigator with the county the Midland, Michigan Holiday Inn during their honeymoon in 1992.
VERDICT: The restaurant offered to settle the case by paying $3,000 to each of the plaintiffs—and later went out of business.

THE PLAINTIFF: William and Tonya P., who booked a room at a Michigan Holiday Inn during their honeymoon in 1992.
THE DEFENDANT: The Holiday Inn.
THE LAWSUIT: William and Tonya claim that a hotel employee walked into their room on their wedding night while they were having sex. They filed a $10,000 lawsuit against the hotel, claiming the unannounced visit ruined their sex life. Holiday Inn does not dispute the charge but says they should have hung up a "Do Not Disturb" sign.
VERDICT: Unknown.

People with heart disease are 2.3 times more likely to have a heart attack when they're angry.

TIPS FOR TEENS

*Teenage girls need all the advice they can get...
so here's more priceless advice from the 1950s.*

BLUE-RIBBON BABY SITTING

Remember, mothers have a remarkable way of comparing notes on sitters. If you are serious about earning a few dollars, shape up!

A baby-sitting job is no time for watching TV programs not permitted at home. *Act as if this is business.* You are being paid. Arrange a definite time for sitting, and inform your family when they may expect you home.

Arrive on time, or a few minutes early to check facts before parents depart. Be sure you have a telephone number where parents, or a responsible adult, may be reached in an emergency.

Bring a book, your homework or knitting. Don't arm yourself with a long list of telephone numbers for a four-hour gab session. Don't treat your employer's refrigerator as a free raid on the local drive-in. Don't glue your nose to TV and overlook sleeping children. Check them every half hour.

Before bed, little ones often need a bottle. No cause for panic. The wiggles, small cries and faces are baby ways of saying, "Where's my nightcap?" Be prepared a few minutes before feeding time to avoid a long hungry roar.

Once the children are bedded down, stay fairly near the telephone. Light sleepers are frequently awakened by its ring.

Should the phone ring, answer as your employer directed. Be sure to write down messages. Never say, "This is Ann. The family is out, and I am baby-sitting with the children" to a stranger. Sad but true, this occasionally leads to harm to you or the children.

The Blue Ribbon Baby Sitter is dependable and completely aware of her responsibility for others. Expect to be out of a job if you eat four hot dogs, two bottles of chilled cola, three packs of snacks, run up the phone bill with unnecessary calls to friends, or permit boy or girl friends to join you without permission!

The average American opens their fridge 22 times a day.

DANGER: LEAVE YOUR GIRLFRIEND'S BOYFRIEND ALONE!

Are you the kind of girl who would dream up an elaborate and ridiculous plot to steal your girlfriend's boyfriend?

Perhaps the compulsion comes to you one day during a geometry test after you have borrowed a pencil from him because something is wrong with your ballpoint pen. You flunk the test. His darling smile keeps coming between you and the angles. At the end of the period, you return the pencil. He hands it back.

"Keep it," he says with a smile. "You'll probably need it in your next class, and I have another."

Another smile! The light in his eyes! You tremble with excitement. This is it! He loves you, and you love him. No one, not even your dearest girlfriend must stand between you.

After school you walk half a block behind him until both he and you are away from the crowds. Then you catch up and "just happen" to appear and join him. In a moment you "just happen" to stumble over nothing so that he must catch you in his arms.

He releases you quickly, a strange expression on his face, and then he strides ahead. You turn back toward your own home on the other side of town, overcome by the wonder of it all. You are sure the boy is too overcome by emotion to speak—that is why he went away so fast.

Unhappily, that evening you see him with your girlfriend. They are so engrossed in each other, neither sees you. Evidently the boy has spoken of your afternoon pursuit, however, for your girlfriend is cool toward you. In fact, you find yourself very lonely these days. You are a pitiful case because you are not only dishonest but ignorant.

TV TRIVIA

• Fonzie's leather jacket, from "Happy Days" is now a part of the Smithsonian Institution's permanent collection.

• The first TV theme song ever to hit #1 on the pop charts was "Welcome Back," by John Sebastian, in 1976. It was from "Welcome Back, Kotter."

Emergency call: In the U.S. you dial 911; in Stockholm, Sweden, you dial 90,000.

REVENGE!

While JFK was president, reporters used to quote the Kennedy family motto a lot: "Don't get mad, get even." Well, we all want to get back at someone once in a while. These guys did—and did it well.

HERE, MY DEAR

Singer Marvin Gaye and Anna Gordy (sister of Motown founder Berry Gordy) had a bitter divorce battle. One of the terms of the settlement: Gaye had to give his ex-wife all the royalties from his next album. Gaye complied. He called the album *Here, My Dear*, and filled it with unrelenting, scathing attacks on her. Predictably, sales were a disappointing (to Anna and Motown) 400,000 copies. Added bonus: The episode got Gaye get out of his contract with Motown—something he desperately wanted. He signed with Columbia Records, where he produced some of the bestselling albums of his career.

NOTABLE EFFORT

"At a London party in the 1920s, Mrs. Ronald Greville slipped an inebriated butler a note saying, "You are drunk. Leave the room at once." He put the note on a silver tray and presented it to the guest of honor, British Foreign Secretary Austen Chamberlain."

—*Esquire* magazine

REWRITING HISTORY

In 1976, Robert Redford put together the film version of *All the President's Men*, the story of how two *Washington Post* reporters broke the Watergate scandal.

Post publisher Katherine Graham signed the contracts approving the project...then started worrying about her newspaper's image. She told her lawyers to try to stop the film—or at least keep the *Post*'s name out of it. This infuriated Redford.

"An early version of the script had referred to her as 'the unsung heroine' of the story,' " writes Stephen Bates, "and Patricia Neal had been considered for the role. Now Redford ordered that the Graham character be *eliminated*." Redford only left in one reference to Graham: the scene in which "John Mitchell tells [reporter Carl]

Bernstein that, if a certain story is published, 'Katie Graham's gonna get her tit caught in a big fat wringer."

—If No News, Send Rumors

HAVE A CIGARETTE, DEAR?

BUCHAREST, Romania—"A man who was heckled by his wife to stop smoking left everything to her on condition she take up his habit as punishment for 40 years of 'hell.'

"Marin Cemenescu, who died at the age of 76, stipulated in his will that in order to inherit his house and $30,000 estate, his 63-year-old wife, Aneta, would have to smoke five cigarettes a day for the rest of her life.

" 'She could not stand to see me with a cigarette in my mouth, and I ended up smoking in the bathroom like a schoolboy,' Cemenescu wrote in his will. 'My life was hell.' "

—San Francisco Chronicle

DRUNKEN VEEP

When President Abe Lincoln ran for a second term of office, he dumped his first-term vice president, Hannibal Hamlin, in favor of Andrew Johnson. Hamlin wasn't too happy about it. But he did get a measure of revenge.

"The morning that Lincoln and Johnson were to be inaugurated," writes Steven Talley, "Hamlin stopped by Johnson's (formerly his) office. Johnson was ill with typhoid and quite nervous about [the event]. When he complained to Hamlin that he could stand a shot of whiskey, the teetotaler Hamlin immediately sent an aide for a bottle. Johnson poured himself a few extra-stiff drinks." Then Johnson gave one of the most embarrassing inaugural speeches in history—long, rambling, completely drunken. "No doubt," says Talley, "Hamlin acted as shocked as the rest of the crowd."

—Bland Ambition

WHAT ISLAND?

"In revenge for England's closing of the Libyan embassy in London, Col. Muammar el-Khadafy ordered that England be deleted from all Libyan maps in the mid-'80s. In its place, he put a new arm of the North Sea, bordered by Scotland and Wales."

—More News of the Weird

Q: What's the fastest two-footed animal on earth? A: The ostrich.

THE BARNEY STORY

Some dinosaurs are extinct...and others we only wish were extinct—like Barney. You have to wonder why anyone thought the Barney blitz would succeed...and then you have to wonder why it did. Here's one version, written by Jack Mingo, the author of How the Cadillac Got Its Fins

How did Barney, a 6-foot, 4 inch purple-and-green dinosaur, capture the hearts and minds of 2- and 3-year-olds everywhere? It depends on who you ask.

THE LEGEND

The story told by the company—and reported in *Time* and other news sources, goes something like this:

Sheryl Leach, a simple mother and schoolteacher, was driving down the highway Dallas in 1988 with her restless toddler Patrick, wondering how to get a little free time for herself.

At the time, the only thing that could hold Patrick's attention was a "Wee Sing" video featuring colorful characters and music. Suddenly, Leach had an inspiration: Why not try making a video herself? "How hard could it be?" she thought. "I could do that."

She got a schoolteacher friend named Kathy Parker to help, borrowed some money, and voila! Barney was born.

THE TRUTH

The real story makes Barney seem a little more like what he is—an extremely clever business venture.

Leach, the inspired mom, was actually working as a "software manager" for a successful religious and education publisher named DLM, Inc.,...which, umm, they forgot to mention was owned by her father-in-law, Richard Leach.

Parker may have been a schoolteacher, but she was working as an "early childhood product manager" for the same company when Barney was born.

And hey, what a lucky break! DLM had just built video production facilities and was looking to branch into the lucrative kids' video market when Leach had her brainstorm. In fact, Leach's father-in-law invested $1 million to develop Barney and even provided the services of a video education specialist who was creating a real-estate training series for DLM at the time.

HOW BARNEY MADE IT TO TV

In *How the Cadillac Got Its Fins*, Jack Mingo writes: "DLM created eight videos starring Sandy Duncan; they sold more than four million copies. One of those copies came to the attention of the executive vice president for programming at Connecticut Public Broadcasting, Larry Rifkin.

"It was Super Bowl Sunday. Rifkin took his 4-year-old daughter to the video store to rent some tapes so he could watch the game in peace. 'Leora walked out with "Barney and the Backyard Gang" and she watched the program and watched the program and watched the program. So I decided to take a look and see what it was she enjoying,' said Rifkin. He tracked down the manufacturer and made a deal to purchase 30 episodes for his station."

From there, the whole phenomenon just took off. Leach and Co. reportedly made $100 million from Barney in 1993 alone.

BARNEY VS. THE WORLD

Maybe it's the color purple…maybe it's that dippy voice. Whatever it is, Barney has aroused some pretty potent passions.

For example:

• The Rev. Joseph Chambers, a North Carolina radio preacher, thinks Barney is proof that "America is under seige from the powers of darkness." He put out a pamphlet called *Barney the Purple Messiah*, charging that Barney is a New Age demon bent on introducing America's children to the occult.

• The University of Nebraska held a "Barney Bashing Day," which featured boxing with a Barney look-alike.

• In Worcester, Massachusetts, a college student jumped out of a car, shouted obscenities and assaulted a woman who had dressed as Barney to help celebrate the opening of a drug store. "I said, 'Why are you doing this to me?' " the woman told police, "And he said, 'Because we…hate Barney!' " One little boy who witnessed the attack said, "I'm going home to get my gun, Barney. And I'm going to shoot him."

MONUMENTAL MISTAKES

Many of our most treasured national landmarks and monuments were neglected—and sometimes almost destroyed—before anyone managed to rescue them. See if you can figure out what happened to them. Answers on page 519.

1. Every year, thousands of people make the pilgimmage to Plymouth Rock. But for 150 years after the original Pilgrims landed, no one paid much attention to it. In the 1770s, pro-American rebels decided it was an historic American landmark and went to preserve it. Where did they find it?

    A) Ten feet under water

    B) Buried in a roadway

    C) In a pile of rocks on the outskirts of town

2. When this president died, his magnificent home and estate were sold to pay off his debts. A few years later, an observer described it as "nothing but ruin and change, rotting terraces, broken cabins, the lawn plowed up and cattle wandering among the Italian mouldering vases." What landmark was he talking about?

    A) George Washington / Mount Vernon

    B) Thomas Jefferson / Monticello

    C) Andrew Jackson / The Hermitage

3. The Statue of Liberty was not immediately installed in New York Harbor, because there was no money available to build a base for it. What private source offered to pay for the base—but was refused?

    A) The company that made Castoria laxative offered to pay for the base if they could put a huge advertisement on it.

    B) Commodore Cornelius Vanderbilt offered to pay for it in exchange for the rights to run the ferry to and from Liberty Island.

    C) The Daughters of the American Revolution offered to pay for it if the inscription welcoming immigrants was removed.

Twelve most-often-used letters in the alphabet: E, T, A, O, I, N, S, K, R, D, L, and U.

4. As the country grew, the number of members in the House of Representatives grew. By 1857, the House had outgrown its chambers and moved to another wing of the Capitol. Today, the area contains statues of famous representatives. But in the late 1850s, it was occupied by:

A) A train station

B) A tourism information booth

C) A root beer stand

5. It was a dry-goods store from 1879 until the turn of the century. Then, in 1905, a hotel chain decided to buy the land, tear it down, and build a modern building on it. They offered $75,000 for it. The owner agreed to sell…unless the Texas legislature wanted to match the offer. But the legislature wouldn't authorize the funds to save it. Was it:

A) The Alamo

B) Sam Houston's birthplace

C) The Emma Lapham house, where the first baby was born to a Texas settler

6. Ford's Theater, where Lincoln was shot, is now a popular Lincoln museum and working theater. But it was almost demolished by:

A) John Ford himself, a Lincoln supporter who was heartbroken to have played any part in the assassination

B) The U.S. government, at Andrew Johnson's command. He thought it was in the nation's best interest to eliminate all memories of the tragedy.

C) An angry mob that gathered after the assassination. They wanted to burn it down, but were dispersed.

7. "Old Ironsides," the *U.S.S. Constitution*, is a tourist attraction afloat in the Boston Navy Yard today. But the famous ship was left to fall apart until 1927, when:

A) Schoolchildren contributed their pennies to save it.

B) The Boston Red Sox played a series of exhibition games to save it.

C) Al Capone, striving for good publicity, donated the money to save it.

INTERNATIONAL LAW

And you thought the U.S. legal system was strange...

Paris law forbids spinning tops on sidewalks...and staring at the mayor.

19th-century Scottish law required brides to be pregnant on their wedding day.

In England it's against the law to sue the queen—or to name your daughter "Princess" without her permission.

The law in Teruel, Spain, forbids taking hot baths on Sunday. (Cold baths are o.k.)

In Rio de Janeiro, it's illegal to dance the Samba in a tunnel.

Gun control: In Switzerland, the law *requires* you to keep guns and ammunition in your home.

Swedish law prohibits trained seals from balancing balls on their noses.

If you're arrested for drunken driving in Malaysia, you go to jail. (So does your wife.)

In Australia it's illegal to hire a woman under the age of 45 to work as a chorus girl.

In Reykjavik, Iceland, it's illegal to keep a dog as a pet.

If you curse within earshot of a woman in Egypt, the law says you forfeit two days' pay.

In pre-Islamic Turkey, if a wife let the family coffee pot run dry, her husband was free to divorce her.

The opposite was true in Saudi Arabia, where a woman was free to divorce her husband if he didn't keep her supplied with coffee.

Horses in Mukden, China, are required to wear diapers; their owners are required "to empty them at regular intervals into specially constructed receptacles."

Toronto, Canada, law requires pedestrians to give hand signals before turning.

English law forbids marrying your mother-in-law.

Red cars are outlawed in Shanghai, China...and other automobile colors are assigned according to the owner's profession.

Tchaikovsky committed suicide by drinking cholera-water.

THURBERISMS

The wit and wisdom of James Thurber, one of America's most respected humorists.

"It is better to have loafed and lost than never to have loafed at all."

"Love is blind, but desire just doesn't give a good goddamn."

"Well, if I called the wrong number, why did you answer the phone?"

"I hate women because they always know where things are."

"Seeing is deceiving. It's eating that's believing."

"You can fool too many of the people too much of the time."

"Early to rise and early to bed makes a male healthy, wealthy and dead."

"Humor is emotional chaos remembered in tranquility."

"It's a naive wine, without any breeding, but I think you'll be amused by its presumption."

"I have always thought of a dog lover as a dog who was in love with another dog."

"Some American writers who have known each other for years have never met in the day time or when both are sober."

"It's better to know some of the questions than all of the answers."

"You might as well fall flat on your face as lean too far backward."

"Love is what you've been through with somebody."

"All men kill the thing they hate, too, unless, of course, it kills them first."

"I'm sixty-five and I guess that puts me in with the geriatrics, but if there were fifteen months in every year, I'd only be forty-eight."

"Sixty minutes of thinking of any kind is bound to lead to confusion and unhappiness."

"Boys are beyond the range of anybody's sure understanding, at least when they're between the ages of 18 months and 90 years."

THE FINGERPRINT FILE

It seems like law enforcement agencies have been catching criminals using fingerprints for ages...but actually the practice is less than a hundred years old. Here's a little background on one of the most important crimefighting techniques of the twentieth century.

WHERE THERE'S A WILL...

In 1903 a convicted criminal named Will West was being processed for entry into Leavenworth penitentiary when prison officials realized that they already had a man matching his name and description at the prison. After doublechecking their records (including a photograph of the inmate), they confirmed that the man being processed was the same Will West who was supposedly already behind bars. What was he doing on the outside?

Prison officials assumed he had escaped without anyone noticing ... until they checked Will West's cell and found he was still in it. The men looked like twins.

At the time, the standard method for criminal identification was the "Bertillon System," a system based on physical descriptions and anatomical measurements. Robert Liston describes the theory behind it in his book, *Great Detectives:*

> If one measurement was taken of a man, his height, for example, the chance of another man having exactly the same height was four to one. If a second measurement was added, his head circumference, say, the chances increased to 16 to 1. If eleven meausurements were taken, the odds against a duplication were 4,191,304 to 1. If fourteen measurements were kept, the odds were 286,435,456 to 1.

It seemed foolproof. But now the Wests had proved it fallible. They resembled each other so closely that the system concluded they were the *same individual.*

WHAT HAPPENED

Left with no alternative, prison officials turned to a new system being developed by England's Scotland Yard. They *fingerprinted* the men and discovered that, although the men appeared to be identical, their fingerprints had almost nothing in common.

More Oklahoma households own dogs than in any other state. Texas comes in second.

FINGERPRINT HISTORY

In 1858 William Herschel, an English civil servant working in India, began collecting his friends' fingerprints as a hobby. Carefully studying the prints over the years, he made two discoveries: no two fingerprints were the same, and each subject's fingerprints remained identical throughout their lives. He brought his hobby to work with him: Put in charge of paying out pensions to Indian subjects, Herschel—a bigot who thought all Indians looked alike—required the Indians to place their thumbprint on the payroll next to their signature. He figured he could more easily spot fraudulent claimants if he took their fingerprints.

In 1880 Dr. Henry Faulds, a Scottish missionary working in Japan, published an article describing how the Japanese had been signing legal documents with their fingerprints for generations. He reported another important discovery: even when their fingers were perfectly clean, people left fingerprints on every surface they touched. Faulds called on British law enforcement agencies to make fingerprint searches a standard part of police investigations; Scotland Yard finally took his advice in 1901.

FINGERPRINT FACTS

• The FBI didn't begin fingerprinting until the 1920s; but by the late 1980s it had more than 140 million sets of prints on file, including those of every government employee and member of the military. An estimated 2,700 criminals per month are identified using the FBI's files alone.

• It is possible to have your fingerprints removed, but it's painful and pretty pointless. Even if you do burn or slice off your prints, the scars that are left behind are as unique as the prints they replaced. There is no known case of a criminal successfully concealing his identity by mutilating their fingertips.

• It's just about impossible to get a set of fingerprints from a handgun; experts place the odds as low as 1 in 1,000. All that stuff you see in movies about cops picking up guns by inserting a pencil under a trigger guard are hooey—there simply aren't enough smooth, flat surfaces on most handguns to get a good print.

• No one fingerprint is *necessarily* unique; scientists figure there's a 1 in 2 quadrillion (about 1 million times the Earth's population) chance that someone on Earth has the same fingerprint you do.

"FORTUNATE" SONS

*We often assume that the children of rich or famous parents have it made.
Maybe not. Here are a few stories to consider.*

W.C. FIELDS, JR., *son of comedy great W.C. Fields*
As a child, Claude Fields hardly ever saw his father...or his father's money. W. C. Fields was as cheap as he was successful. He paid his estranged wife a paltry $60-a-week allowance and refused to contribute a cent to Claude's education. When he died, he left his wife and son only $10,000 each from his $800,000 estate, instructing that the rest be spent founding the W. C. Fields College for Orphan White Boys and Girls, Where No Religion of Any Sort Is to Be Preached. Claude, by then a successful lawyer, contested the will and won.

WILLIAM FRANKLIN, *son of Benjamin Franklin*
William picked up pro-British sentiments while living in London with his father in the 1750s and became an outspoken Royalist and opponent of American independence. Through his connections in the English aristocracy, he had himself appointed Royal Governor of New Jersey. In 1776, he was arrested for trying to rally opposition to the Declaration of Independence in the New Jersey colonial assembly. He languished in prison until 1778, they returned to London in 1782 when it became obvious that England was going to lose the war. Disinherited and shunned by his father (who died in 1790), William died in England in 1813.

HARILAL GANDHI, *son of Mahatma Gandhi*
"Men may be good," Mahatma Gandhi once observed, "but not necessarily their children." He was talking about Harilal Gandhi, his oldest son. But the Mahatma, who was as terrible a father as he was a great leader, had virtually abandoned his son by the time the lad was in his teens. Estranged from his father, widowed, and left to raise his four children alone, Harilal became a womanizer and an alcoholic. In 1936, he converted to Islam, which so deeply embarrassed the elder Gandhi that he issued a public letter condemning the conversion. "Harilal's apostasy is no loss to Hinduism," the letter read, "and his admission to Islam is a source of weakness to it, if

he remains the same wreck that he was before." Harilal remained a drunk in spite of his embracing a religion that forbade the consumption of alcohol, showing up drunk and disoriented at both his mother's funeral in 1944 and his father's in 1948. He died of tuberculosis six months after his father's death.

ALBERT FRANCIS CAPONE, JR., *son of Al Capone*

Believe it or not, Little Al was actually pretty honest. In the 1940s he even quit his job as a used-car salesman when he caught his boss turning back odometers. When the family assets were seized by the IRS after Big Al died in 1947, he had to drop out of college and make a living. So he opened a Miami restaurant with his mother.

In 1965, he was arrested for stealing two bottles of aspirin and some batteries from a supermarket. He pled no contest, telling the judge, "Everybody has a little larceny in him, I guess." A year later, still smarting from the publicity, Capone changed his name to Albert Francis.

ROMANO MUSSOLINI, *son of Italian dictator Benito Mussolini*

He was only 18 years old when his father fell from power at the end of World War II. So Romano spent much of his life in exile going to school, working as a poultry farmer, playing the piano, and developing a taste for jazz music. He eventually formed his own band, "The Romano Mussolini Jazz Band," and either because of talent or novelty was able to book performances around the world.

WILLIAM MURRAY, *son of Madalyn Murray O'Hair, the athiest whose 1963 Supreme Court case resulted in outlawing school prayer*

His mother's famous lawsuit was filed on William's behalf, so he wouldn't have to join in prayers with the rest of his 9th-grade class. But he converted to Christianity in the late 1970s after finding God in an Alcoholics Anonymous support group. William later became a Baptist preacher…and on at least one occasion was barred from preaching in a school auditorium by principals citing his own Supreme Court case.

RICHARD J. REYNOLDS II, *R.J.Reynolds tobacco fortune heir*

Died of emphysema in 1964. His son, Richard J. Reynolds III, died of emphysema in 1994. Patrick Reynolds (R. J. III's half-brother) sold his R.J. Reynolds stock and became an antismoking activist.

The average American gets 20% less sleep than the average American did 100 years ago.

BUILDING THE PENTAGON

It isn't one of the Seven Wonders of the world, but it probably deserves to be. Here's the story of what was for decades the world's largest office building ...and what remains today "the most easily recognized building on Earth."

AMERICA GOES TO WAR

As the United States began gearing up for World War II in the late 1930s, military planners were concerned by the fact that the War Department was located in 17 buildings spread out all over Washington, D.C. Officers wasted hours each day traveling around town from one office to another. This made it almost impossible to plan America's defense quickly and efficiently. And the problem was expected to get much worse: In the second half of 1941 alone, the department of the Army was expected to grow by 25%, enough to fill four more office buildings.

GETTING IN SHAPE

In July 1941, General Brehon Somervell, the Army's chief of construction, gave a team of architects one weekend to come up with a plan for a building that would house the entire military, to be built on a compact site adjacent to Arlington National Cemetery. The architects probably would have preferred a traditional square design, but because a road cut through one corner of the property there wasn't enough room for a square-shaped building. So they designed a building with a pentagonal shape instead.

At first it looked like all of their work had been for nothing. When President Roosevelt learned of the intended site for the Pentagon, he insisted that it be moved farther away from Arlington National Cemetery so as not to desecrate the hallowed burial ground. The architects selected another site about 3/4 of a mile away that was larger than the first site, but stuck with the original pentagonal shape. Why? According to historian R. Alton Lee:

> The original Pentagon pattern was retained for a number of reasons: it already was designed and there was the pressure of time; Army officers liked it because its shape was reminiscent of a 17th-century fortress; and any pattern close to a circular shape would permit the

Japan has far fewer flush toilets than any other modern industrialized nation.

greatest amount of office area within the shortest walking distance. …Roosevelt agreed to the new site, but disliked the architectural design. Why not build a large, square, windowless building that could be converted during peace time into a storage area for archives or supplies? However, [Gen. Brehon Somervell, the officer in charge of construction] liked the pentagonal concept and, as time was vital, told the contractors to proceed.…When the President discovered what was happening, construction had already begun.

THE HEIGHT
The architects also decided on a long, flat building instead of a tall, thin one like a skyscraper. Reason: It was faster and cheaper to build a building without elevators. Also, given that 20,000 to 30,000 people an hour would enter and leave the building during peak traffic times, connecting the floors with wide ramps enabled more people to get where they were going than stairs, elevators, or escalators ever could.

BUILDING THE BEHEMOTH
Because it seemed likely that the U.S. might enter the war at any moment, what took place next was one of the fastest and most massive construction projects ever attempted. Ground-breaking took place on August 11, 1941; soon afterward workers moved more than 5.5 million cubic yards of earth onto the site and then hammered 41,491 massive concrete piles (more than one for each person scheduled to move into the Pentagon) into the ground to form the foundation. Then they built the Pentagon building itself using more than 435,000 cubic yards of concrete made from sand and gravel dredged from the nearby Potomac River. Because speed was essential, 13,000 workers worked around the clock to get the building finished as quickly as possible. The pace was so rapid that rather than take the time to remove all of the heavy equipment after excavating the basement, contractors left some of it in place and entombed it in cement. And given the frantic pace of construction, the architects' drawings barely kept ahead of the construction crews.

The building wasn't built all at once: each of the Pentagon's five sides was built independently of the others in clockwise order, with the occupants of each section moving in as soon as it was finished.

Q: What's the most popular amusement park on earth? A: Tokyo Disneyland.

The last section was finally completed on January 15, 1943, just 16 months after the ground-breaking.

RANDOM PENTAGON FACTS

• Originally budgeted at $35 million, the building ultimately cost $70 million in 1942, about as much as a battleship. Despite the huge cost overruns and the last-minute changes in the plans, Congress barely let out a whimper when it authorized the additional funds needed to complete the building. World War II was in full swing, and even the most penny-pinching politicos kept silent out of fear of jeopardizing—or being *accused* of jeopardizing— the war effort.

• When the Pentagon was in its planning stages, Franklin Roosevelt insisted that the outside of the building not have any windows, believing it would look more dramatic. Furthermore, a windowless building would be easier to convert to civilian government uses once the war was over. But munitions experts talked him out of it, explaining that walls with "blow-out" windows survive bombings better than solid masonry walls, which collapse entirely.

• The Pentagon is designed so that the offices are as close together as they possibly can be—even so, when the building first opened it quickly earned the nickname "Pantygon" because people walked their pants off getting from one place to another.

• To deal with the immense amount of vehicle traffic each working day, architects designed an elaborate system of over- and underpasses arranged into cloverleaf shapes, which enabled thousands of vehicles to drop off passengers and leave again without ever once stopping for a traffic light. The innovative cloverleaf over- and underpasses were so successful that they became a standard feature of the interstate highway system.

• The Pentagon has enough cafeterias and dining rooms to serve more than 17,500 meals a day...but has only 230 restrooms.

• It has 17.5 miles of corridors, 150 stairways, 4,200 clocks, 22,500 telephones connected by 100,000 miles of telephone cable, 25,000 employees, 2 hospitals, its own power and sewage plants, and the world's largest pneumatic tube system. But it only has 1 passenger elevator: the one that the Secretary of Defense uses to get from his parking space in the basement to his office.

WHO HELPED HITLER?

Remember those movies about World War II, when everyone in America pitched in together to fight the Nazis? Well, here's some more amazing info from It's a Conspiracy! by The National Insecurity Council.

While most Americans were appalled by the Nazis and the re-arming of Germany in the 1930s, some of America's most powerful corporations were more concerned about making a buck from their German investments. Here are some examples of how U.S. industrialists supported Hitler and Nazi Germany.

GENERAL MOTORS
The Nazi connection: GM, which was controlled by the du Pont family during the 1940s, owned 80 percent of the stock of Opel AG, which made 30 percent of Germany's passenger cars.

Helping Hitler: When Hitler's panzer divisions rolled into France and Eastern Europe, they were riding in Opel trucks and other equipment. Opel earned GM a hefty $36 million in the ten years before war broke out, but because Hitler prohibited the export of capital, GM reinvested the profits in other German companies. At least $20 million was invested in companies owned or controlled by Nazi officials.

THE CURTISS-WRIGHT AVIATION COMPANY
The Nazi connection: Employees of Curtiss-Wright taught dive-bombing to Hitler's *Luftwaffe.*

Helping Hitler: When Hitler's bombers terrorized Europe, they were using American bombing techniques. The U.S. Navy invented dive-bombing several years before Hitler came to power, but managed to keep it a secret from the rest of the world by expressly prohibiting U.S. aircraft manufacturers from mentioning the technique to other countries. However, in 1934, Curtiss-Wright, hoping to increase airplane sales to Nazi Germany, found a way around the restriction: instead of *telling* the Nazis about dive-bombing, it *demonstrated* the technique in air shows. A U.S. Senate investigation concluded, "It is apparent that American aviation companies did their part to assist Germany's air armament."

STANDARD OIL

The Nazi connection: The oil giant developed and financed Germany's synthetic fuel program in partnership with the German chemical giant, I.G. Farben.

Helping Hitler: As late as 1934, Germany was forced to import as much as 85 percent of its petroleum from abroad. This meant that a worldwide fuel embargo could stop Hitler's army overnight. To get around this threat, Nazi Germany began converting domestic coal into synthetic fuel using processes developed jointly by Standard Oil and I.G. Farben.

• Standard taught I.G. Farben how to make tetraethyl-lead and add it to gasoline to make leaded gasoline. This information was priceless; leaded gas was essential for modern mechanized warfare. An I.G. Farben memo stated, "Since the beginning of the war we have been in a position to produce lead tetraethyl solely because, a short time before the outbreak of the war, the Americans established plants for us and supplied us with all available experience."

• A congressional investigation conducted after World War II found evidence that Standard Oil had conspired with I.G. Farben to block American research into synthetic rubber, in exchange for a promise that I.G. Farben would give Standard Oil a monopoly on its rubber-synthesizing process. The investigation concluded that "Standard fully accomplished I.G.'s purpose of preventing the United States production by dissuading American rubber companies from undertaking independent research in developing synthetic rubber processes."

HENRY FORD, founder of the Ford Motor Company

The Nazi connection: Ford was a big donor to the Nazi party.

Helping Hitler: Ford allegedly bankrolled Hitler in the early 1920s, at a time when the party had few other sources of income. In fact, the Party might have perished without Ford's sponsorship. Hitler admired Ford enormously. In 1922, *The New York Times* reported, "The wall beside his desk in Hitler's private office is decorated with a large picture of Henry Ford." Ford never denied that he had bankrolled the Führer. In fact, Hitler presented him with Nazi Germany's highest decoration for foreigners, the Grand Cross of the German Eagle.

Dream date: Anteaters can stick their tongues out at a rate of 160 times a minute.

CHASE NATIONAL BANK (later Chase Manhattan Bank)

The Nazi connection: Chase operated branches in Nazi-occupied Paris and handled accounts for the German embassy as well as German businesses operating in France.

Helping Hitler: As late as 6 months before the start of World War II in Europe, Chase National Bank worked with the Nazis to raise money for Hitler from Nazi sympathizers in the U.S.

• Even after America entered the war, "the Chase Bank in Paris was the focus of substantial financing of the Nazi embassy's activities, with the full knowledge of [Chase headquarters in] New York. To assure the Germans of its loyalty to the Nazi cause…the Vichy branch of Chase at Chateauneuf-sur-Cher were strenuous in enforcing restrictions against Jewish property, even going so far as to refuse to release funds belonging to Jews because they anticipated a Nazi decree with retroactive provisions prohibiting such a release."

INTERNATIONAL TELEPHONE AND TELEGRAPH

The Nazi connection: IT&T owned substantial amounts of stock in several German armaments companies, including a 28% stake in Focke-Wolf, which built fighter aircraft for the German army.

Helping Hitler: Unlike General Motors, IT&T was permitted to repatriate the profits it made in Germany, but it chose not to. Instead, the profits were reinvested in the German armaments industry. According to *Wall Street and the Rise of Hitler*: "IT&T's purchase of a substantial interest in Focke-Wolf meant that IT&T was producing German planes used to kill Americans and their allies—and it made excellent profits out of the enterprise."

• The relationship with the Nazis continued even after the U.S. entered the war. According to *Trading with the Enemy*, the German army, navy, and air force hired IT&T to make "switchboards, telephones, alarm gongs, buoys, air raid warning devices, radar equipment, and 30,000 fuses per month for artillery shells used to kill British and American troops" *after* the bombing of Pearl Harbor. "In addition, IT&T supplied ingredients for the rocket bombs that fell on London…high frequency radio equipment, and fortification and field communication sets. Without this supply of crucial materials, it would have been impossible for the German air force to kill American and British troops."

ELVIS: TOP GUN

Like many Americans, some of Elvis's favorite toys were his guns. And when he wasn't shooting, he liked to pretend he was a karate champ. Some details:

SHOT OFF THE CAN

You never knew when Elvis might get the urge to engage in a little shooting practice, so it paid to be on guard at *all* times.

On one memorable night, Elvis and some friends were relaxing in the Imperial Suite on the 30th floor of the Las Vegas Hilton after his show. "The very elegant Linda Thompson [Elvis's girl-friend] was sitting in the well-appointed and luxurious bathroom," writes Steve Dunleavy in *Elvis: What Happened?*, "when her reverie was rudely interrupted by a resounding blast. At the same time, a tiny rip appeared in the toilet paper on her right side [and] the mirror on the closet door splintered into shards of glass."

"I think Elvis was trying to hit a light holder on the opposite wall," explains Sonny West, Elvis's bodyguard. "Well, he's a lousy shot and he missed. The damn bullet went straight through the wall and missed Linda by inches. If she had been standing up next to the toilet paper holder, it would have gone right through her leg. If it had changed course or bounced off something, it could have killer her, man."

PLAYING IT SAFE

Elvis had hundreds of guns, and he liked to keep them loaded at all times. But he always left the first bullet chamber empty. "It is a habit he got from me," says Sonny West. "I had a friend who dropped his gun. It landed on the hammer...fired and hit him right through the heart, killing him instantly."

But Elvis had another reason. "Elvis knew what a real bad temper he had," says Sonny. "When he flashed, anything could happen. If he pulled the trigger in a rage, it would come up blank and give him just enough time to realize what on earth he was doing."

It paid off. One evening when the Elvis entourage was at the movies (Elvis rented the entire movie theater and brought his friends with him), Elvis went to the men's room and stayed there for a while. One of the group—a visitor who wasn't part of the regular "Memphis mafia"—started joking around, pounding on the bathroom door. West recalls:

"Elvis yells back 'Okay, man, okay.'

"But this guy just kept banging on the door....Apparently Elvis flashed. 'Goddammit!' he yelled as he charged out the door. Then he screamed, 'Who do you think you are, you m----f----r?,' whipped out his gun, pointed it right at the guy and pulled the trigger. Jesus, thank God, he didn't have a bullet in that chamber; otherwise, he would have blown the man's head clean off his shoulders."

CHOP! CHOP!

Elvis was fascinated with karate. He dreamed of making his own karate movie, starring himself as the evil karate master, and liked to drop in at various karate studios to shoot the breeze and work out.

Dave Hebler, a seven-degree black-belt, remembers their first sparring session in *Elvis: What Happened?*:

"He came in with his usual entourage and shook hands all around. Then he wanted to show-off some moves. Within seconds ...it was obvious to me that one, Elvis didn't know half as much about karate as he thought he did; and two, he hardly knew where he was.

"He was moving very sluggishly and lurching around like a man who'd had far too much to drink....I mean he was actually tripping over and damn near falling on his butt.

"While I couldn't make him look like an expert, I tried to react to his moves in such a way that he wouldn't look half as bad as he could have." Hebler became a regular member of Elvis's entourage.

* * * * *

GOOD ADVICE

"Keep your temper. Do not quarrel with an angry person, but give him a soft answer. It is commanded by the Holy Writ, and, furthermore, it makes him madder than anything else you could say."

—*Anon.*

THE
ANSWER PAGES

THE ELVIS ANSWERS
(FROM PAGE 33)

1. c. He thought he could heal the sick. For example: One time Dean Nickopolous, son of Dr. Nick (Elvis' personal physician), injured his leg sledding in the snow. It hurt so badly that he thought it was broken. Elvis's bodyguard recalls: "Then old psychic healer Elvis comes along. He starts 'laying on the hands' and grabbing the leg. Poor old Dean is nearly passing out with pain." Later in the hospital, the doctor told Elvis and his friends that the leg was only bruised, not broken.

"When Elvis heard from the doctor that the leg wasn't broken, he gave one of those satisfied little know-all smiles," the bodyguard says. "He said, 'I know, it isn't broken. It's okay now.' He was taking credit for the fact that the leg wasn't broken."

2. b. Elvis' vegetarian friend Larry Geller recounts in *If I Can Dream: Elvis' Own Story:*

> Out went the brownies, the ice cream, the chicken-fried steak, the burgers. Elvis ate only fresh, nutritious, healthy foods—for two days. Then it was back to the same old nonsense.

3. c. Elvis hated the show because Karl Malden's character was named Mike Stone. When Priscilla Presley separated from the King, she left him for a karate instructor named Mike Stone. A different Mike Stone to be sure, but that didn't matter to Elvis.

4. a. "Dr. Nick said he didn't recommend the surgery, merely mentioned it as a possibility," Jerry Hopkins writes in *Elvis: The Final Years,* but "Elvis, no stranger to rapid and extreme weight loss schemes, said he wanted the operation that night." Dr. Nick finally talked the King out of the procedure by explaining that if he had it, Elvis would have to stick to a strict diet for the rest of his life. "To celebrate the decision not to have the operation," Hopkins writes,

Americans fill in 54 acres of crossword puzzle space every day.

Elvis "had one of his boys go to a fast-food place in the neighborhood and sneak back with a sack of bacon cheeseburgers and fried potatoes."

5. b. Elvis loved mortuaries. As we told you in *Uncle John's Sixth Bathroom Reader*, Elvis liked to wander through the Memphis funeral home where his mother had been laid out before her burial. "I don't mean he would just go there during the day and look around," Elvis' friend Sonny West recounted to Steve Dunleavy in *Elvis: What Happened?* "I mean he would go there at three in the morning and wander around the slabs looking at all the embalmed bodies. It scared the sh— out of me."

When his friend on the police force died, the King wanted to be there at the mortuary when they worked on him. "I'm sure Elvis was sad about the whole thing, but do you know what he did, man?" says a member of the Memphis Mafia. "He watched the mortician embalm his friend....Can you imagine that? Someone watching someone else slicing into the body of a friend....Elvis could tell us details about embalming that would impress a doctor."

6. a. A friend recalls: "I remember Jimmy Dean, a nice guy, was waiting for him one night. Elvis came out of his bedroom after keeping Jimmy out there for an hour. Jimmy greeted Elvis with a big hello and said jokingly, 'I oughta rip a yard from your ass, keeping me waiting.' And Elvis whipped out his .22 revolver and stuck it under Jimmy's chin and said, 'And I ought to blow your head off for talking to me like that.' "

7. b. His manager, Colonel Tom Parker, botched the invitation by demanding $25,000 for the King to appear. As Jerry Hopkins writes, "The man in the White House was dumbfounded. Finally he regained his composure and said, 'Why, Colonel Parker, no one ever gets paid to perform in the White House.'
" 'Well,' said the Colonel, 'no one ever asks Elvis to play for free.' " Elvis lost the gig...and was never invited back.

8. b. "There's all kinds of speculation about what book Elvis was reading when he died," says his cousin Billy Smith. "It was *The Scientific Search for the Face of Jesus*, the Shroud of Turin book, by Frank Adams."

ANSWERS TO "WOULD YOU BELIEVE..."
(FROM PAGE 89)

1. b) North was testifying before the Iran-Contra investigating committee, and in a supremely cynical gesture, presented the incident as an example of why Congress can't be trusted with secrets. It was too much for *Newsweek*, which had been the recipient of the leaked information. They revealed that the source of their info had been "none other than North himself."

2. c) In an interview with Norman Mailer in *Esquire*, she said: "I think you get to a point with a person that you say, 'I love this person...enough that I don't give a damn what happens to me, I'm willing to take the chance.' "

3. a) Lightner, who was fired by MADD in 1985, began work for the American Beverage Institute—which represents restaurants and breweries. "I assume some people will say, 'Gee, what's she doing working for the industry, the other side,' " she told a reporter, adding: "I don't see it was the other side. They're just as affected by drunk driving as anyone else." Lightner's first project, according to *The New York Times*, was "working against state laws tightening the standards for drunk driving."

4. c) "Her beliefs remain unshaken," said news reports, "even though she had a baby during spring break." The report went on:

> The baby's father was a short-term boyfriend....and the athletic teenager gained only seven pounds during her pregnancy. So she was able to conceal her condition from family and friends until she went into labor during a trip with her present boyfriend. He had planned to take her hang-gliding, but ended up rushing her to a hospital maternity ward at 3 a.m. She told her mother the news the day after the baby was born.
>
> Danyale plans to attend college next year and the child probably will live with her grandmother. When the time comes, the baby will be taught about abstinence. "I still believe in it," Danyale said.

5. a) When Rashwan didn't show up to receive his Fair Play Trophy, David Wallechinsky, author of a definitive book on the Olympics, "went back and looked at the tape of the match and discov-

---

True lies: 57% of Americans say "they look younger than they are."

ered that Rashwan had attacked the injured leg. In fact, it was his first move, 10 seconds into the match."

6. c) "Football and family values—a great marketing concept," wrote columnist Joe Urschel in *USA Today*. "Too bad David Williams was dumb enough to fall for it." He went on:

First, they threatened to fine and suspend him. Then they decided to withhold $111,111 of Williams' pay instead.

Williams' immediate supervisor, offensive line coach Bob Young, took a more personal view of the situation....."Shoot, I had a baby when I was playing," Young said. "Ninety percent of the guys have babies when they are playing, but you never miss games. My wife told me she was having a baby, and I said, 'Honey, I've got to play a football game.' "

7. b) Scot Morris writes in *The Emperor Who Ate the Bible*: "Benjamin Franklin saved his well-earned pennies at Philadelphia's Bank of America. In 1940, accountants audited all of the bank's records —including the earliest transactions. According to their findings, Benjamin Franklin...was overdrawn on his account at least three times each week."

8. b) In 1994, the General Accounting Office of Congress did an audit of the IRS and found that "the agency did things with its books that would put ordinary people in jail." According to one news report, for example:
• The IRS's "inventory records are so poorly maintained that it said a $752 video display terminal had cost $5.6 million."
• "Auditors couldn't account for two-thirds of the money [the IRS] spent in one recent year."
• "When federal investigators wanted to see records for several billion dollars' worth of transactions, the paperwork couldn't be found. So [IRS] employees doctored files to fit."

9. a) According to an account in *If No News, Send Rumors*: "In a summary of Supreme Court actions in 1973, *The New York Times* omitted one Court decision. The Justices had announced that they would not revive a paternity suit in which the defendant was *Times* publisher Arthur Ochs Sulzberger."

THE GRAMMY QUIZ ANSWERS (FROM PAGE 147)

1. b) The Beach Boys. They were nominated for Best Vocal Group in 1966, along with the Association and the Mamas & the Papas. But all lost to the Anita Kerr Quartet, a nondescript middle-of-the-road group. (Anita Kerr just happened to be the vice president of the Nashville chapter of the National Academy of Recording Arts and Sciences—the organization that gives out the Grammys.)

"Good Vibrations" was nominated for 1966's best rock & roll recording...but lost to "Winchester Cathedral." In 1988, the Beach Boys were nominated (and lost) again—this time for "Kokomo."

On the other hand: The Chipmunks won in 1958, for Best Comedy Record and Best Children's Record. Aerosmith was named Best Rock Group in 1990.

2. a) Vaughn Meader did a great impersonation of President John F. Kennedy, and his *First Family* record, which gently spoofed life at the Kennedy White House, was Album of the Year in 1962. In fact, at one point it was certified by the *Guinness Book of World Records* as the fastest-selling album in history. Thomas O'Neil writes in *The Grammys:*

> Meader is remembered in comedy circles today as one of its most tragic figures. He was clearly America's leading political satirist of his day, but [his] career was...shot down the same day that gunfire made history in Dallas on November 22, 1963....

> When Kennedy was assassinated in Dallas, the album was tossed out of homes and record stores across America. While other comics [who] lampooned Kennedy in the past...were able to prevail professionally after his death, Meader was unable to rescue his career, despite countless comeback tries that even included changing his name.

3. c) Yep, it's the Anita Kerr Quartet again, for their immortal album, *We Dig Mancini.* Probably the most scandalous award in Grammy history, because they beat out the Beatles, who were in their prime. The Beatles were nominated for nine awards—and got none. Bob Dylan didn't even get a nomination.

4. c) 1967, for *How Great Thou Art.* In fact, the only Grammys Elvis ever won were for religious music. He was given the 1972 and 1974 Best Inspirational Performance awards, too.

5. c) Sinéad O'Connor. In 1990, she was nominated in four categories, and said: "If I win, I won't accept it and I wouldn't want it near me. As far as I'm concerned, it represents everything I despise about the music industry." She did win a Best Alternative Music award, and turned it down.

6. a) John. George and Ringo won in 1972 for their performances on the *Concert for Bangladesh* album; Paul won one in 1972 for *Uncle Albert* and one in 1974 for *Band on the Run*. Remarkably, the most creative of the quartet got nothing for his solo efforts while he was alive. After (and perhaps because) he was assassinated, he and Yoko won an Album of the Year award for *Double Fantasy*.

7. b) The Rolling Stones. But the Who and the Doors never won anything, either.

8. a) Roseanne Cash. She was nominated for 1982's best female country singer, and didn't get it. After the show, driving down Hollywood Boulevard, she wrote a "tongue-in-cheek…little ditty" that went, "I got my new dress, I got my new shoes / I don't know why you don't want me." She recorded it, and it won her the award for Best Female Country Vocalist in 1985. "I wrote it out of self-pity," she said in her acceptance speech. "How ironic to win with it!"

9. c) Frank Zappa. When he was nominated in 1987 for *Jazz from Hell* (which won Best Rock Instrumental), he said: "I have no ambiguous feelings about the Grammys at all. I know they're fake. I find it difficult to believe that Whitney Houston is the answer to all of America's music needs."

10. a) What Grammys? Each was nominated once—Hendrix in 1970 for an instrumental of "The Star Spangled Banner" and Joplin in 1971 for "Me & Bobby McGee." And that's it.

11. d) Natalie Cole, 1975. It took 17 years. Among the winners in that stretch: Tom Jones, the Carpenters, and Marvin Hamlisch.

12. b) He couldn't afford to rent a tux to go to the awards ceremony. It's a bizarre story. Clark, a blind Nashville street singer, recorded one album for RCA, called *Blues in the Street*. It didn't sell well, but did get a Grammy nomination. For some reason, RCA wasn't interested in promoting it; they didn't even *loan* him the money to go across town and attend the ceremony. So he wasn't there when he beat out Peter, Paul & Mary and Ravi Shankar for Best Folk Recording. In fact, he never recorded again.

According to Thomas O'Neil in *The Grammys*:

> The day after the Grammy ceremony, he was seen still hustling spare change on the sidewalks of the honky-tonk capital. Two years later, he died when a kerosene stove exploded in his trailer home.

13. a) "I tore a ligament in my leg, jumping out of my seat," Popper said; he had to limp up to the stage. What was he going to do with his trophy? "I got a lovely spot for this," he said, as he waved it around. "There's this door that keeps closing…"

THE GODZILLA QUIZ,
(FROM PAGE 342)

1. C) They added Raymond Burr, casting him as Steve Martin, a reporter who remembers the whole incident as a flashback. It starts off with Burr in a hospital bed, recalling the horror he's seen. Then, throughout the film, footage of Burr is cleverly inserted to make it seem as though he's interacting with the Japanese cast.

2. C) *Gigantis*; it was illegal to use the name Godzilla. Warner Brothers brought the film into America, but they forgot to secure the rights to the name Godzilla, so they couldn't legally use it. In this film, by the way, Godzilla crushes Osaka instead of Tokyo, and begins his long tradition of monster-fighting (he takes on a giant creature called Angorus).

3. B) A giant cockroach and a robot with a buzz saw in his stomach. The seatopians, stationed under the sea, are using a metal bird monster with a buzz saw (Gaigan) and a giant cockroach (Megalon)—described as a "metal monster insect with drill arms"— to fight Godzilla on the surface. Godzilla can't take them on alone. He joins Jet Jaguar, a cyborg who changes size to fight monsters.

4. B) A giant moth. The thing is Mothra, who starred in his/her own film a few years earlier. Godzilla kills Mothra—but a giant egg on display at a carnival hatches, and two "junior Mothras" emerge. They spin a cocoon around Godzilla and dump him in the ocean.

5. A) He fought a Godzilla robot from outer space. The film was originally called *Godzilla vs. the Bionic Monster*, presumably to cash in on the popularity of the "Six Million Dollar Man" TV show. But the owners of that TV show sued, and the title was changed to *Godzilla vs. the Cosmic Monster*.

6. C) A three-headed dragon. To defeat them, Godzilla takes a partner again—this time Angorus, his foe from *Gigantis*.

7. A) The Smog Monster—a 400-foot blob of garbage. The smog monster flies around, leaving a trail of poisonous vapors that cause people to drop like flies, especially at discos where teens are dancing to anti-pollution songs. Don't miss the smash tune, "Save the Earth."

8. B) To show a little kid how to fight bullies. The boy falls asleep and dreams he travels to monster Island, where Godzilla and his son teach him how to defend himself.

9. C) A giant lobster. Actually, he might be a giant shrimp. It's hard to tell. His strength: he can regenerate a limb every time one is torn off.

10. C) It was Godzilla's son. Imagine that—Godzilla's a parent!

TEST YOUR "BEVERLY HILLBILLIES" I.Q., (FROM PAGE 447)

1. B) Still smarting from the cancellation of a sitcom called "The Bob Cummings Show" in 1959, Paul Henning, a TV executive, took his wife and mother-in-law on a 14,000-mile automobile trip through the eastern half of the United States. Henning was trying to get his mind off business, but it didn't work—the places he visited kept giving him ideas for new shows. After touring a Civil War site, he thought of creating a sit-com around the concept of an 1860s family that somehow lands in the 1960s...but he couldn't think of a believable way to transport them through time. He later explained:

> I wondered how, without being too magic, such a thing could be accomplished. I subsequently read a little bit about someone trying to build a road through a remote section of the Ozark Mountains and how the residents would try to stop the building of the road. They didn't want to have access. Part of that, I'm sure was that a lot of them made their living moonshining and they didn't want "fereners," as they called it, coming in the remote places.

Turning the concept around, Henning thought that hillbillies moving to California was a good idea for a sit-com. He jotted down some ideas and showed them to executives of Filmways Television over lunch; by the end of the meeting the series had been sold.

2. A) "I told [Filmways] the concept," Henning later recalled. "These hillbillies strike oil and move to a sophisticated urban center, which I first imagined to be New York. But then I got to thinking of the cost of filming in New York and how it wouldn't work. Where else could they land? I thought of Beverly Hills, which is about as sophisticated as you can get on the West Coast."

3. C) Henning and *Beverly Hillbillies* producer Al Simon spent months hitting every hillbilly band and hoedown looking for an authentic hillbilly to play the part of Granny. "Finally," he recalls, "we found someone and thought, 'Gee, this woman's great. This is gonna work out. She sounded great when we talked to her. She said she'd have her nephew, with whom she stayed, help her with the reading. When she came in and faced those cameras, she froze. She couldn't read! She was illiterate, but she disguised it cleverly."

Actress Bea Benaderet got ahold of the script and pleaded with Henning for an audition to play the part of Granny. He told her she was too "well built" for the part. "And when we did the test, she had seen Irene [Ryan] ready to go and do her thing. She said, 'There's your Granny!'" Henning disagreed. "At first they said I was too young," Ryan later recalled, "but I said 'If you get anybody older than I am, she'll be too old to do the series.'" She got the part—and Bea Benaderet got the part of Cousin Pearl. (Note: Did her voice sound oddly familiar to you when you watched the show?

She also provided the voice of Betty Rubble in *Flintstones* cartoons.)

4. B) Bailey "wasn't happy anywhere he was," Henning recalls. "He complained a lot, but he played the part perfectly." The other cast members remember him as arrogant, publicity hungry, willing to argue over just about anything, and frequently insulting, even in public. Paul Henning's wife Ruth remembers one particular incident:

> We were going to a bank opening in Independence, Missouri....Ray got loaded on the plane and when we arrived at Paul's sister's house, a big, historical, Victorian-style home, Ray made a loud remark that it looked like a whorehouse. When Paul's sister stepped out on the porch to greet us, Ray said, "Are you the madam?"

"He alienated himself from everybody," one press agent recalls. "Sometimes people hated to be around him, he complained so much." But according to one California bank official, he was popular in the banking industry nonetheless. "The bankers all love him," the official told *TV Guide* in 1970, "which is unusual considering the way bankers have always been portrayed....I have yet to hear a banker complain about the character of Drysdale." Even so, Bailey's attitude may have cost him his career: according to news reports published after his death, Buddy Ebsen had refused to offer him work on his new series, *Barnaby Jones*. Bailey spent his last years unemployed and bitter. He died of a heart attack in 1980.

5. B) During one break in shooting in 1966, Douglas starred opposite Elvis Presley in his film *Frankie and Johnnie*...and according to some reports, fell in love with the King. "She didn't realize every girl he worked with fell in love with him. She really flipped out," Paul Henning recalls.

6. B) Critics almost uniformly hated the show. "We're liable to be Beverly Hillbillied to death," one observer sniffed, "please write your Congressman." Another complained that *"Beverly Hillbillies* aims low...and hits its target." But the show was an unprecedented hit with viewers. It shot to the #1 ratings slot after only 5 weeks on the air and quickly became the most-watched show in TV history. More than 20 years later, 8 of the top 20 most-watched episodes ever are in history are from the *Beverly Hillbillies*.

7. A) The part of Jed Clampett was made with Buddy Ebsen in mind,

---

The U.S. Congress didn't make "The Star Spangled Banner" the national anthem until 1931.

but he didn't want the part. "My agent had mentioned the hillbillies," he later recalled, "but I wanted to run the other way. I had played a lot of hillbillies, and I just didn't want to get trapped again in that kind of getup with long hair and whiskers."

8. B) The owners were happy for the first three seasons...but only because they had insisted that Filmways keep their address a secret. But in the beginning of the 4th season, *TV Guide* got ahold of the address and published it, and the house, known as the Kirkeby mansion, instantly became one of the hottest tourist stops in L.A. The wife of the owner went nuts. "She had been just beleagured by tourists," Henning later recalled. "She had to get security people, shut her gates...it was a terrible mess. People would actually walk into her house and ask for Granny. Can you imagine?...The tragedy was that we were just about to go to color. This broke before we had a chance to film the exteriors in color. That was a real blow. We had to promise to stay away."

9. B) Tate, who later became famous as one of the murder victims of Charles Manson, played typist Janet Trego in several episodes and even dated Max Baer (Jethro) for a time. She later won the part as one of Cousin Pearl's daughters on *Petticoat Junction*, but was replaced by another actress when *Playboy* magazine published nude photos of her that had been taken before she got the part. "When we first got her," director Joe Depew remembers, "She was very amateurish. It was hard for her to read a line. Then she went to [acting] school and she learned a lot. She was a very pleasant girl and extremely beautiful...a real tragedy."

10. B) Granny was Granny Moses...just like the painter.

THE NUMBERS GAME
(FROM PAGE 457)

1. 7 = Wonders of the Ancient World
2. 1001 = Arabian Nights
3. 12 = Signs of the Zodiac
4. 54 = Cards in a Deck (with the Jokers)

Family attachment: 8 times more women than men buy Father's Day cards.

5. 9 = Planets in the Solar System
6. 88 = Piano Keys
7. 13 = Stripes on the American Flag
8. 32 = Degrees Fahrenheit at which Water Freezes
9. 90 = Degrees in a Right Angle
10. 99 = Bottles of Beer on the Wall
11. 18 = Holes on a Golf Course
12. 8 = Sides on a Stop Sign
13. 3 = Blind Mice (See How They Run)
14. 4 = Quarts in a Gallon
15. 1 = Wheel on a Unicycle
16. 5 = Digits in a Zip Code
17. 24 = Hours in a Day
18. 57 = Heinz Varieties
19. 11 = Players on a Football Team
20. 1000 = Words that a Picture is Worth
21. 29 = Days in February in a Leap Year
22. 64 = Squares on a Chessboard
23. 40 = Days and Nights of the Great Flood
24. 2 = To Tango
25. 76 = Trombones in a Big Parade
26. 8 = Great Tomatoes in a Little Bitty Can
27. 101 = Dalmatians
28. 23 = Skidoo
29. 4 = He's a Jolly Good Fellow (yes, it's a trick)
30. 16 = Men on a Dead Man's Chest
31. 12 = Days of Christmas
32. 5 = Great Lakes
33. 7 = Deadly Sins
34. 2.5 = Children in a Typical American Family
35. 1, 2, 3 = Strikes You're Out at the Old Ball Game
36. 3 = Men in a Tub
37. 13 = Baker's Dozen

MONUMENTAL MISTAKES
(FROM PAGE 491)

1) B. Buried in a roadway. By the time anyone looked for it, say the Whitcombs in *Oh Say Can You See*, "the rock was partially buried in the middle of a roadway leading to a wharf and had to be dug out and hauled to the town square. In the course of several additional moves, the rock fell from a wagon and had to be cemented together."

Tourists were upset that the rock wasn't at the ocean, where the pilgims were supposed to have stepped onto it. So the citizens of Plymouth obliged them, and moved it near the water in 1920.

2) B. Thomas Jefferson/Monticello. A northerner did buy Monticello and restore a part of it, but then the Civil War broke out, and the Confederates confiscated the property and stored grain and cows in it. In 1878, it was described as "desolation and ruin…a standing monument to the ingratitude of the great Republic." Believe it or not, the real effort to save Monticello didn't begin until 1923.

3) A. The company that made Castoria laxative. They agreed to give $25,000 "provided that for the period of one year you permit us to place across the top of the pedestal the word *Castoria*." Imagine how the history of the United States might have been affected if immigrants entering New York harbor had seen, in that inspiring first glimpse of America, an ad for laxatives. What lasting impression would it have made? It boggles the mind. Fortunately, they were turned down.

4) C. A root beer stand. One representative wrote at the time: "I look to see where [John C.] Calhoun sat and where [Henry] Clay sat and I find a woman selling oranges and root beer." In 1864 they turned it into Statuary Hall.

5) A. The Alamo. This landmark, where Davy Crockett and company died fighting against the Mexican Army in 1836, was originally a Spanish mission. When the Mexicans took the Alamo they tried to burn it down. Then they left it, and people who lived nearby took stones from the buildings whenever they liked. In the mid-1800s, the U.S. Army used the Alamo as a barracks. But in 1879, it

---

G.I. blues: Elvis received 10,000 letters a week during his stint in the U.S. Army.

was turned into a grocery/mercantile store. When a real estate syndicate tried to buy it in 1905, the Daughters of the Republic of Texas lobbied the state government to match the offer. They were turned down. It took a private donor—a 22-year-old cattle heiress—to come up with the funds to save it.

6) C. An angry mob that gathered after the assassination. The federal government bought it from John Ford for $100,000 and used it as an office and a storage area. Unfortunately, Lincoln wasn't the only one to die there. In 1893, twenty office workers were killed, and sixty-eight injured, when the building collapsed. It was unoccupied until 1964, when money was appropriated to restore the building to its 1865 condition.

7. A—Schoolchildren contributed their pennies to save it.
The boat got its nickname not because its sides were made of iron, but because its thick wood sides seemed to deflect cannonballs during battle in the War of 1812. After the war, it was abandoned to rot—but in 1830, it was refurbished and used for training. Then, in 1927, it needed work again, and a drive to restore it was led by American scholchildren.
gine how the history of the United States might have been affected if immigrants entering New York harbor had seen, in that inspiring first glimpse of America, an ad for laxatives. What lasting impression would it have made? It boggles the mind. Fortunately, they were turned down.

DOCTOR'S ORDERS

Recently, BRI member Jack Miller sent us this amusing story.

"My friend's dad was an ear-nose-and-throat doctor on the upper West Side, in New York City. He treated a lot of well-known singers, including many from the Metropolitan Opera. He was a very proper old Viennese gentleman.

"One day in the late 1960s, who should walk into the office but Janis Joplin. Dr. Reckford doesn't know her from Adam, but he examines her and delivers his diagnosis:

'Young lady, I don't know what you do for a living, but you've got to stop drinking and shouting so much.' "

People in Salt Lake City eat more Jell-O than citizens in any other city in the U.S.

And No Bathroom Is Complete Without

The Best of Uncle John's Bathroom Reader!

All your favorites—the funniest, oddest, most intriguing articles, quotes, and trivia from volumes 1-7

A Truly Satisfying Experience for the
Connoisseur of Bathroom Reading

AVAILABLE AT YOUR LOCAL BOOKSTORE!

THE LAST PAGE

F ELLOW BATHROOM READERS:

The fight for good bathroom reading should never be taken loosely—we must sit firmly for what we believe in, even while the rest of the world is taking pot shots at us.

Once we prove we're not simply a flush-in-the-pan, writers and publishers will find their resistance unrolling.

So we invite you to take the plunge: Sit Down and Be Counted! by joining The Bathroom Readers' Institute. Send a self-addressed, stamped envelope to: BRI, PO Box 1117, Ashland, Oregon 97520. You'll receive your attractive free membership card, and a copy of the BRI newsletter (if we ever get around to publishing one), and earn a permanent spot on the BRI honor roll!

ᐳ ᐳ ᐳ

UNCLE JOHN'S NEXT BATHROOM READER (OUR 10TH ANNIVERSARY EDITION!) IS IN THE WORKS

Don't fret—there's more good reading on its way. In fact, there are a few ways *you* can contribute to the next volume:

1. Is there a subject you'd like to see us cover? Write and let us know. We aim to please.

2. Got a neat idea for a couple of pages in the new *Reader*? If you're the first to suggest it, and we use it, we'll send you a free copy of the book.

3. Have you seen or read an article you'd recommend as quintessential bathroom reading? Or is there a passage in a book that you want to share with other BRI members? Tell us where to find it, or send a copy. If you're the first to suggest it and we publish it in the next volume, there's a free book in it for you.

Well, we're out of space, and when you've gotta go, you've gotta go. Hope to hear from you soon. Meanwhile, remember:

Go with the flow.